PRAISE FOR CHARLES J. GIVENS'

FINANCIAL SELF-DEFENSE

"Charles J. Givens knows about money because he has been at both ends of the scale—a poverty-stricken child and a multimillionaire. . . . Givens learned by trial and error not only how to make money, but also how to keep it. *FINANCIAL SELF-DEFENSE* gives 183 strategies that can be implemented to provide total control over present and future finances. The attack strategies will help you to use knowledge to make money now. The defense strategies are intended to prevent you from losing the money you will be making."

—*South Bend Tribune*

"An interest-bearing gem. . . . Like a good suspense thriller, this financial self-help book holds your attention; the hunt to save money will engage the reader."

—*Nashville Banner*

"A good book. . . . I must admit after reading *The Wall Street Journal* faithfully for six months that it never once disclosed—as did Givens—that your bank doesn't have to put a hold on your checks. That you should always ask for a cash discount of four percent from any merchant who was prepared to take your credit card. And on and on and on."

—*Fort Worth Star-Telegram*

Other best-sellers by CHARLES J. GIVENS

Wealth Without Risk
More Wealth Without Risk
SuperSelf: Doubling Your Personal Effectiveness
Wealth Without Risk for Canadians

UPDATED AND EXPANDED

FOR 1995 AND BEYOND

FINANCIAL SELF-DEFENSE

HOW TO WIN THE FIGHT FOR FINANCIAL FREEDOM

CHARLES J. GIVENS

POCKET BOOKS

New York London Toronto Sydney Tokyo Singapore

In view of the complex, individual, and specific nature of financial matters, this book is not intended to replace legal, accounting, or other professional advice. Laws vary from state to state and the reader is advised to obtain assistance or advice from a competent professional before making decisions about personal financial matters.

The author and publisher disclaim any responsibility for any liability, loss, or risk incurred as a consequence of the use of this book.

POCKET BOOKS, a division of Simon & Schuster Inc.
1230 Avenue of the Americas, New York, NY 10020

Library of Congress Cataloging-in-Publication Data

Givens, Charles J.
Financial self-defense : how to win the fight for financial freedom / Charles J. Givens.
p. cm.
Includes index.
ISBN: 0-671-51690-6
1. Finance, Personal. I. Title.
HG179.G542 1995
332.024—dc20 94-48464
CIP

First Pocket Books trade paperback printing April 1995

10 9 8 7 6 5 4 3 2 1

Cover design by Barry Littmann
Cover photo by Jeanne Strongin

Printed in the U.S.A.

To my wife, Adena,
and Rob and Chuck, my sons,
and my daughter, Julie Anna,
who are a joy,
an inspiration and, as always,
my greatest supporters

Contents

Introduction

When it comes to handling money, you will end up either the victor or the victim—there is no middle ground. You win when you maximize the use of every dollar to increase your lifestyle and financial security. You lose when, through your financial ignorance, someone else maximizes the use of your hard-earned dollars for his or her benefit and at your expense.

The biggest problem with money is that it doesn't come with an instruction book, and too many of the well-meaning financial decisions you make, including buying, borrowing, investing and paying taxes, end up eroding your personal and potential wealth, producing little or no value, sometimes enriching only those who sold you on "a good deal."

You are already smart enough to spot cheats, thieves and con artists—those who, without conscience, play mental games with you in order to steal your money. Only the greedy or extremely financially ignorant fall prey to sucker scams. But, unfortunately, you have been losing an automatic $10,000 to $20,000 per year every year of your life to perfectly legal schemes dreamed up by bankers, brokers, car dealers, insurance companies, mortgage companies, credit card companies and bureaucracies like Congress and the Internal Revenue Service.

There is an old saying in Las Vegas, "They don't build casinos with winners' money." Multimillion-dollar gambling palaces are all built with losers' money, and other than the entertainment value of the action and the glitter, 95 out of 100 gamblers walk away losers. The same scenario repeats itself every time you buy insurance, borrow money, purchase a home, buy a car and pay your taxes—biggest expenditures in your financial life. The house always has the advantage and has beaten you every time—that is, until now. This book will reverse the odds and put you in control of every financial decision you make from now on, transforming you from financial victim into financial victor.

There's a war going on between you and those trying to get their hands in your pocket, including:

- The insurance industry
- Banks
- Credit card companies
- Car dealers
- Brokers and financial planners
- Mortgage companies
- Federal, state and local tax agencies

As soon as you make it, they try to take it! As a result, 90 percent of all Americans are living paycheck to paycheck no matter how much or how little they earn. Do you believe that—90 percent? I'll bet you do if you're one of the 90 percent.

By following the strategies in this book, you will learn to regain control of your personal finances and keep all the hands out of your pocket except yours. The result? Every year for the rest of your life you will gain the use of thousands of dollars that heretofore have been going to waste—dollars that will get you out of debt and build the lifestyle you want for yourself and your family now, as well as provide the path toward your dreams for your future.

Every family makes two or three major money management decisions every month. Because of a lack of knowledge, these decisions often turn into major financial errors. Knowledge is your first line of defense. What happens to you financially is based totally on what you know and do or, by default, what you don't know and therefore can't do. This book will tell you what you must know to succeed—and what to do about it. Real financial power is created by knowing how to make the right decision at the right time. And for every financial decision there is an optimum strategy. Financial decisions cannot be made in a vacuum. They must be part of an overall financial plan. It has been my experience that with a carefully laid out financial plan and the commitment to follow it, anyone or any family can both:

- build a beautiful lifestyle in the present without sacrificing the future, and
- build a financially sound future without sacrificing in the present.

How? By making every dollar count. By spending, not saving your way to financial success. The concept is simple. All the money you earn, except what resides in the cookie jar, is eventually spent, and you can spend it in only two ways: for your lifestyle (buying goods, services and entertainment) and for your future (buying investments). But what if you had the knowledge to spend so much less when buying goods and services that you would have all the money left over that it would ever take for investing in a sound and happy future? No saving, no sacrificing. Just the right strategies.

For instance, let's say you are spending $900 each year on automobile insurance and you suddenly acquire the knowledge to cut your premium to $450 without sacrificing the quality of your insurance. Your $900 would then buy you:

1. Your automobile insurance
2. A $450 per year investment

In addition to buying your insurance over the next 10 years, you will have $4,500 to invest, which, invested correctly, will grow to $9,500 during the same period. That's almost $1,000 per year of free money produced by a plan that saves you only $450 a year.

In this book, you have at your fingertips 186 strategies that will have the same impact. You can have the lifestyle you want now and a million dollars waiting for you at retirement, all accomplished by how you spend your money, not how it is budgeted or saved. These strategies will help you:

- Create a financial blueprint that gives you total control over your financial future
- Turn financial waste into spendable profits
- Double the purchasing power of your money
- Afford the car and home of your dreams right now
- Free up the money to travel and enjoy your life
- Cut your income taxes in half
- Find the money to build a million-dollar retirement plan
- Get out of debt in half the time with half the money
- Create the lifestyle you want for yourself and your family
- Become a self-confident financial wizard

Becoming a Financial "Magnet"

There are those who seem to attract money and those who can't seem to hang on to a dime. The difference is a function of the mind and not a function of income or assets.

With knowledge, commitment and control, anyone can become a magnet for financial opportunity instead of a victim of continual financial crises. Some people even think they have a financial cloud or curse hanging over their heads. Just when the light appears at the end of the tunnel, the car breaks down, there is an unexpected major medical bill, the credit card bill is twice what's expected or the bank balance is $200 short of what shows in the check register. These are common symptoms of financial ignorance—the inability to control and create financial progress.

Remember way back in science class when we were taught opposite poles attract and like poles repel? Put one south pole and one north pole of two magnets near each other and, clunk, they will be attracted with instant and surprising force. Put the two north or the two south poles together and they will always repel each other with the same force. That is exactly how the mind and financial opportunity work together or, all too often, work against each other. With money, just as with magnets, there is a set of principles that work all the time, and work for everybody, and these principles are carefully described for you in this book.

The same principles that are completely logical to the financially successful are often illogical to the financially illiterate. That's what makes getting out of the financial rut seem so difficult. The approach of the financially illiterate is to do more of what doesn't work. But success is never accomplished by doing more of what doesn't work. If something doesn't work the first time, I promise you it won't work any better no matter how many times you try it.

Doing more of what you are already doing will create plenty of frustration but not wealth. There is an alternative that *does* work—powerful, predetermined, pretested strategies. This book contains two types of wealth-building strategies: attack strategies that will enable you to use knowledge to make instant money, and defense strategies that will keep you from losing it.

ATTACK Strategies: Steps to take immediately to make money and improve your lifestyle.

DEFENSE Strategies: Steps to take to protect your money and ensure your financial security.

By following this total life-changing approach to handling money you will become financially unstoppable—a real pro at winning the fight for financial freedom.

Wealth Building *is* WAR!

Prepare to Win!

PART I

GET ORGANIZED AND GET STARTED

CHAPTER 1

Take Charge of Your Financial Future

Strategic Planning and Control

Ever wonder why some people become superachievers while others just falter and sputter with only talk of what they want to accomplish? *The difference between those who accomplish their dreams and those who only dream of accomplishing them is planning and control.*

There are laws of cause and effect when it comes to reaching objectives, which make success a science and *not* an accident. Anyone who chooses to follow the rules or strategies for accomplishment will be met with a rich, rewarding, satisfying life. Those who are controlled by life instead of controlling life usually end up frustrated, angry, cynical or complacent.

Financial success is the progressive realization of your financial objectives on a timely and preplanned basis. The amount of money required for financial success differs from person to person. The great news about strategies, particularly financial strategies, is that they work independently of the people who use them. Financial strategies like those I'll give you in this book are not theory. They are not good ideas that might work. They are the equivalent of scientific principles that govern the way money, finance and financial institutions *really* work for or against individuals. If ten people stand in front of a concrete wall and each is given the same rubber ball to throw against the wall, no matter which person throws the ball up, the same result will occur. The ball will bounce back. Sometimes it will bounce back higher or lower, depending on the force with which it is thrown, but it will *always* bounce back. The result is predictable. It doesn't matter whether the thrower is tall, short, underweight, overweight, male, female, Hispanic, black or white. The result is the same.

Does that mean that all people can realize their financial objectives with the right strategies? Absolutely. That's the point. No matter who you are, or where you are financially right now, you can use the strategies that I'm about to teach you and achieve the same exciting results that I and the tens of thousands of members of the Charles J. Givens Organization have achieved. A good strategy works all the time, and works for everyone. There should be no exceptions.

But first you must take control of your financial future. Taking control means identifying and accepting where you are and then creating a dynamic plan to take you where you want to go in the minimum time with the maximum satisfaction. Financial strategies, however, mean little unless they are part of a greater plan. Personal or financial success therefore begins, not with strategies, but with a definition of your objectives, what you plan to accomplish.

There are four important parts to your plan of accomplishment, your

Dreams list
Values list
Goals list
Strategies list

Your dreams are the destinations you want to reach; your goals are the signposts of accomplishment that define your path. Your values set the limits for the time and energy you will choose to expend on any dream or goal, and your strategies are the tools of accomplishment. All together they become your blueprint for a rich, rewarding journey and satisfying and fulfilling life.

Goals, to bring true satisfaction, must be in alignment with your values. So first, let's work on choosing your most important goals and identifying your predominant values.

Your Income Does Not Determine Your Outcome

The amount of money that will pass through your hands over a working lifetime is incredible. For example, if you work 40 years and earn only an average of $25,000 per year, you will have made $1 million even without salary increases due to inflation. If you get an annual raise of 5 percent, the $1 million explodes to $3 million. There is no question whether or not you can make a million dollars. The real question is how quickly can you make your first million and how much of it can you keep?

You can create far more wealth by how you use the money you already earn that you can from earning more. It's not how much money you make that counts but how much you get to keep. Being rich is not measured in the number of millions you have accumulated. Being rich is having the money to do what you want to do when you want to do it, and having the attitude to enjoy every minute of the journey.

What would you do if you had more money? A typical family conversation might go like this:

"Brad, if we could only get some extra money, there's so much we could do. Send the kids to college and pay off the mortgage."

"Come on, Brenda! Where is that creative imagination of yours? How about a trip to Europe? A condo in Florida would be nice."

"Well, Brad, I could imagine myself in a new Mercedes!"

This couple is dreaming but certainly not planning, and planning is the connective link between dreams and accomplishment.

An even more typical conversation goes like this:

"How could I have only $5 in my pocket? I just cashed a check for $100 yesterday!"

"Where did it go?"

"Let's see. . . . $15 for dry cleaning, $20 for gasoline, $35 for groceries, $15 at the drug store, $10 for lunch."

"Unbelievable . . ."

"Oh no! Barbara, did you see this Visa bill? It's $847! How can this keep happening?"

These folks are out of control. Right now their dream is limited to having some money left over at the end of the month after all their bills are paid.

Or how about this couple:

"Bob, we've got to be conservative. We can't afford to lose a single dollar. Ever since we retired, costs just seem to be going up, but our income no longer is."

"I know. It would have helped if we hadn't listened to that darned broker. I can't believe he put us into options and commodities. Now we have less money and taxes are just eating us alive."

This couple is scared. They seem to be caught in the retirement trap: the chance that they will be around longer than their money. They have stopped dreaming and started worrying.

All of these scenarios are caused by the same factors: lack of direction, lack of knowledge and lack of financial control. Developing a financial blueprint is the answer for all financial situations. Your blueprint puts you back in control.

Your financial blueprint is made up of four lists, all created by you, of your dreams, values, goals and strategies. All parts of your financial blueprint affect each other and, when aligned correctly, give you practically unlimited power to accomplish anything.

Before learning, choosing and using strategies, it is a must to make a dreams list first, then identify your values, and finally choose your goals. You will then find yourself easily motivated to put your strategies to work. Together these four lists form your financial blueprint. Notice in the chart on facing page how each affects the others.

What you value most, whether peace of mind, security or fame and fortune, determines the dreams you have for your life. Your goals are the stepping-stones that create the path, and your strategies determine the speed and control with which you are able to propel yourself along the paths you have chosen. By doing the exercises that follow, you will quickly create your dreams, values and goals lists. The balance of the book is devoted to the strategies you will employ.

ATTACK #1

Create your dreams list to set the stage for accomplishment.

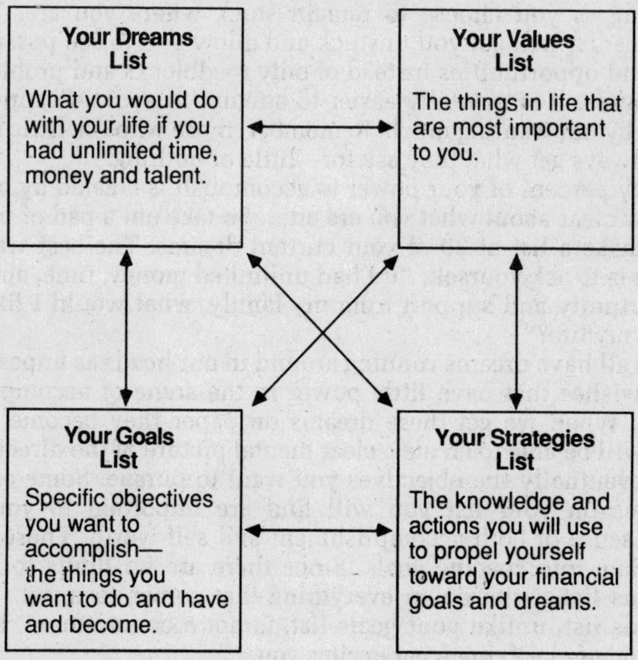

The first step in creating your financial blueprint is to create your dreams list. This strategy is so important to your future that I want you to create your dreams list before you read any further. Your dreams are what you would do, own or become if your life had no limits.

The biggest reason capable people don't realize their dreams is that they see themselves in terms of what they lack—

Lack of money
Lack of time
Lack of ability
Lack of opportunity
Lack of support from family

The truth is that none of these is necessary to begin the journey toward what you want from life. Once you have determined where you are going and what you want to do in life, the things you now see yourself lacking you will find along the path. A bar of gold only a few yards ahead on your path is out of your reach as long as you choose to remain stuck where you are. Your dreams list will get you unstuck and allow you to see possibilities and opportunities instead of only roadblocks and problems. Of course, it is mentally easier to attempt to avoid disappointment by not wanting much. Remember, those who ask little from life always get what they ask for—little or nothing.

Fifty percent of your power to accomplish is created by being totally clear about what you are after. So take out a pad of paper and make a list of 20 of your current dreams. The best way to begin is to ask yourself, "If I had unlimited money, time, ability, opportunity and support from my family, what would I like to do in my life?"

We all have dreams running around in our heads as hopes and idle wishes that have little power in the arena of accomplishment. When we get these dreams on paper they become real. You will be able to create a clear mental picture of the directions and eventually the objectives you want to pursue. Some of the dreams on your list you will find are important to you, to your sense of both accomplishment and self-worth. These will translate into specific goals. Since there are no limits to your dreams list, write down everything that comes to mind. Your dreams list, unlike your goals list, is not a commitment, but a method of clarifying what excites you.

You will find that your dreams can be classified into five categories:

What you would like to have or own
What you would like to do or create
What you would like to go or travel
What you would like to be or become
What you would like to contribute or put back

Encourage your spouse or mate, if you have one, and certainly your children to create their own dreams lists. Make it a fun, fulfilling, exciting family project, not a chore.

Sometimes we get so involved in just making it through the day that our dreams get left in the dust. It's time to get your dreams in front of you where they continually become the major focus of your life. You may be surprised at how many of your dreams require money. The money, believe it or not, is the easy part as long as you are clear about what you are after.

Incidentally, it is not necessary that you and your spouse or mate have the same dreams and values in order to experience a fulfilling relationship. What is necessary is the willingness to support each other's dreams and values without evaluation and criticism.

There are no right or wrong dreams.

ATTACK #2

Identify the values that are the most important to you.

Ideas and beliefs about the relative worth of things in your life are called values. If you value security highly, choosing to leave your job and start your own business could cause a great deal of stress—unless, of course, you changed your values. On the other hand, if you value wealth above security, staying in a safe, secure job at an average wage would be a frustrating experience. You would constantly be looking for opportunity. If, however, you value security and wealth equally, you will experience the frustration of what I call values conflict—the feeling that any decision might be the wrong one and making no decision might be even worse. These emotions and frustrations are all mental and have nothing to do with what is the right or wrong decision.

Values are not facts but simply choices, initially made for us by parents and our childhood environment. As we grow and mature, our values should tend to change and become our own choices. The ability to choose your own values is the freedom to choose the direction for your life.

When you act in accordance with your values, you experience emotional balance, a sense of security and pleasure. When your actions are out of alignment with your values, you can experience fear, guilt, frustration and emotional imbalance. Fortunately, you can get rid of those negative, unwanted feelings. You can either:

1. Change your actions to align with your values, or
2. Change your values to align with your actions.

Of course, you cannot do either until you identify what your values are.

Values are programs in the mind and can be changed only with constant prodding, attention and affirmation. In other words, to change what you value, even if change is in your best interest, you must reprogram what is in your mind. It is far easier, though not usually as rewarding, to change your actions—to get rid of the conflicts and live your life in accordance with what you already value most.

Surprisingly, there are a total of only about 25 major values in life, and these values in different combinations result in the differences in people's actions. The differences in the wants, desires and objectives people set for themselves are the direct result of different values.

By identifying and prioritizing your current values, you will be able to:

- Set your goals to enable you to spend more of your life and money doing and experiencing those things that are most important to you.
- Eliminate values conflict by making certain no two values are pulling you in opposite directions.
- Create an environment of mutual support in your personal relationships by realizing that two people do not need the same values to create a successful relationship, but they must be able to support each other's values emotionally and financially.
- Determine how important wealth building is to the success of your total financial plan.

As you can see, values must be identified before goals are set or it becomes all too easy to establish one or more goals that are in conflict with your values. Reaching a goal should create a sense of accomplishment, self-confidence, excitement and a desire to celebrate, but if that goal is in conflict with an important value, there will instead be a feeling of empty achievement, frustration and sometimes even anger.

Many years ago at a political cocktail party in Washington, D.C., I had the opportunity to talk to one of the most successful attorneys in America. He had spent his life building one of the largest law firms in the country, with over 300 lawyers and offices in Boston, New York and Washington, which provided him and his family with unlimited financial opportunities. I asked him how he felt about what he had been able to accomplish. He hesitated, his voice began to quiver and he said, "You know, when I look back, instead of having the feeling of accomplishment, all I can think about is that today my grown children barely talk to me, because I never got to know them when they were younger. I was too busy with my career. My marriage fell apart after 20 years when my wife left me for someone far less important or successful. Someone who had the time for her." He finished by saying, "If I had it to do over, I would do it differently. That's what I remember about my accomplishment." One important personal value to him was family, but he never realized it and overlooked the conflict in his values until it was too late. Neither business nor family as his most important value was right or wrong. He just never understood how necessary identifying values was to real success.

The truth is that you can have it all. Surprised? To live your life in accordance with your values does not require sacrifice. You must sacrifice only when you are not living your life in accordance with your values. Recognizing what is and what is not important to you is the key. You will be excited when you discover how much easier life becomes after you create and prioritize your values list. It works for everyone.

Your values list will also enable you to choose the dreams on your dreams list that should come first. The accomplishment of those dreams and goals that are in alignment with your top five values will be the most satisfying and personally rewarding. That's where 80 percent of your available energy and time should be spent. Why spend time doing anything else? Time is always limited. Therefore, it is important to prioritize your values once you discover them. It is you and only you who can decide what is important in your life.

Your Values List

First, go through the following list once or twice, and write down on a pad of paper those values that seem important to you. Second, prioritize those values you have listed from most to least important (from 1 to 10). You may, of course, prioritize more than ten values. There are no right or wrong answers.

Peace of mind
Security
Wealth
Good health
A close relationship with spouse/mate
A close relationship with children
Family (spending time with parents or other relatives)
Meeting the "right" person
Meaningful job or career
Fame
Power

Free time
Happiness
Spiritual fulfillment
Friendships
Retirement
Contributing time, knowledge or money to others
Knowing important or famous people
Being in business for yourself
Having no problems to deal with
Living to an old age
Personal possessions—cars, houses, jewelry, etc.
Travel to exciting places
Sense of accomplishment
Respect from others—being thought of as a smart or good person
Other ______________

ATTACK #3

Identify and eliminate destructive values from your life.

Most values are positive but there are destructive values that always lead toward personal and financial failure that must be changed for those who want a successful, fulfilling life. These destructive values include:

1. The desire for something for nothing. Symptoms include gambling, cheating and stealing.
2. The desire to feel superior to others. Symptoms include gossip, prejudice, bigotry, aloofness, criticism and blame.
3. The desire for continuous, instant pleasure. Symptoms include overspending and overindulgence in food, alcohol and drugs.

Identifying destructive values is the most important step in their elimination. Destructive values are parasitic and drain energy that could be spent on the things you value most. A jockey who is overweight by only four pounds can lose a race on even the best horse. Destructive values must be constantly worked on. For some it's a never-ending process of self-evaluation. The long-term rewards, however, are always worth the effort.

Make a list of the values and attitudes that will almost certainly prevent you from reaching your goals. Be honest. Remember, this is *your* list and not for publication.

Do not use your destructive values list to become self-critical. If you value personal success more than anything on that list, simply write out your plan for eliminating destructive values. Don't put roadblocks in the way of success. You can eliminate the negative values by working directly on the symptoms. Once you have identified the symptoms that are affecting your life, making the plan to eliminate them is one of your most important goals.

ATTACK #4

Set your course by defining both your financial and nonfinancial goals.

The next step in creating your financial blueprint is establishing your goals—those specific objectives on which you have decided to invest your time, energy and money. Whereas values are mental attitudes, your goals are your physical objectives. A goal can be accomplished in as little as an hour, like going to the grocery store in order to stock the refrigerator, or your goal may take most of a lifetime, like creating a million-dollar retirement plan.

All goals, to bring satisfaction, must be in alignment with your important values. The higher the priority of one of your values, the greater the satisfaction you will derive from reaching a goal affected by that value.

There are specific parameters that make an objective a goal. To be effective in your blueprint, a goal must:

1. **Be specific and measurable.** You must be able to define your goal in dollars, in numbers or in specific terms, like the specific job you want or the color and model of the car you desire.
2. **Have starting and completion dates.** To become part of an effective ongoing plan, you must choose a time to begin working on your objective and a date by which you intend to have your goal accomplished. When put into your total plan, these target dates will show you where your time will be the most effective.

3. **Be in writing.** A major planning mistake is to have your goals rolling around in your head but not written down. Written goals are concrete and allow you to plan, organize and control the paths to be followed toward achieving them.
4. **Be stated in terms of results and not processes.** A result defines the way your life will be *after* you have accomplished your goal. The process is the means, money, material, time and talent it takes to get there. Defining the results you want will help you find the opportunities you need.

Focus on the result you want and not on what you lack. When you focus on something you lack, it becomes a reason for inaction. For instance, "My goal," you say to yourself, "is a new $35,000 BMW convertible." The process trap: "Since I only have $600 in the bank, I guess I'll never get there." But when you focus on what you want, you have a clear picture of your life with the BMW. You can see yourself driving it, you can feel it, you can almost taste it and your attitude becomes one of, "I will not be denied."

Focusing on the result creates your road map. It is far more effective, when using a map, to first locate where you want to go. The shortest path from where you are then becomes obvious. On the other hand, if you don't identify the location of your destination, but simply follow the red and green lines that mark the roads, it may take you ten times as long to get there. Your destination is the result you want, the roads are the process of getting there. By forming a clear mental picture of each goal and never letting go of that picture, you will always find a way to accomplish your objectives.

Be committed. Your level of commitment to any objective determines how you will handle stumbling blocks along the way. The bigger the goal, the more stumbling blocks you are likely to encounter. The largest concrete blocks can be pulverized with the smallest hammer and enough persistence. Your commitment gives you the persistence to look at each stumbling block as one step closer to your objective. The winning attitude is always:

I Will Not Be Denied.

ATTACK #5

Put your financial goals in writing.

There are certain financial goals we all seem to have in common, although to totally different degrees depending on our values. These categories include

1. Income Goals—the increases in yearly income you want to achieve
2. Career Goals—the type of work you want to do, the company positions you want to attain or the business you want to create
3. Acquisition Goals—the things you want to buy and own
4. Travel Goals—the places nationally and internationally you want to visit and experience
5. Accomplishment Goals—the things you want to do and become
6. Educational Goals—the knowledge you want to acquire for personal, financial and career advancement
7. Recreational Goals—the "fun" things you want to own for recreation and sports
8. Investment Goals—the income-producing, tax-reducing or networth-increasing investments you want to own

Don't just think or dream about your financial goals. Put them in writing. Make lists similar to the ones on the following pages; on these lists, write down each of the goals you have chosen in each category. But don't just make your lists and then file them away. Keep them someplace where you can refer to them from time to time. They will serve as reminders of the financial goals you have set for yourself, and will help you chart your progress toward achieving them.

1. Income Goals

One sure way of having more money to spend on your dreams is to increase your income faster than inflation is cutting your purchasing power. Even if your income is keeping up with inflation, you're running faster just to stay in place. You're not getting ahead. You would be making real progress if you could double your income. But how long would that take? To find out, start by determining how many years it will take you to double your income if your salary and/or net business income continues to increase at the same rate it has during the past two years. Include in your calculations repetitive income such as job, investment, retirement and small business income. Do not include one-time income items such as gifts, inheritances or profits from the sale of your home or other investments. Estimate your total income for this year and compare it with last year's income, or if estimating is difficult or it is too early in the current year to guess at possible raises or other potential income changes, compare last year's income with your income the year before. To do that, simply refer to the gross income you reported on your 1040 tax form for the past two years. Include your spouse's income in your calculations if you have a spouse who works.

How long will it take to double your income?

	(A) THIS YEAR (ESTIMATE)	−	(B) LAST YEAR	=	(C) INCREASE (DECREASE)
Your job income	$		$		$
Your business income	$		$		$
Your investment income	$		$		$
Your retirement income	$		$		$
(D) Your total income	$		$		$
Spouse's job income	$		$		$
Spouse's business income	$		$		$
Spouse's investment income	$		$		$
Spouse's retirement income	$		$		$
(E) Spouse's total income	$		$		$
(F) Combined income (D + E)	$		$ (G)		$ (H)

To determine your percentage increase in income, divide the total increase in family income shown in box H by your combined family income last year shown in box G.

$ ______ (H) ÷ $ ______ (G) = ______% increase in income for one year

Using the following table, "Number of Years Required to Double Your Income," find the increase in yearly income in column A that is closest to the percentage you determined above. Column B represents the number of years it will take you to double your income at your present rate of increase if you do not factor in inflation.

Will your current rate of increase allow you to finance your dreams? That depends on two things: the amount of time it will take you to double your income after inflation is factored in and how much of a hurry you are in to reach your dreams (how importantly you value wealth). Over the past 50 years the inflation rate has averaged about 5 percent per year, meaning that, on the average, the first 5 percent of any increase in your income this year and every year will only allow you to maintain the same purchasing power as you had last year.

Column C shows the percentage increase in purchasing power each year after an inflation factor of 5 percent is subtracted from your actual yearly percentage increase in income shown in column A. Column D is then the number of years required to double the actual purchasing power of your income.

NUMBER OF YEARS REQUIRED TO DOUBLE YOUR INCOME
BEFORE AND AFTER INFLATION

A YEARLY PERCENTAGE INCREASE IN INCOME	B NUMBER OF YEARS REQUIRED TO DOUBLE INCOME —NO INFLATION[1]	C PERCENTAGE INCREASE IN PURCHASING POWER AFTER 5% INFLATION	D NUMBER OF YEARS TO DOUBLE PURCHASING POWER AFTER 5% INFLATION[1]
3	24	−2	—[2]
5	14	0[2]	—[2]
10	7	5	14
15	5	10	7
20	4	15	5
25	3	20	4
30	2	25	3

[1] Rounded to nearest year.
[2] At a growth rate of up to 5%, purchasing power will not increase and cannot be doubled.

If you set yourself the goal of doubling your income you now know how long it will take at your present rate of increase. But now let's look at these same figures in relation to your values, that is, how high a priority you put on building your personal wealth. Read the three statements in the following table and pick the one that most nearly represents your feelings or values about wealth building at this moment. The figure listed in the column labeled "Income Doubling Goal" represents how many years you might set as a goal to double your income based on your values. The number in the next column is the percentage increase in income you must achieve in order to double your income in the time you have allotted yourself in the previous column. The more importantly you value wealth building, the more time and effort will be required to gain the knowledge and do the things necessary to increase your income at the rate you have chosen.

My approach to income goal setting is as follows:

	INCOME DOUBLING GOAL	APPROXIMATE ANNUAL INCOME INCREASE REQUIRED WITH 5% INFLATION
I have a high priority on increasing or doubling my income—"Wealth is one of my most important values."	4 years	23%
I have an average priority on doubling my income—"Wealth building is in the middle of my values list."	6 years	17%
I have a low priority on wealth building—"I love my job or career and am not too concerned about income increases."	10 years	12%

Here is a list of suggestions to get you started toward your income goals, whether you work for yourself or someone else.

Ways to Increase Your Income If You Work for Someone Else

Increase your skill level, education or profile in your present job.
Seek promotion within your department to an existing job.
Create a new, better-paying job in your department and fill it.
Seek promotion to another department.
Ask for raises as you go the extra mile—ask, ask, ask.

Change companies for greater opportunities.
Change to a higher-paying career by getting the necessary skills or education.

Ways to Increase Your Income If You Work for Yourself

Increase sales through hiring more salespeople or spending a greater portion of your time selling.
Create a better advertising and marketing campaign.
Cut your expenses in every area without sacrificing net profit.
Expand your line of products or services.

2. Career Goals

Here are guidelines that will help you determine the directions in which you would like to take your career.

1. Do you want to change careers? Yes ______ No ______
   To what kind of work?
   1. ______ 2. ______
   3. ______ 4. ______
2. Do you want your own business? Yes ____ No ____
   What business ideas do you have?
   1. ______ 2. ______
   3. ______ 4. ______
3. Advances you want to make in your present career:

	POSITION	ANNUAL SALARY
Current	______	$ ______
1 year	______	$ ______
5 years	______	$ ______
10 years	______	$ ______

4. Do you want to change employers? Yes ____ No ____
   When? ______
   Whom would you like to work for? ______
   Salary required for you to change employers: $ ______

3. Acquisition Goals

Make a list of the things you would like to own, how much they cost, and the date by which you hope to acquire them. Include automobiles, stereos, jewelry, furs, furniture, clothes, etc. Some items will come from your dreams list.

	Item	Cost (Approx.)	Target Date (Mo./Yr.)
1.			
2.			
3.			
4.			
5.			
6.			
7.			
8.			
9.			
10.			

4. Travel Goals

Make a list of the top 10 places to which you would like to travel in the United States and abroad. Your list can include the names of countries, states, cities, monuments or other attractions.

	Destination	Target Date (Mo./Yr.)
1.		
2.		
3.		
4.		
5.		
6.		
7.		
8.		
9.		
10.		

5. Accomplishment Goals

Make a list of all the things you want to do and become. Include positions you would like to hold in clubs, groups, your church and your community. Include sports in which you would like to get involved or to excel, as well as social activities or organizations you want to join. Also, list the awards you want to win or other forms of recognition you want to achieve.

	Sport, Activity or Organization	What You Want to Accomplish	Target Date (Mo/Yr.)
1.			
2.			
3.			
4.			
5.			

6. Educational Goals

Make a list of the courses or programs you would like to take and the estimated cost of each. Examples: Speed-reading courses, night school courses, courses to complete your degree, real estate investing programs.

	Program	Approximate Starting Date	Approximate Cost
1.			$
2.			$
3.			$
4.			$
5.			$

7. Recreational Goals

Make a list of the recreational vehicles you would like to own, when you want to acquire them and the cost of each.

	Type	Date to Acquire	Cost
1. Sports car			$
2. Motorcycle			$
3. Bicycle			$
4. Snowmobile			$
5. Sailboat			$
6. Jet Ski/wet bike			$
7. Fishing boat			$
8. Hobie cat			$
9. Sailboard			$
10. Houseboat			$
11. Yacht			$
12. Airplane			$
13. Hang glider			$
14. Motor home			$
15. Camper			$

8. Investment Goals

There is only one reason to invest—to accumulate money to buy yourself something in the future that you can't afford now. For some that means financially safe and secure retirement years. Others have goals that won't wait until retirement, and investing means eventually having the money to make the down payment on a beautiful home or expensive automobile, or having a cushion to quit a job and start a business. Investment accounts, retirement accounts, and your investment in your home and other real estate are all vehicles you can use to achieve your investment goals. Your goals list will help you determine how important your investment plan will become to your future.

Make an Investment Goals Chart similar to the one below to identify where you are now and where you want to be next year, five years from now and at age 65. This chart will also help you measure your progress.

Investment Goals Chart

	THIS YEAR	NEXT YEAR	5 YEARS	AGE 65
Cash in bank	$	$	$	$
Investment accounts	$	$	$	$
Retirement accounts	$	$	$	$
Your home	$	$	$	$
Real estate investments	$	$	$	$
Other investments	$	$	$	$
TOTAL	$	$	$	$

Here are some suggestions that will help you fill in your Investment Goals Chart:

Cash in bank. Include for this year all money in bank-type savings and checking accounts, money market accounts or any other cash. Set your goals for the future on the level of available cash that will give you a sense of security.

Investment accounts. Include all stocks, bonds, CDs, government securities and mutual fund shares you now own, plus what you want to have invested in the future.

Retirement accounts. Enter the amount of money currently in all your retirement accounts. Your retirement accounts will cover the cost of your lifestyle after you are no longer producing income from your job or career. By the time you retire, the amount in your retirement plan should be eight times the annual income you want to have during your retirement years. Although other investments may also produce income during your retirement years, here you will list only the amounts you have and want to have in your retirement accounts, including your IRA, SEP, Keogh, 401(k), 403(b), annuities, federal retirement plan, state retirement plan and union retirement plan.

Your home. Show the current amount of unmortgaged equity you have in your home—what your home is worth minus what you owe. For future years, estimate what you think your home should be worth. If your goal is to buy a more expensive home, adjust your estimated home equity accordingly. If you own or plan to own a second home, show those figures also.

Real estate investments. Show the equity you have in rental real estate or land and the equity you would like to have in the future.

Other assets. Include the value of such noninvestment assets as automobiles, jewelry, furniture, etc.

I can't overemphasize the importance of putting all your financial goals in writing. Focusing on your goals inevitably means you will think about how to achieve them. Putting them in writing will motivate you to take the actions necessary for their accomplishment.

CHAPTER 2

Creating a Records Management System

ATTACK #6

Create a records management system (RMS).

With your financial blueprint developed, the next step is getting yourself organized for action. There is no part of getting organized that is more important to your future than how well you keep records. How many times have you heard yourself say, "I'm such a lousy recordkeeper." When tax time comes, the record gathering process involves looking for receipts, checks and other necessary paperwork in desk drawers, shoe boxes, purses and even the glove compartment of your car. Poor recordkeeping costs time and money—*lots* of time and *lots* of money.

By creating a simple records management system (your RMS) you can organize your important papers in one evening or a Saturday morning, and then spend a minimum amount of time and effort staying organized. If you are one of the very few that already manages your records like a pro, you can skip this chapter or use my strategies to add to your own. If you're not a good records manager, read on. A good RMS will save you hours of valuable time, assure that you get all the tax deductions you deserve, and enable you to know your financial condition at any point in time.

Other reasons for good recordkeeping include:

1. Total control of your financial life
2. Scorekeeping to measure your progress toward your financial goals
3. Proof of loss when filing insurance claims
4. Proof of payments when a creditor's records are incorrect
5. Proving your point in arbitration or litigation
6. Satisfying IRS and legal requirements
7. Exercising warranties and guarantees
8. Having information at your fingertips for completing mortgage and loan applications and financial statements

Records management is simple. It means knowing what records you need and knowing where to find them. In this chapter you will learn how to evaluate your current recordkeeping system and upgrade it to a true RMS.

ATTACK #7

Set up a permanent records management filing system.

Your records management system is important enough to deserve a permanent place of its own. All you need is a work surface—a desk or table top—and a filing cabinet. Also an inexpensive printing calculator will prove invaluable when reconciling your bank and credit card statements and preparing your tax returns.

To create your filing system:

- Purchase 50 regular-size manila file folders
- Purchase a 2-drawer file cabinet if you don't already have one.
- Use the top drawer for this year's receipts, bills, statements, personal papers and contracts and agreements still in force.
- Use the bottom drawer as your history file for the previous years' papers, completed contracts, old tax returns and records, etc. Later I will give you a formula for how long you must legally keep your records. You can combine multiple years of records in your history files, i.e., all previous years' credit card statements from one bank in one file, but you will want to keep your records in order by year. You will

refer to your history file only occasionally, but when you need past records, you want access to them quickly and conveniently.

The next step in creating your filing system is to choose the names or categories you will use and label your file folders. Print clearly with a pen or magic marker so you can read the labels easily.

Here is a suggested checklist to begin your filing system. Check those file names you can use. Add other files you will need to this list. The name of the file folder is shown first. The items that go in the file are shown second.

___ Asset Management Account—monthly statements, prospectuses

___ Bank Account—monthly statements, correspondence

___ Children's File—school papers, birthday and Christmas cards, drawings, awards, diplomas and certificates

___ Credit Bureau Report

___ Credit Card Bills/Receipts (one file for each card)—monthly statement and phone numbers
Enter names of each credit card you have:

____________ ____________

____________ ____________

____________ ____________

____________ ____________

___ Doctor and Hospital Bills—family doctor, address, phone number, medical records, doctor and hospital bills

___ Education—night school, correspondence school, work-related courses

___ Employment Records—employment contract, employee handbook, employee benefits information, retirement plan information

___ Financial Blueprint—your dreams, values and goals lists created in Chapter 1

___ Guarantees, Warranties and Instructions—instructions and guarantees for carpets, tires, stereo equipment, appliances, etc.

___ Home—purchase contract, mortgage papers, home improvement receipts, leases and rental agreements, payment book, canceled checks

___ Important Papers—birth certificates, marriage license, passports, diplomas

___ Insurance, Auto—automobile insurance policy, traffic infractions and accidents, automobile title, driver's license and license plate information

___ Insurance, Health—health insurance policy

___ Insurance, Homeowner's—homeowner's or tenant's insurance policy, umbrella liability policy, personal property inventory list

___ Insurance, Life—life insurance policies, correspondence with company, insurance quotes

___ Investments, Annuities

___ Investments, IRA Accounts

___ Investments, Miscellaneous—tax-sheltered annuities, savings accounts, loans to others, IOUs

___ Investments, Mutual Funds—monthly statements, correspondence

___ Investments, Real Estate

___ Investments, Stock and Bond Certificates

___ Personal—cards, letters, pictures, etc.

___ Receipts—miscellaneous

___ Resume

___ Retirement Plan—papers relating to your employment or small business retirement plan

___ Taxes, Federal and State—tax deductible receipts, tax returns and files for last seven years (one file for each year)

___ Telephone—telephone bills and correspondence

___ Utilities—electric, gas, water, sewer bills

___ Will—copy

Organizing and maintaining your records may seem boring and time-consuming. But with a permanent records management system, recordkeeping is easy, automatic and will end frustration and financial losses caused by lost or misplaced records.

There is another plus to setting up your own permanent records management system. All your expenses—folders, filing cabinet, printing calculator—are deductible as a tax preparation expense.

DEFENSE #8

Don't let your paperwork pile up.

You can have the most sophisticated records management system in the world and it will be worthless unless you use it. It's not necessary to file every piece of paper you want to keep the moment you receive it. But it is necessary to sort and file important papers, bills, receipts, etc., at least once a month. The most convenient time to file is when you sit down to pay your monthly bills. There is one exception to this rule.

Always reconcile your bank statements as soon as you receive them. Keeping your checks organized is one of the most important steps in your RMS. Don't leave canceled checks and statements in envelopes and drawers. File checks in order by check number in a check file box along with deposit slips, deposit receipts and your check register.

There is an absolutely false belief that because a bank uses computers it can't make mistakes. Nothing could be further from the truth. My bank once made a $40,000 mistake in my account, which was fortunately caught by reconciling. Errors of $100 or more can be missed if you don't reconcile your account.

Reconcile each monthly bank statement, using the form printed on the back of the statement. Mark all checks you have written for tax deductible purchases with a "T" in the upper right-hand corner. At tax time you can then quickly pull the checks with the "T's" to compute your deductions.

The steps in reconciling your bank statement are to:

1. Be certain all your deposits were recorded correctly. Compare your deposit receipts with the deposit entries on your statement.
2. Be certain the correct check amounts are deducted from your bank balance. Compare each check returned in your statement envelope to the amount deducted by the bank on your statement. Anything that doesn't agree is a bank error.

3. Identify checks outstanding that have not been deducted from your account. Just check off in your check register all checks returned with your statement. Any check register entries not marked are checks you have written that were not received by the bank by the time your statement was prepared. These outstanding checks must be deducted from the balance shown on your statement to determine the actual balance in your account at the present time.
4. Identify and deduct bank charges. Your bank will charge you for anything it can, including NSF (non-sufficient funds) checks, ATM usage or a minimum monthly account charge. Deduct the total of these charges (once you are certain they are correct) in your check register to adjust your actual balance. By the same token, add any amounts credited to you for interest-bearing accounts.
5. Contact your bank immediately if you find any errors in your account.

How do you know if you are in control of your checking account? You know you're not in control if you ever have to call the bookkeeping department of your bank to check your balance before you write a check!

DEFENSE #9

Store important documents in a bank safe deposit box or a fireproof safe at home.

A few of your records are difficult, sometimes impossible, to replace, and these records should be kept in a fireproof safety storage area. Here is a list of important, hard-to-replace papers that are good candidates for your safe or deposit box:

- Mutual fund shares
- Stock or bond certificates
- Property deeds
- Automobile titles
- Personal property inventory list and photographs
- Marriage certificate
- Will and estate plan
- Birth certificates
- Diplomas
- Military discharge papers
- Passports

You can rent a safe deposit box at a bank or buy a fireproof metal safe for your home. The safe deposit box has the advantage of costing less initially and is available at almost any bank for about $50 per year. The disadvantage is that you continue to pay rent every year, and the bank is not as convenient as your home when you need access to your records.

As an alternative, you can buy a heavy-duty metal combination safe at discount department stores for as little as $80, or a deluxe model from an office supply store for as much as $600. Make sure your safe is fire-rated so your records are protected in case of fire. Most safes can and should be bolted to the floor for extra security. Your home safe is also a good place to store your expensive jewelry. The cost of both a bank safe deposit box and a safe at home is tax deductible.

PART II

How to Win the Automobile Game

CHAPTER 3

Save up to 60 Percent on Every Car You Buy

Car ownership is the third biggest expense you will ever have, behind only income taxes and your home. Nowhere during your life will you be taken more often and for more money than when you buy a car from a new or used-car dealership. The deceptions are so well hidden and so lucrative for the dealers that billions are wasted annually by all car buyers, who love to brag to their friends about what a great deal they got. Even automobile salespeople are often unaware of the incredible front-end and back-end loads that can make car dealership owners some of the wealthiest members of the community. So how do you get a good deal on a new car? You don't. No one has ever gotten a good deal on a new or used car except the dealer. There are no good deals on new cars. Yet owning a car, even the car of your dreams, can be a personal pleasure instead of a financial drain.

Buying a home is an investment that appreciates (becomes more valuable) over time. An automobile, although sometimes a satisfying emotional investment, is never a sound financial investment. It is only an expense, which makes owning a car a financial loss. Your objective is to minimize that loss.

You can overpay for a home, but you will eventually get your money back because of appreciation. When you overpay for a car, you simply add the overpayment and interest on the overpayment to the money you will lose during your lifetime. A two-car family will average a car purchase or trade every three years. That means an average family will buy or lease 20 new and used cars, and spend about $250,000 plus as much as $150,000 on interest, gimmick insurance and unnecessary options. Fifty to 70 percent of that $400,000 will be wasted—that is, unless you use the strategies, principles and knowledge that follow in this chapter.

DEFENSE #10

Don't be seduced by "low, low" interest rates or rebates.

The automobile business has been on a roller coaster ride for many years. One month sales are up, the next month dealers' lots are full of unsold inventory. Because of the huge fixed costs of labor and equipment, the auto makers cannot just close down, as they once did, when demand is light, and then call everyone back to work when people start buying again. Manufacturers and dealers have to resort to unusual methods to sell more cars when few are being brought.

The gimmick that has developed from the plague of too much inventory is to offer a big rebate or a super-low interest rate with every purchase of a new car. The average interest rate on a new car loan is about 10 percent. "Buy now," the TV ad screams, and your rate will be cut to 5 percent or maybe even 2.9 percent. Chrysler has even offered the 0 percent loan. "What a deal," you are thinking. "Their loss is my gain." The truth is that the car companies are not losing, but are actually making huge profits in what appears to be their hour of need.

The lower interest rate offered—the gimmick interest rate—is the result of what the loan industry calls a "buy-down." Home-builders have done it for years, and now the automobile business has joined the game. The average dealer profit on a car with options such as radios and radial tires is about 20 percent. The manufacturer is making another 10 percent. The actual profit on a $12,000 car loaded with extras is as much as $3,600, already leaving the dealer and manufacturer a lot of room to play with your mind. However, with front-end and back-end loading, which you will soon learn about, a dealer can increase the potential profit an extra $5,000, making the amount you end up financing around $17,000 plus interest.

Here is how the buy-down works. To qualify you usually must make a 20 percent down payment and can finance your car for only two years. With cash or trade-in you put up $3,400, leaving a balance of $13,600 to be financed on that $12,000 car. Let's say a bank or finance company will finance all the car sales this month at 11 percent, but the dealer is offering an interest rate of 5 percent to you. The dealer and the manufacturer, therefore, must somehow pay the 6 percent difference themselves. That means they are buying down the interest rate from 11 percent to 5 percent. How much does it really cost them? The total interest on a two-year loan of $13,600 at 11 percent is $1,613. The dealer and manufacturer will pay 55 percent of the total interest, or $887, and you will pay the other 45 percent, or $726.

What has really happened is that the dealer and manufacturer have together conspired to sell you a car for $17,000 that originally contained a total profit of up to $8,600 and offered to give you $887 back in an interest buy-down or, if you prefer, in a rebate for the same amount. Some deal. The painful part, as you will learn, is that you will end up paying well over $20,000 for the $12,000 car you just bought, and even with the interest buy-down or rebate, it is only going to be worth $9,600 the moment you drive it off the lot.

How You Pay More Money for Less Car

When you sign a purchase contract for a new automobile, you are normally paying 250 percent more than the car is worth. That's right, you have obligated yourself for two and one-half times the car's real value the moment you drive it off the lot. Unbelievable? Wait until you read on. To demonstrate how you fall into this trap, let's begin at the beginning—the moment you walk into a new-car dealership.

You walk into a semicrowded showroom lured by an advertisement that proclaimed something like "lowest price in the universe" or promised more in a rebate than you make in a month. Before one of the busy salespeople gets to you, you've bounced across a couple of front seats and headed for the sticker to see how much this baby costs. The so-called retail value of the car is shown by a sticker called the MSRP (Manufacturer's Suggested Retail Price), attached to the rear window by the manufacturer. The sticker shows the base retail price of the car, $10,819 (see MSRP sticker, page 55), which the manufacturer thinks is a fair price and includes a dealer profit of 15 to 25 percent. Underneath the base price is the options list, which includes an upgraded radio for an extra $295, a four-speed automatic transmission for $750, something called an SE-5 sport package for only $579 (sounds like you're the sport) and $52 floor mats like the ones you saw at K mart for $10.

As far as the car itself goes, the big profit margin is in the options, sometimes marked up 75 to 200 percent. The more options the salespeople can dump on you, the bigger the commission and the dealer's profit. In this example, the options add a small but attractive $1,676, or 16 percent, to the base price. The cost of the car has now risen to $12,495 before freight and resale tax.

DEFENSE #11

Never pay overinflated delivery and dealer preparation and setup charges.

Now come the "we had to get it here and fix it up" charges. Typically these include freight, handling and setup. Freight charges are supposed to be what it cost to ship the car from the manufacturer to the dealer. But did you know most dealers can charge whatever they want? I have seen automobile freight charges on a sticker as high as $700 for delivery of a car that could have run no more than $300. The car dealers and manufacturers have great deals with the railroad and trucking companies for the delivery of new cars.

One of the biggest rip-off items you will see on most stickers these days is overinflated "Dealer Setup and Preparation Charges," ranging from $200 to $500. What do they want us to believe, that the car comes in a kit and has to be assembled? In reality the only expense of getting a new car from truck to showroom is a $10 wash job by the kid who is the "dealer preparation" department. If anything is actually damaged or needs fixing, the trucking company or the manufacturer pays for it, but you've been had again.

What should the dealer prep charge really be? Nothing. You don't pay a dealer prep charge when you buy a VCR or washing machine. Why should you pay one when you buy a car?

DEFENSE #12

Never fall for the dealer's sucker sticker.

Suddenly you notice that there is another price list next to the MSRP. It is the deadly sucker sticker. The sucker sticker is a second retail price list the dealer pastes on the car window next to the MSRP sticker, and it has been printed to look just like the manufacturer's MSRP sticker (see page 40). The official-looking sucker sticker adds 5 to 40 percent pure profit for the dealer. On this sticker the dealer adds to the cost of the car anything he wants to, using official-sounding names like dealer markup, dealer adjustment, dealer market value or any number of important-sounding options. It's just dealer excessive profit.

The salesperson also uses the sucker sticker to make sure you think you are getting a great deal. The sticker adds, let's say, $4,000 to the price of the car, and the salesperson then gives you a $1,500 discount. Some discount! Of course, before you get the discount, you have to listen to the salesperson say, "I'll probably get fired for this, but—" or "This is your lucky day. The boss is going fishing this weekend so I think we can catch him in just the right mood."

What's listed on this sucker sticker? Add-ons or options that cost the dealer little or nothing but will cost you a bundle. How about door edge guards for $299 that cost the dealer less than $20? Or an extra delivery charge of $150 that costs the dealer nothing, since the real delivery charge is already on the MSRP sticker?

Here is an example of several sucker sticker items we found on just one vehicle:

clearcoat paint	$ 188
fabric protection, rustproofing, paint sealant	595
wheel lip moldings	79
door edge guards	29
step bumper	149
administration fee	199
tack package with black bumpers	1,190
	$2,429

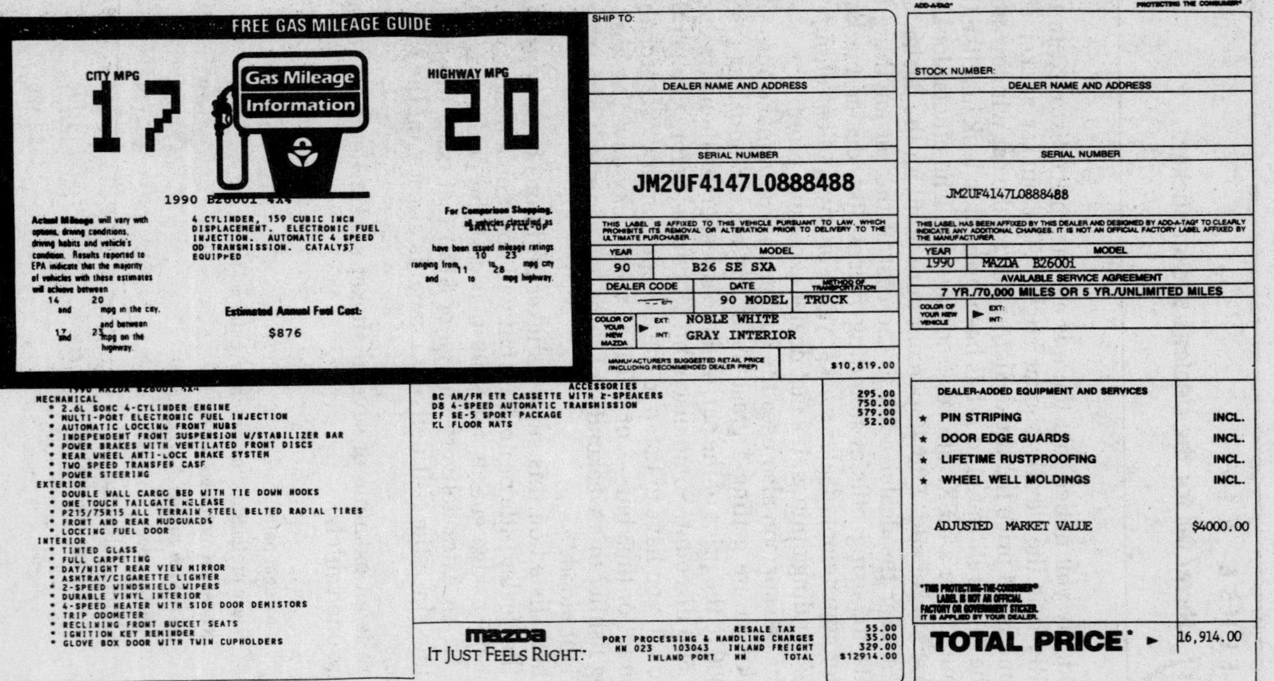

FREE GAS MILEAGE GUIDE

Gas Mileage Information

CITY MPG 17

HIGHWAY MPG 20

1990 B2600I 4X4

4 CYLINDER, 159 CUBIC INCH DISPLACEMENT. ELECTRONIC FUEL INJECTION. AUTOMATIC 4 SPEED OD TRANSMISSION. CATALYST EQUIPPED

Actual Mileage will vary with options, driving conditions, driving habits and vehicle's condition. Results reported to EPA indicate that the majority of vehicles with these estimates will achieve between 14 and 20 mpg in the city, and between 17 and 23 mpg on the highway.

Estimated Annual Fuel Cost: $876

For Comparison Shopping, all vehicles classified as SMALL PICK-UP have been issued mileage ratings ranging from 10 to 23 mpg city and 11 to 28 mpg highway.

SHIP TO:

DEALER NAME AND ADDRESS

SERIAL NUMBER

JM2UF4147L0888488

THIS LABEL IS AFFIXED TO THIS VEHICLE PURSUANT TO LAW, WHICH PROHIBITS ITS REMOVAL OR ALTERATION PRIOR TO DELIVERY TO THE ULTIMATE PURCHASER.

YEAR	MODEL	
90	B26 SE SXA	
DEALER CODE	DATE	METHOD OF TRANSPORTATION
	90 MODEL	TRUCK

COLOR OF YOUR NEW MAZDA ▶ EXT: NOBLE WHITE INT: GRAY INTERIOR

MANUFACTURER'S SUGGESTED RETAIL PRICE (INCLUDING RECOMMENDED DEALER PREP) $10,819.00

1990 MAZDA B2600I 4X4

MECHANICAL
- 2.6L SOHC 4-CYLINDER ENGINE
- MULTI-PORT ELECTRONIC FUEL INJECTION
- AUTOMATIC LOCKING FRONT HUBS
- INDEPENDENT FRONT SUSPENSION W/STABILIZER BAR
- POWER BRAKES WITH VENTILATED FRONT DISCS
- REAR WHEEL ANTI-LOCK BRAKE SYSTEM
- TWO SPEED TRANSFER CASE
- POWER STEERING

EXTERIOR
- DOUBLE WALL CARGO BED WITH TIE DOWN HOOKS
- ONE TOUCH TAILGATE RELEASE
- P215/75R15 ALL TERRAIN STEEL BELTED RADIAL TIRES
- FRONT AND REAR MUDGUARDS
- LOCKING FUEL DOOR

INTERIOR
- TINTED GLASS
- FULL CARPETING
- DAY/NIGHT REAR VIEW MIRROR
- ASHTRAY/CIGARETTE LIGHTER
- 2-SPEED WINDSHIELD WIPERS
- DURABLE VINYL INTERIOR
- 4-SPEED HEATER WITH SIDE DOOR DEMISTORS
- TRIP ODOMETER
- RECLINING FRONT BUCKET SEATS
- IGNITION KEY REMINDER
- GLOVE BOX DOOR WITH TWIN CUPHOLDERS

ACCESSORIES

BC AM/FM ETR CASSETTE WITH 2-SPEAKERS	295.00
D8 4-SPEED AUTOMATIC TRANSMISSION	750.00
EF SE-5 SPORT PACKAGE	579.00
KL FLOOR MATS	52.00
RESALE TAX	55.00
PORT PROCESSING & HANDLING CHARGES	35.00
NN 023 103043 INLAND FREIGHT	329.00
INLAND PORT NN TOTAL	$12914.00

mazda IT JUST FEELS RIGHT.

ADD-A-TAG® PROTECTING THE CONSUMER®

STOCK NUMBER:

DEALER NAME AND ADDRESS

SERIAL NUMBER

JM2UF4147L0888488

THIS LABEL HAS BEEN AFFIXED BY THIS DEALER AND DESIGNED BY ADD-A-TAG® TO CLEARLY INDICATE ANY ADDITIONAL CHARGES. IT IS NOT AN OFFICIAL FACTORY LABEL AFFIXED BY THE MANUFACTURER.

YEAR	MODEL
1990	MAZDA B2600i

AVAILABLE SERVICE AGREEMENT

7 YR./70,000 MILES OR 5 YR./UNLIMITED MILES

COLOR OF YOUR NEW VEHICLE ▶ EXT: INT:

DEALER-ADDED EQUIPMENT AND SERVICES

★ PIN STRIPING	INCL.
★ DOOR EDGE GUARDS	INCL.
★ LIFETIME RUSTPROOFING	INCL.
★ WHEEL WELL MOLDINGS	INCL.
ADJUSTED MARKET VALUE	$4000.00

*THIS PROTECTING-THE-CONSUMER® LABEL IS NOT AN OFFICIAL FACTORY OR GOVERNMENT STICKER. IT IS APPLIED BY YOUR DEALER.

TOTAL PRICE* ▶ 16,914.00

Clearcoat paint? Is that like the emperor's new clothes? Does this vehicle come with no bumpers? Wheel lip moldings must be something like collagen injections for car tires. This dealer is charging $199 just to do the paperwork with an item called administration fee.

We found there are also dealers who just add on thousands without even attempting to justify the increase, like the sucker sticker shown on page 40. Next to the MSRP, you'll notice, is the dealer's sucker sticker, which adds a total of $4,000 for something called the "Adjusted Market Value." What is it really for? Nothing; read the sticker. There is a list of items on the sticker from pin striping to something called wheel well moldings that are supposedly included in the price ("INCL."). These items, of course, have no real value to begin with. If you just glance at the sticker, it also looks as if some kind of warranty may be included: "7 yr./70,000 miles or 5 yr./unlimited miles." When you look closer you realize that it is only an "Available Service Agreement." "Available" is a dealer term for not included. No way, I hear you saying. You can't charge $4,000 for nothing. Oh yes, you can. This sticker came directly off a car on the showroom floor, right off the window (I have an aggressive research staff).

The highest-profit, lowest-value items you'll often find listed on the dealer's sticker are rustproofing, fabric coating and paint sealant. Rustproofing or undercoating can run $200 to $750, fabric coating is usually in the $200 to $350 range and paint sealant adds another couple of hundred.

DEFENSE #13

Don't fall for the undercoating trick.

One of dozens of options you'll find offered when buying a new car is undercoating or rustproofing. Often it is already added into the sticker price. As in all scams, the premise makes total sense. "You don't want the bottom of your automobile to rust out and someday be sitting lower than the center of your wheels," says the salesperson. "Well," you wonder, "is the manufacturer so stupid that he didn't think of that in advance?" But then if the salesperson says, "It's a must," who are you to quibble with an expert? Sometimes you are offered as many as three undercoating options: super, deluxe and lifetime protection. The super is an extra $250, the deluxe $500, and the lifetime protection as much as $750. How can you go wrong? After all, you can add it to the price of the car, which can be financed.

Say "yes" and you're ripped off again. First of all, the undercarriage of the car is already painted with a rustproofing material by the manufacturer, which is all most cars will ever need. The body will rust out long before the undercarriage of your car.

Years ago I hired John Bond to run my printing and publishing company in Manassas, Virginia. At one point in his career John had actually worked for a very "reputable" car dealer in the Washington, D.C., area. He was the undercoating specialist, meaning that his job was to spray the additional undercoating on the endless number of cars on which the rustproofing option had been purchased. John told me the story of the real difference in the super, deluxe and lifetime protection options. "Well," he explained, "to do the super undercoating, I stood under the automobile with a can of pressurized spray paint and carefully coated all the metal, right over the coating the manufacturer had already applied. However, if the customer ordered the deluxe undercoating, I sprayed the undercarriage of the car while standing on one foot. The lifetime protection undercoating process was much more complicated. I stood under the car on one foot and whistled 'Dixie' while I sprayed."

Get the point? Undercoating protection, like so many other options, is a total waste of your money.

DEFENSE #14

Fabric coat your seat covers yourself and forget the paint sealer.

Buy a car with fabric coating done by the dealer and you've just thrown away $200 to $300. Fabric coating is another item that is either already added to the sticker price of a car or pushed by the salesperson as an option. Fabric coating is a process often no more complicated than pulling the car into a bay and spraying the seats and carpets with a can of Scotchgard. Although spraying the seats of any car with $10 worth of Scotchgard or other fabric protection is an excellent idea, why not save a couple hundred dollars by taking 15 minutes to do it yourself? You can buy a spray can of fabric protector for your car at any auto supply or department store.

Paint sealer is another item that is practically 100 percent profit for the dealer. You may have seen cars on which the paint has faded, but they are usually 10 to 20 years old. Your paint will do fine without the paint sealant with just average maintenance such as a waxing every six months. If the paint does eventually begin to fade, a $5 can of fine grit rubbing compound available at an auto parts store is all you need to bring back the luster.

DEFENSE #15

Never give your keys to a car salesperson.

All at once the salesperson notices you've been intently eyeing the sticker and shuffles over to greet you with a reaching hand that is only exceeded in length by the width of his smile. After asking what you're looking for and selling you on the features that only the car you are looking at possesses, he gets down to serious business.

"Give me your keys," he demands, "so my sales manager can drive your car around the block to determine the maximum trade-in we can give you." The purpose of getting your keys is *not* so the sales manager can take it for a ride. He knows what your car is worth within $25 just from the mileage and with one glance at the exterior. The real purpose of getting your keys is to hold you a mental prisoner. It's one of the oldest sales gimmicks still around. At many car dealers there is a parking lot in the back of the building where your car is driven and stored out of sight along with the cars of the other prospects in the showroom. That means the salesperson now has your full attention. If you want to leave, you're going to have to call a cab!

DEFENSE #16

Never use the dealer's Blue Book.

In addition to abusive sales pitches and phony prices, some automobile dealers also have phony Blue Books. These price books are specifically written for the smart-enough-to-be-dangerous buyers who come in and say, "Look, I realize there's a Blue Book and every car has a wholesale price and I will not pay a dime more than what the Blue Book says."

"You got me," the salesperson says. "Gee, you sure are a smart shopper." He reaches into his desk drawer and pulls out a Blue Book with a black cover specifically printed for auto dealers, which shows a price hundreds of dollars higher than the actual value of the car. While the salesperson is playing "you got me," the buyer smiles, figuring for the first time in his life he beat a dealer. Then the salesperson hurries him to the finance department where he is sure to lose several thousand more. As a smart shopper, you will learn the difference between the NADA guide and a phony Blue Book. We'll discuss how to use the NADA book in Attack #22.

There are dozens of ways to get taken when buying a car, and in automobile sales lingo they fall into two categories, front-end loading and back-end loading. Front-end loading is what's added to the price of the car by the salesperson or the dealer's sucker sticker, including:

The inflated delivery and setup charges,
The overpriced options,
The phony discount or trade-in price,
Rustproofing, fabric protection and paint sealant.

But you're not through yet. Once you've cut a deal with the salesperson, you are about to be strong-armed by the finance department into spending at least another $5,000 on items that add absolutely no value to the car. These so-called back-end loads include:

Credit life insurance,
Credit disability insurance,
An inflated interest charge,
The automobile service contract (extended warranty).

DEFENSE #17

Beat the finance department before it beats you.

At a well-run dealership the finance department alone can produce $150,000 a month in extra profit. The finance manager normally gets 7 percent of that profit and, therefore, is highly motivated to use every potential sales gimmick to load you up with every possible high-profit item the dealer has to offer. Finance managers are right there to "help" you finance your car. All you have to do is sign on the dotted line. A good finance manager will earn $6,000 to $10,000 a month loading up car buyers with unnecessary interest, insurance and warranties, all the while making you think you wouldn't be getting the car without his or her help.

Most unaware buyers are so glad to get close to the price and monthly payment they wanted and to be approved for a car loan that they never see what is hitting them from the blind side. When, for instance, the finance department or salespeople can get just another $25 in monthly payments by padding extras into your contract, the dealer makes up to an extra $1,500 profit because you will be paying that measly $25 for 60 months. Add $50 extra to your payment and the dealership pockets $3,000 and pays a bonus to the finance manager of $300. You say, "Well, I can afford $275 a month payments." The salesperson says, "$300 a month and it's yours." You think, "What's another $25 a month?" You have just spent an extra $1,500 when financed for 60 months. If all the padding were taken out, your monthly payments would probably be closer to $230.

It doesn't stop there. After you've agreed to the $300 price figure, the financial manager says, "Look, for only $9 extra per month you get the service contract and you certainly don't want to make a wonderful investment like this without protecting it."

"Okay," you say, and $9 is added to your monthly payment for a total of $540 plus interest. The truth is, if you refuse the extended service contract, you will save much more than $9 per month, since a minimum price for the service contract may have already been added to your monthly payment.

The computer in the finance department is an amazing money machine. Modern automobile dealership computer programs can do anything. Since most buyers are concerned only about the down payment and monthly payments, the finance manager can enter the maximum monthly payment you said you can afford, let's say $310, and the computer will automatically choose and pad your purchase with all of the unnecessary options in order of profit potential to the dealer, and create a loan in which your monthly payments will be exactly $310. Frightening? You bet it is.

An automobile extended service contract, for instance, can cost you anywhere between $300 and $1,800 based solely on the monthly payment the finance manager can talk you into. We discuss the reasons you don't want *any* extended service contract in Chapter 7. If there is only $5 left in the maximum monthly payment you agree to, the extra and unnecessary warranty will cost you $300. If the finance manager still has $30 to play with in your payment, the same warranty will cost you $1,800 plus interest!

Begin thinking this way. Every extra $25 per month you agree to pay on a car financed for 60 months at 12 percent will cost you $1,500 cash, plus interest, over the term of the loan. That's why you never want to buy anything just because you can afford the monthly payments.

DEFENSE #18

Never finance your car at the dealership.

It's one thing to buy a car from a dealer knowing that the price of the automobile has been marked up 15 to 25 percent. How would you feel if you discovered that when you get your loan through the dealer, as most car buyers do, the dealer is also marking up the interest rate 20 to 40 percent?

Oh, I know it's convenient. After you purchase the car, you can walk right into the finance department, the hotbox, and your loan can be handled on the spot. The finance person says he's in touch with all banks and can give you the best interest rate around. The truth is you're probably being charged a rate of 1 to 4 percent more for interest than you would have to pay for a car loan directly from a bank.

How could this happen? The car dealership doesn't finance your loan, a bank does. Unknown to you, a bank has agreed to finance a certain amount of the car dealer's sales at a guaranteed interest rate, let's say 10 percent—guaranteed to the dealer, that is. The dealer can keep everything above the actual interest rate of 10 percent that can be added to your contract. Your financing statement shows an APR (annual percentage rate) of 13 percent which you are told is a great deal in today's market. How did you get sucked into this deal? When you were asked by the salesperson over and over what monthly payment you could afford, the computer raised the interest rate to give you exactly the monthly payments you asked for.

Your defense is simple. Never get your loan from the car dealer. It will cost you an unnecessary fortune. For example, if the dealer's actual interest rate is 10 percent and you finance a luxury car for $20,000, but the dealer clips you for 13 percent for 60 months, you will spend $1,807 in extra interest over the term of the loan—pure profit for the dealer, pure loss for you.

Go into your bank or credit union and finance a car before you begin to shop. Get approved for a loan in whatever price range ($10,000, $15,000, $20,000) you are going to buy. You can then negotiate for a car knowing you already have the loan. You are getting the bank's bottom-line rate, the same approximate rate the dealer would get, and you're not paying the dealer's inflated interest charges.

ATTACK #19

Always buy the car you want, but only after it is two to two and a half years old.

"OK," you're saying to yourself, "this guy is telling me I'll *never* get a good deal on a new car. But I've got to drive, and besides, I like cars. What am I going to do if I don't buy a new car?" Your strategy is to do what I've been doing for 20 years. To get the best value for your money, buy the car you want but *only* after it is between two and two and a half years old.

A new car depreciates about 20 percent the moment you drive it off the lot. That's right, your brand-new $12,500 beauty drops in value $2,500 the minute you take title and the rubber hits the road, and is worth only $10,000! But that's the good news.

Let's go back to our example. The bad news is that after the dealer adds on all the unnecessary high-profit options plus the credit life and disability insurance and the service contract, you just paid $17,914 for a car that is now worth only $10,000. What's more, you signed a 60-month financing contract agreement to pay an additional $6,542 in interest for a total commitment of $24,456. After one day you owe two and a half times what your new car is actually worth! Unbelievable? And then you had the nerve to tell your friends what a great deal you got.

We're not done with the bad news yet. That "new" car will depreciate about another 8 percent the first year and 20 percent on the average the second year, for a total reduction in value the first two years of almost 50 percent. After two years your $12,500 car is worth only about $6,500. From the following table you will see how much an average car depreciates every year for the first 10 years based on its purchase price. The third year your car drops another 16 percent and is worth only about $4,500, or 36 percent of the MSRP sticker price, and only 18 percent of the total amount of $24,456 you are paying for the car.

AGE OF CAR (YEARS)	DEPRECIATION OF PURCHASE PRICE INCLUDING OPTIONS	AGE OF CAR (YEARS)	DEPRECIATION OF PURCHASE PRICE INCLUDING OPTIONS
1	28%	6	5%
2	20%	7	4%
3	16%	8	3%
4	8%	9	2%
5	6%	10	1%

From now on, your objective is to buy a car only after it is two to two and a half years old and has already depreciated almost 50 percent. Since all of the rip-off options like rustproofing, fabric coating, credit life/disability insurance and warranties add no value whatsoever to the car, you, if you bought the car in our example for $6,500 after it was two years old, would be paying 64 percent less for the $17,914 car than the original purchaser—plus all the interest saved. That's how you can buy a beautiful car for the rest of your life at at least up to a 60 percent discount.

You now have two options with your new car-buying knowledge. Either save 60 percent on every automobile you were already going to buy, or begin now buying the luxury cars of your dreams for less than the cost of an ordinary automobile.

I have used this latter strategy for the past 25 years and saved tens of thousands of dollars. Currently I own a fleet of luxury and exotic cars, all bought with the same strategy I just taught to you. A Rolls-Royce costs $145,000 new but I bought mine, you guessed it, a little over two and a half years old for $72,000, a savings of $73,000 or about $35,000 per year for the first two years. My Excalibur cost $84,000 new, but I bought it in mint condition for $27,000 from someone who needed to sell. Adena and I bought my son Chuck a $62,000 BMW for his birthday. Actual price paid, $27,200. Why? Only because it was two and a half years old.

One of the reasons often given for wanting to buy a new car instead of a used car is that you are buying someone else's troubles. That may have been a valid financial concept back in the days when cars cost under $2,000 but it is not true now. When you buy a two-year-old car, you are usually buying one which the original owner spent the first year driving back and forth to the dealership getting all the bugs worked out so that you won't have to. Plus, if you're buying a car for up to 60 percent less, you will have all the money it takes to do the minor repairs.

Let's say you buy a car that has an MSRP sticker showing a retail value of $10,819. What will you typically end up paying for the car and what is it really worth?

THE AMOUNT YOU PAY FOR A CAR VERSUS ITS TRUE VALUE

AMOUNT YOU PAY		ACTUAL VALUE AFTER PURCHASE
$10,819	Base price	$8,655
1,676	4 options	670
419	Freight and handling plus tax	0
12,914	MSRP total	
4,000	Sucker sticker	0
−1,500	Minus "discount"	0
15,414	Actual price of car	
1,500	Credit life/disability insurance	0
1,000	Service contract	0
17,914	Amount financed	
6,542	Interest for 60 months at 13%	0
24,456	Total amount you will pay/actual value of car	$9,325 *

*Value of car if it were to be resold during the first month after purchase.

When you finish paying for this car, you will have shelled out a total of $24,456 for a car that is actually worth only $9,325 when you drive it off the lot, and when you make the last payment in five years it will be worth only about $3,500.

In one hour at a car dealership you have managed to throw away $15,000! Couldn't happen? This scenario currently happens about 20,000 times a day across the country. Never again let it happen to you.

ATTACK #20

Buy a car from an individual instead of a dealer.

When you buy from an individual, you can be assured of getting the deal of a lifetime, every time! Why? Did you ever try to sell a car yourself? It is an absolute nightmare when you don't know how. People are traipsing through your yard day and night, and your phone is ringing off the hook with calls from window shoppers who have no real interest in buying your car. After a couple of weeks of this abuse, coupled with the high continuous cost of advertising, an individual seller is usually just about willing to give the car away. Most eventually give up and either keep the car or get taken in a trade for another car.

When you are shopping the cars for sale by individuals, you have hundreds, even thousands to pick from, while each seller has only one to sell, which immediately puts you in the driver's seat. No one advertises a car for sale until he believes he really needs to sell it. In other words, you have a motivated seller, and armed with the knowledge of how to determine exactly what a car is worth, you are in a position to negotiate your way to luxurious, inexpensive driving.

ATTACK #21

Bargain hunt the classifieds for your ideal car.

First determine one or several models of cars you would like to own. Window shop at the new-car dealers to get a better idea of what you want. But be careful, don't get sucked into a bad deal at a dealership. Instead, you can find the two-year-old car of your dreams by learning how to shop the automobile classified section of your newspaper or your local *Auto Trader* magazine.

It can be a challenge to understand these ads. Because they are normally sold by the line, the fewer lines in the ad, the cheaper it is to run. To cram as much information into as few lines as possible, descriptive codes have been developed and are currently used in almost all newspapers. By learning to decipher the code, you will be able to find several individuals who are selling the car you are looking for.

Automobile Classified Ad Abbreviation Translation

a/c, air = air conditioning
a/t, at, auto = automatic transmission
cass = cassette tape player
cond = condition
conv = convertible
cpe = 2-door
cruise = cruise control
cu in = cubic inches, size of engine
cyl = cylinders (4, 5, 6 or 8)
dlr = dealer is selling the car
exc = excellent condition
h/back, h/b = hatchback or 3-door
hd = heavy duty, as suspension or shocks
hdtp = hardtop, no window pillar
K = number of miles in thousands
lk nw = like new (in almost every ad)
loaded = has lots of options
man trans, mt = manual transmission
mi = miles or mileage
mint = like-new condition
orig owr = original owner is selling
pb = power brakes
ps = power steering
pow seats = power seats
pw = power windows
rdls, rads = radial tires
rear dfg = rear defogger
sac = sacrifice
sed = sedan or 4-door
snrf = sunroof
vnyl = vinyl top
wrnty = warranty comes with car

Here are a few typical classified ads. See if you can decipher them.

TOYOTA CAMRY LE—'92 4dr a/t, PW/Locks, 15k, sac $14,995

SATURN SL1—'93 burgundy/ gray, only 15 mos old, mint cond, 15k mi., book says $11,200, asking $10,000/obo, must see

PONTIAC FIREBIRD—'91, V8 305, Cruise, PS/PB, A/C cass, T-tops, 44k mi., orig owr, black w/ gold pkg., $9,359/obo

NISSAN MAXIMA SE—'91, pearl white, light tan leather, moon roof, BOSE, all power options, clean and well maintained, $16,900

MITSUBISHI 300GT—'93, V6, 5sp, full power, cohv CD, alarm, red, 1 khw, wrnty $23,500

ATTACK #22

Use the NADA *Official Used Car Guide* to determine the value of a car within $25.

The most important step in car buying is to determine exactly what any car you are looking at is actually worth, which is the maximum you will agree to pay. Any car at any point in time is worth exactly what it would sell for that day at your local automobile auction. Every city of any size has an automobile auction at which, once or twice a week, dozens or even hundreds of cars are bought and sold by automobile dealers as they are run across the auction floor in an assembly-line process and at an amazing speed. If you know someone in the auto business, you can attend an auction and even buy a car, but you cannot just show up on your own and start bidding without being a registered automobile dealer.

Most cars on a used-car lot were purchased by the dealer at an auction. Most cars that are traded in by new-car buyers also end up being sold at the auction and not through the new-car dealer's next-door used-car lot.

How do *you* determine the auction price of any car, the maximum that you will pay for a car no matter where you buy it? The simple answer is the NADA *Official Used Car Guide*, the same book used by car dealers and your bank loan officer. The guide is published by the National Automobile Dealers Association (NADA) and until recently was difficult for consumers to get their hands on. Now it's easy.

For the past 25 years, when I needed access to the NADA guide when buying or selling a car, I would simply stop by my local bank and borrow the loan officer's copy, making notes from several pages. You can do the same if you wish. You will find that every banker who makes car loans has a current copy in his or her desk drawer. Many public libraries now subscribe to the NADA guide, and you will find a current copy in the business section. Some bookstores are also now selling the NADA guide for $9.95 each. Other stores have similar books usually called "Used-Car Guides." The automobile dealer's best-kept secret is out.

Since the same automobile's value differs based on geographic area, there are nine editions of the NADA guide published: New England, Eastern, Central, Southeastern, Southwestern, Midwest, Pacific Northwest, Pacific Southwest and Mountain States. The guide is published monthly and the yearly subscription rate is $47. You can also call a toll-free number to get a subscription:

1-800-544-6232

The NADA book is often referred to as the dealers' Blue Book, so when you see one don't be shocked to find that it actually has an orange cover. And don't confuse it with what the dealers like to call their Blue Book.

Using the NADA guide, you will be able to determine within approximately $25 the true value of any domestic or foreign car, van or light truck. Your strategy is simple. Never buy or sell a car without consulting the NADA guide, and never pay more than the auction price. There is a tremendous amount of valuable information in the NADA guide, and learning to decode the data will take just a few minutes of training.

We'll use the same automobile shown on the sticker on page 40. The car on the sticker is a 1990 Mazda B series pickup truck. Let's say that this is what you want, only now we'll go to the NADA guide and find one that is about two years old—a 1988 model. On page 55 you will see the figures from the January 1990 NADA Southeastern Edition as they would appear in the book. From the series number on the sticker, you will find the code UF41, which matches the model number in the book.

In the January edition of the NADA guide, you will find, in addition to the other prices or values, the original MSRP, manufacturer's suggested retail price, which does not include transportation, setup or taxes, items which, of course, add no value to the car. This year the base price from the sticker is $10,819, but two years ago this same vehicle was priced, according to the book, at an MSRP of only $9,849, or a full $1,000 or 10 percent less, which is a part of the savings you will reap by buying a two-year-old vehicle.

There are three additional figures shown for the base price of the vehicle: average trade-in, average loan and average retail. The retail figures are meaningless to you and are supposed to represent, based on reports from dealers, what cars are selling for off the lot, not including all the extras like insurance, warranties and trade-in tricks. The two numbers that are most important to you are Av'g. Trd-in (average trade-in) and Av'g. Loan (average loan value). Nowhere does the book say "auction price." The average trade-in is the auction price and represents what a dealer could buy or sell the car for at an auction. The average trade-in or auction price after adjustment for options, mileage and condition of the car is also the maximum you will offer or agree to pay when buying a car.

Notice that on the Mazda in our example, the current value is shown as $6,600. Now let's add from the same column the two-year-old value of the options that were included on the original sticker on page 40. The options are tape cassette player, four-speed automatic transmission, SE-5 sport package and floor mats (see chart on next page). The current value of the options is shown in the NADA guide at the end of each model year in the left-hand column of the page. Most options listed add value but some, if not included, subtract from the value. Notice with a 1988 Mazda that if the car or truck does not have power steering or air-conditioning, you subtract $150 and $625, respectively. In the front of the NADA guide is a statement that says the editors have found that optional equipment has little or no value on older cars, which is one reason why you don't want to buy a new car loaded with options.

CURRENT VALUE		ORIGINAL COST
$6,600	Base price	$10,819*
75	Cassette tape player	295
475	4-speed automatic trans.	750
300	SE-5 sport package	579
0	Floor mats	52
$7,450		$12,495

*Based on 1990 current replacement cost.

The final adjustments used to arrive at the auction price are made for mileage and overall condition. In the very front of the NADA guide you will find the high and low mileage tables (not shown). For a two-year-old car, the tables show the average mileage is 30,001 to 35,000. Every car and truck fits into one of four mileage categories based on its price, and the categories are shown at the beginning of the section for each manufacturer. Our Mazda fits into category one, and from the high mileage table we would deduct $125 from the value if the mileage was 35,001 to 40,000 and $475 if the mileage was 40,001 to 45,000. If the car was driven less than an average amount, the low mileage table shows that $100 should be added to the value if the odometer reads 25,001 to 30,000 and $150 added if the odometer reads 20,001 to 25,000 miles.

Before you start shopping for your ideal car, develop a True Car Value Calculation Sheet like the one shown on page 57.

Illustration from NADA Guide

January 1990, Southeastern Edition

Auction Price or Maximum You Will Pay

Manufacturer's Suggested Retail Price

What Your Bank Will Lend You

Dealer's Asking Price

I-20 **MAZDA (Japanese) 1988-87**

Av'g. Trd-In	BODY TYPE	Model No.	M.S.R.P.	Wgt.	Av'g. Loan	Av'g. Retail
1988	**MAZDA-AC-PS-Continued**					
7600	Sedan 4D GT	BF22	$11499	2340	6850	8925
5375	Station Wagon 5D	BW62	7849	2230	4850	6550
626-FWD	Veh. Ident.: JM1(Model)()()J1000001 Up					
7400	Sedan 4D DX	GD22	$10499	2590	6675	8825
8350	Sedan 4D LX	GD22	12399	2670	7525	9850
8625	Hatchback 5D Touring LX	GD24	12599	2680	7775	10150
9100	Sedan 4D Turbo	GD22	13999	2760	8200	10700
9400	Hatchback 5D Touring Turbo	GD24	14199	2770	8475	11000
10500	Sedan 4D Turbo (AT,4WS)	GD22	17149	2965	9450	12200
MX6-FWD	Veh. Ident.: ()()()GD31()()J()000001 Up.					
7975	Coupe 2D DX	GD31	$10599	2535	7200	9450
8950	Coupe 2D LX	GD31	12499	2615	8075	10475
9675	Coupe 2D GT	GD31	14499	2705	8725	11300
RX7	Veh. Ident.: JM1(Model)()()J0000001 Up					
11025	Coupe 2D SE	FC33	$15480	2625	9925	12975
11775	Coupe 2D GTU	FC33	17350	2625	10600	13775
12675	Coupe 2D GXL	FC33	19160	2625	11425	14850
13975	Coupe 2D Turbo	FC33	21800	2850	12600	16225
16425	Coupe 2D Convertible	FC35	20500	3003	14800	18825
929	Veh. Ident.: JM1HC221()J()000001 Up.					
13200	Sedan 4D Luxury	HC22	$18950	3282	11900	15425
B SERIES PICKUPS	Veh. Ident.: JM2(Model)()()J()000001 Up					
5000	Pickup	UF11	$7099	2660	4500	6150
5125	Pickup LB	UF21	7599	2730	4625	6275
5525	Pickup Cab Plus	UF31	8599	2790	4975	6700
5675	Pickup LX	UF11	9049	2660	5125	6875
5800	Pickup LX LB	UF21	9549	2730	5225	7000
6200	Pickup Cab Plus LX	UF31	10099	2790	5600	7425
6600	Pickup 4WD	UF41	9849	3190	5950	7875
6725	Pickup LB 4WD	UF51	10349	3225	6075	8000
7125	Pickup Cab Plus 4WD	UF61	11349	3315	6425	8425
7275	Pickup LX 4WD	UF41	12049	3190	6550	8575
7400	Pickup LX LB 4WD	UF51	12549	3225	6675	8725
7800	Pickup Cab Plus LX 4WD	UF61	13099	3315	7025	9150
475	Add Automatic Trans. (Std. 626 4WS)				475	475
75	Add Stereo Tape (Std. 929, RX7, MX6/626 LX & Turbo)				75	75
300	Add SE-5 Pkg.				300	300
100	Add Cruise Control (323, SE, GTU, Pkp)				100	100
200	Add Sunroof				200	200
475	Add Power Sunroof (Std. RX7 GXL & Turbo)				475	475
125	Add Power Windows (Std. Turbo, GXL, 929, MX6/626 LX)				125	125
75	Add Power Door Locks (Std. Turbo, GXL, 929, MX6/626 LX)				75	75
150	Add Power Seats (929)				150	150
50	Add Digital Dash				50	50
175	Add Leather Seats (929, RX7)				175	175
100	Add Alloy Wheels (Std. Turbo, 929, RX7)				100	100
300	Add 2+2 (RX7)				300	300
150	Deduct W/out Power Steering				150	150
625	Deduct W/out Air Conditioning				625	625

1987 MAZDA-AC-PS **Start Aug. 1986, RX7 Turbo March 1986 4WD March 1987, SE April 1987**

Av'g. Trd-In	BODY TYPE	Model No.	M.S.R.P.	Wgt.	Av'g. Loan	Av'g. Retail
323-FWD	Veh. Ident.: JM1(Model)2()H0000001 Up					
3550	Hatchback 3D	BF23	$5999	2060	3200	4550
3775	Hatchback 3D SE	BF23	6699	2105	3400	4800

IMPORTS

Using the numbers from the NADA *Official Used Car Guide*, you will be able to accurately determine the car's auction price and loan value, or the amount of money you will be able to borrow to buy the car. The average retail price will help you calculate the minimum you will save on the car by buying from an individual.

The figures listed in the NADA guide are for a car in good, clean condition. An exceptionally clean car is usually one that has been reconditioned by a dealer and comes with a warranty, not something you are likely to find when buying from an individual. That consideration leads to your next strategy.

ATTACK #23

Offer the NADA price for a car minus what it would cost to put the car back into good, clean condition.

Good, clean condition means that everything on the car works and nothing is about to fall apart. That is what the ads usually promise and what the seller will usually tell you. But how do you know?

Once you and an individual seller have agreed upon the lowest price, take your prospective purchase to a good mechanic and ask him to go through every system and make a list of everything that doesn't work or may soon need fixing, including the price of each repair. A good mechanic will usually charge $50 to $75 to do a thorough check but will end up saving you hundreds in the purchase price now and repairs later on. Never, ever buy a vehicle without going through this process.

You then take the list back to the seller, noting that your offer was for a car in good condition, meaning everything on the car works. You give the seller two choices: either pay for and have the necessary repair work done to put the vehicle in good condition and you will come back next week and pay your first offering price, or if the seller will deduct the cost of repairs, you will take the car now. The seller, if he or she really wants to sell the car, will take your immediate offer at a reduced price, or you can negotiate something in between.

Expect sellers to be shocked when you show them how little their car is really worth by pulling out the NADA guide. Few people are aware of how much they overpay for a new car. Even greater than the sticker shock (seeing for the first time the high price of a new car) is sucker shock, realizing what a mistake you made when you bought it.

If a seller owes thousands more on the car than its NADA value, usually caused by a low or no down payment and 60-month financing, the seller will not be able to sell you or anyone else the car without paying off the balance of the loan that is greater than the sale price. Without the full loan balance paid, the bank or finance company will not release the title to the new owner. When you are calling prospective sellers, the right questions will tell you whether the seller is truly in a position to sell or is going to end up having to keep the car until the debt is paid down to the car's real value.

TRUE CAR VALUE CALCULATION SHEET

Current Date:	January 1990
Year of Car:	1988
Make:	Mazda
Body Type:	Pickup
Model Number:	UF41
Mileage	38,000 Miles

	AVERAGE TRADE-IN AUCTION PRICE	AVERAGE LOAN	AVERAGE RETAIL PRICE
Base Price	$6,600	$5,950	$7,875
Options:			
Tape Player	+$ 75	+$ 75	+$ 75
Automatic Transmission	+$ 475	+$ 475	+$ 475
E-5 Package	+$ 300	+$ 300	+$ 300
Floor Mats	+$ 0	+$ 0	+$ 0
Deduct:			
No Air	−$ 625	−$ 625	−$ 625
Mileage (+ or −) Adjustment	−$ 125	−$ 125	−$ 125
TOTAL	$6,700	$6,050	$7,975

ATTACK #24

Buy the car right and never make a down payment.

Buying a car right means paying the right price, the NADA auction or trade-in price, and not someone's overinflated idea of what the car should be worth. Most banks will allow you to borrow exactly the loan value shown in the NADA guide.

If you offer the NADA price you computed and then deduct the cost of putting the car back into good, clean condition, your required down payment will be either surprisingly low or nonexistent.

Let's go back to our example on page 57, True Car Value Calculation Sheet. The trade-in or auction price you computed was $6,700 for the two-year-old vehicle. The average amount your banker will lend is $6,050, so the maximum down payment you should ever be required to make to pay for the pickup would be $650 ($6,700 − $6,050). Let's say your mechanic found $600 worth of work that needed to be done on the truck, and you finally ended up negotiating an additional $500 discount with the seller and agreed to pay for the repairs yourself. Now the price of the vehicle is only $6,200, which is the $6,700 NADA price minus $500 discount for repairs.

The bank will lend you $6,050, so all you need to do is come up with the difference of $150 cash to buy the car. Best of all, your new purchase will not depreciate much in the next few years compared with the same vehicle when it was new. You will never owe thousands more than your car or truck is worth.

DEFENSE #25

Get a car loan for no more than 36 months.

Another major mistake you can make is financing the purchase of an automobile for 48 or 60 months, whether you get the loan from a dealer or from a bank. Finance a car for 60 months and after two years your car is still worth about $5,000 less than the balance on your loan. You have actually gone deeper in the hole even though you've been making all those big payments. The longer the term of your loan, the greater the percentage of each early payment that goes to pay the interest and not the principal balance of your loan. Your new car is decreasing rapidly in value during the first two years, 10 times faster than you are paying it off!

If you were to totally wreck your car, you might be all right but your bank account won't be. Your insurance company is obligated to pay only the value of the car if damaged beyond repair, not the balance owed on your car loan. After the insurance company pays the value of the car to the bank, the bank will ask you for the $5,000 difference. If you don't have it, the bank will sue you, getting a judgment and ruining your credit. Shocking? Not at all. I hear this story all the time.

Your defense? Never get a car loan for more than 36 months. A 36-month loan allows you to pay off your loan faster than your car is depreciating. A 36-month car loan on a two-year-old car ensures that you can sell your car anytime you want to without losing money. You don't owe more than you own.

Make a commitment to yourself that you will never again get a loan for longer than 36 months no matter how much you want a car. Financial control builds wealth instead of debt. "Well," I hear you saying, "I just can't afford the payments on a 36-month loan." Sure you can if you use the strategies in this chapter. Returning to our example, if you bought the $12,914 new pickup, you ended up borrowing $17,914. If you finance the $17,914 for five years at 12 percent, the payments will be $407.60 per month for 60 months. True, that's less than the $603.59 payments you would make on $17,914 if you financed your car for only 36 months.

But remember, you can buy the same car two to two and a half years old for only about $6,500. The $6,500 financed for three years at 11 percent (you're not paying the dealer's inflated interest charge) has payments of only $212.80 per month, a full $194.80 less per month than the $407.60 per month payments on the five-year loan for the same car new, and you make 24 fewer payments because it is a 36-month loan instead of a 60-month loan. That's how you can afford the car of your dreams now without going deep into debt for the next five years!

As you might suspect, not everyone is delighted with the fact that you and others are wising up about your money. Here are excerpts from a letter I received from the vice president of a Ford dealership in Roanoke, Virginia:

There were two serious prospects who did not purchase their cars from us because you told your audience that if you cannot afford the payments for three years instead of five years don't buy the car. Another who had purchased a car dropped the warranty.

It is obvious that the automobile dealers in the Roanoke area do not need people like you to conduct seminars.

I hope that Roanoke, Virginia, is never on your itinerary again.

These are letters I love to get. It means that I am making progress in helping all Americans learn to handle money.

Finally and maybe surprisingly, I want to say something in defense of the automobile dealers. An automobile dealership 30 years ago was an automatic ticket to financial success. Today, I don't believe most dealers are practicing intentional deception but are trapped in a struggle for financial survival created by the inability of manufacturers to control costs, the high cost of showrooms and, in the case of dealerships that sell American-made cars, fierce foreign competitors with higher quality standards.

No matter what the motivation, however, the end result is the same. Buying automobiles the way everyone else does is enough to break most individuals and families. But you are now armed with the knowledge that will enable you to make driving your car a financial pleasure instead of a financial nightmare.

CHAPTER 4

Sell Your Car Yourself and Pocket an Extra $1,000

After reading the last chapter and becoming a master at the automobile game, one important thought has probably crossed your mind. "If I'm not going to buy from a car dealer and trade in my old car, what about the nightmare that most people go through when selling their old cars? How am I going to get rid of mine?" Getting rid of your old car at top dollar is much easier by following the strategies in this chapter.

ATTACK #26

Make money by selling your old car yourself.

If I told you that you could sell your car yourself with about four hours of effort, without all the problems most people endure, and pocket $1,000 extra in the process, would the extra effort be worth the price? You can.

Trading in a car is almost the same as giving it away. Trade-ins are a nuisance to dealers and require the dealer either to resell the car from his used-car lot or to dump it at a car auction at a rock-bottom price in order to realize the profit from the new car you bought. The dealer's profit is in your old car until it is resold. It's going to cost the dealer plenty of money to take your old clunker as a trade-in, and he is going to get it out of your pocket one way or another. Which brings us to the next principle: *There are no good trade-in deals.*

Don't fall for the dealership trade-in tricks. One reason the manufacturer's and the dealer's sticker prices are marked up so high is to allow the salesperson to offer you what seems to be a good trade-in price for your car, making the offer only with "funny money" built into the inflated price.

Another way the salesperson plays "gotcha" is to get your mind off the amount of the trade-in by getting you to concentrate only on your monthly payments. "Your payments would have been $280 a month," he says, "that is, without the trade-in. But by giving you $3,000 for your old car, we can get them down to just $210, just what you told me you could afford to pay."

If you do know the auction value of your car, you will find that after juggling the numbers a dealer often offers at least $1,000 below the auction price as his profit for handling your old trade-in. You'll be told either that, because there is a current demand for your type of car, you are getting absolutely top dollar, or if you already think the offer is too low, that there is no market for your car right now. Another salesperson's trick is to make you think that you and he are putting one over on his boss by getting such a high trade-in allowance. You start feeling good while you are actually getting clobbered. The dealer makes a profit on the inflated price of the car you are buying—and a big extra profit on the resale of your trade-in. Never trade in an old car.

Here are the steps to follow to get the maximum amount for your car when you sell it yourself.

Step #1: Determine your car's true worth using the NADA guide.

Refer to your NADA used-car pricing guide and determine both the average trade-in (auction) price and the average loan value of your car. Show the NADA guide to a prospective buyer, and he will spot the trade-in price. The average trade-in price is the minimum price you will take for your car, although sometimes you can sell for between the trade-in and retail price if the car is in exceptionally good condition and you are a smooth talker. The average loan value is the amount the buyer will be able to borrow to buy your car. Point out the price in the retail column as the price the buyer would have to pay if he or she went to a dealer, and the big down payment that would have to be made. Then point out your price, which is the average trade-in price you are selling for, and how much that would reduce the down payment required. Tell the buyer he or she will save hundreds just by buying your car—an absolutely true statement.

Step #2: See your banker.

Call or meet with a loan officer at the financial institution that financed your car and ask what would be required for someone to take over your car loan. You will normally be told that the new owner would have to reapply for the loan, but that if his or her credit is good, the institution would be happy to handle the loan. You then can run in your ad, "financing arranged," which will attract many more calls, since most people have no idea how to get a car financed if they buy from an individual owner.

Step #3: Get your car detailed.

The way a car looks is as important to a buyer as the price, and your objective is to fix minor items that will add more to the car's value than the cost of the fix-up. Getting your car "detailed" is the best $75 investment you can make. Detailing goes far beyond washing and waxing and will make your car look and smell new. It's a great idea to have your car detailed every six months or so while you own it, but it is a must when you get ready to sell. You will also want to have the engine steam cleaned and all corrosion removed from the battery cables. Have anything that rattles tightened, and clean out and vacuum your trunk. If the front carpet is a mess, buy some inexpensive floor mats to cover it. Touch-up paint is available in all colors at an auto parts store. Major repairs, as long as the car runs well, are not necessary, as they will normally add more to your cost than to the value. If repairs are required, just say so in your ad and discount the price.

Step #4: Advertise your car.

Buy some space in the classified section of your local newspaper, but avoid the cost of running the ad for an entire week. Many newspapers have specials like: "three days, three lines, $9," and this kind of inexpensive ad is what you're looking for. Key words that inspire potential buyers to call are: low mileage, clean, like new, must sell, financing arranged and financing available. Include your telephone number and the times when people should call. A good idea is to limit the times that people can call by stating, "Call 5–7 pm weekdays, 10 am–5 pm weekends." That way you won't be receiving a lot of phone calls late at night. Putting the asking price in your ad is an absolute must and will save dozens of calls from people who are just window shopping. Set your asking price at $200 to $400 above the trade-in value in the NADA guide.

Step #5: Set up one time for all to view your car.

To save yourself tremendous hassle, set up a specific time and date for all prospects to look at your car. One of the best strategies is to show your car to everyone at once. For instance, if your ad starts on Saturday, you may wish to set up Sunday at 5 o'clock as the time for your prospective buyers to look. When prospects call, you say, "I'll be home at 5 o'clock on Sunday afternoon for you to look at and test-drive the car. Will that be satisfactory for you?"

When the prospective looker says yes, your next statement is the clincher that will prevent the "no-shows." First, ask the person for his name and telephone number so that he knows that you know who he is. Then tell the person that you will be there especially to meet with him or her and your time is valuable, so if for any reason he is unable to keep the appointment to call and let you know. This last step will cut your no-shows by 50 percent.

Show your car to several individuals or families at one time. No one will stall by saying, "I want to go home and think it over." Your prospects will wonder why so many people are interested in this one car, since other cars they have looked at have not attracted this much attention. When you have only one car and several prospective buyers, someone is going to make you an offer.

Step #6: Ride with the potential buyer.

Never let someone take your car for a test drive without being in the car yourself. One of the biggest scams these days occurs when someone shows up as a prospective buyer to look at a car, takes it for a "test drive," and the seller, three hours later, is still standing in the driveway, wondering why the car hasn't come back.

Step #7: Be excited about your car.

Tell prospective buyers what a great time you have had owning the car, that it is one of the most maintenance-free cars you have ever had and give a reasonable, positive reason for selling it. If a prospective buyer says, "Well, this car has several nicks and a dent," your response is, "Isn't that great? That's why you are buying it for a lot less money, as you can see from my price."

Step #8: Pick a rock-bottom price.

To avoid endless dickering about price, start your asking price at about $200 to $400 above the rock-bottom price you will take. Once you're at the rock-bottom price, let the buyer know: "This is the least I will sell for. Please don't waste your time or mine making a lower offer." Tell the prospective buyer that he is welcome to shop around, but he won't find a better car in better condition for the price, and may lose the opportunity to buy your car if he waits too long.

Step #9: Have all the papers and numbers ready.

A prospective buyer may offer to pay cash, but it is more likely that he or she will require financing, and will need to know the model and serial numbers and the options on the car. Have that information ready and handwritten or typed so that a prospective buyer can visit his banker with facts in hand. Or if you have already spoken to your banker, and the prospective buyer doesn't have one of his own, send him there.

Step #10: Accept only cash.

When you have finally negotiated a deal, never take a check or a promise. Once you have written out and signed a bill of sale, if the check bounces, that doesn't give you the automatic right to repossess the car, only to collect on the check. Tell the buyer that you'll accept only cash or a certified check. If the buyer is financing the car, his bank will pay off the outstanding loan balance at your bank, and the difference will come to you. In the meantime take a substantial down payment in cash of $200 to $1,000 to take the car "off the market." If the buyer has only a check, accompany the buyer to his or her bank to cash the check.

If the buyer has financed the purchase of your car, require him to have the necessary insurance, license and proof of ownership before taking the car. If he has paid you cash on the spot and the necessary transfer papers have been signed, he may take possession. But make sure to take off your license plates before the car leaves your driveway.

Step #11: Make sure that you follow your state's transfer rules.

When you sell a car, and before it leaves your possession, contact your state's division of motor vehicles to find out exactly what must be done legally to transfer the car from you to the new owner. Usually, there is a place on the back of the title and the registration for you to sign to effect a transfer. Do not let the buyer take the car if your name is still listed as owner. You may be liable for damages if an accident occurs. Once the necessary legal transfer has been made, prepare and sign a bill of sale, with one copy to the new owner, one copy for you.

Bill of Sale

Sold to ____________________ by ____________________ one ______________________________ (insert the year, model number and make of car) for $__________. Sold as is.

Date ____________ Your Signature ____________________

Step #12: Cancel your insurance only after the car is completely out of your name and your loan shows "paid in full."

Many people sell a car, forget to cancel the insurance and end up paying hundreds before they discover the error. However, never cancel your insurance until the car is in the buyer's name. If you cancel your insurance before your car loan has been paid off, the bank or finance company will add expensive single-party insurance to protect itself and charge the premiums and interest to you. (See pages 253–55.)

Selling a car will never be one of your favorite recreational activities, but doing it correctly will easily save you $1,000.

PART III

How to Save Thousands When You Buy Insurance

CHAPTER 5

The Right (and Wrong) Way to Buy Insurance

Insurance is an economic device whereby you pay a small guaranteed loss—the premium—to protect yourself from the possibility of a larger financial loss—the peril. The greater the possibility of a loss, the greater the cost of the insurance. In the old days, such losses were often the concern of your friends and neighbors, not insurance companies. Remember the stories of how a whole community used to come to the aid of a fellow farmer who had lost his barn in a fire? At no cost the whole village would pitch in to rebuild the barn. The lost barn would be replaced by the combined effort of many in just a few days, something the farmer himself might have required a year or more to do. The farmer's family could have suffered tremendous financial loss if, for that year, their time was spent rebuilding the barn instead of tending crops. The informal insurance agreement was that the farmer who lost his barn would become part of the work party the next time there was a loss suffered by someone else.

Those days were the last time insurance was either cheap or nonprofit. Today, insurance is the biggest and richest industry in the world. The insurance industry in America is bigger than all the banks, brokerage firms and restaurants combined. The basic insurance concept, however, has not changed since the days when everyone pitched in to replace someone else's loss.

The sole purpose of insurance is to protect against the possibility of large unpredictable losses of a few with the smaller guaranteed losses of many. The large potential loss is the peril or risk, and in today's world almost every risk can be insured at some price. Here are some of the most common risks shared by most families:

- Loss of income to a family because of the death of a breadwinner
- Expensive medical bills that couldn't be reasonably paid out of current income
- Damage to a car done by the driver or someone else, or damage done with a car

The insurance business is divided into three major parts—life insurance, health insurance and casualty insurance. Life insurance includes any policy that pays money to someone upon the death of the insured. Health insurance pays hospital and/or doctor bills if the insured is sick or injured and includes disability and dental insurance. Casualty insurance covers just about everything else, and includes:

- Automobile insurance
- Homeowner's insurance
- Liability insurance
- Business insurance
- Rental car insurance

Even though you can buy an insurance policy to cover almost any risk, only a few insurance coverages or policies are good values. The simple fact is that the insurance industry is fraught with false promises and deceptive sales practices, which play on people's financial ignorance and natural fears. It doesn't have to be that way. Don't be wooed or fooled by phony sales pitches and scare tactics used by most insurance salespeople. Use the attack and defense strategies described in the following chapters and maybe you will accomplish what Richard Banks and his family did.

Richard B. of Orlando became a member of the Givens Organization in 1988 and immediately went to work redesigning his total insurance plan using my strategies. Below are Richard's insurance premiums and coverages before and after using the Givens strategies. He was able to cut his total premiums by $6,473 per year, from $11,693 to $5,220. In addition, he received a refund of $1,757 from the cash value of his old life insurance policy. Included in the calculation was an increase in Richard's total life insurance protection from $175,000 to $250,000 and the addition of a $1,000,000 personal umbrella liability policy. Now Richard and his family have the protection they really need and an extra $6,500 every year to live out their dreams.

As you learn more about my insurance strategies, you will see why each change Richard and his family made was the smart move.

TYPE OF INSURANCE	BEFORE	AFTER	SAVINGS
Life Insurance on children Jill, Deb, and Doug @ $18,000 each	$ 180	$ 0	$ 180
Universal Life Insurance			
Richard $174,960	3,858	0	3,858
Term Life Insurance			
Richard $250,000	0	617	(617)
Irma $100,000	265	265	0
Automobile Insurance (2 Cars)	1,194	855	339
Mortgage Insurance	229	0	229
Homeowner's Insurance	248	198	50
Rental Car Insurance (vacation)	112	0	112
Umbrella Liability Insurance ($1,000,000)	0	125	(125)
Disability Insurance	1,800	0	1,800
Health Insurance	3,807	3,160	647
Yearly Savings	$11,693	$5,220	$6,473
Insurance Policy Refund			1,757
Total First Year Savings			$8,230

Insurance and Betting

All insurance is a bet, and the only bet you always hope you lose. You are actually betting your premiums that you will have some accident or injury resulting in loss of life, disability, hospital expenses, or damage to your or other people's property. If you win the bet, you collect in claims from the insurance company usually more than you paid out in premiums, but unfortunately you must suffer some type of loss in order to collect—even, as in the case of life insurance, the loss of your

INSURANCE AND BETTING

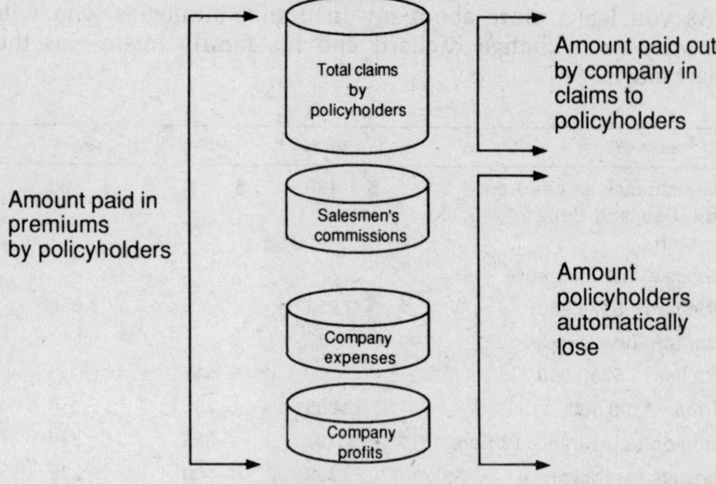

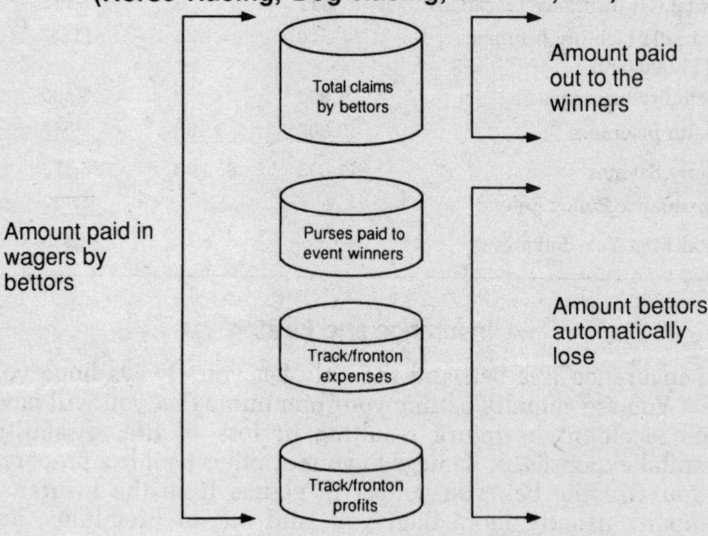

life. When in the end you have paid more in premiums than you have collected in claims you have lost your bet.

The bet would at least be an even bet, like flipping a coin heads or tails, if the total amount paid in premiums by policyholders was eventually paid back to the policyholders in claims plus interest for the time the money was held. For every million the insurance company collected, it would have to pay out a million in claims plus interest. Even though thousands would still pay premiums and only a few would collect claims, at least there would be no question that the premiums were fair and covered the true risk.

But that's not the way insurance works. Instead, insurance is like pari-mutuel betting (at a horse track, dog track or jai alai fronton). None of these businesses pays out in claims or winnings anywhere near what they take in. Look at the insurance and betting chart that follows and you will see a comparison of where insurance and betting dollars really go. Notice that the total amount paid in by policyholders and bettors is divided into four parts, only one of which is paid back.

The truth is that an insurance company pays out far less in claims to policyholders than it collects from them, 25 percent to 80 percent less depending on the type of insurance. Therefore, an insurance bet is never a fair or even-money bet. One goal of the insurance company is to increase premiums taken in but to reduce or limit the claims paid out. For every $100,000 of claims that are not paid, $100,000 is added directly to the company's profits. The portion of the premium that a company charges for sales commissions, company expenses and profits is dictated mainly by market conditions and competition. Paying more in salespeople's commissions usually means more salespeople will agree to represent the company and sales will increase. However, the policyholders will pay more in premiums with no greater potential payout in claims.

If the company can reduce its total claims or reduce its total company expenses as a percentage of the money it takes in, company profits go up. An insurance company reduces the amount of claims it pays in two ways:

1. By attempting to exclude in the policy the risks on which an insured would have the greatest chance of collecting. This limiting process includes deductibles or elimination periods for health, auto and disability insurance. Small claims are the most frequent and expensive claims to process and small claims are eliminated with deductibles. A company also reduces claims with "limited coverage" clauses, which reduce the amount of

coverage for the first two or three years and/or limits the number of years for which the insurance company is liable.

2. By looking for loopholes to avoid paying claims. Claims adjusters are trained to find every possible legal loophole to get out of paying a claim or to negotiate the amount of a legitimate claim to the absolute minimum. If you have ever tried to collect from an insurance company, you already know that what the advertisements and salespeople told you when convincing you to buy has little to do with how you are treated when you file a claim. You begin to wonder if the sales and advertising departments have ever met or talked to the claims department. When you buy an insurance policy, the insurance company is always your friend. When you make a claim on an insurance policy, you may sometimes feel as if the insurance company has immediately become your adversary.

When it comes to winning with insurance, you must put the odds on your side. Your objective and the insurance company's objective may appear to be in total conflict. You want to buy insurance that will protect your real and not imagined risks at the lowest possible price. Some insurance companies, on the other hand, could seem to be motivated to sell you insurance coverage on imagined risks for which you have the least chance of collecting.

I wrote about both life and casualty insurance in my book *More Wealth Without Risk*. The response from my readers was incredible. No one had ever leveled with them about insurance before. And the questions I am asked during my lectures and TV appearances are often about insurance. Everyone wants to know more. So in the following chapters, I'll clarify and expand on my money-saving insurance strategies, and discuss new strategies that have evolved.

By using these strategies, you will be able to protect your assets by creating better insurance bets and in the process save yourself tens of thousands of dollars over the course of your lifetime no longer spent on wasted premiums. When it comes to insurance, you may have often been lied to intentionally or unintentionally by insurance salespeople, financial planners, CPAs and even lawyers, who espouse strategies for what insurance you should or shouldn't carry with little or no knowledge of the mathematical and financial truths about insurance. Anybody who tells you anything different from what you'll learn next, no matter how well-meaning, is lying to you again.

DEFENSE #27

Accept all insurance as a financial alternative and not as a potential financial windfall.

As you have read, there is no way you could possibly win by buying insurance. You can only protect against a major financial loss. The optimum insurance is self-insurance, having the wealth to cover your contingencies or potential risks so that you do not need to rely on a claim funded by overpaid insurance premiums.

To become self-insured as your wealth goes up, take higher and higher deductibles on health, automobile and homeowner's insurance and longer elimination periods if you decide to carry disability insurance. As you become older and more financially fit, you have a reduced need, as you will see, for life insurance, and once the income produced by your assets is equal to the income that could be produced by life insurance, you no longer have a need for life insurance at all.

By reducing your insurance premiums thousands of dollars, you can devote the money you save to enhancing your lifestyle rather than the lifestyles of insurance salespeople and executives. Remember, very few people will ever collect more from an insurance company in claims than they pay out in premiums. Of course, some do—and get very excited about collecting from a policy they shouldn't have bought and didn't need—but most will only watch as extra, wasted insurance premiums vanish.

I am not knocking the concept of insurance. Purchased correctly, with knowledge and without emotion, the right amount of the right kind of insurance is an absolutely essential part of your financial plan. But when you begin to reexamine your own insurance plan, it is important to recognize that you can't possibly protect yourself from everything that could possibly go wrong, nor is it necessary when dealing with small risks. Recognize, too, that it's okay to pay for things that go wrong yourself, that you are not winning just because an insurance company picks up part of the tab. An insurance company, remember, always takes in far more than it will ever pay out.

CHAPTER 6

Create a Maximum-Protection Low-Cost Life Insurance Plan

Life insurance is, though unnecessarily, one of the most expensive parts of a good financial plan. To wrest control of your insurance policy and premiums away from your insurance company and agent, you must understand how the system works.

In this chapter, you'll learn:

- the insurance terms necessary to understand an insurance policy,
- who needs life insurance and who doesn't,
- the amount of life insurance you need to protect your family,
- how to avoid costly life insurance gimmicks,
- why whole life, universal life and single-premium life are three of the biggest investment rip-offs in America,
- how to choose the right kind of term life insurance,
- how to use The Insurance ClearingHouse to find the best and lowest-priced term life insurance,
- how to cancel an old policy and prevent the insurance company from attempting to keep your cash value,
- how to use insurance policy cash values in better investments,
- how to set up your estate plan to correctly distribute life insurance proceeds.

Most families will spend an average of $1,000 to $3,000 every year on life insurance to protect the family financially against loss of the breadwinner. Normally the money goes into some kind of life insurance plus investment plan, like whole life or universal life policies. If life insurance is carried for 50 years, the family has spent between $50,000 and $150,000 just on life insurance, and about 75 percent of that money is misdirected.

Life insurance is a necessary and important part of your total financial plan—that is, if you have a family. But the kind of protection you really need is inexpensive and a true financial benefit instead of a financial drain. However, listen to the pitches of the endless parade of life insurance hawkers and you could throw away more than $1,000 a year for the rest of your life. Your defense? The knowledge and strategies to build a powerful life insurance protection plan. You only have to do it once and the results will last a lifetime.

DEFENSE #28

Don't buy the sales pitches of life insurance salespeople; use knowledge to make your decisions.

The biggest deception in the life insurance business is created through training and brainwashing life insurance agents to sell whatever policies produce the greatest protection and profits for the insurance company, at the expense of the insured. Just as Congress can use tax laws to divert taxpayers' money into any type of investment or action, insurance companies can use commission rates, bonuses and awards to motivate America's tens of thousands of insurance agents to hard-sell prospects into actions that financially benefit the agents.

When recruiting new and inexperienced agents, the main theme of insurance company propaganda is the amount of money salespeople can earn by selling cash value and investment life insurance. More and more life insurance companies are now basing their awards, trips and bonuses on commissions earned, instead of total coverage sold, which rewards salespeople for selling more of exactly the kind of life insurance people don't need.

The entire commission structure of the insurance industry is set up to make failures out of sales agents who sell policyholder protection instead of garnering insurance company profits. Here is an outrageous but absolutely accurate example: Insurance sales Agent A sells five $150,000 term insurance policies every week for 52 weeks. During the year, he would have helped 260 families with the protection they need for an average cost per family of $17.50 per month. Agent A would have brought the insurance company $55,000 of premium income and sold $39 million worth of life insurance. However, Agent A would have earned only about $35,000 for the year by selling term insurance, which are earnings below the industry average, and he would not be acknowledged by most companies in the company bulletin, would not go to the annual convention, and would not receive any plaques or awards. In fact, he may stand the chance of losing his job or having his commission level reduced for poor performance.

Agent B, on the other hand, doesn't work nearly as hard. He makes an average of less than two sales per week with a total of only 92 sales for the year. Because he is selling cash value life insurance, he is able to extract $50 per month from each family, three times the term insurance premium, but provides only $50,000 instead of $150,000 of insurance protection per family. Agent B has brought the company the same $55,000 of premiums but has provided only $4.6 million of insurance protection to his policyholders, 88 percent less than Agent A. However, Agent B has usually earned over $50,000 in commissions, makes the million-dollar club, wins the plaques, take the trips and is well on the road to retirement from the renewal commissions. The insurance commission system is built to reward the people who provide the least protection to the consumer. Most salespeople who sell *only* low-cost term insurance do not survive financially under the current system. Some life insurance companies even require their independent agents to sell a high percentage of whole life or universal life policies rather than term just to maintain their contracts.

Talking to tens of thousands of policyholders who had been misguided into buying overpriced cash value and investment life insurance policies led me to create a new service for members of my organization and those who read this book. What, I thought, could be accomplished if a team of researchers monitored the major life insurance companies rated A or above to find the 1 out of 100 excellent term policies that provide the most protection for the lowest premiums? What if a well-trained, caring staff of insurance representatives not dedicated to any one insurance company could help match families with the right company based on age, amount of insurance required and health of the insured? It can't be done, we were told by experts in the insurance business. If your objective is to locate and sell the lowest-priced non-cash-value term life insurance, the actual commissions are so small per $100,000 of insurance that there is no way you can pay for the staff, the computers and the telephones.

The minute somebody tells me it can't be done, I know I'm on the right track. Along with Buddy and Jo Hewell, longtime friends and consultants to the Charles J. Givens Organization on insurance, annuities and retirement plans, we created what theoretically couldn't be created: a self-sustaining insurance clearinghouse put together for the benefit and financial protection of policyholders. Free access to The Insurance ClearingHouse* is one of the important financial benefits of membership in the Charles J. Givens Organization. As a reader of this book, you will also have access to The Insurance ClearingHouse and will be amazed or even shocked at how little the right amount of life insurance protection can actually cost when you're matched with the right type of policy from a company their research locates for you.

DEFENSE #29

Buy life insurance only when you need it.

Not everyone needs life insurance, but you would never realize that by listening to life insurance salespeople.

First, let's define the purpose of life insurance, and then we'll see who isn't covered by the definition. The main purpose of life insurance is to replace lost family income—income no longer available due to the untimely death of one or both of the family breadwinners. Life insurance, therefore, should be only on the lives of those who produce income for other dependents. Based on the above-stated purpose, there are four groups of people who usually don't need insurance coverage on their lives at all:

1. Single people with no dependents,
2. Nonworking spouses with no dependents,
3. Children,

*This insurance service is not available in all areas.

4. Those who are retired and live off investment or retirement income instead of job or career income.

Why? Because these groups don't produce job or career income for dependents.

Single people with no dependents do not need life insurance because they have no one to protect. Yet because of the incredibly powerful life insurance marketing and sales pitches, about 30 percent of all life insurance in force today is on the lives of—guess who?—single people with no dependents. Who will get the insurance money—the dog, the cat, or parents and other family members who have never been dependent on them financially? Often people ask me, "If I'm single, shouldn't I have a small burial policy so that burden doesn't fall on my parents or siblings?" That can be a consideration. If you don't have enough assets to pay for that unwanted event and the burden would fall on other relatives, you then have someone you need to protect financially and an inexpensive $5,000 or $10,000 term insurance policy makes sense and can be purchased for only a few dollars per year. If you have a group hospitalization policy at work, you may already have a $5,000 to $10,000 life insurance policy included as part of the package and need no additional life insurance.

Children are the most overinsured of all those who fall into the "shouldn't be insured" group. Children should be protected by life insurance, but the insurance should be on the lives of their parents, not on the kids themselves. Remember, the purpose of insurance is to protect the family against loss of income. Normally children don't produce income, unless they happen to have a great job in movies or television.

Parents are easy marks for slick-talking life insurance salespeople. The sales pitch goes something like this: "You do love your children, don't you?" Generally, if it's been a good day with the kids, there's only one answer and that's, "Of course." You are now sucker bait! The next statement from the salesperson is, "Then naturally you'll want a life insurance policy on your child or children; it's the loving thing to do." Life insurance on children is not the loving thing to do. It is detrimental to your wealth as long as you continue to pay the premiums. And if you lost a child, would several thousand dollars of cash help ease the pain?

Another reason life insurance on children makes no sense is the incredibly small chance of a child dying. Look at the mortality table that follows. This table shows at any age how many deaths per 1,000 people in the United States actually occur each year, as well as the average number of years remaining in the life of a person at each age. For instance, locate males age 30 in the first column. In the second column, you will see that only 1.73 deaths per 1,000 people will occur for those at age 30, or a little over 1/10 of 1 percent. The third column shows that at age 30 a person has an average of 43.24 more years to live.

Now let's apply the chart to children. To find the chances of a child dying before age 18, we would total up all the deaths per 1,000 during the years 1–17. The total, 17.07, is the number of deaths per 1,000 children during the 17-year period, or about 2 in 100. There is only a 2 in 100 chance that any child who survives the first year of life will die before age 18. That shows you what a safe bet the life insurance company has made insuring the lives of children. Any premium paid to insure the life of most children is, therefore, a complete waste of money.

To disguise the fact that life insurance on children is such a waste, insurance companies have created deceptive sales gimmicks. "Guaranteed insurability" is one such gimmick. The salesperson tells you that by buying a policy while the child is young, it guarantees his or her insurability later even if your child becomes disabled or is found to have an incurable disease. The chances of those events occurring are even less than the chances of the child dying in the first 18 years. In addition, 99 percent of the people in America who need life insurance are insurable at any age. Yet the statement of guaranteed insurability seems so logical that in my lectures people continually tell me that guaranteed insurability is why they bought life insurance on their children or grandchildren. Never buy life insurance on children now just to provide guaranteed insurability later on.

Insurance as an investment for your child's college education is another sales gimmick. Every parent worries about the ever increasing costs of a college education. Almost every whole life or universal life salesperson has an answer. Buy a whole life policy on the life of your child (or grandchild) and the cash value built up by age 18 will pay for college.

Fact: No one I have ever met has financed even one year of a college education on the money built up in the cash value of a whole life insurance policy or earnings from a universal life policy. I'm sure a few exist, but so do those who have been struck by lightning more than twice and survived.

Giving the insurance company your hard-earned money to use for up to 18 years, while all you receive is a pittance of 3 percent or less per year on a whole life policy, or get ripped off for 10

MORTALITY TABLE
UNITED STATES

AGE	DEATHS PER 1,000	EXPECTATION OF LIFE (YEARS)	AGE	DEATHS PER 1,000	EXPECTATION OF LIFE (YEARS)
0	12.60	73.88	35	1.59	41.43
1	.93	73.82	36	1.70	40.49
2	.55	72.89	37	1.83	39.56
3	.50	71.93	38	1.97	39.63
4	.40	70.97	39	2.13	37.71
5	.37	70.00	40	2.32	36.79
6	.33	69.02	41	2.54	35.87
7	.30	68.05	42	2.79	34.96
8	.27	67.07	43	3.06	34.06
9	.23	66.06	44	3.35	33.16
10	.20	65.10	45	3.68	32.27
11	.19	64.11	46	4.01	31.39
12	.25	63.12	47	4.42	30.51
13	.37	62.14	48	4.88	39.65
14	.53	61.16	49	5.38	28.79
15	.69	60.19	50	5.89	27.94
16	.83	59.24	51	6.42	27.10
17	.95	58.28	52	6.99	26.28
18	1.05	57.34	53	7.61	25.46
19	1.12	56.40	54	8.30	24.65
20	1.20	55.48	55	9.02	23.85
21	1.27	54.53	56	9.78	23.06
22	1.32	53.60	57	10.59	22.29
23	1.34	52.67	58	11.51	21.52
24	1.33	51.74	59	12.54	20.76
25	1.32	50.81	60	13.68	20.02
26	1.31	49.87	61	14.93	19.29
27	1.30	48.94	62	16.28	18.68
28	1.30	48.00	63	17.67	17.88
29	1.31	47.06	64	19.11	17.79
30	1.33	46.12	65	20.59	16.51
31	1.34	45.18	66	22.16	15.85
32	1.37	44.24	67	23.89	15.20
33	1.42	43.30	68	25.85	14.56
34	1.50	42.36	69	28.05	13.93

MORTALITY TABLE
UNITED STATES

AGE	DEATHS PER 1,000	EXPECTATION OF LIFE (YEARS)	AGE	DEATHS PER 1,000	EXPECTATION OF LIFE (YEARS)
70	30.52	13.32	85	107.25	5.96
71	33.15	12.72	86	117.12	5.61
72	35.93	12.14	87	127.17	5.29
73	38.82	11.58	88	137.08	4.99
74	41.84	11.02	89	147.38	4.70
75	45.07	10.48	90	158.68	4.43
76	48.67	9.95	91	171.69	4.17
77	52.74	9.44	92	185.70	3.93
78	57.42	8.93	93	200.23	3.71
79	62.77	8.45	94	214.95	3.51
80	68.82	7.98	95	229.76	3.34
81	75.52	7.53	96	243.38	3.19
82	82.78	7.11	97	256.37	3.05
83	90.41	6.70	98	268.68	2.93
84	98.42	6.32			

percent commissions, fees and mortality charges on a universal life policy, is one of the worst financial moves you can make. Funding a college education for your children is important, but it certainly should never be attempted with life insurance.

If all else fails, the salesperson's final ploy will be to tell you that if you buy life insurance on your children while they're young, you're locking in low lifetime rates. Here are the three reasons not to fall for this deception:

1. Mortality costs on new policies are continually declining as people live longer and longer. The rates on your child's life insurance policy won't be adjusted downward as rates in general come down.
2. Investment yield on the insurance company's investments could continue to increase, but the investment return on your policy won't increase.
3. Insurance premiums are less per $1,000 today than they were 35 years ago, so more protection can be bought for less premium today by an adult than the old outdated policy bought years ago by well-meaning but misinformed parents.

Your defense? Never buy life insurance on children and get rid of any policies that you or grandparents have purchased. Take the cash value, if any, and reinvest in a tax-sheltered investment like an annuity.

ATTACK #30

Determine insurance needs for you and your spouse based on who provides income or family services.

Most families are led to believe by insurance salespeople that there should be life insurance on all adult family members. Not so. Back to our basic concept of life insurance. Insure only those family members who are providing family income, but in addition, insure those whose services, if not available, would eat up part of the income.

Life insurance is meant to protect financial dependents, including spouse, ex-spouse, children or even parents, against loss of income caused by the death of the insured. Included in this category is a spouse whose absence would put an additional financial burden on the remaining income-producing spouse, such as a nonworking parent who stays at home to take care of small children.

Using the next chart, Who Needs Life Insurance?, you and your spouse will be able to determine once and for all which of you needs to be insured. When your situation changes over the years to a different category listed in the chart, your need for life insurance will also change.

Here are the basic rules. The row letters listed below apply to the Who Needs Life Insurance? chart.

A single person with no dependents does not need life insurance (row A). A single parent with dependents does need life insurance (row B).

If one spouse provides income and the other provides family services, insure the lives of both spouses (row C). Life insurance on the working spouse is meant to replace income that could be lost. Life insurance on the spouse at home is meant to pay the replacement cost of the family services now provided by the nonworking spouse, services such as child care, cleaning, cooking and chauffeuring.

If the first spouse provides a majority of family income but the couple has no children or other dependents, insurance should be on the life of the first spouse. The life of the second spouse does not need to be insured (row D).

If one spouse pays alimony or child support to an ex-spouse, and the money is a meaningful or significant part of the ex-spouse's income, the life of the first spouse should be insured so that the alimony or child support would be replaced by a life insurance income plan (row E).

If both spouses work and provide significant family income, then the lives of both spouses should be insured whether they have children or other dependents or not (row F).

ATTACK #31

Decrease the amount of your life insurance as you shift from job income to retirement or investment income.

A group of people who need less life insurance are those who are retired and living primarily off investment and retirement income, rather than job or career income. Why? Because the income of a remaining spouse would not decrease with the loss of the other spouse, but total family expenses would.

Insurance salespeople, however, are trained to go after older people to sell them additional life insurance, not because of their need for more insurance but because older people are likely to have more money to spend. In addition, the concern about death seems to increase in direct proportion to age, and it makes the sale of even very expensive life insurance to older people much easier. Remember, the purpose of life insurance is to replace job or career income. If a couple is living off retirement income or investments, and something happens to one, total income does not decrease, and neither spouse needs life insurance (row G). If a retired person with some job income has no dependents there is also no need for life insurance (row H).

If a retired person or couple is dependent on some job income and there are also others who are dependent on that income, the potential loss of that income should be insured (row I).

WHO NEEDS LIFE INSURANCE?

	1ST PERSON/SPOUSE	2ND SPOUSE	CHILDREN	LIFE INSURANCE NEEDED	INSURED
A	Single	No	No	No	———
B	Single parent	No	Yes	Yes	Single parent
C	Provides majority of income	Provides family services, i.e., child care	Yes	Yes	Both spouses
D	Provides majority of income	Yes	No	Yes	First spouse
E	Pays alimony or child support	Ex-spouse	Yes	Yes	First spouse
F	Provides significant income	Provides significant income	Yes	Yes	Both spouses
G	Retired—no job income	Yes	No	No	———
H	Retired—some job income	No	No	No	———
I	Retired—some job income	Yes or no	Yes	Yes	First person

ATTACK #32

Buy the amount of life insurance that, if invested at 12 percent, would replace your current family income.

A life insurance policy normally has one or more named beneficiaries who receive the insurance policy proceeds in a lump sum. What a mistake. The money can be gone in a year or two. Since life insurance money is meant to replace lost income, you should create your insurance plan to provide income that does not run out after a few years. For instance, a family whose income is $50,000 a year has a life insurance policy with a death benefit of $250,000. The insured dies and the family receives the entire $250,000 at one time with absolutely no experience in handling such a large sum of money.

Studies done over many years have shown that the average lump sum distribution of a life insurance policy is normally gone in less than five years because of bad investments made by the recipients, who usually have a lack of investment knowledge or lack of discipline in controlling the spending of such a large amount of cash. The money is gone, but the cost of raising the kids or providing income for the remaining spouse may not be. In less than five years, the spouse and even the children can be financially destitute, even though at one time there was enough insurance money to produce family income indefinitely.

Generally, do not set up your life insurance policy to give the proceeds to your family or other heirs in a lump sum. The $100,000 to $500,000 of income all in one year with no income in future years just doesn't work. Set up your life insurance plan to have the proceeds invested so income will continuously and automatically be generated for an unlimited number of years or until yearly income is no longer necessary. The best method is the "life insurance trust" discussed in Defense #51.

Where can you invest the money from life insurance proceeds and earn an average of 12 percent over the years? Mutual funds are your best bet. From 1980 to 1990, the average stock fund increased in value 17 percent per year and bond funds 14 percent per year, much above the 12 percent needed in your plan.

The higher the investment return, the less life insurance you need to buy, hence the less you will be paying for insurance each year. If you directed life insurance proceeds into a 3 percent savings account or a 5 percent certificate of deposit, you would have to buy approximately three times as much life insurance to produce the same amount of income from funds invested at 12 percent, which would, over the next 10 to 20 years, amount to thousands of dollars of unnecessary premiums.

In order to determine the amount you would have to invest at 12 percent to replace family income, separately total your and your spouse's job or career income. When both you and your spouse are to be insured, usually the insurance will be written in two separate policies. Total your full-time or part-time job or career income, add any small business net income, and exclude any income you receive from investments or retirement that would continue even after the death of a spouse. Using the following Life Insurance Income Replacement Chart, your objective is to compute exactly how much income could be lost if something happened to either you or your spouse. Multiply the totals for both you and your spouse by 8.5 to determine the amount of money invested at 12 percent that would replace all of your income. That's the amount of life insurance you need.

Life Insurance Income Replacement Chart

You			
Job income	$		
Second job income	$		
Small business net income	$		
Total	$	× 8.5 =	$ Amount of insurance needed
Spouse			
Job income	$		
Second job income	$		
Small business net income	$		
Total	$	× 8.5 =	$ Amount of insurance needed

Now refer to the Life Insurance Planning Chart on page 92–93. You can use this chart to determine your approximate life insurance requirements and premiums. In column A locate the figure closest to the total current income for either you or your spouse. Column B shows you the approximate amount of insurance you will need so that, if invested at 12 percent per year, the investment income would replace 100 percent of your job or career income. Columns C through J show the low annual premium you can pay from age 25 to age 60 on a 15-year level term policy for the amount of insurance shown in Column B. Later, I will show you why 15-year level term is currently your best life insurance alternative.

There is certainly one place that you can find these consistently low annual premiums and that's through The Insurance ClearingHouse. Using a local insurance agent you may find the rates to be as much as 200 to 300 percent higher for the insurance he or she wants to sell you than the rates you will get through

The Insurance ClearingHouse because the agent may work directly for only one company. Should you try to provide the same amount of protection for your family with a whole life or universal life policy, the premiums could be as much as 1,000 percent higher, 10 times what you should be paying.

If you are strapped for cash, living paycheck to paycheck, the minimum amount of life insurance that you should carry is the amount that if invested at 12 percent would replace 50 percent of your current income. Don't buy life insurance only after your bills are paid. Do it now. Your family needs at least the minimum protection. If your family is struggling with the income you now have, think how tough it would be without any income. To compute the minimum amount and approximate cost of the insurance you need, using the following Life Insurance Planning Chart, find your income in column A, and divide the amount of insurance shown in column B in half. The yearly premiums will then be about half of those shown in columns C through J.

The rates shown in the Life Insurance Planning Chart are for a reasonably healthy, nonsmoking male. Rates for females are the same or slightly less. Most nonsmokers will fit into this "best rate" category. If you have a preexisting but nonfatal health condition, such as high blood pressure or high cholesterol count, a good rule of thumb is that the rates will run 25 percent or so higher.

To estimate what the cost of your life insurance should be using the Life Insurance Planning Chart, first calculate the amount of insurance that you need based on your current income and circle the approximate premium you will expect to pay. Separately calculate any additional life insurance required on your spouse, if you have a spouse, and circle the approximate premium based on spouse's income. If you have a health and hospitalization plan at work, you will probably have a small life insurance policy, $5,000 to $10,000, attached to it. Do not include this amount in your calculations since it will not automatically be directed into your insurance income investment plan. This work-related insurance money would give you the cash for final arrangements.

Once you have determined the amount of life insurance you need, call The Insurance ClearingHouse, and they will help you locate what they consider the best and the lowest-priced policy to accomplish your purpose. Although The Insurance ClearingHouse was set up primarily for Charles J. Givens Organization members, since you and I, through this book, are working together on your financial future, you may feel free to use the research services of The Insurance ClearingHouse at no charge. Later in this chapter I will give you the complete instructions.

If you already have life insurance, you will most likely find that you have either too much or too little of the wrong kind and that you are paying hundreds of dollars a year in unnecessary premiums. By the end of this chapter, we will have your entire life insurance plan straightened out once and for all.

Let's look at an example. David and Carol are a hard-working couple. They have two children, Stephanie, age 7, and David, Jr., age 9. David Sr.'s income is $40,000 a year as a retail store manager and Carol's income is $30,000 a year as a nurse. They realize the importance of protecting the family against the loss of one or both incomes but, like most people, are totally confused about how to put together an inexpensive life insurance plan. They have been jerked around by so may life insurance salespeople, all of whom sounded official and knowledgeable but created a gnawing doubt. Now armed with the information in this chapter, they know exactly how to put together their life insurance plan.

On the Life Insurance Planning Chart, they are quickly able to find the amount of coverage they should carry, as well as the lower premiums both should be paying. To replace his $40,000 income with an investment at 12 percent, David finds he needs a $350,000 life insurance policy. At his age, close to 35, David can pay as little as $369 per year for the next 15 years. David circles that amount. To protect Carol's significant family income contribution, a policy should be written with her as the insured for $250,000. As she is closest to age 35 as well, her premiums will only be around $238 a year, guaranteed for 15 years. The beneficiary in both cases should be their life insurance trust, set up according to the instructions in Defense #51, Set Up a Trust to Distribute the Income from Your Invested Life Insurance Proceeds.

For about $617 a year for the next 15 years, the combined life insurance coverage of David and Carol will total $600,000, an amount that, if invested at 12 percent, would totally replace either or both incomes. For about $52 a month, they have once and for all taken control. Up to now they had been paying $1,400 per year for less than half that amount of insurance.

In addition, Carol has an old, $10,000 whole life policy that was taken out by her mother. The couple also has a whole life policy they bought two years before, as well as life insurance on Stephanie and David, Jr. Using the strategies that appear later in this chapter, they cancel all of the old policies, but only after they have received the new ones. Not only have they saved money but they now have many times the amount of life insurance coverage on the right family members.

These are the same steps I want you to go through with your family. Once your plan is in place, there will be very little that you will have to do or be concerned about other than checking every three to five years to be sure that the amount of insurance is increased as your family income increases. You can then confidently get on with the business of living.

ATTACK #33

Choose the life insurance company rated "A" or above with the lowest premiums.

The next step in building your lifetime insurance plan is to learn to pick the correct company, the correct policy options and, most important, the kind of life insurance that is best for you.

Picking the right life insurance company is simple. Since life insurance is life insurance, no matter what cute name the companies call their policies, your objective is to pay the lowest possible premiums per thousand dollars of coverage. However, you also want to be certain that your life insurance company is not in financial trouble. If the insurance company has to pay your beneficiary, you naturally want to be certain the money and the company will still be there.

A. M. Best, an independent insurance industry monitoring organization, checks out life insurance companies based on their financial statements and issues ratings based on financial stability. Acceptable ratings are A, A− (Excellent), A+ (Superior), and A++ (Superior). All mean that the companies are in good financial condition. Some companies are rated lower than A−, and these you will want to eliminate from your list of alternatives. Of course, if you have money invested with the insurance company in a policy like a whole life policy, the ratings become even more important, since the insurance company is holding your money during most of your lifetime. On the other hand, if you have a term insurance policy, the right

LIFE INSURANCE PLANNING CHART

YOUR SPOUSE'S CURRENT INCOME (A)	APPROXIMATE AMOUNT INVESTED AT 12% THAT WOULD REPLACE INCOME 100% (B)	YEARLY PREMIUM COST FOR FIRST 15 YEARS OF AMOUNT OF INSURANCE SHOWN IN COLUMN B							
		(C) AGE 25	(D) AGE 30	(E) AGE 35	(F) AGE 40	(G) AGE 45	(H) AGE 50	(I) AGE 55	(J) AGE 60
$ 20,000	$ 170,000	$ 210	$ 210	$ 217	$ 271	$ 370	$ 543	$ 805	$ 1,230
25,000	210,000	243	243	251	318	439	653	976	1,501
30,000	250,000	275	275	285	365	508	763	1,148	1,773
35,000	300,000	316	316	327	423	594	900	1,362	2,112
40,000	350,000	357	357	369	481	681	1,038	1,577	2,452
45,000	375,000	378	378	390	510	724	1,107	1,684	2,622
50,000	420,000	415	415	428	563	802	1,230	1,877	2,927
60,000	500,000	480	480	495	655	940	1,450	2,150	3,470
70,000	600,000	562	562	579	771	1,113	1,725	2,649	4,149
80,000	675,000	624	624	642	858	1,243	1,932	2,971	4,659
90,000	750,000	685	685	705	945	1,373	2,138	3,293	5,168
100,000	850,000	767	767	789	1,061	1,546	2,413	3,722	5,847
125,000	1,000,000	890	890	915	1,235	1,805	2,825	4,365	6,865
150,000	1,250,000	1,095	1,095	1,125	1,525	2,238	3,515	5,438	8,563

175,000	1,500,000	1,300	1,300	1,335	1,815	2,670	4,200	6,510	10,260
200,000	1,750,000	1,505	1,505	1,545	2,105	3,103	4,888	7,583	11,958
300,000	2,500,000	2,120	2,120	2,775	2,975	4,400	5,950	10,800	17,050
400,000	3,400,000	2,858	2,858	2,931	4,019	5,957	9,425	14,661	23,161
500,000	4,200,000	3,514	3,514	3,603	4,947	7,341	11,625	18,093	28,593
750,000	6,250,000	5,195	5,195	5,325	7,255	10,888	17,263	26,888	42,513
1,000,000	8,400,000	6,958	6,958	7,131	9,819	14,607	23,175	36,111	57,111

All rates are guaranteed 15-year level term. *Rates shown are for a preferred risk non-smoking male in good health. Female rates are equal or less. Call The Insurance ClearingHouse at 800-522-2827

The Insurance ClearingHouse services are not available in all areas.

kind of life insurance, your only concern is that the company has the funds to pay your beneficiary when due.

When you are working with The Insurance ClearingHouse, you are automatically dealing with companies that are rated A– or above. The ClearingHouse has done the checking for you. But should you wish to check out the A. M. Best rating for any life insurance company on your own, you can do so with a quick trip to the business section of your local public library.

Never buy from a life insurance company simply because you recognize the name. There is a tendency to believe that because you've heard names like Metropolitan, Prudential or Equitable, somehow the insurance offered by these companies must be better. Some recognition comes from the amount of money a company spends on advertising, money that is ultimately charged to policyholders as extra premiums. From our research we've discovered that because of the higher overhead, higher advertising costs and high commissions paid to salespeople, even term policies from the old-line recognizable companies are usually much more expensive than from lesser-known companies with equally acceptable ratings. Choose your insurance company based on acceptable ratings and lowest premiums, not name recognition.

DEFENSE #34

Don't buy life insurance from a company because it pays dividends.

Companies that sell life insurance are divided into two groups: stock companies and mutual companies. Stock insurance company policies are sometimes called "nonparticipating" because policyholders don't receive dividends. Mutual insurance company policies are often called "participating" because policyholders do receive dividends, as if they were participating in the profits.

Stock life insurance companies are owned by stockholders and are run like any other private corporation. The stock is normally sold on the major stock exchanges, and the profits earned are returned to the stockholders as dividends. Most stockholders do not own a life insurance policy from the insurance company in which they own stock.

Mutual companies are theoretically owned by their policyholders instead of stockholders. The stated objective of mutual companies is not to earn a profit, but supposedly to provide the lowest-priced life insurance to their policyholders. Therefore, when a mutual company has taken in more money during the year than it needs for expenses and paying claims, it is supposed to return the excess money to policyholders as so-called dividends.

In truth, the concept of mutual company dividends is another insurance scheme. The insurance companies may call the returned money a "dividend" but it is not. Even the IRS and state insurance departments see through the veil and define and treat such dividends not as participation in insurance company profits but as a return of overcharges on premiums. Even so, some salespeople of mutual company life insurance will try to convince you that buying a policy makes you an owner of the company and your return of dividends is a share of the profits, which makes your policy cheaper than one from a stock or nonparticipating company.

To find out if the dividend idea actually reduced insurance costs or was just another scheme, we examined over 100 similar policies from both stock and mutual companies. The results were a real eye-opener.

Here's what we found. The average premiums on participating life insurance policies issued by mutual companies were higher per $1,000 of insurance coverage. How much higher? Higher by about the amount of dividends the company returns to the policyholders. The dividends therefore are nothing more than overpaid premiums. See the Life Insurance Premium Comparison Chart, columns G and H, for a comparison of premiums for two similar participating and nonparticipating policies (pages 122–23).

If you overpay your premiums, the insurance company has free use of your hard-earned money until it is returned. Of course, insurance companies never like to give up control of your money once they have it, and they will try to use your overpaid premiums as future premium payments, to buy extra coverage or for so-called paid-up insurance—all ploys that benefit the insurance company, while possibly deceiving you.

Life insurance policy dividends are not free money. Overpaying insurance premiums to get dividends is like the folly of overpaying your income taxes so you will receive a refund. In both cases, you are getting your own money back, which you never owed in the first place. Get out your life insurance policy and check to see if it is participating (dividend paying). If the answer is yes, it is a good bet you can save unnecessary premiums by switching to the best nonparticipating policy.

DEFENSE #35

Refuse or drop the "disability premium waiver," "double-indemnity" coverage and other costly life insurance gimmicks.

Once you've agreed with the life insurance salesperson on how much insurance you're going to buy, suddenly the options list will be pulled out, and you will have an opportunity to increase your annual premium significantly. The two main add-on options are the disability premium waiver (DPW) and double-indemnity coverage, both of which add little protection for you but create huge extra profits for the insurance company.

Disability Premium Waiver

"For just a few dollars more" goes the salesperson's eternal cry, and in this case those not so few dollars go toward buying you disability insurance on your life insurance premium payment. The purpose of the disability premium waiver is to exempt you from paying your life insurance premiums if you become permanently disabled. It sounds so logical and so necessary, and yet the chances of ever benefiting from the disability premium waiver are so small and the premiums for the coverage so incredibly high when weighed against risk that the disability premium waiver is something you don't want to consider.

Whom does this waiver of premium really benefit? The insurance company, of course, since your payment for the disability premium waiver guarantees that the insurance company, even when it waives your payment of life insurance premiums, will continue to receive premiums. If you don't become disabled, the insurance company keeps the premiums as profit. In most policies, you are required to have been continuously disabled for six months before the insurance company is obligated to pick up a premium payment. In addition, if the policy has some sort of cash value, your policy already states that the premiums can be paid from that cash value.

Does anybody ever benefit from this kind of coverage? Of course, a few people do, but as with every type of gimmick insurance, hundreds of dollars of premiums are being paid in for every dollar of premiums that are waived. Remember, a life insurance policy does not lapse if the insured becomes disabled. The premiums still have to be paid, but if the right kind of life insurance was purchased at the right price, your life insurance is not a major cost, and the premiums do not need to be directly protected by disability insurance.

Double Indemnity

When you buy the double indemnity or accidental death option with your life insurance, twice the face amount of the policy will be paid to your beneficiary, but only if you die of an accidental death within a specified period of time after the accident, usually 90 days.

The cost per $1,000 for double indemnity is more expensive in some nonsmoking policies than the base cost per $1,000 of an annual renewable term insurance policy. For example: on a 35-year-old, nonsmoking male, the base cost of a term insurance policy is about $.90 per $1,000. Accidental death insurance is around $1.00 per $1,000, even though only 6 out of 100 will die from accidental causes. In addition, there are myriad exclusions—causes of accidental death that the double indemnity premiums don't cover, making the insurance even less of a value. Based on the chances for accidental death, the true cost of the double indemnity insurance should be about $.05 per $1,000 of coverage, not $1.00. Double indemnity insurance is overpriced by nearly 2,000 percent!

Drop it if you have it, and do not take double indemnity when you buy an insurance policy. The base premium on a life insurance policy pays a death benefit for every type of death, not just accidental. Rather than spending money on double indemnity, increase the base policy to a higher death benefit for whatever the cause. You could actually pay the entire premium on a low-priced term insurance policy for the cost of the accidental death premium on a whole life policy.

Even though your chances of collecting on gimmick life insurance add-ons are small, the premiums are not. Over a 30-year period, double indemnity and disability premium waiver could cost you about $4,000 if you are now age 35 or $15,000 if you are now age 55. On page 99 are comparisons of the cost of disability premium waiver and double indemnity coverage on both whole life and term insurance policies from three major companies. Look in the total extra premium columns and you will be shocked at how many thousands of dollars of extra premiums are added during your lifetime by life insurance add-on gimmicks. You can stop this drain on your lifetime wealth.

ATTACK #36

Choose the right kind of insurance based on the maximum protection for the minimum premium.

In 1979, the Federal Trade Commission published the results of its two-year investigation into the practices of the life insurance industry. The study disclosed that American consumers were losing billions of dollars yearly because of lack of training and information on how to make correct life insurance decisions. That hasn't changed.

No matter what salespeople tell you, or what companies name their insurance polices, there are just three major kinds of life insurance: whole life, universal life, and term insurance. All policies, no matter what the gimmicks or promises, fit into one of those categories. The first two are absolute rip-offs, and the third is usually the right kind of life insurance for your financial plan once you learn how to buy the best life insurance for the least premiums.

Whole Life Insurance

Whole life or cash value insurance is often the worst type. The only good thing you can say about whole life insurance is that it is named correctly. "Whole" life is where your money goes down in a "hole" never to be seen again. You overpay your premiums by 1,000 percent to create something called cash value, which neither you nor your heirs will probably ever see. Due to a slick maneuver in the policy (which we'll cover later), when the insured dies, the insurance company and *not* the beneficiary gets to keep every dollar of the cash value. Not 10 percent, not half, *every dollar* up to the face value of the policy. Why would you want to overpay your premiums by 1,000 percent to build something you'll never see?

Single-premium whole life is an outdated offshoot of the original whole life concept. With single-premium life, you pay

HOW THE DISABILITY PREMIUM WAIVER AND DOUBLE INDEMNITY ACCIDENTAL DEATH ADD THOUSANDS TO YOUR PREMIUMS

Extra premiums for $100,000 whole life and term policies taken out at ages 35 and 55.
Term rates are for 10-year level term.

		Age 35				Age 55			
COMPANY	POLICY TYPE	DISABILITY PREMIUM WAIVER ONE YEAR	DOUBLE INDEMNITY ONE YEAR	TOTAL ONE YEAR EXTRA PREMIUM	TOTAL EXTRA PREMIUM OVER 30 YEARS	DISABILITY PREMIUM WAIVER ONE YEAR	DOUBLE INDEMNITY ONE YEAR	TOTAL ONE YEAR EXTRA PREMIUM	TOTAL EXTRA PREMIUM OVER 30 YEARS
Northwestern	Whole Life	$40	$76	$116	$3,480	$197	$109	$306	$ 9,180
	Term	$19	$70	$ 89	$2,670	$181	$109	$290	$ 8,700
Lincoln Nat'l	Whole Life	$55	$91	$146	$4,380	$326	$130	$456	$13,680
	Term	$27	$75	$102	$3,060	$231	$118	$349	$10,470
Penn Mutual	Whole Life	$53	$85	$138	$4,140	$461	$114	$575	$17,250
	Term	$26	$80	$106	$3,180	$470	$106	$576	$17,280

SOURCE: A. M. Best *Flitcraft Compend and Review* 1990. Dated Information. A. M. Best no longer provides this data in Flitcraft Compend. Figures may vary or no longer be available.

your lifetime premium in one lump sum in the belief that you can borrow earnings from the policy tax-free. That is no longer true. New federal legislation now makes single-premium life a poorer idea than it was originally. Variable life is the latest twist to the whole life scam. With variable life, the interest rate you earn on your cash value is supposed to change with other market interest rates, but what does it matter since the insurance company is going to end up with the cash value anyway?

Universal Life Insurance

Universal life insurance is a good idea gone astray. Universal life combines a term insurance policy, the right kind of insurance, with an investment plan. You pick a specific amount of premium to pay each year. Your premium money first goes to pay the yearly increasing cost of the term insurance, and the balance is supposedly put into a tax-deferred investment plan. In many universal life policies you can choose your investment in the same way you can in a mutual fund family. There are, however, several deceptions in a universal life policy. The term insurance is often too expensive, and there are big commissions taken out of your premium or cash value. Commissions paid to salespeople can range from 75 to 90 percent the first year and then 5 to 10 percent thereafter, based on the total premium paid each year. In addition, you pay huge surrender charges should you change your mind and wish to withdraw your cash value.

A study done by the Federal Trade Commission found that although universal life insurance ads claim to pay you 8 to 10 percent per year, because of all the charges, you are actually losing at least 5 percent per year for the first five years. Why would you ever put money in an investment with a guaranteed loss?

Term Insurance

Term insurance is insurance, plain and simple. No bells, bows or whistles. It is the least expensive form of life insurance, yet does everything that a life insurance policy is supposed to do: protect the family or the heirs against financial loss. One hundred percent of your premiums go into protection for your heirs.

In order to help you pick the best insurance at the least cost, we will explore each of these three forms of life insurance, and I will show you *exactly* what happens with each type of policy, something the insurance companies hope that you never discover. Don't misunderstand, I'm not slamming the concept of life insurance, only that the majority of policies that claim to protect you are actually only protecting the insurance company at your expense.

Like any winning financial strategy, the selection of the right kind of life insurance protection for your family is a simple straightforward process—that is, once you understand the rules.

DEFENSE #37

Never buy a whole life insurance policy.

Once the life insurance industry discovered it could make more money from selling investments than from selling life insurance, the concept of whole life insurance was born.

When you buy a whole life insurance policy, you are guaranteed a fixed premium per year as well as a fixed amount of life insurance or death benefit. You are given a schedule for the life of the policy showing how much of your premium is going into an account called cash value. Cash value is theoretically the amount of your money you could borrow while the insurance is in force, or that you would receive from the company if you canceled the policy. Neither concept is totally true, as you will soon see.

You are told that the advantage of the whole life policy is that you'll be earning interest on your cash value and that your life insurance dollars don't totally disappear as they do with term insurance. You're sold on the fact that your insurance policy is a tax shelter and in many cases that your policy will eventually be paid up as if at that point the company will start paying your premiums for you. The sales pitches are so effective that hundreds of billions of dollars of whole life coverage have been sold by over a thousand different life insurance companies.

The truth is there are no good whole life policies. Not one, not for anybody. Even the concept, in my opinion, is a flagrant abuse of financial ignorance. To illustrate the deceptions in the whole life sales pitches, we don't have to look much further than the promise of cash value.

The Disappearing Cash Value

Whole life is sold as life insurance with an investment plan. But there is actually no investment at all. Your cash value is really the property of the insurance company from the moment you began to build it. When the insured dies, the beneficiary receives only the face value (death benefit) of the policy or the cash value, whichever is greater, but not both. You may be thinking, "You mean I spent 20, 30, 40 years paying huge insurance premiums to build cash value, something that I may never get?" Absolutely true.

Let me give you an example. At age 35 a father buys a whole life policy under the following terms: The death benefit is $100,000, the yearly premiums are $1,300 and after 20 years, at age 55, he will have accumulated, according to the policy, $35,400 in cash value. At age 55 the father unexpectedly dies. Of course he might have thought that his family would receive the death benefit of $100,000, plus the accumulated cash value of $35,400 for a total of $135,400. What his family actually receives is the death benefit, $100,000, and no cash value. The entire cash value of $35,400 becomes the property of the insurance company.

Term insurance, which can be as much as 80 percent less in cost, pays the death benefit but has no cash value, producing exactly the same results as a whole life policy. Whole life is, therefore, just a grossly overpriced term insurance policy.

The Disappearing Insurance Value

Another way to look at a whole life policy is in terms of the disappearing insurance value. Since the maximum the company is responsible for paying upon the death of the insured is the death benefit of the policy, and if we consider the first money paid to the heirs as the cash value, then the insurance company will have to pay only the difference between the cash value and total death benefit out of its own funds.

To illustrate the point, refer to the Disappearing Insurance Value chart that follows and notice that as the cash value of the policy grows, the insurance company's liability shrinks. Up to year five there is no cash value. The insurance company, in the unlikely event of death during the first five years, would pay the insured's beneficiary the full $100,000 from insurance company funds. After 10 years of paying premiums, the insured has built a cash value of $5,000 in the policy. If the insured dies at that point, the death benefit or amount received by the heirs would still be only $100,000. So after the insurance company returns the $5,000 cash value, it has to put up only $95,000 of its own money. The insured is now paying part of his own death benefit! After 20 years, the cash value is $20,000, which means that the insurance company is liable for only $80,000. After 30 years the cash value has built to $50,000, which takes the insurance company off the hook for half of what the beneficiaries are paid. Remember, any way you slice it, the total paid upon death of the insured is $100,000.

If you look at a whole life policy in terms of the disappearing insurance value, it is nothing but a decreasing term insurance policy. Decreasing term insurance is a policy where the premiums remain constant but the amount of life insurance decreases as the insured gets older. Look at the chart below. As the cash value increases, the actual amount of insurance is decreasing.

THE DISAPPEARING INSURANCE VALUE: WHOLE LIFE INSURANCE POLICY

YEAR	YOUR CASH VALUE		AMOUNT INSURANCE COMPANY WOULD PAY AT DEATH		TOTAL DEATH BENEFIT
5	$ 0	+	$100,000	=	$100,000
10	$ 5,000	+	$ 95,000	=	$100,000
20	$20,000	+	$ 80,000	=	$100,000
30	$50,000	+	$ 50,000	=	$100,000

On a radio show in Oklahoma City, after exposing the ills of the whole life insurance industry, I received a call from an ex-whole life salesman who related the following story:

"When I was young and less wise, I became a whole life salesman for a major insurance company. My second month I sold a whole life policy to a young couple in their early 20s with two small children. The premiums were high, but the amount of insurance was only $20,000 because the majority of the premium went to build the so-called cash value. Three years later the husband, the insured, died in an automobile accident, leaving the kids with no father and the family with no income.

"When the wife turned in the insurance claim she received $20,000 but, of course, there was no cash value. The money barely covered the funeral arrangements and a few months of family expenses.

"I realized," the ex-salesman said, "that had I done what was good for the family instead of what was good for me and the insurance company, I would have sold the family a term policy. For the same exact premium, I could have sold the family almost $1 million of life insurance with no artificial savings plan and the wife and children would have been taken care of financially for the next 20 years or more.

"This experience," he continued, "shook me emotionally so badly that I quit the life insurance business forever. I honestly felt because of my knowledge and their lack of it that I had stripped this family of the protection and help they really needed."

Don't make the same mistake. Separate your life insurance from your investments, and use your life insurance dollars to buy the maximum necessary protection for those you love and want to protect.

Borrowing Your Own Money

Another deception in a whole life policy is the idea that you are able to borrow your cash value. The concept is that if you get yourself in financial trouble during your life and need quick money, it's always available from your life insurance policy. Remember, your so-called cash value is built solely from the overpayment of unnecessary insurance premiums. Once the insurance company gets its hands on your money, the money is treated as if it belongs to the insurance company and not you. How do you know? Because the insurance company will actually charge you interest on the borrowing back of your own money. The insurance company tries to tell you it is a benefit because the interest rate you'll pay on the borrowed money is only 5 percent to 8 percent, much less than market rates. But should you pay any interest at all if the money is truly yours? And to compound the crime, if the insured has borrowed the cash value of a whole life policy and dies, the insurance company pays the death benefit *minus* the cash value which has been borrowed and minus any unpaid interest.

The Disappearing Interest

Insurance salespeople will also tell you that a whole life policy is great because your money is earning tax-sheltered interest. In a study done by the state insurance commissioners about 15 years ago, it was discovered that the average interest paid on a whole life policy amounted to less than 3 percent per year. Who cares if it's tax-sheltered? The real problem with the interest is that you never receive it. When you buy a whole life policy, the interest on your cash value is not paid to you in quarterly or annual installments, it is credited to your cash value account, money your beneficiary will never receive, since the insurance company keeps your cash value when you die. By adding interest earned to your cash value account, the insurance company is actually paying your interest to itself and not you. After spending many years examining whole life policies, I have yet to find a good one, or even a marginal one.

Some years ago I had the opportunity, on *The Today Show*, to debate an editor of a financial magazine on the whole life issue. Incredible as it may seem, his position was that whole life insurance is good because most Americans are basically too stupid to save or build wealth on their own. Since a whole life policy in no way builds wealth, only those who don't understand whole life insurance could take that position.

By the way, one of the producers of *The Today Show* told me that within 30 minutes after one of my segments on life insurance, the top executives of four of the nation's biggest whole life insurance companies called NBC and threatened to cancel their advertising if NBC allowed me ever again to talk about whole life insurance. Not one of them said I was wrong. They just threatened to cancel their advertising.

Single-Premium Whole Life (Modified Endowment Contract)

If paying yearly premiums to buy a rip-off like whole life insurance could make insurance companies wealthy, wouldn't it be even more profitable if companies could get you to pay your entire lifetime's whole life premiums in advance? "Nobody would fall for that," you think. Tens of thousands of policy buyers have and still do through the purchase of a life insurance gimmick called single-premium whole life insurance. Here's how a single-premium whole life policy works. You deposit $5,000 to $500,000 of your money in a one-time premium payment with the insurance company. You're sold on the idea because you're told the money is going into a life insurance contract and you can borrow back your money plus the earnings tax-free. What a tax shelter, you think. You have use of your money plus all of your interest tax-free, in addition to an insurance policy paid up for life.

Sold so far? Well, let me unsell you. First of all, you are buying a whole life policy, which is one of the most expensive and worst forms of insurance available. The expensive premiums and the disappearing cash value are cleverly disguised in the salesperson's pitch about the tax-free borrowing. And you don't borrow free. As with all cash value, once the insurance company has your money, it won't let go without a fight, in this case charging you interest on borrowing your own money. The interest eats up any tax benefit and is not normally tax deductible.

The real slam dunk the insurance companies created was based on their knowledge of how financially ignorant policyholders would act. Even though the policy's supposed big benefit was tax-free borrowing, companies knew that most policyholders would never set up a plan to borrow the money. They were absolutely right. Score another one for the life insurance companies. They created a pipeline in which single-premium life policyholders would attempt to beat tax reform by handing over hundreds of millions to grinning life insurance salespeople and stockbrokers who, because of the large sums involved, were earning unthinkable commissions. The pipeline was virtually plugged at the other end, however, because policyholders, as predicted, were reluctant to borrow money from their own policies. They felt more comfortable to let it sit. Because of the huge surrender charges that would be levied if the insured canceled, few policies have been canceled even by those who discovered they'd been had. Some uninformed members of the media unfortunately played a major role in the proliferation of this bad idea. Since almost every financial planner, broker and life insurance salesperson was pushing single-premium life, financial writers bought into the scheme and increased sales hundreds of percent with glowing articles.

Through my contacts in Washington, I know that many members of Congress considered the creation of single-premium life insurance a complete rip-off of the tax system. Single-premium life appeared just after Congress had given the insurance industry in 1988 several tax exemptions for which the insurance lobbyists were begging. In 1988 Congress closed what was considered a tax loophole in some insurance policies by creating a class of life insurance called modified endowment contracts (MECs). Instead of directly naming single-premium life policies as tax scams, Congress took the very rules that made these policies attractive and turned them into potentially taxable events instead of tax shelters.

To get single-premium life policies into the modified endowment contract class, Congress defined MECs as insurance policies that had premium payments higher than necessary to fund the future death benefit. In a whole life policy, the entire amount paid is considered the premium, and where the premium, as in a single-premium life policy, includes instant cash value, it is obviously much higher than necessary to fund the death benefit.

Here are the tax penalties for single-premium life policies:

- The first money you borrow from your plan is treated as your earnings and is taxed as an investment income. Only after the amount you withdraw or borrow exceeds your earnings is any balance treated as withdrawal of nontaxable principal. In other words, you pay income taxes on the earnings you *borrow* from a single-premium life policy.
- Loans or withdrawals made before age 59½ are subject to a federal government 10 percent early withdrawal penalty unless you became disabled or agree to take small annuity payments over your lifetime. Even though only your earnings are subject to the penalty, you can't take out the penalty-free principal until you have paid the penalty on your entire earnings.

If your policy is with a mutual life insurance company, even the dividends are included in your earnings and are subject to the withdrawal tax and penalties.

Single-premium life contracts purchased before June 21, 1988, are exempt from this rule but you still have to live with rules that favored the insurance company in the first place. Even if you have a single-premium life policy you are better off replacing it with a term policy and transferring your cash value to a self-directed tax-deferred annuity, which can be done without tax penalties.

There may be only one reason to keep any whole life policy, and that is if your health has deteriorated since you bought the policy, and you've become one of the only 1 percent of Americans who is no longer insurable.

DEFENSE #38

Never buy universal life insurance.

Universal life is an insurance product that was created in the early eighties when interest rates on other forms of investments were rising. Many informed policyholders were taking their money out of the cash values of their whole life policies, which were paying less than 3 percent interest, and investing where they could earn 10 percent or more. To stop this outflow, the insurance companies created universal life. Universal life is a generic name. Each insurance company has its own specific name for its universal life policies, such as Appreciable Life, Target Life, Future Plan, etc.

On the surface, universal life insurance seems to have overcome all of the faults of whole life insurance. Universal life insurance is a combination of term insurance, which is the right kind of life insurance, with a savings plan which seems to pay a competitive tax-deferred return.

A universal life policy allows you to choose your total premium. The first portion of the premium goes to pay the term insurance cost for the amount of insurance you select. The balance is supposed to go into the investment plan. You can decide to increase or decrease the amount that you are putting into the investment portion of your policy by increasing or decreasing the yearly premium. With some universal life policies, instead of accepting a fixed interest rate, you can choose to invest in an assortment of mutual funds.

You are told that after a certain number of years you can stop making premium payments altogether and convert to a paid-up policy. It sounds as if the universal life policy will do everything for you except give you a ride to work. Unfortunately, the benefits of universal life policies available today are, without exception, deceptive. The universal life policy doesn't do any of the things it appears to do, but wastes tens of thousands of your insurance dollars.

What's wrong with universal life insurance? The first problem is that companies tell a legal lie in their advertisements about the return you can expect. You've seen magazine advertisements for universal life that proclaim: "Earn 9 percent tax deferred." What the ad does not tell you, not even in small print, is that the hidden commissions and fees you pay each year on your entire premium amount to as much as 10 percent. It doesn't take you more than third-grade math to figure out that if the insurance company is charging you 10 percent on the entire premium but paying you only 9 percent after the expenses, commissions and insurance costs are deducted, you're losing money.

If you invested in a certificate of deposit at a bank and the banker said, "We keep 10 percent of your money to cover our expenses and commissions," you would laugh and leave. Yet because of the confusing ways that universal life policies are written, coupled with the confusing sales pitch, it is practically impossible to know what you have really purchased. The interest rate quoted on a universal life policy is known as the gross rate and is not the actual net return on your policy. In 1986, Joseph Bell, professor of insurance at Indiana University, was quoted in *The Wall Street Journal* as saying, "The universal life gross rate is a sales gimmick only."

In 1985, A. M. Best published a study of 125 universal life policies to compare the real rates of return paid on the cash value of a $100,000 policy against the published and advertised rates of return. The study used an example of a male nonsmoker, age 35, to compute what the policy actually paid after 10 and 20 years. The advertised rates in those days of higher interest rates varied from 8.5 percent to 12 percent. The company with the actual highest net rate was advertising a current rate of 10.5 percent but, after 10 years with all charges deducted, actually paid 5.19 percent per year and only 8 percent per year after 20 years. The 125th company on the list quoted a return of 11 percent per year, but in truth, after all charges were deducted, the real return after 10 years was minus 4.9 percent per year and after 20 years was only 2.4 percent per year.

How can any insurance company, let alone all of them, get away with these kinds of deception? The reasons are twofold. There is no "truth in life insurance" act that makes insurance companies state only the facts, and insurance companies are regulated primarily by state insurance commissioners, who are often ex-insurance company executives, many of whom once sold for a living the policies they regulate.

Here is a good example: One of the biggest sales gimmicks with universal life is that the premiums remain the same each year, so you need not worry about increased life insurance costs as you get older. That is nonsense. Because the insurance portion of a universal life policy is like annually renewable term insurance, the premiums on the insurance portion increase every year. Since the total premium you are paying for both insurance and investment stays the same, you never see it happening. As your term insurance premium increases each year, less and less is left to go into your investment account.

So many times I have heard policyholders say, "What I got is not what my agent told me I would be getting." If you read your insurance policy, you'll see a clause that says that the only agreements and conditions you are accepting are those in writing in the policy and that no spoken representations made by the salesperson are valid. What this clause means is that it doesn't matter what the agent told you or that you used the agent's representations in deciding to buy the policy. You're stuck with what's written, the stuff that only an insurance lawyer can possibly understand.

Here are the factors that make a universal life insurance policy as bad a financial decision as a whole life policy.

1. The rate you are quoted as a return is not the real rate you actually get because of the deductions of commissions, management fees, mortality charges and other expense factors.
2. The cost of the term insurance in a universal life policy is exceedingly high. You are usually paying more in a universal life policy than you would pay for the same amount of term insurance coverage through The Insurance Clearing-House or often through the same insurance company.
3. The hidden charges in a universal life policy take a big chunk of your premium yet are very hard to find without reading your entire universal life policy and adding the individual charges together.
4. You are always better off to separate your insurance from your investments and get the best deal on both. The best rate on term insurance and the best return on tax-sheltered investments are seldom if ever from the same company.
5. Most universal life companies have a huge surrender charge, making it emotionally difficult to change your mind once you are in a universal life policy. The surrender charges can amount to 30 to 150 percent of your cash value. Often I am asked, "You mean if I cancel my policy, the insurance company is going to send me a bill for the amount I owe above my cash value?" Although the insurance company would like to, the answer is no. On a universal life or whole life policy the insurance company may keep all your cash value in the early years, but it can't

come after you for more. Those companies with the lowest up-front first-year fees normally have the biggest surrender charges.

If there were any way you could win with a universal life policy, I would have found it! Your strategy: Never buy a universal life policy.

If you currently have a universal life policy and you are in good health, there are no good reasons for continuing the premiums. You can always do better separating your life insurance from your investments. Use the strategies for canceling a life insurance policy explained later in this chapter, and move any cash value into a self-directed, tax-deferred annuity.

The fact that I have not seen a good universal life policy doesn't mean there couldn't be one designed. In my lectures over the years, I've had dozens of universal life salespeople come up to me and tell me that their policies are the one exception to the rule, that they, indeed, have a great universal life policy with none of the drawbacks. In all cases, I have asked those salespeople to send me the plans for evaluation and so far I have yet to receive one.

Let's design the ideal universal life policy the way it would be if it benefited the consumer as well as the insurance company, and challenge some forward-thinking insurance companies to come up with such a policy. Here would be the parameters:

1. Low cost of the term insurance, as low as any annually renewable term insurance offered by the same company
2. Standard term insurance commission paid only on the insurance portion of the policy
3. No commissions paid on the amount of the premium that goes into the investment
4. Maximum surrender charge of 6 percent the first year declining to zero after the sixth year
5. No-load mutual funds as choices for the investment portion of the policy, with no more than a 1 percent management fee

As you can see, the ideal universal life plan is not difficult to design. It's just that, to our knowledge, one currently does not exist. Almost good doesn't count. Once again, you will become much wealthier by separating your insurance from your investments.

DEFENSE #39

Don't fall for the paid-up policy scam.

Another ploy that the life insurance industry has used to generate billions is the paid-up policy gimmick. You are told, when sold a whole life or universal life policy, that your policy will be "paid up" after 7, 9 or 15 years, depending on which plan you're being pitched. Paid up means that you are required to make no more annual premium payments. It sounds as if the insurance company now likes you enough to give you free insurance.

There is no such thing as free insurance in a paid-up policy; the concept is a fraud. In reality, the only reason you are able to stop paying premiums on a policy is that you dramatically overpay your life insurance premiums every year until premiums stop. The overpayments are put into a fund which is earning you a small rate of interest, and the interest on your own money is then used to pay your future premiums. Still sound like a good deal? Not when you learn how little you are receiving in interest and how much you could have earned with the same overpaid premiums if invested elsewhere.

There is no such thing as a good deal on a paid-up policy. When you finance an automobile, you would never think of giving your bank or automobile finance company thousands of extra dollars up front so they could earn big interest on your money and then eventually make your car payments for you. What a mathematical smoke screen.

Look at the Paid-up Policy and Term Plus Annuity Comparison Chart that follows and you will see how this deception works. This chart compares the yearly premiums for 25 years on paid-up insurance vs. 10-year level term insurance with the difference invested in a self-directed, tax-deferred annuity.

The rates in this chart are based on a male nonsmoker who is age 40 in year 1 and age 65 in year 25. At first it seems that because of the shorter time you pay premiums on the paid-up policy (column B), you come out better financially. The exact opposite is true.

Column B shows the $1,470-per-year premium that would be paid for 10 years on a paid-up life insurance policy with a $100,000 death benefit. After 10 years the premiums would end, with no premiums from years 11 to 25. Because the paid-up policy is a form of whole life insurance, it accumulates a cash value. In column F you see the yearly cash value of the policy at the end of each year for years 1 through 25. At the end of 25 years, there would be a cash value of $30,372. The insured would have paid in a total of $14,700 and could extract $30,372 at the end of the 25-year period by canceling the policy or borrowing with interest paid to the insurance company and a corresponding reduction in the death benefit. Sound like a great deal? It's a lousy deal when you take a look at your alternatives.

Column D shows the premiums for a 10-year level term policy for the same 25 years. The premiums for the first 10 years are $200 per year; for the second 10 years they are $297 per year. For the balance of 5 years the premiums total an average of $654 per year with the insurance amount reduced from $100,000 to $50,000.

During the first 10 years, the insured would actually pay $1,270 per year less for the term insurance than for the paid-up life insurance, a savings of over 80 percent. Even though premiums are paid for 15 years longer on the term insurance, the total premium is just $8,235, which is $6,465 less than the paid-up life premium. But, you may say, the paid-up life policy builds cash value. In order to compare accurately a policy that contains cash value to a reasonable alternative, let's invest the money saved with the term insurance at an average of 12 percent per year in a tax-deferred, self-directed annuity which offers the same kind of tax-shelter protection as a life insurance policy.

We will choose a total outlay for term insurance plus the annuity as shown in column C of $1,470 a year for the first 10 years, the same as the premium on the paid-up life policy in column B. As shown in column D, $200 of the $1,470 each year for the first 10 years goes to pay the term insurance and $1,270 is left to deposit in the annuity (column E).

Here are the incredibly different results of using the two options. By investing $1,270 a year in the self-directed tax-deferred annuity for just 10 years (which represents the difference between the term insurance premium and the whole life premium), at the end of the 25-year period, you would have $117,781 in your annuity account (column G), which is $87,409 more than the $30,372 cash value of the paid-up policy! To make the comparison equal, the term insurance premiums shown in column D after the 10th year have been deducted from the balance in the self-directed, tax-deferred annuity account, column G. So, in 10 years, using money from your annuity account,

PAID-UP POLICY AND TERM PLUS ANNUITY COMPARISON CHART

40-Year-Old Male Nonsmoker

	10-YEAR PAID-UP POLICY	TERM PLUS ANNUITY			COMPARISON OF CASH VALUE AND ANNUITY ACCOUNT VALUE		COMPARISON OF TOTAL DEATH BENEFIT	
(A)	(B)	(C)	(D)	(E)	(F)	(G)	(H)	(I)
Year	*Annual Premiums*[1]	*Term Plus Annuity Annual Outlay*	*Term Premium*[2]	*Annuity Annual Deposit*	*Paid-up Policy Cash Value*	*Projected Annuity Values*[3]	*Paid-up Policy Death Benefits*	*Term Plus Annuity Death Benefits*
1	$ 1,470	$ 1,470	$ 200	$ 1,270	$ 1,188	$ 1,392	$100,000	$101,392
2	1,470	1,470	200	1,270	2,443	2,951	$100,000	102,951
3	1,470	1,470	200	1,270	3,768	4,698	$100.000	104,698
4	1,470	1,470	200	1,270	5,169	6,654	$100,000	106,654
5	1,470	1,470	200	1,270	6,647	8,845	$100,000	108,845
6	1,470	1,470	200	1,270	8,207	11,299	$100,000	111,299
7	1,470	1,470	200	1,270	9,858	14,047	$100,000	114,047
8	1,470	1,470	200	1,270	11,621	17,126	$100,000	117,126
9	1,470	1,470	200	1,270	13,481	20,573	$100,000	120,573
10	1,470	1,470	200	1,270	15,441	24,434	$100,000	124,434
11			297		16,172	27,003	$100,000	127,003
12			297		16,936	29,881	$100,000	129,881
13			297		17,737	33,104	$100,000	133,104
14			297		18,572	36,714	$100,000	136,714
15			297		19,445	40,757	$100,000	140,757
16			297		20,356	45,285	$100,000	142,285

17			297		21,305	50,357	$100,000	150,357
18			297		22,293	56,037	$100,000	156,037
19			297		23,324	62,399	$100,000	162,399
20			297		24,399	69,524	$100,000	169,524
21			537		25,511	77,235	$100,000	127,234
22			588		26,664	85,814	$100,000	135,814
23			642		27,860	95,359	$100,000	145,359
24			712		29,096	105,974	$100,000	155,974
25			786		30,372	117,781	$100,000	167,781
Total	$14,700	$14,700	$8,235	$12,700				

[1]John Alden Life
[2]10 + 10 year level term renewable to age 95
[3]Self-directed annuity

you can stop paying your term insurance premiums out of your pocket.

Since the same salesperson who can sell you the paid-up life insurance has the option of selling you term insurance plus a tax-sheltered annuity, why would the salesman, who is supposed to be looking out for your best interest, ever consider offering a paid-up life insurance policy?

But that's not all. Notice in column H that the death benefit of this paid-up life policy is always limited to $100,000. If the insured were to die anytime during that 25-year period, the death benefit to the heirs would be $100,000 and the insurance company would keep the cash value of up to $30,372. If the insured used the term insurance plus self-directed annuity, however, the heirs would get $100,000 from the term insurance policy plus 100 percent of the money in the self-directed annuity, as shown in column I, a total of up to $167,781 in year 25. Notice that if the insured died in the 20th year, the family would get $169,524, which would be the total of $100,000 of insurance plus the full amount in the annuity account of $69,524.

In years 21 to 25, the insured, who is now between 61 and 65 years old, could drop the death benefit on his term policy from $100,000 to $50,000, which make the premiums average $654 per year shown in column D for years 21 through 25. The insured no longer needs $100,000 worth of life insurance because there is more than $100,000 in the total of insurance plus the annuity account. If the insured died at age 65, the heirs would get $167,781 total as shown in column I, instead of the $100,000 shown in column H, even though the insured is now carrying only $50,000 of life insurance. Now you can begin to see how millions have thrown away billions of dollars on life insurance premiums.

The life insurance company is taking your extra money for its own use while making you believe you got a good deal. For instance, if you overpay $10,000 on a paid-up life insurance policy and the insurance company decides to reward you with a 5 percent return, it can then pay your $500 insurance premium every year out of your own money while making you think you're getting it free. Don't fall for it. Just because you already have a "paid-up" policy does not mean that you shouldn't convert to term insurance and start paying premiums again. There's no mathematical reason to keep a paid-up policy. Get your money back and use it for something beneficial while paying premiums on inexpensive term insurance.

ATTACK #40

Replace universal life with the least expensive term policy coupled with the best self-directed annuity.

Since the objective of a universal life insurance policy is insurance plus a tax-sheltered investment plan, you should wonder if there is an effective way to achieve the same results without:

High commissions,
Huge surrender charges,
Overpriced term insurance,
Hidden policy fees and charges.

There is. The ultimate approach is to buy the lowest-priced level term insurance from one company and invest in the best tax-deferred annuity from another.

Use the strategies that appear later in this chapter to buy the least expensive term insurance. Use the chart on pages 138–39 to choose what I consider the best self-directed annuities (tax-deferred mutual funds) in which to invest your money to achieve high return, tax-free compounding.

Let's look at the advantages the term insurance plus annuity approach has over universal life.

FINDING THE ULTIMATE COMBINATION

Universal Life: Since both the term insurance and the tax-deferred investment are included in the same universal life plan, you have no option for finding the best of each. It is improbable that the insurance company that has the best rate on the term insurance also offers the best returns on tax-deferred investments.

Term Insurance Plus Annuity: This approach gives you the option of finding the lowest rate on life insurance from one company and the highest return on tax-deferred, self-directed annuities from another.

AMOUNT OF COMMISSIONS PAID

Universal Life: The average commission paid to the salesperson is 80 percent of the first year's total premium. On a yearly premium of $1,200, the commission paid out of your premium is $960 the first year.

Term Insurance Plus Annuity: The average commission paid to the salesperson is 50 percent of the first year's premium on the term insurance and only 5 percent on the annuity portion. Is it surprising that salespeople vigorously push universal life and neglect to tell you that you would do far better with the annuity for your investment money? Out of a $1,200 total insurance plus annuity investment, only $100 commission is paid on the insurance and $50 on the annuity the first year, for a total of $150 instead of a $960 commission.

SURRENDER CHARGE

Universal Life: The surrender charge, if you decide to cancel in the early years, can run into thousands of dollars, even up to 100 percent of the money you have paid in.

Term Insurance Plus Annuity: The surrender charge is on the average 7 percent in the first year, decreasing 1 percent each year until it reaches zero after the seventh year.

The term insurance plus annuity plan is the hands-down winner.

ATTACK #41

Buy the least expensive term life insurance and devote the rest of your money to prosperous living.

Term insurance is the correct life insurance under all circumstances. But there are three different types of term insurance and choosing the right type is as important as choosing term insurance itself.

- Decreasing term
- Annually renewable term (ART)
- Level premium term (LPT)

Decreasing Term—No

Your yearly premiums remain constant when you buy decreasing term insurance, but the amount of insurance coverage decreases each year. Decreasing term is used primarily for mortgage life and credit life insurance and is overpriced by as much as 600 percent. (See Chapter 7 on gimmick life insurance.) Decreasing term has little value other than making insurance companies wealthier. As you saw earlier, whole life could be considered a form of decreasing term insurance.

Annually Renewable Term (ART)—Only Under Special Circumstances

The policy term of annually renewable term (ART) insurance is one year, as implied by the name. The policy is automatically renewable each year up to the age you choose without another physical as long as you continue to make the required annual premium payment. Since theoretically you are buying life insurance coverage for one year, the premium is based only on your chances of dying that year. Look at the following mortality table and you will see that your statistical chance of dying in any one year from disease, accident or any cause is extremely small at any age.

MORTALITY TABLE

The Chances of Dying in Any One Year

AGE	NUMBER WHO DIE PER 1000	PERCENTAGE CHANCE OF DYING
25	1.47	0.15%
35	1.88	0.19%
45	4.06	0.41%
55	8.78	0.88%
65	20.01	2.00%
75	51.22	5.12%

As you get older, your chances of expiring in any one year increase. The premiums, therefore, on an annually renewable term policy also increase, as they should.

As you can see from the Life Insurance Premium Comparison Chart on pages 122–23, column A, ART premiums are the lowest of any form of life insurance in the first year and increase each year as long as you continue the policy. From the preceding mortality table you will notice that there is a four times greater chance of dying at age 55 than there is at 35, 8.78 per 1,000 versus 1.88 per 1,000. Look again at column A, page 123, and you will see that the one-year premium for ART insurance at age 54 is $593, about four times higher than the premiums of $143 for someone 36 years old. Because of the rapid rise in yearly premiums, annually renewable term is the best choice for term insurance only under the following special circumstances:

1. *Short term need for insurance coverage.* There may be times during your life when you need a life insurance policy for less than five years. For instance, you obtain a business loan on which the bank requires you to be covered with life insurance. If the loan is for only three years, and you want to drop the insurance after the loan is paid off, the total premiums for an ART policy would be lower than the premiums for a level term policy. Many insurance companies offer the first three years of annually renewable term insurance at an artificially low rate as an inducement to buy the policy.

2. *Limited budget.* If you are struggling financially, you may need to have the absolutely lowest possible premiums on your life insurance policy during the next few years. In this case, annually renewable term, until you get yourself on your financial feet, may be your best choice. While level term may be the best value, the ART rates the first couple of years will be lower than the level term premiums.

3. *Future habit changes.* The third reason to consider ART instead of level term is that you have a habit that increases your life insurance rates and you intend to change the habit over the next couple of years. These habits can include smoking or overeating that has caused obesity or high cholesterol. Rates for people in these groups are about 25 to 100 percent higher than for others because of the increased health risks. Instead of locking in a higher rate for level premium term for 5 to 20 years, you can do better with the short-term ART rates now until you qualify for low nonsmoker or better health rates later.

Level Premium Term (LPT)—Best

With a level premium term policy you choose a policy period, 5, 10, 15 or 20 years. Both your yearly premium and the amount of insurance remain constant over the entire period. The only disadvantage is that your level term premiums are slightly higher in the first few years than the premiums on an annually renewable term policy. Level premium term insurance with its fixed premium guarantees that the total amount you pay over a 20-year period will be less. With a choice of a guaranteed premium for 5, 10, or 20 years, how do you know which term is mathematically best? What if we were to find the lowest-priced term policies in every category, total the premiums that would be paid over a 20-year period and then select the type of term insurance with the lowest overall premium? We could even compare the various forms of term to the total premium that would be paid over the same 20 years for typical whole life and universal life policies. Well, we've done just that and the astounding results are shown in the Life Insurance Premium Comparison Chart on pages 122–23. Columns A through E show a 20-year comparison of the premiums that would be paid by a 35-year-old, nonsmoking male for $100,000 of the lowest-priced term insurance policies uncovered by The Insurance Clearing-House in each category. Columns F through G show the premiums over the same 20 years for whole life and universal life policies.

There are six different ways to buy term insurance, not including decreasing term, as shown in the next table.

WAYS TO PURCHASE TERM INSURANCE AND COMPARATIVE COSTS
(From Life Insurance Premium Comparison Chart)

	COLUMN	1ST YEAR PREMIUM	TOTAL PREMIUM OVER 20 YEARS
1. Annually renewable term, not switching companies	A	$135	$6,483
2. 5-year level term	B	$135	$4,950
3. 10-year level term	C	$141	$3,950
4. 10-plus-10-year level term	D	$156	$3,740
5. 20-year level term	E	$215	$4,300

Remember these are the best possible rates we could find from companies rated high enough to be considered acceptable. You will note that on the best-priced ART policy, the premiums for $100,000 of insurance are only $135 the first year, but with the yearly increases you would pay a total of $6,483 over 20 years—not the best value of all the types of term insurance but far better than the $24,800 to $29,380 you would pay for the whole life insurance policies shown in columns F and G. ART rates are priced artificially low in the first one to three years to attract business. Once the insurance company has you "on the books," it figures that out of habit or inconvenience you will continue to pay the premium, which becomes much higher as time goes on. There is a better way.

LIFE INSURANCE PREMIUM COMPARISON CHART

$100,000 Coverage, Male Nonsmoker

Premiums over 20-Year Period at Age 35

	TERM INSURANCE					TYPICAL WHOLE LIFE		TYPICAL UNIVERSAL LIFE	
AGE	(A) A/R/T	(B) 5 YEAR LEVEL TERM	(C) 10 YEAR LEVEL TERM	(D) 10 + 10 YEAR LEVEL TERM	(E) 20 YEAR LEVEL TERM	(F) NON-PARTICI-PATING WHOLE LIFE	(G) PARTICIPATING WHOLE LIFE	(H) HIGH CASH BUILDUP	(I) LOW CASH BUILDUP
35	$ 135	$ 135	$ 141	$ 156	$ 215	$ 984	$ 1,469	$ 1,200	$ 650
	143	↓	↓	↓	│	│	│	│	│
	154	↓	↓	↓	│	│	│	│	│
	168	↓	↓	↓	│	│	│	│	│
	184	↓	↓	↓	│	│	│	│	│
40	201	$ 210	↓	↓	│	│	│	│	│
	219	↓	↓	↓	│	│	│	│	│
	241	↓	↓	↓	│	│	│	│	│
	266	↓	↓	↓	│	│	│	│	│
	293	↓	↓	↓	│	│	│	│	│
45	324	$ 270	$ 218*	$ 156 $ 218	│	│	│	│	│
	348	↓	│	│	│	│	│	│	│
	373	↓	│	│	│	│	│	│	│
	398	↓	│	│	│	│	│	│	│
	426	↓	│	│	│	│	│	│	│

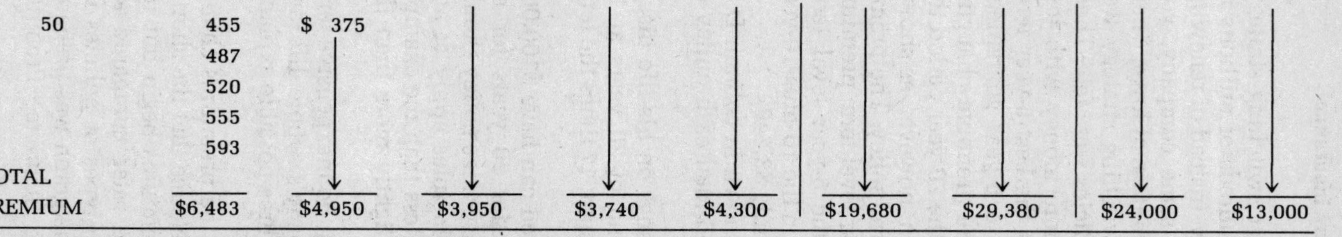

Age	A	B	C	D	E	F	G	H	I
50	455	$ 375	↓	↓	↓	↓	↓	↓	↓
	487	↓							
	520								
	555								
	593								
TOTAL PREMIUM	$6,483	$4,950	$3,950	$3,740	$4,300	$19,680	$29,380	$24,000	$13,000

*not guaranteed rate, must requalify for renewal of future rate

Companies used in preparing Life Insurance Premium Comparison Chart:

Column	Company	Column	Company
A:	Jackson National	F:	Jackson National
B:	USLICO	G:	Federal Kemper ('90)
C:	Manhattan National	H:	Life USA
D:	Manhattan National	I:	Life USA
E:	Midland Mutual		

Years ago we developed the ART 5-year switching strategy, which helped tens of thousands save hundreds of millions in life insurance premiums. With this strategy, instead of renewing your insurance every 5 years with the same company, you applied to different companies to take advantage of lower "new customer" rates. At the time the ART switching strategy was developed, good low-priced level term policies were few. There are more now and you can save even more money with less hassle. In column B, you will notice that the best 5-year term policy for a person age 35 begins with a 5-year guaranteed premium of only $135 each year, with the premium changing once every 5 years at renewal time. Over the 20-year period the total cost is $4,950. The best overall option, however, as shown on the chart, is a 10-plus-10-year level term policy. The premiums are $21 per year higher than the 5-year level term premium for the first 5 years but $52 less than the 5-year level term premium by the 10th year. The total paid on the 10-plus-10-year level term policy over a 20-year period is only $3,740.

The 10-plus-10-year level term policy shown in column D at this time represents the lowest guaranteed total cash outlay of all of the various types of policies.

If the 35-year-old had invested the savings on his life insurance in a tax-deferred annuity, at the end of 20 years at 10 percent he would have $67,000 in the account, 17 times the total cost of the term insurance!

At age 35, as in our example, the insured can have $100,000 of continuous life insurance protection for 20 years for an average of $235 per year. That's all a life insurance policy should cost using these strategies. The same principles apply at any age, but the average cost per year will be less than the example if you are currently under age 35 and slightly more than the example if you are over age 35.

The thousands of agents who could sell the inexpensive term insurance instead push the same company's whole life and universal life policies. There can be only three possible explanations—fear, greed or ignorance.

The graph that follows illustrates how the premiums change on a 5-, 10- or 20-year level term policy. Notice that the shorter the term of the policy, the lower the premiums begin but the higher they end up 20 years later. The rates compared are the lowest premiums found on the three types of policies for companies rated A or above by Best's. The graph was prepared using the premiums shown in the Life Insurance Premium Comparison Chart.

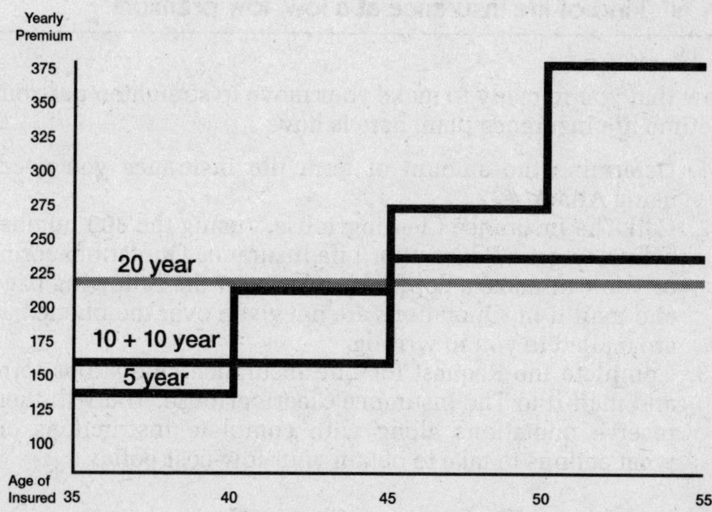

One final warning. You must constantly be on your guard against potentially misleading advertising methods used by the life insurance industry. One example was an A+ rated life insurance company that had sold over $2 billion of a policy which it marketed as "the lowest level premium in the world." The policy was called "permanent term," which is in itself a contradiction. For $100,000 of insurance, the "preferred premium" was $336 per year forever. (Well, not really forever, just to age 100, which for a 35-year-old would seem forever!) At the end of 20 years, the insured would have paid $6,720 in premiums, so it would beat none of the true term plans in the Life Insurance Premium Comparison Chart. The "permanent term" plan accumulates a small projected cash value at the end of 20 years, so the policy was really a type of ordinary or "universal" life with an incorrect name. If the insured dies, remember that the company keeps the cash value.

You may wonder, "How in the world do they sell this type of expensive policy?" First of all, by not calling it what it is, "expensive term"; second, by paying up to 105 percent commission; and third, not everyone has read this book—yet!

ATTACK #42

Call The Insurance ClearingHouse to get the right kind of life insurance at a low, low premium.

Now that you're ready to make your move to straighten out your lifetime life insurance plan, here is how:

1. Determine the amount of term life insurance you need, using Attack #32.
2. Call The Insurance ClearingHouse,* using the 800 number below, to get a Request for Life Insurance Quotations form, or you can make a copy of the form on the following page and mail it in. Quotations are not given over the phone but are mailed to you in writing.
3. Complete the Request for Life Insurance Quotations form and mail it to The Insurance ClearingHouse. You will then receive quotations along with complete instructions on what actions to take to obtain your low-cost policy.

The Insurance ClearingHouse
400 West Main Street
Leesburg, Florida 34748-5180
1-800-522-2827

The Insurance ClearingHouse is a huge organization that has brought the relief of low-cost life insurance to thousands of Americans. The ClearingHouse occupies its own three-story national headquarters building in Leesburg, Florida. By matching Givens Organization members with the best life insurance policies and least expensive term insurance available through ClearingHouse research, it has written an average of over $1 billion of the least expensive term insurance every year, stretching computer and administrative systems to the limits. The required paperwork is measured in tons and shows what can be accomplished by a group of highly motivated, well-trained and caring people.

The Insurance ClearingHouse will provide you with the most current and best life insurance rates available from its ongoing research. Jo and/or Buddy Hewell, the directors of The Insurance

*This insurance service not available in all areas.

Request for Life Insurance Quotations
The Insurance ClearingHouse

400 West Main Street
Leesburg, Florida 34748-5180
Telephone: 1-800-522-2827

Name ______________________ Date ________
Address ________________________________
City ______________ State ______ Zip Code _____
Birth Date ________ Sex (M) ____ (F) ____
Nearest ________ Last ________ (Do not complete this line)
Have you smoked or used ANY tobacco products in the past 12 months?
Yes ____ No ____ If yes, specify: Cigarettes _____ Cigars _____
Pipe ___ Chewing Tobacco ___
HEALTH: (Answer YES or NO) Do you have or have you ever had:
Coronary Disease ____ Diabetes ____ Cancer ____ Alcohol or Drug Treatment ____ Blood-Related Disorders ____ High Blood Pressure ____ High Cholesterol ____
Height ____ Weight ____
Amount of Insurance Desired $ ____________
How long will you need coverage? ________

SPOUSE/OTHER

Name of Spouse/Other (if also to be insured ____________
Birth Date ________________ Sex (M) ____ (F) ____
Nearest ________ Last ________ (Do not complete this line)
Have you smoked or used ANY tobacco products in the past 12 months?
Yes ____ No ____ If yes, specify: Cigarettes _____ Cigars _____
Pipe ___ Chewing Tobacco ___
HEALTH: (Answer YES or NO) Do you have or have you ever had:
Coronary Disease ____ Diabetes ____ Cancer ____ Alcohol or Drug Treatment ____ Blood-Related Disorders ____ High Blood Pressure ____ High Cholesterol ____
Height ____ Weight ____
Amount of Insurance Desired $ ____________
How long will you need coverage? ________
Phone: (Applicant) __________ (Other) __________

ClearingHouse, are currently licensed to do business in all states. There is no charge for this service. The expenses of The ClearingHouse are paid by commissions received from the insurance companies with which the policies are placed.

Preferred rates. All rates quoted will initially be preferred rates. Preferred rates apply to healthy, low-risk-profile individuals. These are people who have no personal history of high blood pressure, diabetes or cancer, have no personal or family history of coronary artery disease, are nonsmokers who are not overweight, and have a cholesterol level of less than 230. Since 90 percent of the applicants using The ClearingHouse fit the preferred category, this is the rate quoted. Don't be disappointed if you don't fit into this category. The Insurance ClearingHouse will attempt to find the best rate possible for a person in your general condition.*

Standard rates. People who do not qualify for preferred rates may pay a standard rate which is a bit higher than the preferred rates, but still is among the best standard rates. Standard rates are normally about 25 percent higher than preferred rates. Occasionally, in the case of preexisting health problems, a person is individually rated based on the degree of risk involved. You will always be notified in advance if your condition requires a special rate, which you can choose to accept or reject.

Smoker or nonsmoker. Another factor affecting rates is whether you smoke. To be classified as a preferred nonsmoker you must *not* have smoked or used any tobacco products within the past 12-month period—no exceptions. The new technology for detecting nicotine in the body is so advanced that if you smoke or chew tobacco only once or twice during the year, it will become apparent in your blood and/or urine test. There is no honor system here; the insurance company checks. So answer the question on the application honestly. The Insurance ClearingHouse has discovered some companies that provide rates far more favorable to smokers than other companies.

The Insurance ClearingHouse will choose from the companies they recommend the company that is best for you based on your age, health and amount of insurance you need and give you specific written instructions for completing the particular application you will receive for the recommended company.

*This insurance service is not available in all areas.

Policy issue time. The usual time is 6–8 weeks if there are no delays in getting all necessary information.

Binding receipt. Your insurance will be in effect with most companies upon completion of all medical requirements. Always include a check made out to the insurance company with your application. When the insurance company accepts and deposits your check, and if you have answered all questions truthfully, binding coverage is in effect up to the binding limits set by the company.

DEFENSE #43

Fill out your insurance policy application truthfully, even if you know your answers will increase your premiums.

Ever wonder how a life insurance application gets accepted or rejected? I know you do if you've ever been rejected. Understanding the underwriting process means giving yourself the best chance of obtaining the best insurance for your situation and condition at the best rates. Understanding the process will also give you the self-confidence to move ahead with your new plan and understand the inside secrets of how insurance companies operate.

Every individual who fills out an application for life insurance coverage goes through a qualifying process called underwriting. The person at the insurance company who processes and accepts or rejects applications for life insurance coverage is called the underwriter. In general, the decision is based on these considerations:

Medical information. Most life insurance companies require that a medical examination be conducted by a paramedic organization. These tests will include a blood profile, a urinalysis and a paramedic examination (an abbreviated examination by a medical technician), all done at no cost to you. The paramedic organization will contact you to make an appointment for the exam, which can be done at your home or office. Set up your appointment as quickly as possible to avoid delays. The medical exam takes only a few minutes. The insurance company may also use the Medical Information Bureau (MIB) to gather additional information about you. The MIB is a nonprofit organization of life insurance companies that operates an information exhange on behalf of its members and keeps a medical history on just about everyone who has ever purchased life insurance. The answers to medical questions on your application are often checked against MIB records to see if you are telling the truth or forgot to mention anything material.

You can find out what is in your MIB file if you wish. Upon receipt of a written request from you, the MIB will disclose any information it may have in your file to your personal physician for your review. If you question the accuracy of your file, you may seek correction in accordance with the procedures set forth in the Federal Fair Credit Reporting Act (see page 270). The address of the MIB's information office is Post Office Box 105, Essex Station, Boston, Massachusetts 02112.

Inspection report. Generally, an inspection report is required only on larger amounts of coverage, $300,000 or more. This investigative consumer report is information compiled through personal interviews with neighbors, friends, or others with whom you are acquainted. The inquiry includes information as to your character, general reputation, personal characteristics and mode of living. This report usually is done through Equifax Services.

Occasionally you may be contacted directly by the insurance company by telephone. Be honest but cautious in answering any type of personal question via telephone. Some people give information actually detrimental to their own case. Be especially wary of questions relating to your intent to replace life insurance coverage you already have.

Financial justification. There must be financial justification for any amount of life insurance you are securing. The larger the amount, the more rigorous the qualifying process. Most life insurance companies will require a simple financial statement if the amount is $500,000 or more. A rule of thumb for determining the maximum amount of coverage you may request is 10 times your annual income. Other criteria such as business obligations and/or debts may be used to increase the maximum amount of insurance coverage for which you qualify. The life insurance you already have is added to the amount you are requesting, and the total is used in the qualifying process.

ATTACK #44

Once you've obtained inexpensive term insurance, dump your old policies.

Now that you understand how to get the right policies, you should also know how to cancel those you don't want without getting ripped off by the insurance company in the process.

Here are the steps to take in making the transition to a better life insurance plan.

Step 1: Get together all existing life insurance policies you own, including those on children, and make a list of your coverage amounts, types of policy, company names, addresses and policy numbers.

Step 2: Locate and buy the best and lowest-priced term life insurance policy for the amount of life insurance you need.

Step 3: When you have your new coverage (but not before!), cancel your existing whole life, universal life or over-priced term policies, using the strategies that follow.

Step 4: Transfer any cash value from canceled policies to self-directed tax-deferred annuities. See pages 136 to 140.

You can also get help moving cash values into tax-sheltered annuities by calling The Insurance ClearingHouse at 1-800-522-2827.

ATTACK #45

Stop paying premiums and revoke automatic withdrawals to cancel a life insurance policy.

You may think that canceling a life insurance policy is simple and straightforward. Not at all. The insurance company uses several tricks to prevent you from canceling to keep your cash value.

If you stop paying premiums, your life insurance policy

should automatically lapse after the 30-day grace period. If your premiums are automatically withdrawn from your checking account, send a letter to your financial institution revoking the authorization and request that no future drafts be honored. Here is a form for you to use. The letter can be handwritten but be certain to keep a copy.

TO: (Bank name and address)

____

____

DATE: ____/____/____

REFERENCE: (Name of your insurance company)

MY BANK ACCOUNT NUMBER: (Account that is debited)

I intend to cancel my life insurance policy. Effective immediately, I am, therefore, revoking my authorization for the above-named insurance company to directly charge my account for premiums.

(Your signature)

After 30 days from the premium due date most policies will lapse.

ATTACK #46

Withdraw your cash value during the 30-day grace period to stop automatic conversion to a paid-up policy.

Many life insurance policies contain an automatic provision to convert the cash value in the policy to a reduced paid-up life insurance policy. The provision gives the company the right to borrow enough money from your cash value to pay the premium necessary to keep the policy in force. In addition, the company charges interest on each loan and makes new loans to pay the premiums plus the interest until all of the cash value has been depleted. Because of these life insurance gimmicks, you must take additional steps to cancel your life insurance policy.

Follow these steps to liquidate your life insurance policies and get back your cash value.

1. From your insurance records, photocopy:
   a. the declaration sheet,
   b. cash value tables and surrender values,
   c. the application.
2. Write, print or type a simple letter or memo of instructions to the home office of the insurance company with your name, Social Security number, policy number and a request for the total cash surrender value to be mailed to you immediately. Use the sample letter that follows.
3. Sign the letter or memo exactly as your name appears on the policy application. If the beneficiary is an adult, have him or her sign the letter also.
4. Photocopy the letter and store it in your file.
5. Enclose your original policy with your letter. Direct the correspondence to: The Home Office, Attention: Policyholders Service Department. Mail your letter "return receipt requested," which will require a trip to a post office.
6. Place the post office receipt in your file. When the dated and signed receipt is returned to you, put it in the same file.
7. You should have your check within 7–10 working days after the signed post office receipt is returned to you. If there is a discrepancy between the amount you receive and the amount shown in the surrender value tables, you must contact the company.
8. If you have any problems, call the insurance company using their 800 number or call collect. Write down the name of every person with whom you speak. Start by asking for the president.
9. If you are unable to get satisfaction, file a complaint against the insurance company with your state insurance commissioner. The phone numbers of all the state insurance commissioners' offices are shown on pages 134–35.

Date:

To: Big Bucks Life Insurance Company
Tall Office Building
Some Large City, USA 12345

From: Your Name, SS#

Subject: Policy #20987654321

Upon receipt of this letter and policy, please liquidate the above-referenced policy and remit 100% of the cash value to the owner immediately. Mail to the following:

Your Name
Street Address
City, State, Zip Code

I am not replacing this policy with a permanent life insurance policy from another company. I do not wish to have an agent or other company representative contact me.

Print your name *Print name of beneficiary*

Your signature *Signature of beneficiary*

cc: copy retained for State Insurance Department

You will get the results you are after if you follow these steps. Otherwise the insurance company will beat you almost every time.

State Insurance Commissioners' Offices

Alabama
205-269-3550

Alaska
907-465-2515

Arizona
602-912-8400

Arkansas
501-686-2900

California
415-557-9624
(San Francisco)
213-736-2572
(Los Angeles)
916-322-3555
800-927-4357*
(Sacramento)

Colorado
303-894-7499

Connecticut
203-297-3800

Delaware
302-739-4251

District of Columbia
202-727-7424

Florida
904-922-3100
800-342-2762*

Georgia
404-656-2070

Hawaii
808-586-2790

Idaho
208-334-2250

*The 800 numbers are in-state WATS lines only.

Illinois
217-782-4515
(Springfield)
312-814-2420
(Chicago)

Indiana
317-232-2385

Iowa
515-281-5705

Kansas
913-296-7801

Kentucky
502-564-3630

Louisiana
504-342-5900

Maine
207-582-8707

Maryland
410-333-6300

Massachusetts
617-521-7777

Michigan
517-373-9273

Minnesota
612-296-6848

Mississippi
601-359-3569

Missouri
314-340-6830

Montana
406-444-2040

Nebraska
402-471-2201

Nevada
702-687-4270

New Hampshire
603-271-2261

New Jersey
609-292-5363

New Mexico
505-827-4500

New York
212-602-0429
(New York City)
518-474-6600
(Albany)

North Carolina
919-733-7349

North Dakota
701-224-2440

Ohio
614-644-2658

Oklahoma
405-521-2828

Oregon
503-378-4271

Pennsylvania
717-787-5173

Rhode Island
401-277-2223

South Carolina
803-737-6117

South Dakota
605-773-3563

Tennessee
615-741-2241

Texas
512-463-6464

Utah
801-538-3800

Vermont
802-828-3301

Virginia
804-371-9741

Washington
206-753-7301

West Virginia
304-558-3386
800-642-9004*

Wisconsin
608-266-0102

Wyoming
307-777-7401

DEFENSE #47

Never replace a policy until a new policy is issued.

The strategies to replace whole life, universal life, single premium life, and other cash value policies, which attempt to combine investing and life insurance protection, are prudent for the majority. The strategies of replacing various types of term insurance with new policies that will provide either the same amount of life insurance protection for *less* premium, or *more* life insurance protection for the same premium is a mathematically intelligent decision, but you should never quit paying for any insurance policy that you may replace until a new policy providing all the protection you and/or your family need has been issued by the new insurance company and *they have accepted your premium payment.* It is vital that you do not go one minute without the insurance protection you need. It is better to pay one month's premium to two companies for double protection than risk a loss while not insured.

ATTACK #48

Transfer your insurance policy cash value to a tax-deferred annuity.

A sales pitch that the insurance agent who sold you a whole life or universal life policy will use to dissuade you from canceling the policy is to tell you that your cash value will be taxed when taken out of the policy. That is not totally true. The only portion that is subject to taxes is the tax-deferred interest or earnings that the policy built up over the time you kept it, usually very little, if any. Your principal, the amount of premium that went into the investment, is not taxed because you had already paid taxes on the money before you bought the policy.

You can avoid any taxes when canceling a life insurance policy by using a little-known tax law. You have the right to transfer your cash value without taxes into a tax-deferred annuity with the same or a different insurance company. When you use the "insurance policy to annuity transfer rules," the exchange is not counted as a withdrawal and none of your money is taxed, but it can end up in a better investment. You can then leave the money in your tax-deferred annuity with earnings compounding tax-free until you choose to withdraw any or all of it. Only at that time will you be subject to taxes on the earnings. Tax-deferred annuities are the best alternative to the tax shelter that you can get from a life insurance policy. You don't have to buy a whole life or universal life insurance policy in order to invest in an annuity. The transfer must be handled within the company or between the two insurance companies in order for you to avoid the taxes.

You can get help with the life insurance to annuity transfer through The Insurance ClearingHouse. The best annuities are those that offer you mutual funds as investment choices instead of a small guaranteed interest rate. On the following pages you will see, based on our research, what we currently consider to be the best annuities for either life insurance transfers or regular tax-deferred investments. For further information, you can call The Insurance ClearingHouse at 1-800-522-2827.

Definitions

Company The name of the company that issues the annuity.
Annuity Name The name of the annuity plan offered by the company.

GENERAL INFORMATION

Issues Ages to The last age at which you can open or start the plan.
Minimum Initial Deposit The minimum investment required to open the account.
Statements How often you receive a statement of your account.
States Not Approved The states in which the company is not licensed to sell.

FEES

Mortality Fees/Expenses Represents the percentage per year charged to guarantee payout plans and for company operating expenses.
Investment Fees The percentage charged for investment management. The average is .5 percent.
Administrative Fees A flat charge assessed against your account as an administrative charge. The average is $30 per year.
Transfer Charges The amount you are charged, if any, to move your money from one investment to another within the annuity plan.

SAFETY

A. M. Best Rating The safety rating assigned by the A. M. Best Company. All recommended companies are acceptable.

RECOMMENDED TAX-DEFERRED ANNUITIES

COMPANY ANNUITY NAME	NATIONWIDE BEST OF AMERICA IV	GUARDIAN INVESTOR	ANCHOR NAT'L "POLARIS"
General Info			
Issue Ages to	0–76	0–75	0–80
Min. Initial Deposit	$1,500-1st year	$500	$2,000 (qualified plan) $5,000 (unqualified plan)
Additional Deposits	$10 or $25	$100	$20 or $250 or $500
Retirement Plans Avail.	All	All	All
Statements	Quarterly	Semi-annually	Quarterly
States Not Approved	None	None	NY, MI
Fees			
Mortality Fees/Expenses	.80%/.45%-.05%	1.0%/0.1%-0.28%	1.02/.35%–.15%
Investment Fees	See prospectus	0.5%	0.12%–0.90%
Admin. Fees	$30	$35	$35
Transfer Charges	0	0	0 for one through 15 ($25 thereafter)
Safety			
Year Company Established	1929	1970	1965
Assets	19.2 Billion	2.5 Billion	$5.2 billion
A. M. Best Rating	A+ Superior	A+ + Superior	A Excellent

Flexibility			
Investment Options	(Portfolios)(24)	(Funds)(8)	SunAmerica
	Oppenheimer	Stock	Anchor
	Fidelity	Bond	13 total funds
	Neuburger-Berman	Cash/MM	
	Van Eck	Conturion	
	Twentieth Century	Value Line	
	Nationwide*	Real Estate	
	Yes	Yes	
	V = 100% anytime	V = 100% anytime	
	F = 1st mo** contract yr.	F = 1st mo** contract yr.	
Transfer			Anytime
Written or Phone	Either	Either	Either
Performance			
Stock	91 92 93 %	91 92 93 %	New Anchor Product—
Bond	37 7 9	34 19 19	formerly American
Money Mkt.	4.4 2.0 1.4%	4.3 2.0 1.4%	Pathway II. See
Fixed	6.7 5.2 4.5	6.0 5.0 4.5	prospectus for details.
Liquidity			
Surrender Fees	7%-6-5-4-3-2-1	5%-5-5-5-5	7%-6-5-4-3-2-1 rolling
Charged Against	Deposits	Deposits	Deposits
Partial Free Withdrawal	10% of Dep.	10% of Dep.	10% of Dep.

For information on the above annuities, call The Insurance ClearingHouse at 1-800-522-2827
—variable rate investment
—fixed rate investment

FLEXIBILITY

Investment Options The different mutual funds or fixed-interest accounts in which you can invest your money.

Transfer How often you can move your money from investment to investment.

Written or Phone The method(s) you can use to move your money from one investment to another. "Written" requires a letter or special form; "phone" requires only a phone call and gives maximum convenience.

PERFORMANCE

The percentage of growth for the year shown of each type of investment offered. Where more than one investment is included in a category, the average is shown.

LIQUIDITY

Surrender Fees The year-by-year deferred sales charge assessed if you withdraw your money all at once. Example: "7%-6-5-4-3-2-1" means that 7 percent is charged if you withdraw your money the first year, which decreases by a percentage point each year until it reaches zero the eighth year and after. Surrender fees for these companies apply only to purchase deposits and not to earnings.

Partial Fee Withdrawal The amount of your account balance that you may withdraw each year without paying a surrender fee.

ATTACK #49

Earn a spread by reinvesting borrowed insurance policy cash value.

A spread is the difference between money borrowed at a low interest rate and invested at a higher rate of return. What happens if you find that your current state of health makes you no longer insurable but you have a significant amount of cash value in a whole life or universal life insurance policy that you've built over the last 10 to 40 years? Your best strategy is to earn every dollar you can on the cash value—but that won't usually happen by letting the insurance company keep your money. Most every whole life policy allows you to borrow your own cash value at an interest rate ranging from 5 percent on the old policies to 7 percent on the newer ones. Some policies now loan you money from a general fund at 2 percent more than you are being paid. Either way you are paying interest on your own money!

By borrowing and reinvesting your cash value in a mutual fund and averaging 12 to 15 percent, you can earn up to 8 percent more than the insurance company was paying you. In many cases the money you are borrowing from your life insurance policy, used for investment, is eligible for a tax deduction for the interest that you pay. Interest on money borrowed to reinvest is tax deductible. To qualify for the tax deduction, keep the insurance money you borrow separate from your regular bank account. You must be able to trace the insurance funds from the source into your new investment to take the tax deduction.

Some policies require that you pay interest on any cash value you borrow on a periodic basis. A few companies simply deduct the interest from any additional cash value that you are earning. In either case, keep the necessary statements for tax purposes.

Here are the steps to take to utilize the loan provision of a cash value life policy:

Read the "Loans," "Policy Loans" or "Loan Values" section of your policy to understand your interest rate, your required repayment schedule and any important consequences of failure to repay the loan.

Either call your insurance company's policyholders service department and request a "Policy Loan Request" form or prepare your own request, typed or printed, like the one on the following page.

Some companies may require that signature(s) be notarized or have a signature guarantee from a bank.

Require the company to furnish a letter or printout that clearly discloses your current loan value, the amount of money needed to pay the interest each year, and the projected cash value of the policy with or without future interest payments after the loan. Add this request to the letter or in the "remarks" section of the company's "Policy Loan Request" form.

Date:	
To:	Big Bucks Life Insurance Company Tall Office Building Some Large City, USA 12345
From:	(Your Name and SS#)
Subject:	Policy # ____________

Upon receipt of this request, please forward a check for 100% of the loan value of the above-referenced policy to the policy owner. Mail to:

Name ______________________________

Address ______________________________

Beneficiary Name ______________________________

(*Signature*)

____

ATTACK #50

Don't buy life insurance to pay estate taxes; buy a guaranteed insurability rider.

If you are married you can pass an unlimited amount of cash or property to your spouse with no estate taxes. If you are single or if you are a surviving spouse, everything over $600,000 in your estate will be taxed at the rates shown on the Unified Gift and Estate Tax Rates table on page 144.

One error in judgment often made in estate planning by those whose estates are over the taxable limit is to assume that the estate tax must be provided for while living. Let's say that your taxable estate is $1,350,000, exceeding the $600,000 exemption limit by $750,000. From the Unified Gift and Estate Tax Rates table, you will notice that the taxes your estate would pay would be 39 percent of $750,000, or a total of $248,300.

Whole life insurance agents would love to solve the problem for you by selling you an incredibly expensive $250,000 whole life insurance policy so that the cash would be there to pay the estate taxes. But when you buy a life insurance policy to pay estate taxes, all you are doing is paying estate taxes before you die, instead of after. That's like paying income taxes on money you haven't earned yet. Realize that the insurance company must bring in more money in premiums than it pays out in death benefits or it cannot stay in business. Therefore, a majority of the people who buy life insurance to protect an estate will have paid more into the plan in terms of premiums and the interest they could have earned with other investments than will come out of the plan to pay the estate taxes. This one hard fact of life is often hard for me to get across, because the amount of money just doesn't seem as significant when you're making yearly payments in premiums and not seeing the investment return the insurance company is earning on your money. Ask yourself, does it really matter whether your heirs split $1.35 million or $1.1 million? Of course not. Instead, set up a plan to give your heirs estate-tax-free money or property while you are living, not after you're gone. That way at least your heirs will get the extra money instead of the insurance company using it for years at your expense.

The insurance companies have done an admirable job of terrifying wealthier people about estate taxes. Even if you agree with me that it's okay to pay the estate taxes after death rather than before so you can use the majority of your money for living, planning is still required.

If your estate, as in our example, is $1.35 million and the taxes to be paid about $250,000, you will want to make certain that your investments are structured so that it will be fairly easy to convert $250,000 of your estate to cash to pay the taxes when due. In any case, the executor of your estate will not have to come up with $250,000 cash in a day or two, or even a month or two. You will want to be sure that $250,000 of your $1.35 million estate is in investments like money market funds, annuities, your retirement plan or securities such as stocks and bonds that could be converted to cash. If your entire estate, for instance, is in a piece of undeveloped land or invested in an ongoing business you owned, it will be more difficult to raise cash to pay the estate taxes. The most loving thing you can do for your heirs is set up a plan so that the cash will be available for estate taxes, not to buy a whole life insurance policy.

UNIFIED GIFT AND ESTATE TAX RATES

IF TAXABLE AMOUNT IS OVER	BUT NOT OVER	YOUR TAX IS	PLUS %
$0	$10,000	$0	18
$10,000	$20,000	$1,800	20
$20,000	$40,000	$3,800	22
$40,000	$60,000	$8,200	24
$60,000	$80,000	$13,000	26
$80,000	$100,000	$18,200	28
$100,000	$150,000	$23,800	30
$150,000	$250,000	$38,800	32
$250,000	$500,000	$70,800	34
$500,000	$750,000	$155,800	37
$750,000	$1,000,000	$248,300	39
$1,000,000	$1,250,000	$345,800	41
$1,250,000	$1,500,000	$448,300	43
$1,500,000	$2,000,000	$555,800	45
$2,000,000	$2,500,000	$780,800	49
$2,500,000	$3,000,000	$1,025,800	53
$3,000,000		$1,290,800	55

In the absence of a revokable living trust, there is a great estate planning strategy of which few people are aware—buy a guaranteed insurability rider for your insurance policy. A guaranteed insurability rider is an addition to a life insurance policy that guarantees that upon the death of one spouse, the other may purchase up to 10 times the amount of his or her own current life insurance without regard to health or medical history. For example, if each spouse were insured for $100,000, and one of them died, the other would have the option of purchasing up to $1 million of additional life insurance, which could then be used upon the death of the second spouse to pay the estate taxes for the heirs. Your life insurance salesperson would rather that you pay tens of thousands of dollars in premiums over the next 10 to 20 years to protect your estate—as well as his income. With the guaranteed insurability rider, you pay premiums for the additional insurance only after the death of the first spouse. Part of the insurance proceeds from the death of the first spouse can actually be used to purchase the additional insurance. Normally you must purchase the additional insurance, guaranteed by the rider, within 90 days of the death of the first spouse, so the purchase should be part of your will or estate plan. Using this strategy, instead of falling for the normal life insurance estate plan sales pitch, should save you thousands. The right policy for handling estate taxes at the minimum premium is a level term policy with the guaranteed insurability rider.

Let's look at an example: Bill is 55 and his wife, Ethel, is 53. Both are nonsmokers in excellent health and they each have $100,000 worth of insurance protection. They estimate that their estate will be about $1,100,000, of which $500,000 would be taxed when given to anyone other than a surviving spouse. Using the Unified Gift and Estate Tax Rates table, they determine that approximately $150,000 will be needed to pay their estate taxes after the second spouse dies. Unless an RLT is in existence, they can purchase a 15-year level term policy giving them guaranteed insurance rates for 15 years of $610 for him and $368 for her. They can also purchase a guaranteed insurance rider which provides that either could purchase an additional $150,000 of life insurance within 90 days of the other's death and the added insurance cost for the rider is just $228 a year for Bill and $209 a year for Ethel. If their estate were bigger and the surviving spouse could buy $1 million worth of insurance to pay estate taxes, the rider for the $900,000 difference would cost $1,368 per year for Bill and $1,251 per year for Ethel.

With this type of insurance at these rates, which will effectively handle the estate taxes, you are looking at premiums that amount to peanuts compared with the high-priced, high-profit, whole life and single-premium life insurance policies that are being marketed by the insurance companies as estate planning tools. It's amazing how a little knowledge and forethought can save you thousands, even tens of thousands of dollars, when handling your estate.

When you are buying insurance to pay estate taxes, remember that any insurance proceeds become part of your estate and are taxed if above your exclusion. If you're in the 39 percent estate tax bracket with an estate of $1,350,000, as in our first example, and buy $250,000 worth of life insurance to pay estate taxes, 39 percent of the insurance you buy the government will take in taxes. Therefore, to fully cover estate taxes with life insurance, you will want to add in an amount sufficient to pay the estate tax, if any, on the insurance proceeds.

One of the biggest lies told by life insurance salespeople, many of whom don't know the truth, is that life insurance is tax-free. That is absolutely incorrect. Life insurance is *income-tax-free*, but then none of your estate is subject to income taxes. Life insurance proceeds are only estate-tax-free if your estate, including the addition of the life insurance, is below the $600,000 estate tax limit, transferred to your surviving spouse, or set up in an insurance trust.

DEFENSE #51

Set up a trust to distribute the income from your invested life insurance proceeds.

By setting up a life insurance trust you can create an income stream from life insurance proceeds that would take care of your kids, spouse and/or other heirs. Your primary objective in setting up the trust is to make certain that lost family income is immediately replaced and will continue until no longer necessary.

There are three additional important reasons for creating a life insurance trust:

1. To insure that your life insurance proceeds, should something happen to you, are invested according to your instructions
2. To prevent one or more of your heirs from acquiring the insurance money in a lump sum, thereby threatening the future income from the investment
3. To enable the life insurance proceeds to flow into the trust, effectively removing the money from your estate for estate tax probate purposes.

A trust is a legal document that puts into action how you want your money handled and distributed. The beneficiaries of the trust are your heirs. You choose a trustee (a family member or your attorney), who is responsible for seeing that the money is invested according to the instructions you set up in the trust document. If the money is invested in mutual funds, for example, the trustee will instruct the fund to send a check to your heirs each month in the amount you specify. The gift tax rules normally do not apply, since only the premium and not the value of the policy is counted for gift tax purposes and is normally under the $10,000 not-taxed limit per year.* The amount and terms of the distribution are up to you. The trust document should state how much of the investment income or appreciation should be paid from the investment each period.

I recommend that the money be invested in mutual funds to produce the maximum safe return on your investment. You may even choose to have the trustee move the money from one type of mutual fund to another as interest rates change to increase the investment return. (See *More Wealth Without Risk.*) Here are some suggestions for the payout based on the type of mutual fund in which the money is invested.

Bond Mutual Fund—Pay out all interest income plus appreciation of the shares above the original amount of principal.

Stock Mutual Fund—Pay out dividends plus appreciation above the original principal.

Money Market Mutual Funds—Pay out dividends.

To even out the income, making it easier for your heirs to plan, you could instead set a minimum or fixed payout at 1 percent per month or 12 percent per year no matter what the earnings of the fund.

In your life insurance policy, name the trust and not your heirs as the beneficiary. If your heirs include younger children and your primary purpose is to make certain that income is available from your insurance trust until they are grown, you may decide to distribute eventually all the money in the trust rather than just the income. Here are some alternatives:

1. When your children reach age 18, distribute the trust money equally between your children and your spouse.
2. Continue the income plan until the children are age 22, which is about the time they would finish a four-year college education, and then distribute the balance of the money in the trust to your children and spouse.
3. When each child reaches age 18, allow him or her to tap one quarter of his or her share of the trust money each year for four years to pay for college expenses, with any remaining balance to be distributed at age 22.

To help you get started you will find a sample insurance trust declaration in the Resources section prepared by the CJGO legal

*The cash value of an existing insurance policy would be considered for gift tax purposes if the cash value of the policy exceeded $10,000.

department. Fill in the blanks and take it to your local estate planning attorney or contact the CJGO product services estate planning administrator at 1-800-365-4101. You will want to add to your insurance trust document the instructions for how you want the money invested and distributed.

Never put a whole life or other cash value type policy into an insurance trust. The insurance trust is an irrevocable decision, and if you want to get out your cash value from the trust you cannot, not even by borrowing. On the other hand, if the policy that is connected to the trust is a term policy with no cash value, you simply stop paying the premiums to effectively revoke the trust. You would lose nothing.

DEFENSE #52

To avoid probate, make your life insurance payable to a beneficiary, not to your estate.

Probate is the part of the legal system that is supposed to make sure that your estate is split up among your heirs as you direct. In reality the probate system has become a scheme whereby attorneys and courts can legally get their hands on 8 to 15 percent of your estate. In addition to protecting yourself from estate taxes, you must protect yourself from the probate system. Many people mistakenly make their estate the beneficiary of their life insurance policy, thinking that the executor of the estate will then have the money to pay the estate taxes. Insurance proceeds payable to an estate are subject to probate, and must go through the probate system. The proceeds of your life insurance policy are not subject to probate as long as there is a named beneficiary. The beneficiary, if you choose, then can use the money to pay estate taxes, if any, without the insurance going through the probate nightmare. However, insurance proceeds are included in any calculation of estate taxes, whether they have gone through probate or not.

Until you set up an insurance trust for the distribution of investment income from your life insurance proceeds, be certain that your beneficiaries and not your estate are named in your life insurance policy. After you have set up a trust, name the trust as the beneficiary of your life insurance policies. An insurance trust is not subject to probate or to estate taxes.

CHAPTER 7

Get Rid of Hidden Insurance That Is Costing You $2,000 a Year

Out of the dozen types of insurance there are six absolute rip-offs that almost everyone knowingly or unknowingly has purchased. The cost/value relationship of these coverages is so low you might as well be financing the next search for the fountain of youth. These insurance gimmicks fall mainly into two categories—insurance attached to purchases and insurance attached to loans. In addition, there are dozens of gimmick life and health insurance policies sold through television and direct-mail advertising. Insurance attached to purchases includes extended warranties and automobile service contracts that are supposed to cover repair costs of stereos, appliances, automobiles or other major purchases that the manufacturer's original warranty does not cover. Insurance attached to loans is actually life or disability insurance with fancy names like credit life, credit disability, mortgage life and Chargegard. These are intended to pay off your loans if you lose your ability to work or lose your life.

In the Six Hidden Insurance Rip-offs table that follows, you will see how several of these insurance gimmicks can cost families $2,000 to $3,000 every year or $20,000 to $30,000 every 10 years. These are the highest-profit gimmicks in the insurance business, with profit margins of up to 80 percent for the insurance company, which then pays up to 60 percent of the profit to the banks, car dealers, credit card companies and credit unions that sell the insurance.

Many times these insurance contracts and clauses are slipped into purchases and loans without the complete awareness of the buyer or borrower. One study showed that 40 percent of those who were paying hundreds of dollars for credit life and disability insurance weren't even aware that they had bought the optional insurance. Your objective is first to search your purchase and loan papers to find and then cancel the unnecessary coverages you do have, then mentally gear yourself to refuse ever again to buy these high-priced gimmicks, no matter what the sales pitch. You will pocket $2,000 to $3,000 per year for the rest of your life.

SIX HIDDEN INSURANCE RIP-OFFS

INSURANCE	ATTACHED TO	AVERAGE YEARLY COST
Extended warranties	Stereos, TVs, VCRs, appliances	$ 200
Auto service contracts	Auto purchases	$ 300
Credit life	All loans—personal or business	$ 300
Credit disability	All loans—personal or business	$ 200
Mortgage life	Home or rental property mortgages	$1,500
Chargegard	Credit cards	$ 300
Your loss—		$2,800

DEFENSE #53

Never buy or finance extended warranties on appliances and electronics.

Repair insurance or extended warranties on electronics, appliances or almost anything costing over $100 is a complete rip-off. The real purpose of an extended warranty is to add to the dealer's profit at your expense. An extended warranty will pay the cost of repairing the item you buy after the manufacturer's warranty runs out. What happened to the good old days when manufacturers tried to get us to believe that their products were fail-proof?

Audio and video equipment usually comes with a 90-day manufacturer's warranty; appliances, like washers, dryers and microwaves, usually have one to three years to break down at the manufacturer's expense. The extended warranty, created and sold by the retail store, not the manufacturer, kicks in when the manufacturer's warranty expires. There are a number of good reasons why extended warranties are a financial mistake:

- You pay for the warranty in advance even though you get no benefit until the manufacturer's warranty runs out.
- If you finance the amount of the extended warranty, you will be paying interest on the cost of a contract that won't be in effect for as much as one to three years.
- Once you sell, replace or discard the item, the money you spent on the extended warranty becomes worthless.
- The warranty is a limited guarantee and does not cover normal wear and tear or rough handling or, in the case of a video recorder or camera, dropping the equipment. These are the major causes of repairs.
- The cost of the warranty is astronomical compared with the amount of money the dealer actually pays for the real repairs. Less than 15 percent of all the extended warranty monies collected by a dealer is paid out in repairs. The rest is profit.
- Salespeople are normally paid big commissions for intimidating you into saying yes to extended warranties.

Why then do people fall for the extended warranty scheme so easily? Most people will mistakenly buy anything that seems to contribute to peace of mind or a sense of security with no idea of how to calculate the value. Everyone has had something break and need repairs. You will save big money over time, however, by paying for these repairs yourself instead of buying extended warranties.

DEFENSE #54

Never buy the service contract on an automobile.

More than half of all new- and used-car buyers are coerced into a service contract (automobile extended warranty). The service contract technically pays for repair or maintenance not covered by the manufacturer's warranty or after the original warranty runs out. A typical service contract costs $800 to $1,800, depending solely on how much the salesperson can get you to pay, and is therefore one of the most expensive options associated with buying a car. Sixty percent of these warranties are written by manufacturers like Chrysler, Ford and General Motors. The other 40 percent are sold through dealers by independent companies. But there are so many loopholes, conditions and limited chances of collecting that an extended warranty turns out to be one of the biggest potential rip-offs in your financial plan.

The first problem is with independent companies. Should you buy a warranty and the company goes out of business, as often happens, you're out of luck and get no help from the dealer. Here are other gimmicks that insure you will seldom collect:

- The warranty normally does not cover preventive maintenance, towing if your car breaks down or rental expenses while your car is in the shop. These items often amount to more than the actual repairs.
- The service contract on a new car does not start until the original warranty runs out, so you have paid in advance for something you won't need for three to seven years.
- If you add the cost of the warranty to your car loan, as most do, you end up paying as much as 40 percent extra because of several years' interest.
- Many warranties, particularly those from independent companies, require you to pay the bill and be reimbursed later. But it always seems difficult to collect from the company.
- Most service contracts have a deductible, like $100. With some service contracts you will be charged the deductible for every visit to the repair shop. Most automobile repairs fall within the deductible range or allow you to collect only a few dollars after the deductible is applied.

An automobile dealership charges you up to $55 an hour for repairs which are actually costing the dealer about $15 an hour. If the repair work requires three hours and $50 worth of parts, at cost, the dealer actually has less than $100 in the repair, but your bill shows $150 worth of labor and $100 of parts, so you think you've gotten a wonderful deal. By paying the $100 deductible you believe your insurance has paid the difference, or $150. In reality, the dealership made a profit on the $100 deductible that you paid.

Some dealers will also do just about anything to get out of paying. While I was discussing automobile warranties on my

What's Typically Not Covered Under an Automobile Service Contract

Battery and cables, belts and hoses, brakes (front hub, drums, shoes, lining, disc rotors and pads), coolant, exhaust system, filters, fluids, lights (bulbs, sealed beam and lenses), lubricants, manual clutch assembly, shock absorbers, spark plugs and wires, squeaks and rattles, tires, tune-up, wheel balance and alignment, wiper blades.

Exterior—adjustments (glass and body parts), bright metal (outside ornamentation), bumpers, glass, moldings, paint, rust, sheet metal, sideview mirror(s), water leaks, wheel covers and ornaments, wind noise.

Interior—carpet, rearview mirror, trim upholstery.

Repairs due to recalls by the manufacturer or repairs caused by damage or unreasonable use (damage from road hazards, accident, fire or other casualty, misuse, negligence, racing or failures caused by modifications or parts not authorized or supplied by Ford).

Repairs resulting from lack of required maintenance (failures caused by the owner neglecting to perform the required maintenance services set forth in the Owner's Guide for the vehicle). Costs of these routine maintenance services are not covered.

Damage from the environment (airborne fallout, acts of war, tree sap, salt, hail, windstorm, lightning, road hazards, etc.)

Maintenance service and wear item replacements are not covered during the period covered by this contract unless the Maintenance and Wear Option was purchased.

Repairs needed to a covered part caused by the failure of a noncovered part.

Repairs to the vehicle if the odometer is altered, broken or repaired/replaced so that the actual mileage cannot be determined.

To the extent allowed by law, loss of use of vehicle including loss of time, inconvenience, commercial loss or consequential damages.

Repairs to the vehicle performed outside the 50 states and Canada and repairs required because of the use outside the 50 states and Canada.

Repairs made on or before the enrollment date of this contract are not eligible for reimbursement.

radio show, a lady called and said that she had just attempted to collect on an extended warranty from a dealership representing a major U.S. manufacturer. It appeared there had been a leak in the oil pan, the oil ran out, the engine froze and the repairs amounted to hundreds of dollars. The dealership refused to fix her car under warranty, however, because they required her to prove that she had put oil in the engine in the first place. And, of course, she, like most people, had kept no receipts for engine oil.

The salespeople who sell service contracts promise to take care of you should you need a repair. But when it comes time to collect, the attitude in the service department is all too often one of "we'll take you" instead of "we'll take care of you," and the salesperson is nowhere to be found or, at best, of no help at all. Your best repair insurance, if you're constantly short of cash, is to get a no-fee MasterCard or Visa card that you keep in your top dresser drawer. There's no cost or interest unless you need to use the card to charge an occasional repair. You'll save thousands of dollars in unnecessary service contract premium costs.

Now for the service contract clincher. It's what's not covered that counts. On page 153 is a list of what's excluded from repairs under Ford's extended service contract, which is similar in most respects to other warranties and service contracts. Once you finish reading the list, you may begin to wonder what is covered. One of the biggest gimmicks in the automobile service contract business is that if you do not replace the original parts with overpriced parts from the same manufacturer, your warranty may be no good. Also, if you don't bring your car in at the required time for the required maintenance, and pay an exorbitant price for an oil change and checkup, the warranty is also worthless. Cost of the routine maintenance, of course, is not covered by the original warranty or the service contract, and the dealer makes enough profit from the required routine maintenance to afford several repairs on your car.

ATTACK #55

Hire a moonlighting mechanic.

Don't buy warranties on new or used cars. Instead find a moonlighting mechanic who will charge you only $7 to $12 per hour to fix your car in the evenings when he is not working for the dealer who charges you $55 per hour for the same repairs. Your car can be fixed at your home or his and usually at your convenience—even on weekends. I started using this strategy 25 years ago and have saved tens of thousands of dollars in automobile repair costs. You will too.

ATTACK #56

Cancel your extended warranties and get a refund.

Normally you can have an extended warranty or automobile service contract canceled and recover the unused portion of the cost. Put your cancellation request in writing and include the loan number and the date purchased. If there is nothing to the contrary in your warranty agreement, it can be canceled. Ask for a refund of the unused portion of the insurance or to have one or more payments knocked off the end of your loan.

A new gimmick in the lucrative extended warranty business is to put in the contract that the warranty is not cancelable, which you could probably have declared invalid by small claims court. Most extended warranties are cancelable because banks and finance companies will not finance extended warranties that are not. Financing institutions require the dealer to reimburse them for any warranties that are canceled. A few of the new extended warranty contracts, however, like other forms of insurance, have a high cancellation penalty, which simply allows the dealer to keep the unused portion of your extended warranty money even if you cancel.

Some dealers underwrite or cover the cost of repairs covered by warranties themselves. Other dealers buy an inexpensive repair policy from an insurance company and pocket the difference between what they collect from you and what they actually pay the insurance company.

Read your contract and act now. There is no question that after the manufacturer's warranty runs out you will have occasional repairs, some minor, some major, but overall your total cost of repairs will equal only 15 to 20 percent of what you would spend on extended warranties and service contracts during your lifetime.

DEFENSE #57

Never buy credit life and credit disability insurance when getting a loan.

Wherever and whenever you borrow money, the loan officer or financial institution will attempt to attach credit life and credit disability to your loan. All loans are targets for this overpriced insurance, including auto loans, boat loans, personal loans and business loans.

Credit life insurance pays off the balance of your loan should you die. Credit disability makes your loan payments for you should you become disabled or unable to earn income. Both are usually included as a package and financed as part of your loan. What's wrong with the concept? Credit life and disability are overpriced by 800 percent! You will never get wealthy overpaying for anything by that much. Up to 60 percent of the premiums go as commission to the car dealer, bank, credit union or other lender. Only a few states have enacted laws limiting this abusive practice, and even in those cases the commission is up to 30 percent.

Lenders are always very aggressive in pushing credit life and disability, and finance managers usually receive big bonuses or commissions if you are coerced into buying the insurance. They will use scare tactics, mild threats or even gloss over any verbal discussion and simply include the insurance in the payments, waiting to see if you catch it. Most buyers don't even understand what hit them. Many lenders will even indicate that if you don't take the credit life/disability you won't get the loan. In truth, it is against federal law for anyone to require that you take credit life or credit disability unless the cost is included in the finance charges and interest rates, which in many states would violate usury laws.

Credit life insurance is actually a form of decreasing term insurance, meaning that the insurance pays off only the balance of your loan even if you are down to your last one or two payments. If you finance $18,000 for the cost of an automobile and were to die the first month, the insurance would pay off the full $18,000. However, at the end of the term of the loan, often 48 to 60 months later, the amount paid off would be as little as one month's payment: $400.

Credit life actually protects the financial institution and not your heirs. Your heirs get nothing from the policy; it only guarantees that the financial institution will collect its money if something happens to you. The cost of the credit life and disability itself can equal as much as four or five of your car payments. If something were to happen to you, remember, the bank or financial institution does not call the balance of the loan due or repossess your automobile. The payments are simply due as usual. If the insured were to become disabled or die, it is likely that a second family car would be sold anyway and the loan paid off. The credit life and disability premiums would then amount to a monumental waste of money. The chances of dying or becoming permanently disabled are so small during any three- to five-year loan period that hundreds of millions of dollars each year are earned by financial institutions solely because of ignorance and fears of the borrowers.

Here is a typical example of the cost of credit life and disability straight from a bank loan officer. The amount of the loan is $12,000 at 13 percent. The monthly payment if the credit life and disability insurance is declined is $321.94. If the insurance is accepted, the payment becomes $353.76 per month, an increase of $31.82 or a total cost of $1,527.36 for the 48 months of the loan. Credit life and disability insurance is usually financed into the loan, meaning you end up paying compounded interest on insurance you never needed in the first place. These two insurance gimmicks, with interest, can add as much as 10 percent to the cost of anything you purchase and finance.

Most disabilities last for 30 days or less, and as you might suspect, credit disability insurance doesn't cover the first 30 days. Often because of the proof required and the insurance company's reluctance to pay claims, it's 60 to 90 days after a disability before you can get your first payment. During that time you are still required to keep your payments up to date. By the time you collect, if you ever do, you are back to work and the problem is solved by your paycheck, not credit life disability insurance. If you have disability coverage at work or on your own, your income is protected anyway.

If you feel strongly about having your loans paid off if something should happen to you, don't buy credit life and disability insurance. Substitute inexpensive level term insurance for expensive credit life insurance, and your premiums will drop more than 90 percent, saving you hundreds of dollars a year for the rest of your life. Total up the loans you would like paid off, add the total to your level term policy (see Chapter 6, Create a Maximum-Protection, Low-Cost Insurance Plan), and add to clause to your will requiring the executor of your will to pay off the car or other loans.

Money to make loan payments should you become disabled can be generated from a spouse's income, from an income disability policy or from your investment plan. The truth is your chances of becoming so disabled as to collect on credit disability insurance or any disability policy are so small compared with the cost that disability insurance is not a good value.

ATTACK #58

Remove all credit life and credit disability insurance from your existing loans.

If you already have credit life and disability insurance on your loans, can you get it removed? Of course you can, and save hundreds of dollars a year in the process. If you don't remember whether you took the credit life and disability insurance the last time you obtained a car or other loan, guess what, you've got it. Get out all your loan papers and find the credit life insurance clause and premiums. Go back to the financial institution or car dealer that made you the loan, walk in head held high and say something like, "Chuck Givens told me to get this trash off my loan. Would you take care of it for me, please?"

After the initial shock, minor resistance and two or three excuses, you will get the job done. If you paid for credit life in cash in advance, you will get a refund for the unused portion of the insurance. If, on the other hand, you financed the credit life into your payments, as most borrowers do, the lender will usually knock payments off the end of your loan. Either is acceptable.

A member of my organization walked up to me in Orlando and told me the story of how this strategy had helped her save big dollars. "My husband and I moved to Orlando six months ago," she said, "and when we got a car loan the bank told us we had to get the credit life and disability since we had been in the area for such a short time. We paid $1,300 in cash for the insurance. When we realized it was a mistake, we took your strategies and statements back to the bank, but the loan clerk kept telling me I had to keep the credit life, that is, until I explained it the way you explained it. The loan clerk excused himself and went to a bank officer and both came back all flustered and apologetic. Before I had left the bank, they had written me a cashier's check for the full $1,300. I never felt so smart and in control of the situation," she said, smiling.

ATTACK #59

Replace expensive mortgage life insurance with inexpensive term insurance.

Another gimmick in the lucrative insurance business is mortgage life insurance. The sales pitch is logical. If you die, wouldn't you like your home mortgage paid off so the payments wouldn't be a burden to your family? Of course you would, but mortgage life insurance is certainly not your best alternative. Mortgage life is nothing more than a decreasing term insurance policy where the beneficiary is your mortgage company and not your heirs. As you get older the amount of insurance, which is equal to the balance of your home mortgage, is decreasing as your mortgage balance decreases, but your premiums remain the same.

The concept of mortgage life insurance is certainly sound. The problem is the cost. If you buy mortgage life insurance from your mortgage company, the premiums are overpriced by 200 to 400 percent. The money that can be thrown away on mortgage life insurance far exceeds even what you can lose on credit life and disability on your other loans.

The premiums on mortgage life insurance are usually based on your age or your and your spouse's ages at the time you buy the insurance. In one policy we examined, at age 54, $100,000 of mortgage life insurance cost over $1,200 per year, or about $100 a month. For the same premium, the same homeowner could buy $500,000 of term insurance or, conversely, spend 70 percent less for $100,000 of level term insurance.

If you want your home mortgage paid off if something were to happen to you, your strategy is to add the amount of your mortgage payoff to an inexpensive term policy. For instance, $100,000 of term insurance at age 54 with a rate guaranteed for five years would be a little over $250 a year, saving about $1,000 per year for exactly the same amount of insurance. Over the next 10 years, using term insurance instead of mortgage life insurance, you would save $10,000, money that can be applied to living. As the insured gets older and the premiums per $1,000 of term insurance increase, the amount of insurance necessary to pay off the home will decrease, since the mortgage balance is decreasing, allowing the homeowner to decrease the amount of term insurance necessary to pay off the mortgage. The premiums per year, therefore, will remain about the same, particularly if this strategy is coupled with a 15-year mortgage or the extra mortgage principal payments strategies (see Chapter 15), which pay off your home mortgage at a far faster rate. In addition, mortgage life insurance proceeds go directly to the mortgage company, so mortgage life protects the mortgage company far more than it does the insured. The proceeds of your term policy either go to your heirs or can be directed to the payoff of your mortgage, as you choose.

Let's go over, step by step, a mortgage life insurance application so you can see what transpires. Opposite, you will see an exact reprint of an application for mortgage life insurance offered through a Florida mortgage company.

When you first apply for the mortgage, either the mortgage salesperson or closing attorney hits you with a sales pitch about protecting your wonderful new purchase, your home. Of course, the mortgage company and often the closing agent are receiving huge commissions or kickbacks from the insurance company. That's why the insurance is so overpriced. Notice on the application that the beneficiary is already typed in, and it is the mortgage company, not your heirs.

The mortgage company buys the insurance from the insurance company at one price and then sells it to you at a much higher price. If you didn't buy mortgage life when you got your loan, the mortgage company will attempt to sell it to you later. The mortgage company computer goes through all of its mortgage

FRONT OF APPLICATION FOR MORTGAGE LIFE INSURANCE

MORTGAGE DECREASING TERM LIFE INSURANCE

CALL TOLL FREE • 1-800-438-1058 (NC ONLY 1-800-438-1057)

MONTHLY COST OF INSURANCE . . . . YOUR PREMIUM WILL NOT CHANGE BECAUSE YOU GROW OLDER

AGE	18-34	35-39	40-44	45-49	50-54	55-59	60-64	65-69
INDIVIDUAL	$27.44	$33.32	$49.00	$80.36	$113.68	$152.88	$264.60	$386.12
JOINT	$44.10	$52.92	$78.40	$128.38	$182.28	$245.00	$423.36	$617.40

JOINT RATES ARE BASED ON AGE OF OLDER INSURED

NAME AND ADDRESS

************* 5-DIGIT 32779
CHARLES GIVENS
Longwood, Fl 32779

BENEFICIARY
MORTGAGE SERVICES
RELATIONSHIP

APPLICANT	DATE OF BIRTH	STATE OF BIRTH	SEX	HEIGHT	WEIGHT
			☐M ☐F	FT. IN.	LBS.
HOME PHONE NUMBER	WORK PHONE NUMBER	OCCUPATION			
( )	( )				

JOINT APPLICANT	DATE OF BIRTH	STATE OF BIRTH	SEX	HEIGHT	WEIGHT
			☐M ☐F	FT. IN.	LBS.
HOME PHONE NUMBER	WORK PHONE NUMBER	OCCUPATION			
( )	( )				

IF ANY ANSWER IS YES, INDICATE PERSON TREATED, DATES, NAMES AND ADDRESSES OF DOCTOR(S) BELOW.	APPLICANT	JOINT APPLICANT
	YES NO	YES NO
1. During the last (5) years have you been hospitalized or have you consulted a physician for any reason? (INCLUDE PHYSICAL EXAMINATION)	☐ ☐	☐ ☐
2. Have you ever been treated for or been advised that you had		
A. Cancer, diabetes; high blood pressure; nervous disorder; tumor; ulcer; or disorder of the blood, heart, intestines, kidneys, liver, lungs, lymph nodes or stomach? (CIRCLE APPLICABLE ONE)	☐ ☐	☐ ☐
B. Acquired Immune Deficiency Syndrome (AIDS), or test results indicating exposure to the AIDS virus?	☐ ☐	☐ ☐

These answers are complete and true to the best of my knowledge and belief. I agree that the answers will form a part of the certificate, if issued. I agree that the insurance will not be in force until this application has been approved by the Company, the certificate issued, the first premium payment made prior to any change in my health and the loan proceeds paid. To determine my insurability, or for claims purposes, I authorize any medical practitioner or institution, insurance company, the Medical Information Bureau or other organization, institution or person that has any records or knowledge of me or my physocal or mental health, including alcohol or drug abuse, to give to Insurance Corporation or its reinsurers any such information. A photocopy of this authorization will be as valid as the original. I have read this authorization and the enclosed notices. I understand that I may request and receive copies. The authorization is valid for 30 months from the date the application is signed. ☐ I (we) elect to be interviewed if an investigative consumer report is prepared in connection with this application.

APPLICANT'S SIGNATURE	DATE	JOINT APPLICANT'S SIGNATURE	DATE

TO BE COMPLETED BY INSTITUTION

NAME OF INSTITUTION	CITY	STATE	ACCT #	ID NO.
MTG. SERVICES	ORLANDO, FL		04-683	

LOAN NUMBER	LOAN BALANCE	INITIAL PREMIUM	INITIAL AMOUNT OF INSURANCE	TERM OF INSURANCE	LOAN CLOSING DATE
0000001749176711			$96,000	YRS	

loans to find those who did not take mortgage life insurance when they first borrowed the money and then, on a periodic basis, sometimes monthly, sends out a computer-printed application. Look at the application for mortgage life insurance. Near the bottom, notice that the computer has printed in the loan number and the initial amount of insurance, which is the current balance of the mortgage, and the balance of the loan in years. This application is one I personally received for one of my rental properties. The mortgage company's computer obviously did not figure out that I didn't live in the home, but that's no problem, since the company would just love to write mortgage life policies on all rental properties as well. Profits are the same, whether the insurance is sold to homeowners or landlords.

You are told in the advertising that a physical is not required, but looking in the middle of the application on page 161, you will see three questions about your physical condition: "During the last five (5) years have you been hospitalized . . . ?" "Have you ever been treated for or been advised that you had: cancer; diabetes; high blood pressure; nervous disorder; tumor; ulcer;" etc.? "Acquired Immune Deficiency Syndrome (AIDS), or test results indicating exposure to AIDS?" If you or your spouse check "yes" to any one of these questions, you can be assured that you will be required to take a physical. If your answers are not truthful, the insurance company may not have to pay any claim. Notice how question one is phrased. "During the last five (5) years, have you consulted a physician for any reason? (INCLUDE PHYSICAL EXAMINATION)." Few people could check "no" to that question.

On the back of the application, the insurance company puts you on notice that it will do a lot of checking on you. The clauses from the back of the application are shown on page 163. Here are the important statements: "We may request that an investigative consumer report be prepared." In the MIB disclosure notice, the company is telling you that even for life insurance to pay off your mortgage, it is going to check your records at the Medical Information Bureau. For an explanation of the Medical Information Bureau, see the life insurance chapter (Chapter 6). If you check "no" to all of the boxes relating to medical questions, the insurance company still checks the Medical Information Bureau's computer, assuming that you're probably lying. The insurance company's goal, of course, is not to pay claims, but to write insurance only on those who statistically have less chance of collecting.

Back of Application for Mortgage Life Insurance

NOTICE OF INSURANCE INFORMATION PRACTICES

To issue an insurance policy or certificate, we need to obtain information about you. Some of that information will come from you. Some will come from other sources. We may request that an investigative consumer report be prepared. You may be interviewed in connection with that report. The information collected by us may be disclosed to third parties as allowed by law without your specific authorization.

You have a right of access and correction with respect to the information collected. This right does not apply to information which relates to a claim or civil or criminal proceeding.

If you wish to have a more detailed description of our information practices, please contact your agent.

MIB DISCLOSURE NOTICE

Information you provide will be treated as confidential, except that Life Insurance Corporation or its reinsurers may make a brief report thereon to the Medical Information Bureau, a nonprofit membership organization of life insurance companies that operates an information exchange on behalf of its members. Upon request by another member insurance company to which you have applied for life or health insurance coverage or to which a claim is submitted, the MIB will supply such company with the information it may have in its files.

Upon receipt of a request from you, the Bureau will arrange disclosure of any information it may have in your file. (Medical information will be disclosed only to your attending physician.) If you question the accuracy of information in the Bureau's file, you may contact the Bureau and seek a correction in accordance with the procedures set forth in the Federal Fair Credit Reporting Act. The address of the Bureau's information office is Post Office Box 105, Essex Station, Boston, Massachusetts 02112, telephone number (617) 426-3660.

Life Insurance Corporation or its reinsurers may also release information in its files to other life insurance companies to whom you may apply for life or health insurance, or to whom a claim for benefits may be submitted.

Now let's look at the incredibly high cost of mortgage life insurance. To appreciate just how high it is, you must remember that mortgage life is a decreasing term life policy. The premiums remain the same each year but the amount of insurance decreases. If the initial amount of the mortgage to be insured was $98,000, with a 30-year mortgage term, after 29 years and with only one year to go, the mortgage balance would be only about $5,000. The homeowner would have paid over $25,000 in premiums to the mortgage company but the company, if the insured homeowner died, would pay off only the $5,000 mortgage balance. The insurance company advertises, "Your premium will not change as you grow older." Your premium doesn't need to increase, because your insurance coverage decreases over time, reducing the insurance company's risk. During the last 10 years of the 30-year mortgage, the amount of insurance coverage drops five times as fast as it did in the early years. Look at the graph on the following page, How Mortgage Life Insurance Coverage Decreases as Your Mortgage Balance Decreases, and you will see how the insurance coverage on a mortgage life policy drops as your principal balance drops. As the coverage drops, the cost per $1,000 of insurance increases. But you still make the same yearly premium payment no matter how small your life insurance coverage becomes.

Unlike most insurance policies, mortgage life insurance premiums are quoted on a monthly basis, and the premium amount is added to your monthly mortgage payments, disguising the truly astronomical yearly cost of the insurance.

Why would anyone continue paying the same premiums when the mortgage principal becomes dramatically smaller? Most Americans make financial decisions out of habit instead of with knowledge and good sense. The mortgage company knows that once a policyholder becomes accustomed to making a payment with the life insurance premium included, it is likely the payments will continue to be made until the mortgage is completely paid.

As an example, look up an individual in the table on page 166, taken from the policy application mentioned before, who is 45 to 49 years old. The monthly premium of $80 would continue for 30 years, for a total of $960 per year for life insurance coverage that decreases every year. The total amount paid during the 30 years is $28,800, almost 30 percent of the original mortgage amount!

This graph shows how the mortgage balance and, hence, the amount of mortgage life insurance coverage drops over the 30-year term of a $98,000 mortgage. Since the mortgage life insurance insures only the mortgage balance, both drop at the same rate.

How Mortgage Life Insurance Coverage Decreases as Your Mortgage Balance Decreases

Initial Mortgage Amount and Life Insurance Coverage: $98,000
Mortgage Term: 30 years
Interest Rate: 11%

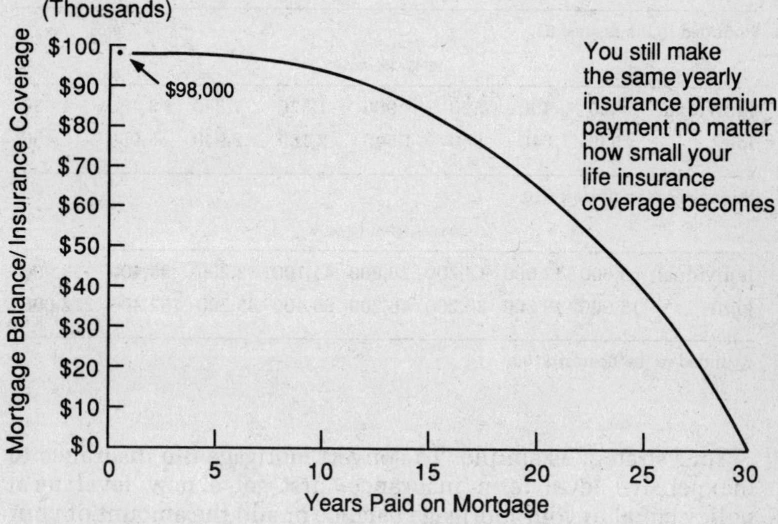

Now look at the table on page 167, Comparing the Cost of 10-Year Level Term and Mortgage Life Insurance. If you use a 10-year level term to insure the $98,000 mortgage balance, the total premium for the same amount of insurance will be only $13,744. In this example, the insured would save $15,000 just by using level term instead of mortgage insurance.

The younger you are when you buy either mortgage life insurance or 10-year term, the less the total premiums you will pay before your mortgage is paid off. If the home buyer was only 35 years old when the insurance was purchased, the total premiums for 30 years of mortgage insurance would be $12,000, but level term insurance premiums for the same period would be correspondingly less.

TOTAL MORTGAGE LIFE PREMIUMS FOR ONE YEAR AND THIRTY YEARS

Mortgage Amount = $98,000

MONTHLY PREMIUM AS SHOWN IN THE POLICY								
Age	18–34	35–39	40–44	45–49	50–54	55–59	60–64	65–69
Individual	27	33	49	80	114	153	265	386
Joint	44	53	78	128	182	245	423	617

Rounded to the nearest $1.

YEARLY PREMIUMS								
Individual	320	400	590	960	1,370	1,840	3,180	4,630
Joint	530	640	940	1,540	2,180	2,940	5,080	7,400

Rounded to the nearest $10.

30-YEAR TOTAL PREMIUM								
Individual	9,600	12,000	17,700	28,800	41,100	52,200	95,400	138,900
Joint	15,900	19,200	28,200	46,200	65,400	88,200	152,400	222,000

Rounded to the nearest $100.

Your strategy is simple. To convert mortgage life insurance to inexpensive level term insurance, first get a new level term policy equal to your mortgage balance or add the amount of your mortgage to your existing term policy. You can get the best rates on term insurance by calling The Insurance ClearingHouse at 1-800-522-2827. When a new term insurance policy is in effect, then cancel your mortgage life insurance policy. You will have better insurance coverage, and your monthly mortgage payments will drop dramatically.

COMPARING THE COST OF 10-YEAR LEVEL TERM AND MORTGAGE LIFE INSURANCE

Beginning Age 45 Male Nonsmoker[1]

Original Mortgage Amount = $98,000
Interest Rate = 11 percent
Term = 30 years

			10-Year Level Term Insurance		*Mortgage Life Insurance*	
AGE OF INSURED	BALANCE OF MORTGAGE TERM, YEARS	MORTGAGE/ DECREASING INSURANCE AMOUNT	1-YEAR PREMIUM	10-YEAR TOTAL PREMIUM	1-YEAR PREMIUM	10-YEAR TOTAL PREMIUM
45	30	$98,000	$265	$ 2,650	$960	$ 9,600
55	20	$88,000	$471	$ 4,710	$960	$ 9,600
65	10	$59,000	$794	$ 6,384	$960	$ 9,600
75	0	0				
30-Year Total				$13,744		$28,800

[1] Rates for female nonsmokers are about 20 percent less.

DEFENSE #60

Use the income from invested life insurance proceeds to make mortgage payments.

If you add the amount of your mortgage principal to your term insurance policy, you could have your mortgage paid off at once from the policy proceeds if something happened to you. But a better strategy is to have the life insurance proceeds invested in a stock or bond mutual fund and use the 12 to 15 percent growth and earnings from the fund to make the home mortgage payments for your heirs. The entire process can be set up through your will.

Not only would the mortgage principal and interest be covered by a 12 percent mutual fund return but when the mortgage is paid off, the entire amount invested will still be in the mutual fund. For example, if the insurance amount designated to pay off the mortgage was $100,000, a 12 percent return in a mutual fund would provide $1,000 per month income indefinitely to apply to mortgage payments. The $100,000 would still be intact after the mortgage was paid off.

ATTACK #61

Cancel Chargegard insurance on your credit cards.

The latest wrinkle in the continuing insurance marketing saga is the inclusion of credit life and disability insurance on MasterCard and Visa cards and other revolving credit accounts. Usually called Chargegard, the concept is always the same: your balance will be paid or your payments will be made if something happens to you like death, physical disability or being fired from your job.

Chargegard Payment Assurance for Your Credit Card Account*

Unemployment and disability benefits will pay your Visa or MasterCard minimum monthly payment due if you're employed full-time in a nonseasonal occupation and you lose your job involuntarily, or if you're disabled because of an accident or illness and are unable to work. Benefits are paid retroactive to the first day of unemployment or disability, following a waiting period of 30 consecutive days. Benefits continue until you reach a maximum of $10,000, or you return to work. Retirement is not covered.

Life benefits will pay your outstanding balance up to $10,000 if you or your spouse (or other cosigner) die as a result of an illness or accident, or if you're dismembered in an accident. Suicide for the first from the effective date is the only exclusion.

The premium of $.66 per $100 of your average daily balance will be charged to your credit card account. You may enroll for this coverage through age 70. This is a brief description only. The certificate(s) you will receive when you purchase coverage will contain full details.

________ YES. Please protect my account with Chargegard. I understand it is not required to obtain credit and will not be provided unless I sign and agree to pay the additional costs disclosed.

*Example given is for Florida residents. Others may vary.

A good idea, you think? Let's read the small print. Here is an example of the Chargegard portion of a credit card application. Read the unemployment and disability benefits section.

Notice the ambiguous statement that says, "Benefits are paid retroactive to the first day of unemployment or disability, following a waiting period of 30 consecutive days." What do you suppose that means? Does it mean the payments are made from the first day of unemployment or from the 31st day? It means from the 31st day. Moreover, the insurance does not pay off your entire balance when you become unemployed or disabled; only the minimum monthly payments are made. If your minimum monthly payment is $40 and you're off work 90 days, even with a balance of $3,000 the insurance would pay only $80. Since most disabilities do not last for more than 30 days, the insurance company seldom has to pay. The same holds true for periods of involuntary unemployment. No one is going to put off taking a job for 30 days just because he has Chargegard.

Half of the cardholders who buy this kind of insurance never go through the paperwork required to get the insurance company to make the payments; most don't even remember they have the insurance. The premium is automatically charged to your credit card account so that you never really miss the money and the premiums are outrageous! Notice that on the application shown, the cost is $.66 per one hundred dollars of average daily balance; that is $6.60 per thousand per month. If your credit card balance is $5,000, you're paying about $33 per month, or almost $400 per year, just for the insurance. That is the equivalent of an additional 8 percent interest rate! Your chances of collecting any real money on a policy of this type are unbelievably small, so the bank wins, the insurance company wins and you lose.

Check now to see if you have Chargegard on your MasterCard, Visa or other charge accounts. If so, send a letter similar to the one below to your credit card companies. Watch your bill for the next month to be sure that the charge has been removed.

> To the Accounting Department:
>
> Please cancel as of date of receipt any and all forms of credit life and disability insurance such as Chargegard that I may be carrying on my account and stop charging me the premium.
>
> Thank you.

DEFENSE #62

Don't buy life or medical insurance from slick television or direct-mail ads.

Direct-mail and TV celebrity ads have been incredibly effective at selling low-value, high-cost medical and life insurance through a combination of deception and fear. Sleazy is the nicest word you can apply to those marketing ploys that promise to:

- Insure the lives of those age 50 to 80
- Pay $50 a day, in addition to your hospitalization coverage
- Provide insurance against dreaded diseases like cancer
- Provide special coverage for select groups such as veterans

The premiums are at least 400 percent too high for the potential payoff, and the restrictions guarantee that few will ever collect. Most of the ads play on fears of old age and use deceptive mathematics to sell policies.

Even though policyholders lose, paid celebrities do not. If your movie career begins to fade, or if your passing arm won't deliver the ball, you can always get a job pitching life insurance on TV or through direct mail. The fees paid to the stars are staggering, but the benefits delivered by the insurance are minimal compared with the advertising claims.

The marketing costs of companies who pay stars for endorsements, buy expensive television time, and use direct mail with an average response of only 1 in 200 are so huge that 40 to 60 percent of every premium dollar paid by policyholders is used just to pay the marketing expenses. There is little money left for the insurance or to pay legitimate claims from policyholders. The insurance companies must, in order to make a profit (and they do make a profit), design policies that promise the moon and deliver green cheese.

The Veterans-Only Plan

One such insurance plan is targeted only to veterans of the armed services as if they had been singled out for their contribution to America. Roger Staubach, the great Dallas Cowboys quarterback, and Glenn Ford, the actor, have carried on this supersuccessful television campaign for years.

The ads imply that if you are a veteran or the widow of a veteran you are entitled to special life insurance policies not available to nonveterans. The ads imply that the policies are:

- guaranteed coverage
- easy to get
- part of an entitlement, implying that an act of Congress created the program
- low cost

In truth, the offer does not guarantee coverage to all veterans but only to those who pass a health questionnaire. On a cost-per-$1,000-of-insurance basis, the policies are incredibly expensive and the insurance company has absolutely nothing to do with the government.

The 50-to-80 Folly

Another group specifically targeted for high impact television advertising are those age 50 to 80. As people get older, there is a false belief that life insurance becomes harder to get, since the big life insurance companies don't seem to market to older Americans. Along comes a TV campaign that promises easy, no-hassle approval, no physical, no health questionnaire and sometimes even "approval guaranteed." Then comes the clincher: the rates appear to be unbelievably low, and the policy cannot be canceled by the company except for nonpayment of premiums. Thousands run to the phone to dial the toll-free number for the bargain of the century.

But is this life insurance and its cost really what it appears to be? Not on your life! The price for the insurance is quoted in units, says the unreadable small print that flickers momentarily on the bottom of the TV screen. The death benefit on one unit of insurance decreases over time on most of these policies, but the price shown is the fixed-price premium per month. Even though the premium is, let's say, $7 per month per unit, the real, totally hidden insurance cost depends on the amount of insurance. If the insured takes five units, the cost is $35 per month, $420 per year, but the amount of life insurance is as little as $500 to $5,000. Let's examine how. The policy states:

"Limited benefits the first two years"

In one $10,000 policy I examined, the death benefit for a 50-year-old man for the first year was only $100 per every $1,000 unit of insurance. At $7 per unit per month, his cost for 10 units was $840 the first year for $1,000 worth of insurance, making this type of life insurance the most expensive in history. Imagine paying $840 to get $1,000 of life insurance for one year! The second year, the death benefit went up to $250 per unit, making his cost $336 per $1,000 of insurance. No way that an insurance company can lose with rates like that! Beginning the third year, the amount of insurance went up to $1,500 but the $840 per year premium remained fixed, so the cost of $1,000 worth of insurance became $56. Better deal the third year? Sure. Rip-off? Absolutely! A man 50 years old can buy $100,000 of term life insurance for as little as $160 the first year through The Insurance ClearingHouse. The cost per thousand is $1.60, not $56.

Here is a word-for-word description of the benefit limitation from the literature of Colonial Penn, one of the biggest direct-response marketers.

"If you are under age 65 your beneficiary will receive 15% of your certificate's face amount the first year, 30% for death from natural causes the second year."

How can they collect two full years of premiums from hundreds of thousands who certainly can't be that stupid? They tell you it's for the policyholder's benefit. Here's the pitch:

"By now you're probably thinking this all sounds too good to be true . . . and you're probably asking yourself . . . How can we afford to make such a guarantee?"

You are darn right they can afford it. And make a lot of money by convincing you that collecting money from you with practically nothing in return is in your best interest. By the end of the third year you have paid three years' premiums for what amounts to full coverage for only one year.

Colonial Penn's policy was called Modified Benefit Group Whole Life. Maybe it should have been called Nullified Benefit Whole Life! But why pick on that company when there were a dozen others, like National Home Life, getting away with the same thing. Another similar policy was issued by Goudchaux Maison Blanche Life for those ages 45–80. The coverage stated in the policy, called the "protected amount" for marketing effect, ranged from about $1,000 to $6,000 depending on your age and when you buy the policy. But when you read the policy closely you discovered:

"In the first year you are insured in the amount of $200, in the second year a minimum of one-third of the full protected

amount and in the third year a minimum of two-thirds the protected amount. After three years you have 100% protection."

Terrific. So why were you paying 100 percent premiums all three years? The company even had the nerve to call this rip-off Increasing Benefits for Nonaccidental Death.

Here are other sales pitches and what they really mean.

"You can apply only if you're ages 50–80."

This ploy is to make you feel special, as if these policies are designed for your benefit and conditions. The advertising makes it sound as if the insurance company is doing you a favor by offering you insurance you can't get anywhere else. What nonsense!

"You can apply without a medical exam."

The coverage is so small, under $10,000, that no medical exam could be afforded by the insurance company for the amount of premium you are paying. However, if you answer the company's medical questions with the wrong answers, you will either be denied or have to take an exam. Notice that the clause says, "You can apply without a medical exam"; you are not guaranteed you can get the policy without an exam.

"Your policy builds cash savings you can use or borrow."

This ploy is aimed at the masses who believe that cash value is something free. Nowhere in the literature do the cash value tables ever appear, since the most you can borrow after a few years would barely pay for lunch. At age 55, let's say you would pay premiums of $150 per year, which amounts to a total of $750 in five years or $1,500 in 10 years. Your cash value after five years is $200 and a whopping $600 after 10 years. All you had to do to build the cash value was to overpay your premiums by 1,000 percent with virtually no coverage the first two years.

"Your policy cannot be canceled except by you."

The insurance company *never* wants to cancel the policy. Remember the insured is overpaying premiums by 1,000 percent.

"Your monthly payments never change."

This ploy plays on the fears many senior Americans have about increasing insurance rates. In fact, these rates or payments don't have to increase because the insurance company will get its money back many times over from the excess premiums paid and the interest earned on policyholders' money. The fixed premiums are so artificially high, the insurance company cannot lose, but the policyholder paying these premiums can. And not many claims are ever paid because the cancellation rate after a few years is higher on these policies than on other, more legitimate life insurance plans.

The mail order/TV insurance business has become, for the insurance companies involved, a huge money machine. If you want to put your money in a machine, go to Las Vegas.

DEFENSE #63

Don't waste money on Medigap or any other insurance that covers only deductibles.

Medigap, or what could better be called "medicrap," insurance appears to be just the supplemental policy needed to pick up what federal Medicare coverage doesn't include. The television and direct-mail ads for Medigap also play on the fears of senior adults. These fears have even resulted in many retired individuals and couples buying not one but several different overpriced, unnecessary Medigap policies. One Florida woman bought 14 such policies in 5 years. And the people who sold her these policies collected commissions of up to 60 percent the first year and 15 percent thereafter.

The schemes now used to generate hot prospects for Medicare supplemental policies are becoming legendary in the insurance business and increasingly dangerous to the wallets of senior citizens. There are numerous companies not involved in insurance that specialize in generating leads which are sold to insurance companies and agents for as much as $20 each. Companies that market the insurance or generate leads use primarily direct-response mailings or compelling celebrity TV ads with an 800 number. Here are the marketing tricks used to generate responses without letting prospects know what they are actually responding to:

Misleading Company Names

Lead-generation companies choose names that are often meant to deceive you into believing that the mailing you receive is from a government or nonprofit agency looking out for your welfare—names like Senior Citizens Health Services, Retired Persons Information Center, or how about this one: Medicare Division, Information Distribution Office? In America you can name your company anything you choose, and these insurance-lead-generation companies certainly are creative.

Masquerading as an Information Service

Rather than promoting insurance, which would probably turn off prospects, this deceptive pitch of these lead-generation companies often talks about information you *must* have on Medicare, Social Security or retirement. It is usually worthless information most people already have. Here is an example: *"Send in the reply card today to receive information on how you can protect yourself against costly hospital, doctor and nursing expenses."* Nowhere does it say that the information will come in the form of a policy-toting insurance salesperson trained to mentally muscle his way into your living room. Once there, the salesperson's deceptive pitch is so slick that one of your potential answers seldom seems to be "no." Respond to an outfit called the National Federation of Retired Persons and you get reprints of government pamphlets, which can legally be reprinted by anyone. You get the junk mail, and a generation company gets your name and address and earns $20 by selling this "qualified" lead to an insurance company.

Fear

Half-truths or remote possibilities peppered with words meant to terrify have a tremendous impact on the number of leads that can be generated. Here are a few statements that would probably scare any financially ignorant senior citizen.

"Congress and the President have proposed new stopgaps in your Medicare coverage . . . previous information is invalid . . . respond now for important changes in your coverage."

In truth there are no adverse changes pending, although I suppose an offhand remark by a member of Congress could be construed as a proposal by the above definition.

"Because of new regulations, hospitals are transferring patients to low-cost nursing homes or extended-care facilities."

You certainly wouldn't want yourself, your spouse or a parent in a cheap, run-down, cockroach-infested, low-cost facility simply because you weren't smart enough to buy Medigap insurance. In reality, a Medicare supplement policy, because it costs so much but covers so little, has never made the difference in the type of facility a patient is in.

"The federal Medicare system pays only about 50 percent of your medical expenses, and your benefits are being significantly reduced."

Actually Medicare pays for 100 percent of the hospital bill except for the deductibles, plus doctor's fees whether you are in or out of the hospital. The only mathematical way Medicare would pay just half is if your total bill were so low that your deductible represented 50 percent of the total bill.

There are already both state and federal laws on the books that should have stopped this nonsense long ago, but they are not enforced. Laws in almost all states require the word "insurance" to appear next to the word "plan" in insurance advertisements, so that consumers know exactly what is being sold. The same advertising rules state that brochures, flyers and TV ads must be truthful and not misleading or create undue fear or anxiety. Florida, California, Wisconsin and Oregon have begun enforcing these rules. In Florida, for instance, an investigation and action by the state insurance commission caused great embarrassment to celebrities who have lent their names to the promoting of insurance, among them Betty White, Eddie Albert, Dick Van Dyke, Tennessee Ernie Ford and Ed McMahon.

The coverage you think you're getting is seldom what you may actually receive due to the subtle deceptive differences between the advertisement, the sales pitch and the policy itself. It's true there are deductibles in Medicare insurance—but not many. No insurance is free, and the deductibles help keep the cost down while insuring against the greater threat of a large financial disaster. Medigap insurance covers *only* the few Medicare deductibles at a cost that is overpriced by 1,000 percent. How else could these companies afford celebrity spokespersons and expensive direct-mail and television campaigns? But even then their policies have significant exclusions. One sales trick Medigap insurance companies use is to guarantee that the policy will be issued without a medical checkup to anyone who applies, but the policy itself excludes coverage for custodial care, alcohol and drug addictions and even mental disorders. Also, the policies often contain an additional *time* deductible. Coverage doesn't even begin until the eighth day of hospitalization.

Insurance underwriters have determined that the average hospital stay is seven days or less, which minimizes your chance of collecting. The advertising carefully conceals the fact that you are not covered for the amount of time most likely spent in the hospital, a maximum of seven days.

Your best weapon against all forms of gimmick insurance is knowledge. If you have such insurance, get rid of it. If you're told you can't live without it, now you know you can—and save a lot of money in the process.

CHAPTER 8

Save Big Money on Your Automobile Insurance

Automobile insurance is another of the most expensive parts of your financial plan. Yet if you drive you must buy it. It's the law. If you have been listening to your automobile insurance agent, I promise you you're paying double what you need to pay. Most families are paying between $600 and $3,000 per year to protect themselves against potential damage caused by or to themselves and the cars they drive. But automobile insurance, like all insurance, is often purchased out of fear instead of with good strategies. As a result, 98 percent of automobile insurance policies contain the wrong amounts of the wrong kinds of coverage.

A driver is involved in a car accident an average of once every 8 years. About half of those accidents involve personal injury or serious damage to the car. There is a 50 percent chance the accident could be your fault instead of the other driver's, and that means that you stand a 1 in 40 chance each year of being involved in a serious crash for which you are at fault. There is a 1 in 80 chance for anyone born today that a car wreck will be fatal. Sounds frightening until you learn that you have an 11 times greater chance of dying of cancer and 15 times greater chance of dying of heart disease.

Before discussing the insurance companies' responsibilities, let's talk about what *you* can do to assure your safety. Fatalities in your car are fairly easy to prevent. The secret is seat belts. According to Jack Gillis, considered one of the top automobile experts in the country, the force of impact on your body in an accident at just 10 mph is equivalent to the force of catching a 200-pound bag of cement dropped from a first-floor window. At 35 mph there is no possible way that the strength of your arms and legs can stop you from hitting the steering wheel, dashboard or windshield. That's what causes almost all serious injuries and fatalities. Seat belts keep you right where you should be, pinned against the seat. The chance of a fatality is 2,500 percent greater if you go through the windshield.

Therefore, the greatest insurance policy that you can ever give yourself, your family and other passengers is to insist that all seat belts are fastened before you move the car. The big mistake is getting lax about wearing seat belts, when driving around the neighborhood. In truth, three out of four accidents happen within 25 miles of home. The percentage of accidents that occur on city streets is much higher than on highways. Eighty percent of serious injuries and fatalities occur at speeds under 40 mph. It is incredibly difficult to hurt yourself badly if you have your seat belt on. Of course, you can't control the other driver. That's why it is even more important to buckle up.

I may sound like a crusader today, but until a few years ago I had tremendous resistance to wearing seat belts. I felt that it was an admission that I could be hurt in an automobile, and I just didn't want to believe it. Now I do. And I'll tell you why.

My son Chuck and I went to Skip Barber's professional driving school to learn to race open-wheel Formula Fords, and our instructor told us how much safer he felt driving over 100 mph on the racetrack, within two inches of another car's wheels, because of the seat belt, harness and the skill of the other drivers, than he felt driving down a public highway or city street. That thought made a lasting impression on me, and since then the seat belt of my personal car has always been buckled.

Chuck and I both ended up trying to mimic dummies in a crash test, which hammered home the point. While racing each other at the Indianapolis Speedway, Chuck attempted to get around me on a curve that was just too tight for the speeds we were going. His car lost traction and he slammed into a concrete wall. I caught it in my rearview mirror but couldn't see what happened until I got through the curves of the next lap. When I could see him again, there he was dusting himself off and walking away from what little was left of his car, all because of his seat belt. He had bounced off the wall at 90 miles per hour and it hardly knocked the breath out of him.

The same thing happened to me two months later. Early Friday morning, after giving a lecture in Miami the night before and with far too little sleep, I climbed into my race car at Sebring, Florida. My response time just wasn't what it needed to be. After an hour on the track, the car got away from me on a sharp S-turn, slammed into a curb, bounced into the air and the undercarriage was torn out in the process—all at a speed you would never come close to on a highway. When the dust finally settled, I reached down with my left hand, flipped the lever on my two-strap shoulder and lap belt and walked away without a scratch. The greatest damage, other than to the car, was to my pride.

Americans love to create controversy, even about things that should not be controversial. Arguing about the value of seat belts, which ensure the safety of you, your kids or other passengers in the car, is just nonsense. Maybe, like me, you are not fond of the federal government telling you what to do with your life and your automobile, but in the case of seat belts, that argument doesn't really matter.

ATTACK #64

Redesign your automobile insurance policy to cut your premiums by up to 50 percent.

To understand what your automobile insurance is costing you and how the insurance company or agent has padded your policy with unnecessary coverage, you must first become familiar with the Declarations page, which is usually the first page of the policy (see example on page 181). On the Declarations page you will find seven to twelve different coverages and endorsements for which you are charged individual premiums. If you pay your premiums every six months, as most drivers do, you are actually paying each year double the premiums shown. In truth, there are only two to four coverages that you actually need to adequately protect yourself. They are bodily injury liability, property damage liability and, if your car or truck is worth over $2,000, comprehensive and collision coverage.

Automobile Insurance

THE DECLARATIONS PAGE

Coverage is provided where a premium and a limit of liability are shown for the coverage.

COVERAGES	LIMIT OF LIABILITY		PREMIUM AUTO 1	PREMIUM AUTO 2	PREMIUM AUTO 3
A. Liability					
Bodily Injury	$ ____	Each Person			
	$ ____	Each Accident	$ ____	$ ____	$ ____
Property Damage	$ ____	Each Accident	$ ____	$ ____	$ ____
B. Medical Payments	$ ____	Each Person			
C. Uninsured Motorist	$ ____	Each Person			
	$ ____	Each Accident	$ ____	$ ____	$ ____
D. Damage to Your Auto	Actual Cash Value Minus				
1. Collision Loss	$ ____	Deductible	$ ____	$ ____	$ ____
2. Other Than Collision Loss	$ ____	Deductible	$ ____	$ ____	$ ____
E. Towing and Labor Costs	$ ____	Each Disabled	$ ____	$ ____	$ ____
F.			$ ____	$ ____	$ ____

Endorsements Made Part of This Policy at Time of Issue:

Endorsement Premium $ __________

	Total Premium Per Auto	$ ____	$ ____	$ ____
	Total Six-Month Premium	$ ____________		

Loss Payee
Name and
Address

Countersigned: By ______________________
Authorized Representative

In many states, however, lawmakers have jumped into the automobile insurance business. You may be required to take an additional coverage or two which are highly profitable to the insurance company simply because the insurance lobby in your state has done such a good job of misrepresenting the truth and contributing to the right political campaigns. These coverages can include personal injury protection (PIP), no-fault insurance and uninsured/underinsured motorist insurance. You will find the requirements for each state at the end of this chapter.

Once you have become familiar with your state requirements and know the coverages you already have, here are the steps to take to redesign your automobile policy:

1. Determine which coverages you actually need from the strategies that follow.
2. Determine the amount or limits of the necessary coverages you should carry. Some limits will be determined by your current financial situation.
3. Learn why each available coverage is or is not needed in your policy. Self-confidence comes from knowledge of how your policy works.
4. Contact your insurance agent to add, delete or change coverages and amounts.
5. Enjoy year after year the hundreds of dollars of savings you will automatically generate from the right amount of the right kind of automobile insurance.

In the process of redesigning your policy, we will also explore the misleading and false statements automobile insurance salespeople make when selling you a policy. First, let's look at the automobile insurance coverage and limits you do need; then we'll explore those you don't.

DEFENSE #65

Carry bodily injury liability insurance equal to two times your net worth or total equities.

Bodily injury liability insurance covers injury or death caused by you as a driver and resulting from an automobile accident to:

1. people in other cars,
2. pedestrians,

3. passengers in the car you are driving,
4. you and your family while driving someone else's car, including rental cars.

Your objective in choosing your bodily injury liability limits is to carry enough insurance to adequately protect your assets and net worth but not so much that you are throwing money away on unnecessary premiums. A good rule of thumb is to carry bodily injury liability insurance equal to twice the amount of your net worth. Net worth is the value of what you own minus what you owe. The more you have in home equity, retirement plans, investments and/or business net worth, the higher you will want your liability limits to be.

If you owe more than you own and most of what you do own has a lien or mortgage attached to it, you have negative net worth, and taking your state's minimum required bodily injury liability limits not only will be enough protection but will save you money to help get you out of the hole. (See Auto Insurance Requirements by State at the end of this chapter.)

I have seen policies for people with no net worth that contain bodily injury limits of $100,000/$300,000 and policies for people with a quarter million dollars of net worth that contain limits of only their state required minimum of $10,000/$20,000. Both approaches are dangerous to your wealth. Never let your insurance agent make this important decision for you.

There are normally two numbers separated by a slash (/) shown for bodily injury liability limits on the Declarations page of your policy. The first and smaller number is the maximum your insurance company will pay to any one person injured or killed in an accident that was determined to be your fault and the amount includes attorney's fees and cost of litigation. The second, larger number is the maximum your insurance company will pay per accident no matter how many people were involved. The maximum per accident is normally two to three times the maximum per person coverage.

Your policy limits, which are normally in the format "25,000/ 50,000," are sometimes abbreviated to "25/50." Both means $25,000 maximum bodily injury liability coverage per person per accident and $50,000 total liability coverage per accident.

Every state now requires that its resident drivers carry a minimum amount of bodily injury liability coverage determined by state legislators. The required limits range from a low of $10,000/$20,000, in states like Florida, Louisiana, New York and Oklahoma, to a high of $50,000/$100,000 in Alaska. For the minimum requirements in your state, check the Auto Insurance Requirements by State chart at the end of this chapter.

If you are involved in an accident that injured or killed someone else for which you are liable or at fault, here is how the settlement process works. No matter what your liability limits, your insurance company provides an attorney or claims adjuster to negotiate a settlement with the other party's attorney, who is provided by his or her insurance company. Most claims are settled out of court and within the policy limits of the party at fault. Any extra medical or other expenses are then paid by the injured party's insurance company up to his or her policy limits.

Only if it is discovered that you have net worth greatly exceeding your bodily injury liability coverage is there a good chance that the injured party's attorney would attempt to collect more from you personally. Otherwise, it would be a waste of time. Although there is no guarantee that, if a driver who caused an accident were grossly negligent or intoxicated, a court award might not be higher than any possible liability limit, the strategy above will adequately cover most circumstances.

Why do you need coverage equal to twice your net worth? Because attorney's fees in an extensive litigation can run 30 percent or more of the settlement amount. The attorneys have developed an incredible system in which they are going to get paid whether you win or lose.

Which of the two liability limit numbers do you use with the "twice your net worth formula"? The first, the insurance company's liability limit per person. Although you may be able to choose liability limits in any increments you wish, standard liability limits are:

$10,000/20,000	$100,000/200,000
$15,000/30,000	$100,000/300,000
$20,000/40,000	$250,000/500,000
$25,000/50,000	$500,000/1,000,000
$50,000/100,000	$1,000,000/2,000,000

Choose the limit for your policy nearest the one you need from those offered by your insurance company. The limits you need are the same for all the cars you own.

There are some instances in which net worth will not give a true picture of the liability limits you need. For example, you have significant equity in your home, business, investments or retirement plan but your overall net worth is low because of other heavy debt. In this case, substitute your *total* equities for net worth and carry liability coverage equal to two times your total equities.

DEFENSE #66

Carry property damage liability coverage equal to twice your net worth or total equities up to a maximum $50,000.

The second coverage on your policy is normally property damage liability. This insurance covers damage you could potentially do, not to other people, but to other people's property. Usually the damage done is to someone else's automobile, but property damage liability even covers damage to a noninvolved party's personal property, like rosebushes or mailboxes. Occasionally property damage liability is paid to repair or replace property owned by a city or utility, like street signs or telephone poles.

When redesigning your automobile policy, you will have to pick a single number limit or maximum amount for property damage coverage. This limit applies per accident and is the maximum amount the insurance company will pay out for the actual cost of property damage plus legal fees. The choices are normally $5,000, $10,000, $25,000, $50,000 or $100,000.

Every year automobiles become more and more expensive to buy and certainly more expensive to repair. There are now more automobiles costing $30,000 to $50,000 on the highway than ever before. For this reason, plus the fact that you could potentially do damage to more than one car in an accident, the minimum property damage liability coverage you should include on your policy is twice your net worth or total equities up to a maximum of $50,000. Equities, remember, are the sum total of your equities in property, investments, retirement plans and your business. If you have a net worth of about $25,000, carry $50,000 of property damage liability coverage but in no case do you need more than $50,000 or coverage to be adequately insured for 99 percent of all potential claims. Any additional insurance is a waste of premium dollars. On the other hand, if you are in that low or negative net worth category, the minimum required by your state will be your best value.

You need not feel morally obligated to carry higher limits of property damage liability. Should you do damage to someone else's car, if your insurance coverage does not pay the full amount, the other driver's collision insurance coverage makes up the difference. The full amount of liability you would have for damage to someone else's car is limited to the cost of repair or replacement and is much easier to estimate and agree on than bodily injury damages.

Remember, the insurance company claims department's job is to pay out the least amount of money possible and not to make certain that you are protected financially. Any limits in your automobile insurance policy will be strictly adhered to by the insurance company, regardless of whether you consider them fair or not.

Occasionally you will find all liability limits on a policy written as a group such as 25/50/10. The first two numbers are the bodily injury liability limits, in this case $25,000 per person and $50,000 per accident, and the third number is the property damage liability limit, $10,000 per accident.

DEFENSE #67

Cover $1 million of personal liability with an inexpensive umbrella liability policy.

One of the best and least expensive types of personal liability coverage is an umbrella liability policy. Umbrella liability coverage applies to bodily injury claims and legal costs resulting from any type of accident for which you are deemed to be personally liable. Unfortunately, umbrella liability coverage does not cover claims arising from your business or profession. Whereas your automobile liability coverage applies only to automobile accidents and your homeowner's liability coverage applies primarily to liability arising from damages at or around your home, umbrella liability insurance covers all personal liability. Umbrella coverage is powerful, inexpensive and, if you have over $50,000 of net worth, a must for your insurance plan.

Umbrella liability is usually sold as an individual policy, an endorsement or rider to your automobile or homeowner's policy. To qualify for the coverage, you normally must have both policies with the same company and take minimum liability limits on both your automobile and homeowner's policies of about

$100,000/$300,000. The umbrella liability policy then covers you for up to $1 million per accident. As insurance goes, umbrella liability coverage is extremely cheap, and the average cost, depending on where you live, is generally between $125 to $200 per year. If you have net worth or equities of $50,000 or less, umbrella liability is not necessary, but if you do have significant net worth, umbrella liability coverage will give you maximum protection and peace of mind.

Almost all companies offer the umbrella liability supplement, but if yours doesn't offer the coverage, or requires that your basic limits be higher than those you have determined as necessary, or you get any hassle from the agent, change companies.

ATTACK #68

To cut premiums dramatically, become self-insured for the first $500 to $1,000 of damage to your car.

Coverage for damage to your automobile is always divided into two parts: "collision," which covers damages to your car done while colliding with another vehicle or object, and "comprehensive," which covers loss or damage not done by collision, such as theft, fire or vandalism. By dividing possible damage to your automobile into two parts, the insurance company has found a slick way to charge you two premiums.

There are two deductibles that you choose for your policy: one for collision and one for comprehensive coverage. To save money on premiums, your basic strategy for "comprehensive" and "collision" is to raise your deductible on both coverages to at least a $500 minimum. There are two reasons.

First, never file an insurance claim for under $500 even if you have the insurance. Your automobile insurance company never intends to lose, and if you file one or two small claims, it will either raise your rates or cancel your policy altogether. To pay even the smallest claim will cost your insurance company $500 to $700 in administrative, claims adjustment and processing expenses. To the insurance company, a small claim of a couple hundred dollars paid to you becomes a much bigger expense.

Second, the premiums you pay for low deductibles far outweigh the amount of damages you could ever collect. Over your lifetime, no matter how poor a driver you are, you will pay out many times in premiums for low deductibles what you could recover in claims. You always lose with deductibles of less than $500.

Raise your deductible from $100 to $500 and insurance premiums for comprehensive and collision insurance will drop about 40 percent. That means the first 40 percent of your collision and comprehensive premiums have been insuring only $400, the difference between a $100 and a $500 deductible. The other 60 percent of your premiums insures the total value of your car above the $500. What a difference in the cost of the insurance! If you are paying $200 a year for comprehensive and collision, you will save about $80 a year. If you are paying $600 a year on more than one car, your yearly premiums will drop about $240. The greater the number and value of cars that you own, the more you will save by raising your deductible. If you own a business that has company cars or trucks, you will find that you will save a huge chunk of the premiums by following this one simple strategy.

If your deductible is currently $100, by raising it to $1,000 you become self-insured for an additional $900, which will cut the cost of your comprehensive and collision premiums by as much as 60 percent. The better driver you are, the less you are already paying and the less you will save, but the savings will still amount to approximately 40 percent of what you are now paying. The worse you are as a driver or the more expensive your automobile, the more you are already paying for comprehensive and collision and the greater number of dollars you will save.

What are the real chances of having to pay a deductible yourself? According to the National Safety Council, one in eight people is involved in an accident every year which involves collision damage. You are responsible for the deductible only if the accident is your fault or if the insurance company is unable to collect from the other party. If and when your insurance company collects from the other party, which is usually 80 percent of the time, you are reimbursed for your deductible.

So, let's say that during your lifetime half the accidents in which you are involved are your fault. That would mean that there is only a 1 in 20 chance in any one year that you would be responsible for paying any deductible, or about once every 20 years. The premiums that you will pay over the 20 years to get the lower deductible will far outweigh the few hundred dollars that the insurance company might occasionally reimburse you.

A scare tactic used by automobile insurance salespeople is, "If you don't take a low deductible and we can't collect from the other driver's insurance company, you'll have to pay the deductible yourself." So what? That's an acceptable risk. What's not an acceptable risk is paying thousands of dollars extra during your lifetime for low deductibles that are not a good value.

If your car is financed, you may find a clause in your loan that requires you to carry no greater than a $250 or $500 deductible. Most people when getting an auto loan never notice the clause or understand its meaning. Since banks or loan companies are not paying your premiums, why shouldn't they ask for everything? Most banks or finance companies will allow you to raise your deductible to $500 even if your contract says differently, particularly if you indicate that financing your next car with them is dependent on their cooperation now.

From now on your strategy is to get the finance company to agree to a $500 or $1,000 deductible when you first apply for your auto loan. You will be surprised at how many of the terms of an auto loan are negotiable.

ATTACK #69

Drop your comprehensive and collision insurance when the value of your vehicle drops below $2,000.

Is collision and comprehensive insurance on an older, less valuable car a good value? Not when you do the arithmetic. The cost of repairing a five-year-old car is approximately the same as the cost of repairing the damage to a new car, even though the older car is worth only a fraction of the new one. The costs of a fender and a door, for instance, are the same whether they're put on a new or an old car. While your car is depreciating rapidly in value each year, your collision insurance premiums won't go down as much, but the amount you are likely to collect drops dramatically. Your insurance company, for instance, can choose not to repair your car and instead pay you only the book value. If your car is worth only $700, but the damages are $3,000, the company will write a check for only $700 *minus* your deductible, no matter how much you loved that old car.

The greatest risk the company insures under comprehensive

coverage is theft of your automobile. The less the value of your car as it depreciates, the less the insurance company is going to pay you if your car is stolen. However, thieves tend to steal only newer and not older cars. The jail sentence is exactly the same in either case, but the illegal profit potential is not.

Once your car is worth less than $2,000, the cost of your yearly comprehensive and collision premiums is so high that it is far better for you to risk the $2,000 loss than to pay the premiums. Remember that the insurance company is liable for only the value of your car. After filing a claim, you would end up with practically nothing, so why pay the premiums?

DEFENSE #70

Take the minimum required PIP or no-fault coverage and ask for a deductible.

One of the most expensive parts of an automobile insurance claim has always been determining who was at fault for the accident. If there is a question, the attorneys' fees and court time become astronomical. The attorneys, of course, end up with a good portion of the money from any settlement. Many states, therefore, decided to adopt no-fault insurance systems. The original concept was a good one. Each person's losses in an accident would be paid for by his or her own insurance company no matter who was responsible for the accident and the expense of litigation would be unnecessary, significantly bringing down the high cost of automobile insurance.

No-fault insurance was designed to cover:

- reimbursement for medical expenses,
- reimbursement for lost income,
- compensation for death, permanent injury or disfigurement,
- reimbursement for property damage.

In most states no-fault has not worked for three reasons. First, by the time the state legislators finished messing around with the concept, final no-fault laws had little in common with the original purpose. Second, in several states the auto insurance rates have gone up dramatically despite the enactment of no-fault laws because of state lawmakers' refusal to restrict severely or eliminate lawsuits due to the lobbying influence of lawyers in those states. Ask the automobile-insurance-poor people of

New Jersey who were supposed to be helped by no-fault laws. Third, insurance companies have used no-fault laws to minimize payment for claims instead of to reduce premiums.

In many states, no-fault laws require the payment of an additional premium for coverage called personal injury protection (PIP). If the no-fault laws are supposed to bring down the high cost of insurance, why should you be required to pay an extra premium for PIP?

PIP is nothing more than duplicate insurance coverage for hospitalization, personal disability, workman's compensation, Social Security disability, life insurance and collision insurance coverage you already have or should have. In some states PIP is offered as an option and should be declined. If PIP insurance is required in your state, you have no choice but to pay. You can tell from the list below whether or not your policy must contain personal injury protection to satisfy state requirements. Your strategy? Always take the minimum. Your insurance agent may have upped your PIP coverage to as much as $50,000.

There are 13 states and one territory in which personal injury protection (PIP) is required. The minimum coverage for the states that require it is shown below, but in some states you can cut premiums by asking for a little-known deductible also shown in the chart.

STATE PIP INFORMATION

Revised June 1, 1994

STATE	PIP MINIMUM	POSSIBLE DEDUCTIBLE
Colorado	$50,000	yes
Delaware	$15,000 (1 person)	$0
Florida	$10,000	yes
Hawaii	$20,000 (1 person)	$0
Kansas	$4,500	$0
Massachusetts	$8,000	$100 to $8,000
Michigan	lifetime medical unlimited	$300
Minnesota	$40,000	$300
New Jersey	$15,000 (1 person)	$250
New York	$30,000	$0
North Dakota	$30,000	$0
Oregon	$10,000	$0
Puerto Rico	unlimited medical for up to 2 years	$0
Utah	$10,000	$500

ATTACK #71

Consider dropping the uninsured/underinsured motorist coverage, if not required by your state, after you have otherwise provided for disability insurance.

Once you have determined the insurance you do need, the next step is to consider the insurance coverages you don't need. The first of these is so-called uninsured or underinsured motorist coverage, another gimmick that makes auto insurance companies rich. The premiums can increase the cost of your automobile insurance several hundred dollars per year.

Most people falsely believe that the main purpose of uninsured/underinsured motorist coverage is to fix your car if it is hit and damaged by someone without insurance. Not so. Damages to your car are already covered by the collision premiums you are paying no matter who caused the damage. That, however, has not stopped the insurance companies in several states from tacking on an additional premium for collision damage under the uninsured motorist coverage. Several states even require that you carry the coverage (see list at the end of this chapter).

The real concept behind uninsured motorist coverage is that your automobile insurance company will pay you the amount that a court would have awarded to you if you were injured in an automobile accident caused by someone who should have had bodily injury liability insurance but didn't. Uninsured/underinsured motorist coverage applies only if the other driver is not insured or underinsured. Otherwise the driver's liability coverage pays the claim. Sounds like an important, necessary form of insurance, doesn't it, especially since up to 30 percent of the drivers in some states are driving without insurance? It is not, for two reasons. First, the insurance doesn't do what it is supposed to do, and second, it is just more duplicate coverage for which you are paying big additional premiums.

The uninsured motorist coverage applies not only to you but also to any liability you may have to passengers in your car if they were injured in an accident with an uninsured or underinsured motorist. To pay premiums for this protection is nonsense, since if the accident is someone else's fault, insured or not, you have no liability. In addition, your passengers are already covered under the liability section of your policy. Your policy states: "*We will pay damages for bodily injury for which you become legally responsible because of an auto accident.*"

Your policy also states: "*Any amount otherwise payable for damages under uninsured motorists shall be reduced by any sum paid under the liability coverage of this policy.*" That means that you are paying premiums for *both* liability and uninsured motorists but the insurance company has to pay only once.

Uninsured motorist coverage is also supposed to pay you for lost income resulting from disability caused by an accident plus reimbursement for the nebulous concept of "pain and suffering." If you are concerned about becoming disabled, your strategy is to buy or create a 24-hour-a-day disability policy that covers both illness and accident and not one that covers you only part time while driving a car. (See Chapter 10.) Most permanent disabilities do not arise from auto accidents and are already covered totally or in part by Social Security or worker's compensation insurance. In fact, the uninsured motorists section of your policy says: "*Uninsured motorists coverage shall be reduced by all sums paid or payable because of bodily injury under any worker's compensation, disability benefits law or any similar law.*"

Well, that leaves only "pain and suffering" on which you can possibly collect under this coverage. "Pain and suffering" is a concept under current law that, in my opinion, is responsible for the high cost of insurance caused by huge, unreasonable jury awards that make only attorneys rich through the court-ordered redistribution of wealth. Money pays medical bills and replaces lost income but is in no way a substitute for pain or suffering. The real pain and suffering is the lifelong financial burden imposed by this outdated concept through the ever increasing liability and uninsured motorists insurance premiums forced on millions of drivers. While it is true that some people collect on uninsured motorists coverage, the chances that you will be one of them versus the amount of premiums you will pay are, in my opinion, simply not worth the money.

UNNECESSARY AUTOMOBILE INSURANCE COVERAGES

There are lots of coverages on an auto policy for which you are paying duplicate premiums, for which you can be insured better by other full-time policies, or that you don't want at all. Here is a list.

COVERAGE	WHERE YOU'LL FIND IT IN YOUR AUTO POLICY	YOUR SUBSTITUTION
Funeral Expenses	No-fault, Uninsured Motorists	Term Life Insurance
Death and Dismemberment	Death and Dismemberment	Term Life Insurance and Health Insurance
Medical Expenses (you and your family)	Uninsured Motorists, No-fault, PIP	Health Insurance
Medical Payments (nonrelated passengers in your car)	Uninsured Motorists, PIP, Medical Payments	Your Liability Insurance, Passenger's Health Insurance
Lost Wages	Uninsured Motorists, No-fault, PIP	Disability Plan
Loss of Life	Uninsured Motorists	Life Insurance
Pain and Suffering	Uninsured Motorists	No Insurance
Consortium (loss of companionship due to death of a spouse)	Uninsured Motorists	No Insurance

The premiums and profits on uninsured motorist coverage are so high that in California, where automobile insurance rates are limited by law through Proposition 103, many auto insurance companies, but not the state government, began requiring that Californians take the uninsured motorist coverage so that the insurance companies can increase their profits and effectively circumvent the law.

One final note. Your policy Declarations page may state "stacked" or "unstacked" next to the uninsured motorist limits. Stacked requires a yet higher premium and raises the insurance company's limits of liability to the sum total of the coverage for all of your cars if you have more than one. Since, as you can see, your insurance company has little additional liability under uninsured motorist coverage anyway, increasing the limits through stacking is detrimental only to your pocketbook, not to the company's.

Some people falsely believe that uninsured motorist coverage is beneficial because it provides a way of getting around having to sue for damages. The policy specifically states, "We will pay damages which a *covered person* is *legally* entitled to recover from the owner/operator of an uninsured motor vehicle." But here's the catch. The only way that you could establish what you would be legally entitled to recover in damages is to go to court and sue the uninsured motorist. However, many insurance companies have prevented you from doing that by inserting a clause in your policy which states that "any judgment for damages arising out of a suit without our written consent is not binding on us."

Instead, the insurance company will come to you and say, "Let's settle this out of court," and then offer you a fraction of what you might have received in court. In your desire to avoid a lawsuit, you will normally agree to a lesser amount and the insurance company gets away with paying you only a minimum amount under the uninsured motorist coverage.

If you and the insurance company disagree about whether you are legally entitled to recover damages and in what amount, again the insurance company is protected. Your policy may contain an arbitration clause similar to the one below that allows the insurance company through forced arbitration legally to get out of having a jury award you a large settlement on behalf of the liability of an uninsured motorist.

If you and your insurance company disagree, probably the company will demand arbitration. That is how it will normally

Part C—Arbitration

If we and a covered person disagree whether that person is legally entitled to recover damages from the owner or operator of an uninsured motor vehicle or do not agree as to the amount of damages, either party may make a written demand for arbitration. In this event, each party will select an arbitrator. The two arbitrators will select a third. If they cannot agree within 30 days, either may request that selection be made by a judge of a court having jurisdiction. *Each party will pay the expenses it incurs, and bear the expenses of the third arbitrator equally.* Unless both parties agree otherwise, arbitration will take place in the county and state in which the covered person lives. Local rules of law as to procedure and evidence will apply. A decision agreed to by two of the arbitrators will be binding.

be able to stay out of court and make a very reasonable settlement with you. But notice the arbitration clause also says that each party will pay the expenses of the arbitrators.

Your strategy? Drop the uninsured and underinsured motorist coverage from your policy immediately if not required by your state, and make sure you have bought or created a twenty-four-hour-a-day disability policy that covers both illness and accident. Make sure you are carrying only the minimum required uninsured motorist coverage if it is required by your state. You may find your agent has upped the limits to increase the premiums. You may also want to spend some time working toward kicking out of office those state legislators who support these required rip-off automobile insurance coverages.

The 25 states (plus District of Columbia) that have gotten in on the plot to unnecessarily increase auto insurance rates through the requirement of uninsured/underinsured motorist coverage are as follows:

STATE	MINIMUM UNINSURED MOTORIST REQUIRED LIMITS
Connecticut	20/40—
Illinois	20/40/15
Kansas	25/50/—
Maine	20/40/10
Maryland	20/40/—
Massachusetts	20/40/—
Minnesota	25/50/—
Missouri	25/50/—
New Hampshire	25/50/—
New Jersey	15/30/5
New York	10/20/5
North Dakota	25/50/—
Oregon	25/50/—
Rhode Island*	25/50/—
South Carolina	15/30/5
South Dakota	25/50/25
Vermont	20/40/10
Virginia	25/50/20
West Virginia	25/40/10
Wisconsin	25/50/10
Washington, D.C.	25/50/—

*If you carry the minimum liability you can waive Uninsured Motorist. If you carry above 25/50 in liability, you must carry Uninsured Motorist of at least 25/50.

ATTACK #72

Drop the medical payments coverage from your automobile policy.

Medical payments coverage on your automobile insurance policy promises to pay reasonable medical expenses or the cost of a funeral for *anyone* who is injured or dies while riding in *your* car. You and your family members are also covered if hit by a motor vehicle while walking.

Why is medical payments insurance usually a waste of your money? Medical payments insurance is just a duplicate of the hospitalization or life insurance coverage you already have or should be securing on you and your family, or your automobile liability insurance, which covers the potential medical expenses of any passengers riding in your car—if you are legally responsible for their injuries.

If you have a group hospitalization policy covering you and your family, why pay premiums again for automobile medical payments insurance? If you don't have a hospitalization policy, your strategy is to get one that covers you 24 hours a day for all forms of illness or accidents, not just those resulting from an auto accident.

Automobile medical payments coverage allows you to choose limits of usually $5,000 to $50,000, depending on the amount of premiums you want to pay, and covers you only an hour or two a day while you are in your car, walking across the street, or riding in some other vehicle. Your group or individual hospitalization (medical) policy could pay you and your family up to $1 million for illness or injuries caused by an automobile accident or any other reason. Included in most group medical policies is a minimum of $5,000 of life insurance, which is, in essence, the same coverage as the funeral expense portion of automobile medical payments insurance.

Don't fall for sales pitches in the form of scare tactics. If you say that you don't want the medical payments insurance on your policy, your auto insurance agent may have been trained to ask, "Then who is going to pay for the medical expenses of other passengers in your car?" The truth is that your passengers already should be adequately insured. Your immediate family members should already be covered by your group or individual hospitalization policy and nonfamily members are covered by the bodily injury liability portion of your policy if you are at fault, for which you are already paying premiums, as well as by their own hospitalization insurance.

Another pitch is that automobile medical payments insurance will pay any deductible not paid by your group or individual hospitalization policy. The purpose of a deductible is to lower your premiums in the first place, and since a great majority of people will never collect a claim for injuries sustained in an automobile accident, buying expensive medical insurance to pay deductibles is a waste of hard-earned dollars.

Paying premiums twice for the same coverage, like medical insurance, does not give you greater protection or allow you to collect twice. Here is an "other insurance" clause from one company's auto policy:

"If you have auto medical payments insurance coverage we will pay only our share. Our share is a proportion that our limit of liability bears to the total of all applicable limits."

This clause can get your automobile insurance company out of paying almost anything if you have other hospitalization coverage. For instance, if your work-related group policy limit is $1 million and your auto medical payments coverage is $5,000, the above clause can mean that your auto insurance company is liable for a percentage of the bill equal to $5,000÷$1,000,000, or about one out of every $200 of the claim. If your medical bill were $5,000, your auto medical insurance might pay 1/200, or $25, leaving your group policy to pay $4,975.

Companies that write group and individual hospitalization policies, however, have a method of fighting back. Look in your individual medical policy and you will find a clause called "second to pay insurance." This clause says that your regular medical plan will pay only if there is anything left after the primary insurer, in this case your automobile insurance company, has paid up to its total limits. Sounds like nobody wants to pay? You've got it, and that is why you must select your insurance so carefully, never throwing away money on duplicate or unnecessary coverage.

Even though it is pure nonsense, most drivers have medical payments coverage on their policies. So do most automobile insurance agents, who you would think would know better! There is one reason to consider medical payments coverage as a part of your auto policy—if it is required by your state. In that case, it is usually called PIP or personal injury protection and is part of the no-fault laws.

ATTACK #73

Dump the death, dismemberment and loss of sight coverage.

Auto insurance companies seem to prey on the very afraid and the very dumb, especially with optional auto insurance coverage like death and dismemberment. This coverage is nothing more than an extremely overpriced and even more limited combination life insurance policy and lottery. The life insurance included usually gives you a choice of a $5,000 or $10,000 death benefit, but the premium is more than you would normally pay for an equivalent $50,000 of real life insurance—and the insurance covers you only part-time, while you are in your car. Another limitation is that you must die *from* the automobile accident. It doesn't count if you have a heart attack while driving and lose your life, even if the heart attack causes the accident. You must also hurry and die. If you live 90 days in the hospital before you die, the company doesn't have to pay. You want life insurance that covers you 24 hours a day for all causes of death in an amount equal to 8.5 times your income, not $5,000 or $10,000 worth, which would certainly not protect your family's financial future.

Get the point?

Now let's examine the "dismemberment and loss of sight" part of the coverage. The amount you can collect is determined by how many fingers, feet, eyes or hands you can manage to lose in an accident. It reminds me of the slot machines in Las Vegas or Atlantic City. You pull the handle and get paid based on what comes up. The better the combination, the more you collect. Here is the unbelievable stuff the companies actually put in the policy. The amount of coverage, A or B, is chosen at the time of policy purchase.

To begin with, a few hundred dollars isn't going to ease the pain or financial burden caused by the loss of sight or limbs; and second, you have a better chance of dying and collecting on your life insurance policy than qualifying for a dismemberment claim under the above definitions. This kind of insurance is not

SCHEDULE

LOSS OF:	COVERAGE A	COVERAGE B
hands; feet; sight of eyes; one hand and one foot; or one hand or one foot and sight of one eye	$5,000	$10,000
one hand or one foot; or sight of one eye	$2,500	$5,000
thumb and finger on one hand; or three fingers	$1,500	$3,000
any two fingers	$1,000	$2,000

only wasteful, it is insulting. And the chance of collecting, or for that matter the desire for collecting, is incredibly small.

ATTACK #74

Drop emergency road service and rental car reimbursement coverages.

Rental car reimbursement is supposed to provide the cost of a rental car if yours is damaged and in the shop, and emergency road service pays part of the cost of a tow truck if your car breaks down on the side of the road or some labor/service costs if repairable at the scene. It's the little premiums over time that add up to big dollars.

Rental car reimbursement adds $15 to $25 per year per car to your premiums and emergency road service adds another $4 to $10. Every 10 years you could be paying as much as $350 per car for insurance you will seldom if ever use. If you have two cars the 10-year cost is $700 or over $1,000 for three cars.

Some people never file a claim for a rental car since the amount the insurance company will pay is so small and the volume of paperwork so large. Most policies limit the amount they will pay for a rental car to $15 or less per day, and many limit the reimbursement for towing charges to $25. The last time you could get a tow truck for $25 was the early sixties! Instead of renting a car, a more common practice is to use a second family car while one is in the shop or to get a ride to work temporarily with a friend. In addition, if an accident was the fault of another driver, you can ask for rental reimbursement as part of your settlement.

Putting the Automobile Insurance Strategies Together

Look at the automobile insurance policy declarations page on page 202. John Stevens, single, owns two older cars and is paying $1,044 per year for auto insurance. He uses the Cadillac as his primary car and doesn't drive the BMW more than 100 miles per year.

Using what you've learned, let's rip his policy apart, redesign it and cut the premiums to a minimum. Premiums for these coverages, of course, do vary from state to state.

Part A—Liability

Bodily Injury Liability John owns his home with about $10,000 in equity and has only a couple thousand in investments. Not much in assets to protect, but his agent sold him $300,000 of liability protection. By cutting the coverage to $25,000/$50,000, roughly two times his net worth, he will save $75 per year.

Property Damage Liability John has a limit of $25,000, approximately two times his net worth, so no change is required here.

Part B—Medical Payments

John has a good hospitalization policy at work. Why should he carry at any price medical payments insurance that just duplicates the coverage he already has? He should drop the medical payments insurance, saving $15 per year.

Part C—Uninsured Motorist

John could cut his auto insurance $262 per year, or 25 percent of his total premium, just by dropping this unnecessary coverage.

Part D—Comprehensive and Collision

By raising the deductible for each to $500 from the current deductible of $50 for comprehensive (shown as "other than collision loss") and $100 for collision loss, John will save $25

MAII MCH-MH-1

RENEWAL OF

STATE	03	04			Veh	POLICY NUMBER
FL	005	005			TERR	106 32 76U 7102 8

POLICY PERIOD (1201 A.M. standard time)
EFFECTIVE APR 05 1994 TO OCT 05 1994

Name Insured and Address
JOHN STEVENS
PO BOX 678735
ORLANDO FL 32867-8735

01John Stevens

Description Of Vehicle(s)

VEH	YEAR	TRADE NAME	MODEL	BODY TYPE	ANNUAL	IDENTIFICATION NUMBER	VEH USE STM		WORK/SCHOOL Miles One Way	Days Per Week
03	88	BMW	3201	2DR SD	100	5435375 8 P	8	P		
04	90	CADILLAC	DEVILLE	SED4D	6000	1G6AD6984D9187221	12	W	10	5

The Vehiche(s) described herin is principally garaged at the above address unless otherwise stated

*W/S=Work/School, B=Business, F=Farm., P=Pleasure

VEH 03 ORLANDO FL 32817
VEH 04 ORLANDO FL 32817

This policy provides ONLY those coverages for which a premium is shown below.

COVERAGES LIMITS OF LIABILITY ('ACV' MEANS ACTUAL CASH VALUE)	VEH 03 6-MONTH D=DED AMOUNT	PREMIUM $	VEH 04 6-MONTH D=DED AMOUNT	PREMIUM $	VEH D=DED AMOUNT	PREMIUM $	VEH D=DED AMOUNT	PREMIUM $	TOTAL PREMIUMS PER YEAR*
PART A - LIABILITY									
BODILY INJURY EA PER $100,000									
EA ACC $300,000		64.31		68.79					266.00
PROPERTY DAMAGE EA ACC $ 25,000		25.81		27.61					107.00
PART B - MEDICAL PAYMENTS									
EA PER $ 5,000		3.58		3.85					15.00
PART C - UNINSURED MOTORISTS STACKED									
BODILY INJURY EA PER $100,000									
EA ACC $300,000		57.50		73.50					262.00
PART D - DAMAGE TO YOUR AUTO									
OTHER THAN COLL LOSS ACV LESS	D 50	11.47	D 50	20.12					63.00
COLLISION LOSS ACV LESS	D 100	49.37	D 100	68.56					236.00
OTHER COVERAGES									
PERSONAL INJURY PROTECTION									
MAXIMUM BENEFITS $500,000		14.45		15.00					59.00
RENTAL REIMBURSEMENT		5.00		5.00					20.00
EMERGENCY ROAD SERVICE		4.00		4.00					16.00
TOTAL SEMIOANNUAL PREMIUM $522.00									1044.00

LOSS PAYEE
VEH 03 NATIONAL BANK, WICHITA KS

ENDORSEMENTS: ADDED 04-05-94 5301(02) 5611(08) 564(08)
REMAIN IN EFFECT (REFER TO PREVIOUS POLICY) - 5699(02) 5000(03) 5302(02)
6325(01) 5613(05) 5681(01) 5883(02) 5801(01) 5804(01) 5653(02)
INFORMATION FORMS (NOT PART OF POLICY) - 40FL(01) 55FL(02) 334(03) 1465U(03)

03	812129	000	00	N	04	812229	000	00	N

per year on comprehensive and $94 per year on collision premiums, or about 40 percent of these premiums.

Personal Injury Protection

This unnecessary insurance is required in John's state but the minimum is $10,000 and there is a little-known rule that allows him to take a $2,000 deductible. John's agent slapped on $50,000 coverage. By changing to the minimum he will save $24 per year.

REDESIGNING JOHN STEVENS' POLICY

COVERAGE	*Yearly Premiums* BEFORE	AFTER	YEARLY SAVINGS	SAVINGS AFTER 10 YEARS	STRATEGY NUMBER	STRATEGY
Bodily Injury Liability	$ 266	$191	$ 75	$ 750	65	Reduce to 25/50 (two times net worth)
Property Damage Liability	107	107	0	0	66	O.K. as is
Medical Payments	15	0	15	150	72	Drop
Uninsured Motorist	262	0	262	2620	71	Drop
Comprehensive (other than collision)	63	38	25	250	68	Raise deductible to $500
Collision	236	142	94	940	68	Raise deductible to $500
Personal Injury Protection (PIP)	59	35	24	240	70	Change to state minimum
Rental Reimbursement	20	0	20	200	74	Drop
Emergency Road Service	16	0	16	160	74	Drop
Total Premiums	$1044	$513	$531	$5,310		

Rental Reimbursement/Emergency Road Service

By dropping both of these coverages John will cut his yearly premiums by another $36.

Death and Dismemberment

John does not have death and dismemberment coverage. I wonder how his agent missed the opportunity.

The premiums on John's policy were $1,044 per year. By redesigning his policy using the strategies outlined in this chapter, he has cut his yearly cost to $531, a savings of almost 50 percent. Over the next 10 years he will save over $5,300!

Automobile Insurance Audit Chart

Using the Automobile Insurance Policy Audit on page 205, you can redesign your own policy for big savings. Take out your own automobile insurance policy declarations page to see what coverages you now have and what you are paying. Then refer to the list of Auto Insurance Requirements by State below and use all of the strategies we've covered to redesign your automobile policy. I guarantee you it's worth the effort.

Auto Insurance Requirements by State

Alabama	
BI/PD Minimum	20/40/10
PIP Required	No
Uninsured Motorist	No
Alaska	
BI/PD Minimum	50/100/25
PIP Required	No
Uninsured Motorist	No
Arizona	
BI/PD Minimum	15/30/10
PIP Required	No
Uninsured Motorist	No
Arkansas	
BI/PD Minimum	25/50/15
PIP Required	No
Uninsured Motorist	No
California	
BI/PD Minimum	15/30/10
PIP Required	No
Uninsured Motorist	No
Colorado	
BI/PD Minimum	25/50/15
PIP Required	$50,000
Uninsured Motorist	No
Connecticut	
BI/PD Minimum	20/40/10
PIP Required	No
Uninsured Motorist	20/40
Delaware	
BI/PD Minimum	15/30/10
PIP Required	$15,000
Uninsured Motorist	No

(Continued on page 206)

Automobile Insurance Policy Audit

Total Six-Month Premiums for All Cars

Check minimum requirements for your state at the end of the chapter.

Date _____ / _____ / _____

	Coverage	CURRENT LIMITS OR DEDUCTIBLE	DESIRED LIMITS	CURRENT PREMIUMS	NEW PREMIUMS	STRATEGY
1	Bodily Injury Liability	/	/	$	$	Change to 2 × net worth
2	Property Damage Liability					Change to 2 × net worth
3	Comprehensive		$500 deductible			Change to $500 deductible (Drop if car worth is less than $2,000)
4	Collision		$500 deductible			Change to $500 deductible (Drop if car worth is less than $2,000)
5	No-Fault (PIP)					Only if required
6	Uninsured/Underinsured Motorist	/ /	0			Drop if not required
7	Medical Payments		0			Drop
8	Emergency Road Service		0			Drop
9	Towing		0			Drop
10	Death/Dismemberment		0			Drop
11	Rental Car		0			Drop
12	Umbrella Liability	/	/			Only if you need liability coverage of over $100,000/$300,000
13	Total Premiums (Add Lines 1–11)			$	$	This represents 6 months or one-half your yearly premium
14	Total Yearly Premium (Line 13 Times 2)			(A) $	(B) $	

Savings, 1 Year = (A) − (B) $_____

×10

Automobile Insurance Savings Next 10 Years $_____

District of Columbia
BI/PD Minimum 25/50/5
PIP Required No
Uninsured Motorist 25/50/5

Florida
BI/PD Minimum Property only 10
PIP Required Yes
Uninsured Motorist No

Georgia
BI/PD Minimum 16/30/10
PIP Required No
Uninsured Motorist No

Hawaii
BI/PD Minimum 25/unlimited/10
PIP Required Yes—min. $20,000
Uninsured Motorist No

Idaho
BI/PD Minimum 25/50/15
PIP Required No
Uninsured Motorist No

Illinois
BI/PD Minimum 20/40/15
PIP Required No
Uninsured Motorist 20/40/15

Indiana
BI/PD Minimum 25/50/10
PIP Required No
Uninsured Motorist No

Iowa
BI/PD Minimum 20/40/15
PIP Required No
Uninsured Motorist No

Kansas
BI/PD Minimum 25/50/10
PIP Required Yes
Uninsured Motorist 25/50

Kentucky
BI/PD Minimum 25/50/10
PIP Required No
Uninsured Motorist No

Louisiana
BI/PD Minimum 10/20/10
PIP Required No
Uninsured Motorist No

Maine
BI/PD Minimum 20/40/10
PIP Required No
Uninsured Motorist 20/40/10

Maryland
BI/PD Minimum 20/40/10
PIP Required Yes
Uninsured Motorist 20/40

Massachusetts
BI/PD Minimum 20/40/5
PIP Required Yes
Uninsured Motorist 20/40

Michigan
BI/PD Minimum 20/40/10
PIP Required Yes
Uninsured Motorist No

Minnesota
BI/PD Minimum 30/60/10
PIP Required Yes
Uninsured Motorist 25/50

*Mississippi
BI/PD Minimum 10/20/5
PIP Required No
Uninsured Motorist 20/40

Missouri
BI/PD Minimum 25/50/10
PIP Required No
Uninsured Motorist 25/50

Montana
BI/PD Minimum 25/50/25
PIP Required No
Uninsured Motorist No

Nebraska
BI/PD Minimum 25/50/25
PIP Required No
Uninsured Motorist No

Nevada
BI/PD Minimum 15/30/10
PIP Required No
Uninsured Motorist No

New Hampshire
BI/PD Minimum 25/50/25
PIP Required No
Uninsured Motorist 25/50
Medical Required $1,000

New Jersey
BI/PD Minimum 15/30/5
PIP Required Yes
Uninsured Motorist 15/30/5

New Mexico
BI/PD Minimum 25/50/10
PIP Required No
Uninsured Motorist No

New York
BI/PD Minimum 10/20/5
PIP Required $50,000
Uninsured Motorist 10/20/5

North Carolina
BI/PD Minimum 25/50/15
PIP Required No
Uninsured Motorist No

North Dakota
BI/PD Minimum 25/50/25
PIP Required Yes
Uninsured Motorist 25/50/25

Ohio
BI/PD Minimum 12.5/25/7.5
PIP Required No
Uninsured Motorist No

Oklahoma
BI/PD Minimum 10/20/10
PIP Required No
Uninsured Motorist No

Oregon
BI/PD Minimum 25/50/10
PIP Required Yes
Uninsured Motorist 25/50

Pennsylvania
BI/PD Minimum 15/30/5
PIP Required No
Uninsured Motorist No
Medical Required $5,000

Rhode Island
BI/PD Minimum 25/50/25
PIP Required No
**Uninsured Motorist No

South Carolina
BI/PD Minimum 15/30/5
PIP Required No
Uninsured Motorist 15/30/5

South Dakota
BI/PD Minimum 25/50/25
PIP Required No
Uninsured Motorist 25/50/25

Tennessee
BI/PD Minimum 25/50/10
PIP Required No
Uninsured Motorist No

Texas
BI/PD Minimum 20/40/15
PIP Required No
Uninsured Motorist No

Utah
BI/PD Minimum 25/50/15
PIP Required Yes
Uninsured Motorist No

Vermont
BI/PD Minimum 20/40/10
PIP Required No
Uninsured Motorist 20/40/10

Virginia
BI/PD Minimum 25/50/20
PIP Required No
Uninsured Motorist 25/50/20

Washington
BI/PD Minimum 25/50/10
PIP Required No
Uninsured Motorist No

West Virginia	
BI/PD Minimum	20/40/10
PIP Required	No
Uninsured Motorist	20/40/10

Wisconsin	
BI/PD Minimum	25/50/10
PIP Required	No
Uninsured Motorist	25/50/10

Wyoming	
BI/PD Minimum	25/50/20
PIP Required	No
Uninsured Motorist	No

Puerto Rico	
BI/PD Minimum	No
PIP Required	Yes
Uninsured Motorist	No

*Auto insurance of any kind is not compulsory in Mississippi.
**If you carry the minimum liability, you can waive Uninsured Motorist. If you carry liability above the minimum 25/5, then you must carry Uninsured Motorist of at least 25/50.

BI/PD Minimum = BI per person/per accident/property damage.
PIP (no fault) Required = Personal injury protection required.
Uninsured Motorist = Uninsured motorists coverage requirement. Limits, if shown, are for minimum coverage required.

CHAPTER 9

Money-Saving Health Insurance Strategies

Health Insurance

You know the story; you see it everywhere. The cost of doctor and hospital care is going up and up. Health insurance, also called medical or hospitalization insurance, has become one of the most expensive parts of your entire financial plan. One way or the other, you're paying big dollars. Even if your employer pays for part or all of your health insurance premiums, he does so by paying you less in wages. Who's kidding whom? You can't have both. If you're paying part of your health insurance costs at work, particularly the part that covers your family, you're outraged by the fact that your health insurance is practically as expensive as Social Security or income taxes. For some it's more, since you get no break on health insurance premiums because of a lack of income. If you're not covered by a health insurance plan at work and have to seek an individual policy on your own, the premiums you are quoted are enough to make you ill, no matter what condition you were in before. The average cost of health insurance for a family of four is over $300 per month or $3,600 per year.

If you are one of the 40 percent of Americans who does not have a paid-for health plan, by following the strategies in this chapter you can cut the high cost of health insurance for you and your family by up to 50 percent. Even if you do have health insurance provided now, you may not always. A young employee today will change jobs seven times before retirement, usually to one or more jobs where medical insurance is not provided, and then ends up having to find an individual policy at retirement when the company's group plan no longer applies. Use the strategies in this chapter and you should not have to worry.

The biggest part of the problem, as in every part of your financial life, is nobody ever told you the truth about health insurance: about what you need and don't need, about what coverage and limits benefit you versus what benefits the insurance company's profit picture. In addition, your company plan is only as good as the limited knowledge of the people in your company who chose that plan.

As with every form of insurance, there seems to be an abundant number of companies that provide health coverage. Yet there are usually one or two best companies and policies that will protect the greatest part of your real risk with the lowest premiums. You have about a 1 in 250 chance of finding that policy through luck. If you have no health insurance coverage now, because of the high cost, by using my strategies you will soon find that you can afford it. But first, let's look at how your health insurance premiums are determined.

Although every health insurance company has different rates for the same or similar coverage, your premiums are usually determined by the following factors:

- Age of the primary insured—The primary insured in the case of a company group policy is the person who works for the company. On individual policies, it is usually the age of the oldest applicant or spouse that is used in determining rates. Premiums may increase every five years; thus a person 35 to 39 would pay more than one age 30 to 34. When you are over 50, health insurance becomes more and more costly, but usually the kids are grown by then, which helps cut your total premium.
- Your spouse—Your premiums, as you might suspect, are dramatically higher if a second adult, like a spouse, is included in the policy.
- Where you live—Your zip code causes you to pay more or less based on the average doctor, prescription and hospital costs in your area. The population, pollution, and crime rates are also factors. All zip codes are placed in rating

categories, with each succeeding category becoming more expensive. Two zip code areas next to each other may have totally different rates. You may pay the lower rate automatically by living in the lesser-rated zip code area, even though it is your right to cross zip code or county lines to use the more expensive hospital facilities.

- Number of children—Each child under 18 can be covered for an equal premium. The age of your children is not a factor.
- The company—All health insurance companies determine their own rates. Choosing the wrong company or even the wrong employer can double your insurance premiums.
- Current state of health—The lowest premiums are for those policyholders classified as preferred risks, those with no serious health problems. Rates can increase based on health conditions to the point where a person becomes uninsurable or has limited benefits for the first couple of years the policy is in force.
- Type of insurance plan—The lowest rates are usually for an employment-related group plan, but companies with fewer than 15 employees usually do not qualify. Regular individual policies are the most expensive, unless you use the strategies in this chapter. The Insurance ClearingHouse has found policies for individuals at lower group rates, which will be discussed later.
- Options chosen—Options to a medical policy like maternity benefits, dental and supplemental accident will dramatically increase the monthly premiums.

Your objective with health insurance, as with any insurance, is to maximize your protection while paying the minimum premiums. To show you how to accomplish this goal, let's design the ideal policy. In the following list, What You Want and Don't Want in a Health Insurance Policy, you will see what an ideal policy has and doesn't have. If you have a group plan through your employer, use the list to check your policy to see how good your plan really is. If you have an individual hospitalization policy or need one, this list will help you choose or change to a better plan. You probably won't find all the ideal options in any single policy, but the list will enable you to compare.

What You Want and Don't Want in a Health Insurance Policy

OPTION	DON'T WANT	WANT
Rates	Higher individual rates	Lower group rates
Deductible	$250	$1,000
Stop-loss	80/20 to $1,000	80/20 to $5,000
Refund	No refund	P.P.O. refund
Claim time	6 weeks	14 days
Company sells	In one or two states	In 40 or more states
Company Rating	Below A	A or above
Coverage	Maternity Dental Supplemental accident Prescription drug card	

Let's look first at the options you don't want, and why. Then I'll tell you how you can find a policy with the options and coverages you *do* want.

ATTACK #75

Raise your deductible to $1,000 to cut your premiums 35 to 45 percent.

The amount of the direct deductible has the greatest effect on the premiums you pay for a health insurance policy. The higher the deductible, the lower the premium. The deductible is the portion of any claim for which you are responsible before the insurance company has to pay. A normal low deductible is $150 to $250 and may make you feel more secure but it is a financial drain. Your strategy? Raise your deductible to $1,000 or more and over the long run you will pay far less in net premiums even if you occasionally pay the extra deductible on a claim. Your real risk is not the first thousand dollars of a claim but tens or hundreds of thousands of dollars of medical expenses caused by a serious illness or accident to you or a family member.

If you have a $1,000 deductible you are responsible for the first $1,000 of any claim, and the insurance company then pays the rest of your claim up to $1 million or the limits of your policy, less the amount of your coinsurance (see Defense #76). The difference to you is that the premiums are about 40 percent less than a policy with a $100 deductible. You can save as much as $700 to $1,200 per year with the higher deductible. If you have substantial assets, a $2,500 deductible could save you up to 50 percent.

Although it may feel good to know that claims of a few hundred dollars are paid by the insurance company, over time you will pay two to three times in extra insurance premiums what you could ever collect in claims. To pay your claim of $400, it costs the insurance company in paperwork and administrative expenses an additional $500. No insurance is free. Administrative costs are added to the premiums for low-deductible policies. By taking a major medical policy with a $1,000 or more deductible, you have, in effect, stopped paying the administrative expenses for other policyholders' small claims. The fewer claims you make, the more money is wasted with low deductibles. Become self-insured for the first $1,000 or more of your medical expenses and watch your premiums drop dramatically.

Here is a typical comparison of monthly and annual premiums for a 30-year-old male with a 30-year-old spouse and two children, living in Altamonte Springs, Florida. Based on the deductible chosen and an 80/20 to $5,000 stop-loss. (See next defense for an explanation of stop-loss.)

PYRAMID LIFE INSURANCE COMPANY
MAJOR MEDICAL DEDUCTIBLE COMPARISON

DEDUCTIBLE	MONTHLY PREMIUM	ANNUAL PREMIUM	SAVINGS OVER $500 DEDUCTIBLE $	%
$500	$301.26	$3,503.00	—	—
$750	$273.31	$3,178.00	$325.00	9%
$1000	$245.53	$2,855.00	$648.00	18%
$1500	$222.22	$2,584.00	$919.00	26%
$2500	$181.03	$2,105.00	$1,398.00	40%
$5000	$147.32	$1,713.00	$1,790.00	51%
$10000	$106.73	$1,241.00	$2,262.00	65%

These rates are for individual policies for a state without mandated riders and our base area factor of 1.00.

Notice that as the deductible is increased over the basic $500 deductible, the yearly premiums drop dramatically. Raise the deductible from $500 to $750 and the savings are $325 per year, or 9 percent, and all you are doing is agreeing to pay an extra $250 if you have a claim! Raise the deductible from $500 to

$1,000 and the savings are $648 per year, or 18 percent. The best value for most people is a $1,000 deductible.

There are two ways that health insurance can hurt you financially: paying too much in premiums or having too little coverage to pay a major claim. The older you get, the greater the chances are of having a serious illness that could cost megadollars. Health insurance that covers catastrophic illness is the answer for some. A catastrophic policy is one with low premiums because of a substantial deductible ranging from $5,000 to $20,000 and is meant to pay only huge claims, but it is a huge claim that could destroy the entire estate of a retired person or couple. The trade-off is that you are covered for a major illness but would have to pay all small hospital and doctor bills yourself. Why would you consider the catastrophic policy? Because if you are over age 65 or your state of health is not the best, your yearly health insurance premiums with a low deductible can be $5,000 to $8,000 annually. You would more than likely lose more in premiums with a low deductible than you would stand a chance of collecting in claims.

If you are under age 65 and you and your family are in good health but have to buy health insurance as individuals, a catastrophic policy may be an alternative. You have the advantage of low premiums coupled with coverage for any major medical financial expenses.

DEFENSE #76

Select a higher stop-loss, like 80/20 to $5,000, to further reduce your premiums.

In addition to the direct deductible in health insurance policies, there is a second hidden deductible known in the insurance business as the stop-loss or coinsurance. Here's how it works. If you have a claim, you first pay the entire amount of the deductible on your policy, but you are then also responsible for paying 20 to 50 percent of the next $3,000 to $10,000, depending on the company and policy. The insurance company then guarantees it will pay everything above that amount to a lifetime maximum, which can be a million dollars or more. For example, if you or someone in your family has a $10,000 medical bill, you first pay the deductible, let's say $1,000. If your policy reads that the company pays 80 percent of the first $5,000 minus your deductible, that means it pays $3,000 of the first $5,000 and you pay 20 percent or up to a maximum of another $1,000. On your $10,000 medical bill, you would actually pay $2,000, or 20 percent, and the insurance company would pay $8,000. By increasing your stop-loss you can decrease your premiums even further, although in reality you are just increasing your potential deductible.

Choosing a higher direct deductible will save you the most money as a percentage of your premiums, but also agree to a higher stop-loss. The best value is a policy that pays 80 percent of the next $5,000 plus 100 percent of any claims above $6,000.

DEFENSE #77

Buy from a company rated A or above that is a leader in the health insurance business.

A bigger consideration than premium costs is dependability. You want the company to which you have been paying your hard-earned money to be around to pay a claim if and when you have one.

Buddy Hewell, co-director of The Insurance ClearingHouse, relayed the following story to me. Recently at a meeting conducted for our insurance staff, the vice president of a large health insurance marketing firm told the group that his firm uses a service that compiles information on over 1,500 life and/or health insurance companies and noticed that 500 of these companies in 1988 had total premium income from health insurance sales exceeding $100 million. In 1989 nearly half, over 200, of these companies had either gone broke or withdrawn from the health insurance business.

Your strategy? Buy your health insurance at the lowest possible cost, but only from a substantial, well-established company like those listed below.

EXAMPLES OF THE LEADING COMPANIES IN THE HEALTH INSURANCE INDUSTRY

COMPANY	A.M. BEST RATING
American National	A++
Celtic Life	A
Durham Life	A+
Golden Rule	A+

COMPANY	A.M. BEST RATING
Mutual of Omaha	A+
Pan American Life	A
Provident Mutual Life of Philadelphia	A+
Time Insurance	A+
United of Omaha	A+
Woodman Accident & Life	A

Companies that are big in the health insurance business also have the most stable rates over the long term. In a study just completed by The Insurance ClearingHouse, we found that some companies sometimes make huge rate increases in one year, up to 25 percent. The major companies in the health industry have a track record of much smaller increases.

One way to determine the leaders or more established companies is the number of states in which they have been licensed and approved to offer their policies. A good rule of thumb is to look at companies licensed in over 40 states and avoid, no matter what the cost, companies licensed in only a few states.

Finally, because of the competitive nature of the health insurance business, most companies that are leaders in health insurance create a new and better policy about every two years. When a new policy comes to market, it is purposely underpriced to attract business away from other companies, which can allow you to take advantage of those new lower rates. If after a couple of years you can do better with a new policy from another company, it may be worth the change.

As with life insurance, the A. M. Best rating of the insurance company from which you are going to buy a policy is important. Do business only with companies rated A or above. Since companies are rated primarily on financial strength, choosing a company with an acceptable rating helps ensure that the money will be there to pay any claims you may have. At the end of this chapter, there is a list of companies that offer health insurance coverage and their A. M. Best ratings.

DEFENSE #78

Don't pay for maternity benefits with your health insurance.

If you are planning to have another child, you will certainly want to make sure that expensive maternity bills are covered. Does that mean that health insurance maternity benefits are a good buy? The truth is, you're going to pay for the birth of your next child whether you first give the money to the insurance company as a maternity benefits premium or whether you pay it yourself in cash or through payments you work out with the hospital. Maternity benefits have incredibly overpriced premiums, which are seldom recovered in a maternity claim. Since most people don't understand the mathematics of insurance, they are unaware of what a lousy investment maternity coverage can be.

A senior vice president of marketing for a major health insurance company was visiting our offices and called maternity coverage a sucker's bet. Let me show you why. The maternity benefits coverage is designed so that you always pay hundreds of dollars more than you will likely collect. The insurance company limits its total exposure by setting a maximum maternity benefit, and, of course, there is always the deductible and stop-loss. On a typical policy, the maximum maternity benefit is $3,000 to $5,000 and the premium is an extra $200 a month. To prevent people from waiting until they decide to have children to take out the maternity coverage, there is a waiting period of nine months to a year during which you pay premiums but coverage is not in effect. At $200 a month, you've paid up to $2,400, or most of the maximum you could possibly collect. And what if that year you don't have a child? You've just thrown away $2,400 or more. If you wait until the second year to have a child, you've paid in as much as $4,800. All you've done is given the insurance company the benefit of your money with no interest if you do have a child, and if you don't, you've thrown it away.

One major concern is "What if there are complications after birth that require intensive care?" Don't worry. If you own a policy that covers both spouses with or without children included, your newborn will be automatically covered as long as you comply with your company's procedures as to notification and paying a proper premium. Most companies require notification within 30 days to 90 days to activate "automatic" coverage. Read your policy ahead of time so that you won't lose this valuable option. Without the required notification your company can get out of paying, but if you follow the procedure your child is covered from the moment of birth.

If you have a policy that insures only yourself and not a spouse, you need to arrange for coverage for your expected child *before* birth. Contact your insurance company at least six months before the "due date" of the child and find out about the procedures and time requirements necessary to add your newborn to your policy.

Why not take the extra premium money you can save on maternity benefits and put it into a no-load mutual fund where you might average 15 percent a year? Invest that $200 a month and let it continue to grow until you do have a child. Anything left over you can use to start your child's college investment plan.

Speaking of insuring your child, another form of insurance you will be offered when your child enters school is a $15- to $40-per-year accident policy. If you have structured your basic family health policy correctly, an accident policy with a $500 or $1,000 maximum limit is just insurance that covers deductibles. It's a waste of money. Don't buy it.

DEFENSE #79

Don't buy health policy options like dental, supplemental accident or prescription drug cards.

All optional health policy coverages are attractive, sound, logical and make you feel as if you ought to have them. But that's why some American families and companies are overpaying their health insurance premiums by 50 percent.

Dental Coverage

Dental coverage has been a big seller since its inception, and yet it is one of the highest-profit items for the insurance companies. Dental insurance is bought out of fear. We all know that we will have some family dental bills and we think the insurance company will freely, and out of goodwill, chip in to take care of the expense. Let me tell you what really happens. Statistics show that the average claim for dental coverage is a cleaning bill and an occasional filling about once a year. The average amount spent for a cleaning bill is about $60. In other words, the worst case scenario for most families is an average expenditure of $60 per person per year. But the average cost of dental coverage is about $38 per month or $456 a year. There's also a deductible per person of around $50. All those premiums just so the health insurance company will pick up only a few dollars of your annual dental bill. Even if you and your family run up large bills, the maximum benefit is usually only $1,000. Occasionally, you or someone in your family may require dental surgery, which could run into many thousands, but in that case you are normally covered under the surgical section of your medical policy even without dental insurance. Check your own policy.

Supplemental Accident Coverage

Supplemental accident coverage pays your policy's deductible if someone in your family is injured in an accident, and the coverage requires an extra premium. It's another high-profit, low-risk coverage for the health insurance company! Here's why. Only about one out of six claims on a medical insurance policy is caused by an accident. The insurance company wins again. Supplemental accident coverage is easy for insurance companies to sell but absolutely one of the worst values for you. Your goal is to take a higher deductible in order to save money on your health insurance, not to spend extra money on insurance that pays the deductible.

Prescription Drug Cards

The prescription drug card gimmick requires an additional premium that gives you the convenience of a credit-type card to pay for prescriptions. Pay a $5 to $10 deductible and the insurance company pays the balance. Unless you already have a chronic illness which requires monthly medicine worth over $30 a month, you probably will not profit from a prescription drug card. And if you already have a chronic illness when you apply for insurance, that illness will more than likely be excluded from your health insurance policy.

ATTACK #80

If you need health insurance, call The Insurance ClearingHouse for individual policies at low rates.

A number of companies offer individual health insurance policies. If you are paying your own premiums, how do you know you have the best policy with the right coverage at the lowest possible premiums? Look at the list at the end of this chapter, Companies That Offer Health Insurance Coverage, and you will see that finding the best policy yourself could require years of research.

To solve that problem, we created The Insurance Clearing-House for members of the Givens Organization. As a reader of this book, you also qualify to use its services for free. The research staff at The ClearingHouse checks policies and rates offered by various companies and helps our members find a policy that could cover their needs. When you request a quote or coverage, The ClearingHouse staff can find a recommended policy for someone in your circumstances. That way you can use the health insurance strategies we just covered to tailor the policy to your individual needs, including money-saving deductibles and only coverages that are a good value. When you are working with staff members of The ClearingHouse, they will automatically design your policy to fit the strategies in this chapter.

If you are covered at work but pay for your other family members yourself, there is an excellent chance The Clearing-House can save you money on coverage for the rest of your family. If your employee is paying all or most of your health insurance premiums, you already have the lowest premium possible and don't need to contact The ClearingHouse. If you are an employer who does not qualify for low group rates for your employees, The Insurance ClearingHouse may also help.

Call The Insurance ClearingHouse at:

1-800-522-2827

At this point you will want to review your health insurance plan. If you have a "cafeteria" plan at work which allows you to design your own benefits package, following the strategies in this chapter will enable you to make better use of every benefit dollar. If you find that your employer's group plan is not up to par with the ideal medical policy we've designed, these strategies will help your employer develop a better insurance benefits package for you and all of your fellow employees. If you are an employer, applying these strategies will give your employees the best possible benefits at the least cost to you.

If you have an individual health insurance policy because you are not covered by group insurance, use the "shop-and-drop" approach. Shop for the best policies at the best rates using these strategies, and drop any policies or coverages you already have that are not a good value.

Companies That Offer Health Insurance Coverage

The letter after the name is the *A. M. Best* rating. Choose a company rated A, A+ or A++.

Aetna Life Insurance Company A
AIG Life Insurance Company A+
Alexander Hamilton Life A+
Alfa Life A+
All American Life A+
Allianz Life Ins. Co. of North America A+
Allstate Life of NY A+
American Enterprise Life A+
American Family Life Assurance A+
American Family Life Insurance A+
American Fidelity Assurance A+
American Franklin Life A++
American General Life A++
American Health & Life A++
American Investors Life A
American Life A−
American Mayflower A+
American Mayflower Life A+
American National A++
American United Life A+
Americans Life Insurance A+
Ameritas Life A+
Bankers Security Life A
Bankers United Life A
Beneficial Life A+
Benefit Trust Life A
Boston Mutual A
Celtic Life Insurance A
Central Life Assurance A
Central States Health and Life of Omaha A−
Chubb Life Insurance A+
Combined Insurance A+
Commercial Life Insurance A−
Connecticut National Life A
Continental Assurance A+
Crown Life A−
Durham Life A+
The Equitable A+
Equitable of Colorado, Inc. A−
The Equitable Life Assurance Society A−
Equitable Life Insurance Co. of Iowa A+
Equitable Reserve Association A
Equitable Variable Life Insurance Co. A−

Federal Home Life A+
Federal Kemper Life A−
Fidelity & Guaranty Life A−
Fidelity Security Life A−
First Colony Life A++
Garden State Life (GEICO) A−
General American Life A+
Golden Rule Insurance Co. A+
Great-West Life Assurance (The) A++
Guarantee Mutual Life A
Guardian Life of America A++
Hartford Life and Accident A++
Home Life Financial Assurance A
Jackson National Life A+
Jefferson National Life A
John Alden Life A+
Lamar Life Insurance A
Life Ins. Co. of North America A+
Life Ins. Co. of Virginia A+
Life Investors A+
Lincoln Benefit Life A+
Loyal American Life A−
Manhattan National Life A−
Manufacturers Life A++
Massachusetts Mutual A++
Merit Life A+
Merrill Lynch Life A
Metropolitan Life A++
MId-Continent Life A+
Midland Mutual Life A
The Minnesota Mutual Life A++
Monumental Life A+
Mutual of Omaha A+
Mutual Life of New York (MONY) A−
National Life A+
Nationwide Life A+
New York Life A++
North American Company A+
North American Co. For Life & Health of NY A
North American Co. For Life & Health A
Northern Life Insurance A+
Northwestern Mutual Life A++
Northwestern National A
The Ohio National Life A+
The Ohio State Life A
The Old Line Life A+
Old Republic Life A−
Pacific Mutual A+
Pan American Life A
Philadelphia Life A
Phoenix Home Life Mutual A
Presidential Life A
Principal Mutual Life A++
Protective Life A+
Provident Life & Accident (TN) A+
Provident Life Insurance A
Provident Mutual Life of Philadelphia A+
Pyramid Life Ins. Co. A−
Security Benefit Life A+
Security-Connecticut Life A+
Sentry Life Insurance A+
Southland Life A+
Time Insurance Company A+
Transamerica Occidental Life A+
The Travelers Insurance A−
United Life Insurance A
United of Omaha A+
William Penn Life A
Wisconsin National Life A+
Woodmen Accident & Life A

CHAPTER 10

Designing a Disability Income Plan Without Insurance

Disability insurance should more properly be called "lost income" insurance. It pays a monthly income to replace part or all of the income lost if you become totally disabled and are unable to work at a job, career or business. Premiums are based on age, amount of income you want per month if you become disabled and the amount of time you are willing to wait before you can collect.

Because so much depends on family income, naturally there is a great fear of what would happen to the family if that income was lost. Such fear has created an incredible opportunity for those insurance companies willing to issue disability insurance. Disability insurance is considered part of the health insurance industry and is offered by both life and health insurance companies. But the truth is that the premiums on disability insurance are so high, the definitions of disability are so narrow and the chances of collecting so small that most people waste their money when buying a policy.

There are some people, however, who absolutely need disability insurance: those who are clumsy or accident-prone. Here's a good test to see if you fit into this category. When you wake up in the morning, do you walk into the wall before you make it to the bathroom? If so, you may be an accident waiting to happen and certainly should consider disability insurance.

As with most insurance, the concept of disability insurance is great, but insurance companies do not like the prospect of paying anyone monthly income for 10, 20, 30, 40 years or longer. As a result, the premium levels are chosen to protect the insurance company and not you. A disability policy, depending on the monthly benefits and options you choose, will typically cost $800 to $2,500 per year.

Don't confuse disability with just feeling bad and staying at home for a week or two. Disability insurance normally pays only for *total* disability. The extent of your disability is not a determination you make; it is one that your insurance company makes based on the fact that one or more doctors state in writing that there is no way you can work at your job or in many cases any job. Let's look at a disability definition clause from a typical policy:

> "Total disability" means that because of injury or sickness:
> a. You cannot do the main duties of your occupation; and
> b. You are under a physician's care; and
> c. You are not engaged in any other gainful occupation.

By definition, if you sit at a desk or computer terminal as the main function of your job and lose the use of your feet to frostbite, you could not collect on your disability policy.

Some policies, like the one above, prevent you from doing any work if you want to collect. Others stop paying after two years if you can work any job and even provide retraining. If you were an engineer and couldn't perform the main duties of your job but could be trained to sling hamburgers at a fast-food restaurant, the company might get out of paying the monthly income.

It's true that some people who have disability insurance will collect more than they pay in. However, they are so few that disability insurance for the most part is more expensive than it's worth. Why, then, are millions of dollars' worth of such policies sold? The advertising done by the disability companies and their salespeople is, at best, totally deceiving and, at worst, an outright fraud. One company tells you in its national advertising that between the ages of 25 and 65, three out of four people will become disabled, so everyone should have disability insurance. The real truth is that three out of four will become totally disabled for a period of between 1 and 30 days, not for a lifetime as the ads would lead you to assume. The greatest number of disabilities are caused by a bump on the head, a cut finger, a pulled muscle or a broken bone. These short-term temporary disabilities are not even covered by a disability policy.

As with health or automobile insurance, disability insurance has a deductible. But rather than a dollar deductible, it has a time deductible called the elimination period. When you buy a policy, you choose the amount of time you will agree to be disabled before the insurance company has to start paying. The minimum is, you guessed it, 30 days, the time when most Americans will be going through that once-per-lifetime temporary disability. The shorter the elimination period you pick, the higher your premiums become.

Disability insurance is expensive, no matter how you slice it. Let's look at the arithmetic. If your premiums for disability insurance are $2,000 per year and you pay those premiums for 40 years, you have paid a total of $80,000. The real value of the money that you paid the insurance company, if invested instead at 12 percent, is over $300,000. What are your chances of collecting $300,000 from a disability policy? Practically none, less than 1 in 1,000, since you would have to receive $1,500 per month for about 17 years to break even. Even then the odds are the insurance company won't have to pay out the face value or amount promised because of the benefit reduction gimmick. Here is the benefit reduction clause from a typical policy:

> We will pay the maximum monthly benefit amount reduced by:
> 1. 100% of Social Insurance Benefits for which you are eligible;
> 2. 100% of the Employer Sponsored Benefits for which you are eligible; such reduction not to exceed 80% of the maximum benefit amount.

This clause means little when you buy the policy, but when it comes time to collect it means that the insurance company will get out of paying you 10 to 80 percent of the amount you thought you were going to collect. Here are the disability payments most people will receive even without disability insurance.

GOVERNMENT DISABILITY ASSISTANCE

Social Security pays all those who can prove total disability, and the monthly income provided is $500 to over $1,700. Social Security is automatically subtracted from the income you were promised on your disability policy. If your disability policy were for $2,000 per month and Social Security pays you $1,500 per month, your disability insurance income would be reduced by $1,500 or 75 percent. Other government disability benefits are paid to federal employees, veterans, civil service workers, plus those who qualify under the Medicaid rules. They, too, can reduce the payments from your disability policy.

WORKER'S COMPENSATION

If you were injured on the job, the place where 40 percent or more of accidents occur, you will receive disability income because of the mandatory worker's compensation premiums your employer is paying. This amount can also be deducted from your disability policy monthly income.

EMPLOYER DISABILITY PLAN

Most medium and large companies pay disability income to employees for three months to one year. That amount will also be deducted by your disability insurance company. If you have accumulated sick leave time, you would continue to receive your full salary during that period. Most employers in New York, Hawaii and New Jersey pay disability benefits for about six months and in California for up to one year. If you work for a big company anywhere, chances are you have some disability protection. Check this week.

If you become disabled and your disability policy had a monthly income benefit of $1,400 per month but Social Security, worker's compensation and employer benefits totaled $1,200 a month, your disability insurance company might get out of paying you all but $200 of what it promised. But not to worry—most policies guarantee to pay a minimum of 20 percent of the income you were paying 100 percent of the premiums to get!

And finally, here's the hook that benefits the insurance company, not you. If you do become disabled, disability insurance will not cover you for the rest of your life, perhaps another 10 to 40 years. You receive disability income only to age 65, unless, of course, you want to pay an even greater premium. Therefore, if you were age 55 when you bought the policy and became disabled, the policy would provide income for a maximum of 10 years. You would have no job or disability income after age 65.

If you still feel that disability insurance is something you would like to have for emotional reasons rather than mathematical probabilities, there are strategies you can use that will cut your premiums by as much as 50 percent.

DEFENSE #81

Buy a disability policy that replaces only 50 to 60 percent of your income.

Most policies limit the maximum amount of income you can choose on a disability policy to 80 percent of your current earnings, so that there will not be more incentive to stay home than to go back to work. However, the amount of coverage you really need is far less than 80 percent.

Your expenses would drop dramatically if you became permanently disabled. The biggest expense that would disappear is income taxes. Although you pay income taxes on disability income you receive from your employer, if any, there is no income tax on money you receive from a disability insurance policy. You will save up to 33 percent on federal and 7 percent on state taxes alone. You also save another approximately 7 percent because Social Security payments are not required.

Your commuting-to-work expenses will disappear, as well as the need to keep your wardrobe up to date. You will be eating lunch at home instead of expensive lunches at work and you would probably drop your golf, tennis or health club memberships. Any increases in your medical expenses will, in most cases, be covered by your health insurance. There is nothing pleasant or appealing about cutting your personal expenses by becoming permanently disabled, but expenses will decrease nevertheless. You will need only 50 to 60 percent of your current income to pay the bills and feed the family. The lower the amount of income you need disability insurance to replace, the lower the premiums will be.

DEFENSE #82

Choose a longer elimination period on disability insurance to cut premiums up to 40 percent.

The time deductible, or what the insurance company calls the elimination period, can usually be chosen at 30, 60, 90, 180 or 365 days. That's the period of time that will elapse before you can begin to collect on the policy. Your objective, remember, is to give yourself the greatest disability protection for the least amount of premium. Your money-saving strategy is to choose the longest possible elimination period. Become self-insured for the first year and then let the disability policy cover you until it terminates, usually at age 65 and you'll save a bundle.

Here is the disability insurance rate schedule from Jefferson Pilot Life Insurance Company. Notice with a 30-day elimination period, the premium is $1,736 per year. But with a 365-day elimination period, the premium is only $1,093 per year, a premium savings of $643 a year, or 37 percent.

BASIC BENEFIT $4,000 PER MONTH

ELIMINATION PERIOD CHOSEN (DAYS)	YEARLY PREMIUM	SAVINGS COMPARED WITH 30-DAY	SAVINGS COMPARED WITH 30-DAY
30	$1,736	—	—
60	$1,484	$252	15%
90	$1,352	$384	22%
180	$1,189	$547	32%
365	$1,093	$643	37%

Statistics show that your chances of becoming disabled for any significant period during your lifetime are relatively small and during any one year are almost infinitesimal. You could pay almost $700 a year more to receive an extra 11 months of coverage at $4,000 per month or $44,000 total. That means you would pay an extra $7,000 every 10 years, which if invested at 12 percent would have an equivalent value of almost $20,000. In 20 years you will have paid the insurance company the equivalent of the $44,000. If the money were invested instead, it would be there for you whether or not you ever became disabled.

The insurance company is guaranteed to win if you pick a short elimination period.

If you do choose a short elimination period like 30 days, you will pay the extra 37 percent in premiums every year for 10, 20, 30 years or as long as you carry the disability income insurance. However, if you become disabled, you can collect the extra few months of income only one time, the year in which you become disabled.

Disability insurance is like a decreasing term insurance policy. The premiums stay the same, but your coverage decreases. The more you pay, the less maximum coverage you have. Because disability insurance covers you only until age 65, the maximum potential amount you can collect from the insurance company decreases each year as you get older. And, as you can see from the Disability Insurance Rate Comparison on the following page, the older you are when you take out a disability policy, the higher the premium for less coverage.

DEFENSE #83

Substitute the free disability protection in your IRA or retirement plan for expensive disability insurance premiums.

A far better alternative than disability insurance for protecting your job, career or business income is available through little-known retirement plan rules. Normally, if you were to withdraw money from your IRA, Keogh, 401(k) or other retirement plan before age 59½, you would pay a 10 percent penalty. But if you become permanently disabled, the rules allow you to withdraw your money at any age with no penalty.

Instead of buying expensive disability insurance, commit to putting the maximum each year into your retirement plan. By investing the money in stock, bond and money market mutual funds, available in most all retirement plans, you can average a growth rate of up to 15 percent per year, doubling your money every five years. In the unlikely event you become permanently disabled, you have created your own insurance fund. At 15 percent per year, every $100,000 in the fund will return to you $15,000 of yearly income indefinitely.

There are exceedingly few "permanent" disabilities that keep a person from working for over a year and fewer still that require

DISABILITY INSURANCE RATE COMPARISON*

Best Occupational Class, Nonsmoker, To Age 65 Benefit Period, 90-Day Elimination, Level Premium, $2,000 Monthly Benefit.

	Monthly and Yearly Premium and Age									
	30		35		40		45		50	
Company	*Mon.*	*Yr.*	*Mon.*	*Yr.*	*Mon.*	*Yr.*	*Mon.*	*Yr.*	*Mon.*	*Yr.*
Lincoln	$57.54	$690.48	$66.70	$800.40	$81.20	$974.40	$106.14	$1273.68	$133.22	$1598.64
Paul Revere	57.78	693.36	70.74	848.88	90.12	1081.44	111.76	1341.12	138.28	1659.36
Northwestern	58.00	696.00	69.20	830.40	82.60	991.20	101.00	1212.00	118.40	1420.80
Guardian	61.14	733.68	73.18	878.16	88.84	1066.08	107.84	1294.08	129.24	1550.88
UNUM	61.38	736.56	73.86	886.32	90.46	1085.52	104.20	1250.40	126.62	1519.44
Provident	61.60	739.20	74.68	896.16	91.54	1098.48	112.92	1355.04	140.68	1688.16
Monarch	65.80	789.60	79.40	952.80	98.40	1180.80	124.20	1490.40	156.00	1872.00

SOURCES: *Guardian NC 95 Rate Book Pub. 1294*
Lincoln Pro Add Rate Book 24165-1
Monarch CDR A+ Rate Card 59259 Rev.
Northwestern MM Rate Book 90-1859
Paul Revere Preferred Professional (960) 9409 Rev.
UNUM Rate Book 902-85
Provident 337 Rate Book A-30783

*Based on 1990 figures.

a full or partial recovery time of over five years. In the example that follows showing the five-year IRA withdrawal plan, if you were to withdraw both the principal and interest from a $100,000 retirement plan over a five-year period, you could withdraw $25,000 the first four years and the balance of a little over $31,000 the fifth year. Your income from your retirement plan is not reduced by other disability income like social security or worker's compensation as insurance disability income would be.

How long will it take to get $100,000 into a retirement plan if you haven't started one yet? Over the next 10 years, the maximum allowable contribution to a 401(k) will be an average of $8,000. To accumulate $100,000 at $8,000 per year if the account is earning 15 percent will take just 7 years!

FIVE-YEAR IRA WITHDRAWAL PLAN
ORIGINAL AMOUNT = $100,000

YEAR	YEARLY WITHDRAWAL	=	NEW BALANCE + INTEREST ON BALANCE	BALANCE END OF YEAR
1	$25,000	=	$75,000 + $11,250	$86,250
2	$25,000	=	$61,250 + $ 9,187	$70,437
3	$25,000	=	$45,437 + $ 6,816	$52,253
4	$25,000	=	$27,253 + $ 4,088	$31,341
5	$31,341	=		

If you feel you need a minimum of disability insurance while building your own retirement insurance account, follow the strategies in this chapter. If you already have sufficient money in your IRA, Keogh, 401(k) or other retirement plan, you are protected and should stop wasting money on disability insurance premiums.

ATTACK #84

Buy a renewable term disability policy to cut premiums in half.

Renewable term disability (RTD) is like annual renewable term life insurance in that the premiums are initially lower but increase as you age. Premiums on renewable term disability begin as much as 50 percent less than a policy with a level premium and increase every five years. Lower premiums can be important during the years when you are struggling financially. Pay too much in insurance premiums and other unnecessary expenses and chances are you may never be in a position to get ahead.

If you are building a disability insurance fund using your retirement plan (see previous strategy), renewable term disability is ideal, since your intent will be to reduce and finally cancel the disability insurance as your retirement account builds. Below is a comparison of rates between typical level premium disability and renewable term disability insurance.

Notice that for the first 15 years the policies are in effect, the annual premium for the renewable term is less than for the level premium. And after 25 years, the total premiums paid for the renewable term are still less than for the level premium. Of course, you'll never see that money again when you cancel the renewable term policy, but at least you will have had the same amount of protection for the same length of time for less money.

Monthly Benefit: $2,500 *Initial Age: 30 years old* Age	*Elimination Period: 90 days* *30-Year Period* *Level Premiums*		*5-Year* *Renewable* *Premiums*	
	1 YEAR	5 YEARS	1 YEAR	5 YEARS
30–34	$785	$ 3,925	$ 396	$1,980
35–39	785	3,925	464	2,320
40–44	785	3,925	620	3,100
45–49	785	3,925	880	4,400
50–54	785	3,925	1,199	5,995
Total		$19,625		$17,795

DEFENSE #85

Substitute the income of your spouse for a disability income insurance policy.

All decisions about buying disability insurance should be based on your understanding of the statistically small chance that you'll ever collect more than the premiums you pay. Being a two-income family is the best disability protection you can possibly have. If both you and your spouse have good jobs, and one were to become disabled, the other's income would keep the family going. It is true that one income would not provide the same lifestyle as both incomes, but paying disability insurance premiums is guaranteed to eat into your lifestyle for almost your entire lifetime whether you collect or not.

The income of even a lesser-paid spouse, if at least 60 to 70 percent of the income of the higher-paid spouse, is an acceptable substitute for the high cost of disability insurance. If your spouse doesn't work but currently has the skills or ability to work if necessary, you have the same second-income protection.

As you can see, disability insurance is not very high on my list of recommendations. Far better, in my opinion, is to design a disability income without disability insurance.

What are the true chances of becoming permanently disabled? No one seems to know or has ever been able to gather the facts. So far, all that is known is that some disability insurance advertisements are at best deceptive.

Part of the problem lies within the definition of disability. To collect on a disability policy you must prove permanent disability, which means any disability that prevents you from working longer than the elimination or waiting period on a disability policy. In no case does the term "permanent disability" mean that you have to be disabled for the rest of your life. No less than 90 percent of those declared permanently disabled during their working years are back to work within five years.

Permanent disability is often defined as a disability that prevents you from performing the main duties of your job. Many policies after two years will stop paying if you can work at any job. Almost all who qualify as disabled can work at something.

Maybe one of the best methods of determining the real chances of collecting on a long-term disability policy is to look around you. Worker's compensation pays those who are disabled while at work, so we'll eliminate that now. Ask yourself how many people under age 60 out of the hundreds you know have been so disabled for over five years from a non-job-related illness or accident that they could not work any job? I don't know any, and out of all the times I have asked the question in my seminars, zero is the most common answer, with most others replying just one.

In reality, the chances of fitting the real definition of total, permanent disability are so remote, and the chances of collecting any significant amount of money small enough, that for most people disability insurance premiums would be far better used if invested in a financial plan that would provide income in the unlikely event that you do become disabled. In the more likely event that you do not, you will still have the investments and will not have wasted thousands of dollars for insurance you will never collect.

CHAPTER 11

Making Sense Out of Nursing Home Insurance

Although nursing home or long-term care insurance is not likely to become a fully paid-for Medicare benefit any time soon, that doesn't mean you will profit by running out and buying a nursing home policy now. The long-term care insurance business will soon be another multibillion-dollar insurance company cash machine, mostly because of the misunderstanding by policyholders of what the insurance covers and the real chances of collecting. Twenty major corporations have now made long-term care part of their optional benefits package, but even under a group plan, the premium for two people can run from $1,000 to $3,000 a year long before there is any real chance of being in a nursing home. Individual policies cost even more. Once again, you're paying far more than you're likely to collect.

Long-term care or nursing home coverage is another form of insurance bought out of unrealistic fears. Almost every person imagines himself or his parents ending up in a nursing home and the cost breaking the family financially. The word "burden" has become the sales pitch of the long-term care industry. You don't want to be a "burden" to your spouse or kids, do you? Of course, the answer is always no, but that does not mean that long-term care is the solution.

You are told by the salesperson that those who do buy long-term care coverage will *never* have a chance of becoming a burden on their families, financially or personally. That statement is totally untrue. Long-term care is really not long term at all. It typically covers a nursing home stay of only three to five years. Sometimes the maximum benefit is stated in terms of total dollars rather than years, but the effect is the same. Moreover, long-term care coverage can be difficult to get if there are any health problems. Since companies want to insure only the best risks, the rejection rate of applications is up to 30 percent.

Don't forget that if you need nursing home care you are not left out in the cold even without private insurance. Medicare pays for 100 percent of the first 20 days in a nursing home, the period of greatest risk, and all but $87.00 a day for the next 80 days, for a total payment period of 100 days. For those whose income and assets are below the state Medicaid limits, all types of long-term care are already covered by Medicaid.

There is no question that long-term care for the elderly is expensive. Even custodial care for those not sick enough to be hospitalized but who need help just getting through the day can cost $1,500 a month. There are two major problems that currently make nursing home or long-term care insurance a lousy investment. First, the coverage now available from over 100 companies does not cover what people fear the most: someone ending up in a nursing home for 10, 20 or even 30 years. Many current policies limit the coverage to 3 to 5 years, and pay for nursing home stays for medical reasons only, not because a senior adult might need a supervised place to live. Second, because of inexperience with this new kind of coverage, insurance companies have priced long-term care coverage so that it contains a huge margin for error—in their favor. If there are potentially more claims than expected, the insurance company will not lose.

As with any kind of insurance, it is important to know your chances of collecting. The risk that any one person will enter a nursing home or require long-term care during his or her lifetime for even one week is only 40 percent, or 4 out of 10. So, 6 out of 10 people who buy long-term care coverage will never collect anything. The chance of using long-term care coverage increases, of course, as the insured gets older, but you will be shocked to learn how little chance there is of someone being in a nursing home under the age of 85. Under age 65, the chances of ending up in a nursing home for even a day are about 1 in 500. Between ages 65 and 74, the chances of ending up in a nursing home for 30 days or more are only 1 in 1,300. Between ages 75 and 84, when you would logically think the need for long-term care would be the greatest, only 6 in 100 people end up with nursing home or long-term care expenses. At age 85 and older, for the few who get that far, there is still only a 25 percent chance that any one person will use nursing home facilities.

The insurance companies have these facts; you don't, or didn't. So you can see that with the current expense of nursing home coverage it is not a good deal. Even if you or a loved one goes into a nursing home at age 70, the coverage doesn't last a lifetime. Although huge premiums are paid, the coverage, remember, only lasts for 3 to 5 years, depending on the policy. If the insured were to need medical care in a nursing home at age 70 but needed care to age 85, the insurance coverage would still only last until age 73 or 75. In truth, what value is it?

If you look at nursing home insurance mathematically, the axiom might be, "If you can afford it, don't buy it because you don't need it, and if you do need it, you can't buy it because you can't afford it." If you still feel that nursing home or long-term care insurance is something you want for yourself, your spouse or your parents because of emotional rather than financial reasons, let me give you the strategies for buying the best for the least, cutting the total amount you'll spend by 50 percent.

DEFENSE #86

Don't buy nursing home insurance until after age 65.

The chances of being in a nursing home before age 65 are so small—remember, 1 in 500—that spending money on premiums before age 65 is an absolute waste. Of course, the insurance costs more at age 65 than it does at age 45 or 55, but your money is not magically going into some savings policy. You are only insuring the year following the date you make your premium payment. Look at the chart at the end of this chapter, Comparing Nursing Home Insurance Costs and Coverage, and you'll see that premiums run from about $500 to $2,000 per year from age 60 to 70. By waiting until after age 65 or even age 70 to buy a long-term care policy, you are using your money most effectively. Once you've purchased the policy, it cannot be canceled except for nonpayment of premiums.

DEFENSE #87

Buy a policy that covers expenses at home after a nursing home stay.

Some policies include coverage for home care; others require you to buy a rider. Home care coverage furnishes money to pay a home care worker to come in and feed or bathe a patient who is convalescing at home. Most quality plans now cover adult day care, although some do not. There is a tremendous variation in how insurance companies pay for home care. Some policies require that you spend 30 days in a nursing home for each 30 days of home care that will be paid for by the insurance company. This requirement is in AIG Life's Nursing Home plan and Aetna's long-term care Plan B. Sentry Life pays $25 a day for home care to the maximum of the policy but will pay for up to 12 years. Travelers, on the other hand, pays 80 percent of the actual at-home cost for up to 5 years and requires no previous nursing home stay. Although home care, on the average, costs only 50 percent of what nursing home care costs, the coverage under this section can be as important as the basic nursing home coverage.

DEFENSE #88

Buy a policy with no more than $80-a-day coverage.

All nursing home policies pay a specific amount per day for a specific number of years, while the insured is in what is referred to in the policy as a "covered nursing facility." As with any kind of insurance, it is all right to be self-insured for part of the potential cost yourself, which will dramatically cut the premiums. Coverage is available for as much as $150 a day from many companies, but the premium cost per year goes up proportionately. The average cost in a nursing home today is about $80 per day, although more expensive facilities certainly do exist. The winning strategy for buying nursing home or any other kind of insurance is to protect the biggest portion of the risk and become self-insured for the rest. The $80-a-day coverage gives you a balance between premiums and coverage and can save you up to 40 percent.

DEFENSE #89

Buy a policy with inflation protection.

Because of inflation, in about 12 years the money you collect from a nursing home policy could be worth only one-half as much as it is today. Nursing home care costs will have at least doubled. Many policies do offer an optional inflation protection, which certainly adds to the cost of the policy. A 5 percent per year inflation increase is adequate. Pick a policy with which you can buy automatic inflation protection so you do not have to remember every three years or so to upgrade your daily coverage amount. From the chart at the end of this chapter, notice that all companies listed, except Sentry Life and John Hancock, have inflation protection as an option.

DEFENSE #90

Choose a plan with at least a 30-day elimination period.

Part of your premium is determined by the elimination period or time deductible you choose for your policy. You can buy nursing home insurance with elimination periods ranging from 0 to 365 days. Most policies offer an elimination period of 30 or 100 days, and you can save about 30% per year in premiums just by picking a policy with a higher deductible. If you have a choice, remember the longer the elimination period, the lower the premiums. Since a maximum of only 1 in 4 will ever collect on nursing home insurance, it certainly makes sense to increase the waiting period to the point where the premiums are the lowest, but where the most expensive part of the risk (the possibility of care for three to five years) is covered.

DEFENSE #91

Buy a long-term care policy with 3-year instead of 5-year coverage.

Eighty percent of nursing home stays are less than 3 years. The average stay is about 20 months for those over age 75, and even though 1 in 10 will stay in the nursing home 6 years or longer, the most important part of the coverage is the first 3 years. The longer the coverage period, of course, the greater the premium you will pay each year. From the chart below, Comparing Nursing Home Insurance Costs and Coverage, notice that New York Life's Nursing Home Plan, which has a 5-year benefit period, is an average of $400 more per year at age 60 than those policies that offer a 3-year benefit period. To get the most important coverage at the best price, buy a long-term policy with 3-year coverage.

COMPARING NURSING HOME INSURANCE COSTS AND COVERAGE

All companies listed below are rated A or above by A. M. Best. Daily benefits average $80 per day. The policies shown are a sampling from the 100 or so policies available and not necessarily a recommendation.

COMPANY	PLAN NAME	APPROXIMATE ANNUAL PREMIUM Beginning Age 60	Beginning Age 70	INFLATION PROTECTION OPTION	BENEFIT PERIOD (YEARS)	WAITING PERIOD (DAYS)
Aetna	Plan B	$500	$1750	5% per year	4	20
AIG Life	Nursing Home	$500	$1450	7% per year	3	20
CNA	Convalescent Care	$500	$1200	5% per year	3	30
John Hancock	Protect Care	$650	$1800	N / A	3	20
New York Life	Group LTC	$900	$2100	5% per year	5	20
Sentry Life	Nursing Home	$600	$1600	N / A	4	90
Travelers	Independent Care	$550	$1750	Increase tied to consumer price index	3	20

PART IV

Winning with Other People's Money

CHAPTER 12

Beating the Bank

The banking industry includes banks, savings and loans, credit unions and all other institutions that offer checking and savings accounts and loans. Banking is a highly regulated industry, governed by the FDIC and FSLIC, but that doesn't seem to have affected the lousy decisions and investments made in the eighties by owners and executives that almost caused the entire system to collapse. Although you may have had trouble getting a business or car loan at your local bank even after having been examined under a microscope, the same banks seem to have had no problem in putting depositors' money in high-risk investments and loans that went belly up. At no time since the Great Depression have so many screwed up so badly as they did during the eighties in the banking industry.

Once your bank or savings and loan was a friendly, neighborhood place run by local people, and although it never wanted to pay you much interest on your savings account or on CDs, at least you felt secure knowing your money was safe in the hands of honest, conservative folks. Today America has become known as the place where your checks clear but the banks bounce!

Your local bank or savings and loan has probably been taken over by a bigger bank or savings and loan, maybe even one from out of state, and is now run by people who may never have been to your neighborhood, let alone the branch where you have always done business. Banking institutions now look only at the bottom line. If, in order to make a bigger profit, your bank is forced to give you some kind of extra service, then the willingness is there. Put quite simply, banks use your money to make more money, which goes into their pockets, not yours. And for that privilege, even the smallest deposits should be treated with fairness and consideration.

The banking business has changed, and to succeed with your money you've got to change your banking habits. You must develop strategies that will allow you to beat the bank instead of the bank beating you. In this chapter we'll go over those strategies, and you'll learn how to handle all the new bank schemes like bad check fees, nonrecorded deposits, oversecured loans and automatic rollovers for CDs.

DEFENSE #92

Place your checking account in a bank that won't hold your deposit checks.

For many years now, banks have been glad to allow you to make a deposit, but often they won't show the money credited to your account for several days. Your bank's excuse is that with so many deadbeats around, the chances of somebody having written you a bad check are high enough that, until the bank actually receives the money, you don't get credit in your account. The truth is that your bank, S&L or credit union actually receives the money for the check that you deposited from the Federal Reserve Bank within approximately 24 hours. It doesn't matter whether the check was local or from out of the area. It seems that the Federal Reserve trusts you more than your local bank does.

Of course, you're just being had. Your bank is using your money absolutely free! Prior to a new law enacted in September 1988, banks were in the habit of holding noncredited deposits for up to three weeks. In other words, somebody wrote you a check that was considered "legal tender," you deposited the money in the bank, funds that your bank could get immediately, but you couldn't use the money. Holding deposits allowed financial institutions to get free use of billions of dollars. Federal law now limits the bank holding period to three days for local checks, five days for out-of-town checks, and seven days for out-of-state checks. Of course, the bank still gets its money within 24 hours, but at least the greed has been limited by law.

Most banks won't make any exceptions to those legal limits. Even if the bank has held your deposit for a couple of days and collected the money, should you write a check against the so-called uncollected funds, the bank will bounce your check and charge you up to $25 "nonsufficient funds" fee. How's that for a great financial strategy? The bank not only has your money, but it's also collecting up to $25 from you! If the check you deposited was for $100, the bank is getting up to 25 percent one-day interest return.

There's no federal law that says the bank has to hold any of your checks, whether local or out-of-state. If you become a good customer of the bank, maybe even have your car loan or mortgage with the bank, introduce yourself to the branch manager and get an agreement that none of your funds will be held. Not ever, not for any reason. You might think that if you have an overdraft, the bank would simple transfer the money from your savings account to your checking account. Not so; you could have a million dollars in savings and overdraw your checking account by $10, and no transfer from savings to checking would be made. According to banking law, you must give permission to your bank in writing to withdraw money from your savings account.

Illogical? Yes. Hard to handle? No. Simply get to know your banker personally and make the necessary agreements.

I first ran into this little-known "we can't touch your savings account" rule during a trip abroad in 1973. I'd made a lot of money in real estate in North Carolina and decided to retire for a while. Bonnie and I took our kids, Chuck and Rob, who were then eight and six, to Europe. We were like gypsies going from country to country just to experience the sights, sounds and tastes. But because of the incredible inflation rate in Europe during that period, I was spending twice as much money as I anticipated. One of my goals was to stop at every major gambling casino on the continent and apply my newly practiced skills of card counting to the game of blackjack.

Today, I'm not a gambler. I like winning too much, and even in those days I only gambled small amounts, enjoying the thrill of victory, often walking away from the tables with an extra $100 or $200 to pay for the next couple of days' hotel and food expenses. By the time we got to Monte Carlo, not only was I low on money, but because of my winning streak, from the Boule tables of Amsterdam to the blackjack tables of the magnificent casino in Baden-Baden, I was starting to get a little cocky.

We had left our kids at the hotel in Nice with a baby-sitter, and I parked myself at the blackjack table in Monte Carlo with Bonnie looking over my shoulder. One thing about European casinos is that they are boring. Croupiers don't smile, all the gold glitters, but there's no circuslike environment as there is in Las Vegas or Atlantic City. After about an hour I was still breaking even, but then I heard yelling and screaming from the craps table. Now I know better than to get involved in something I know just enough about to be dangerous, but for 30 minutes the same man had been on an incredible winning streak. Well, I thought, this is simple. I'll just back his bets. When he wins, I win, and he hasn't lost yet. My money followed his, and I managed to win on his first two rolls of the dice. After that it was straight downhill. He rolled seven losers in a row, and my bankroll dropped to $50. Bonnie had another $50. So here we were, the whole family in Europe, a $400 hotel bill due the following Friday, no credit cards, no traveler's checks and only $100 left in cash. "Not to worry," I said. "Let's get out of here and have some fun." So we took what money was left, went to the magnificent Sky Roof restaurant in the hotel next to the casino and enjoyed a sumptuous meal with seven waiters and wine stewards in attendance. We felt like royalty, even though after the meal we were royally broke, having about $20 to finish the week.

Our budget plane trip home originated in Luxembourg on Icelandic Air, and here we were hundreds of miles away on the Riviera. Fortunately we had a tank of gas. But I knew that once the hotel found out that I was without sufficient funds to pay the bill, the smiles would turn to a quick call to the gendarmes, and it was going to be tough to get through the border owing money. So, like all good travelers, the next morning I quickly made my way down to the American Express office and wired my banker, Jim Robertson, at NCNB in Banner Elk, North Carolina. The wire was simple: "Help, send money from my savings account."

In those days I didn't have an American Express or any credit card, so Jim was my last hope. A smirking clerk looked up at me and snapped, "Don't you know that your bank cannot take money out of your savings account without your signature? Tell them to take it out of your checking account."

"My checking account is out of money," I replied.

"You're out of luck," she giggled, trying to hand me back the unsent wire.

"Send it," I said. "He'll figure it out, if he ever wants me to make another car payment."

Twice a day, for the next two days, I showed up at the American Express office looking for my North Carolina windfall. "Nope," the American Express clerk kept saying with an "I told you so" smile. At 10:00 A.M. on Friday the situation was desperate. We were told by the hotel that we must check out by noon that day, since the room was rented to someone else. Checking out means paying your bill, and the money still hadn't been sent. Every half hour I ran to the American Express office, and finally at 11:30 A.M., 30 minutes before truth-telling time, lo and behold, the money arrived. When I got back to Banner Elk a few weeks later, I told Jim the true story, and he told me that legally even a bank can't withdraw money from a savings account, but he had, at his own personal risk, advanced me the money on an unsecured loan. What a banker!

There have been many times in my life when a banker I knew personally has come to my rescue, even acting contrary to regular banking policies or procedures, because we had established a personal relationship. That's why it's so important for you to turn an impersonal banking relationship into a personal friendship. If your bank won't give you special benefits, like placing a note on your account that it won't hold your checks, or notifying you if you overdraw your account before they charge up to $25, then you either haven't made a friend at the bank or you're working with the wrong bank. If so, change banks and let your friends know which is the better bank.

DEFENSE #93

Open a bank account with automatic overdraft privileges.

All too many people assume that if there are still checks in the checkbook, there must be money in the bank. Let's say you've written a check to a local merchant who sends it on to the bank. The bank stamps NSF (nonsufficient funds) on your check, sends it back to the merchant and charges your account up to $25 for the trouble. Then comes the snowball effect. The merchant redeposits your check, hoping that the funds will be there this time. If not, the bank once again returns your check and charges your account another bad check fee of up to $25 and stamps your check "endorsement canceled" so that it cannot be deposited a third time. The merchant is now furious with you, calls you everything but deadbeat and makes you bring in cash to cover the bad check, plus charges you another $15. Unfortunately this process occurs not because you or others are trying to bilk the bank, but because you made a simple, unintentional error in reconciling your account balance, or because the bank held one or more of your deposits. If you run your checking account close to the wire, that extra bad check charge can now start the chain reaction of bouncing other checks, even if they were written for only $5 or $10 each. It is not unusual for this process to cost a depositor $100 to $200 before the runaway train is stopped.

"Well," some may say, "so what? The bank should be compensated for all of the trouble it must go through to process an NSF check." This will shock you. It costs the bank about $.79 to process an NSF check. Bad check charges have become one of the biggest profit centers in the banking business. Next time your bank is abusive and belligerent and attempts to intimidate you into feeling guilty for an accidental overdraft, remember how much it is actually making. Most banks today will even bounce the check if your account is only $.10 or $.20 short. In other words, if you write a check for $98 and you have $97.80 in your account, the noncaring, nonfeeling computer automatically sends the check back and charges your account the NSF fee.

Deal with a bank or banker that won't brand you a loser simply because you made an error in your account. Get the bank's policies on nonsufficient checks in writing so you know what to expect. Arrange to have any overdraft charged to your savings account, your MasterCard or Visa card or to a small line of credit that the bank has set up for you. Most important, get to know your banker. He or she has the right to be notified by the bank's accounting department if your account is overdrawn. Once the banker is your friend, you may get a call and a few hours' "grace time" to make an additional deposit. That's the kind of banking relationship you want to establish.

You'll be surprised sometimes how much a friend at the bank can help you. When I was working for Genesco in Nashville in the 1960s, we had a branch of the First National Bank right in the Genesco world headquarters building, not 200 feet away from my desk. Because I was a typical lousy money manager and was constantly outspending my next paycheck, NSF checks were the terror of my bank account. Whenever I was in the bank, Effie, the assistant manager, and I would talk for a few minutes. Considering herself a friend, she began to collect my NSF checks as they came in, sticking them in a bottom drawer and often holding them until my next paycheck was deposited a few days later. After about a year of what seemed to me to be good, friendly banking practices, I got in the habit of writing checks and dealing with funds later. One morning Effie didn't show up at work and Sam, the manager, while looking for some papers in Effie's desk, ran across not one but 27 of my NSF checks all in a neat pile. It was still three days to payday when I got a call from Sam, who said, "Chuck, you've got 30 minutes to cover these checks, or they all go back." Being in my typical paycheck-to-paycheck rut, and working with others who could barely raise money for lunch, let alone loan me the money to cover my checks, I was out of luck. Twenty-seven NSF checks and the corresponding late charges gave me the eye-opening cure I needed. I stopped writing checks until my deposits had cleared, no matter how badly I needed the money. And Effie ended up with more storage space in her desk.

ATTACK #94

Get to know a loan officer at your bank and find out his or her lending limit.

Cultivating friends in the financial world is one of the best assurances of getting your way more of the time, particularly when you are looking for a loan. You will have an easier time at a newer, smaller bank that is looking for business or at a small neighborhood branch of a larger bank. But wherever you do your banking, get to know the loan officer and make certain he or she knows you. I can promise you that during my early years I got a dozen loans that would never have been made otherwise simply because I had cultivated a friendship before I asked for the loan.

When you are actually applying for a loan, always ask the loan officer personal questions. Get people to talk about themselves, and you've made friends for life. Here are some questions I have always used successfully:

"How long have you been with this bank?"

"What got you interested in banking?"

"What are your goals in the financial world?"
"How many kids do you have?"
"Where do you borrow money when you need it?"
"Do you ever have good deals on bank repo cars?"

Find out the loan officer's hobby or interests, and always be prepared to discuss them.

All loan officers have a lending limit, which is the amount they can approve for a loan without going to the bank's board of directors. The lending limit can range from $5,000 to $50,000 depending on the size of the bank and the title or stature of the loan officer. In small branches, the loan officer will often be a vice president. Although that designation is more a title than an accurate job description, a VP will have the highest lending limit of all the loan officers and is the best person with whom to cultivate a friendship. Automobile loans, except for luxury or exotic cars, always fall within the loan officer's lending limit. Ask the loan officer what his or her lending limit is, and more often than not he or she will tell you. By asking for personal or business loans within the loan officer's lending limit, you have a far greater chance for approval. The more a loan officer sees you and knows about you, the more automatic trust he or she will have at loan time.

ATTACK #95

Invest your money in money market funds, never in money market accounts.

These days there are so many new investments and savings accounts that it's difficult to tell the difference. Two similarly named investment accounts that are very different are money market accounts in banks and money market mutual funds offered by mutual funds families and brokerage firms. Since the early eighties, billions of dollars were taken out of bank CDs and savings accounts by investors and moved in to money market mutual funds. Bankers roared in protest and tried to come up with ways to combat the cash drain. Someone came up with the great idea of renaming a form of the old bank savings account and calling it a "money market account." So what's the difference? In 1988 and 1989 the difference was about 3 percent on your money. Money market mutual funds paid an average of 9 percent, while money market accounts at banks paid an average of only 6 percent. Since those early years the difference in returns has decreased to one percent or less in 1993 and 1994. Bankers thought that if they used the term *money market account* investors and savers would be duped into leaving their money in banks, and it worked! Today there are billions in money market bank accounts that could be earning more in money market mutual fund accounts.

The name *money market* comes from the types of investments that a real money market mutual fund makes. These investments include jumbo bank certificates of deposit, U.S. Treasury bills, repurchase agreements that finance transactions of the major brokerage houses and bank acceptances, which finance imports and exports. All of these money market fund investments are extremely safe, and they earn higher-than-average short-term interest rates. In a money market fund, the daily interest is divided proportionately between all shareholders and distributed as dividends. The money market fund keeps about one-half of 1 percent as a management fee. The interest money market mutual funds pay to investors fluctuates with overall market conditions and has been as high as 17 percent in 1981 and as low as 3 percent in 1993 and 1994. On the other hand, the money in bank money market accounts is not invested in the money market but becomes part of the regular loan portfolio of the bank and is used for automobile, personal and commercial loans. There are some similarities between the two types of accounts, but the interest rates are not one of them.

ATTACK #96

Keep the minimum required balance in your checking account and the rest of your cash in a money market mutual fund.

Don't keep any more money in your checking account than what you need for immediate personal expenses. Banks pay interest on some checking accounts these days, but only if you maintain a minimum balance in the account, money that could be earning higher interest elsewhere. To encourage you to maintain a minimum balance, banks will generously forgive per-check service charges that have become nothing short of highway robbery. In essence, a less than minimum balance in your account is money your bank is using that you will be charged for, and on which the bank is still earning interest. How's that for service?

Banks will tell you that the great advantage of their checking, savings and money market accounts is their liquidity. You have instant access to your money. It's true, and you pay for that convenience. But how much money do you need instant access to? Keep your bill-paying money or the minimum balance required to avoid service charges and no more in your checking account, if only to stay on friendly terms with your banker and to be able to use your bank's ATM (automatic teller machine). Any spare cash should be invested in a money market mutual fund, which also provides instant liquidity and pays more interest. If you have a large or unexpected expense, you can transfer the money immediately to your bank checking account or write a check on your mutual fund account. Keeping more money than necessary in a checking account is not a sound financial strategy. Investing in a money market mutual fund is.

DEFENSE #97

Open a money market mutual fund as a high-interest business account.

One of the biggest rip-offs in the banking business is that banks do not pay interest on business checking accounts, even though all deposits increase the bank's loan capabilities. If you are in a business or profession that accumulates money for quarterly tax payments or accounts payable, or your business is just plain highly profitable and you need a temporary place to store money, a money market fund is the answer, not a bank account.

You can make deposits of any amount, every day if you wish, into your money market mutual fund and earn the high interest rate on the balance with interest normally credited to your account on a daily basis. When you need part or all of the funds, you can simply write a check on your money market mutual fund account for deposit in your bank business checking account. If you are dealing with a money market fund that is out of your area, you may be concerned about the lost interest for the day or two it takes your deposit to reach the fund. The lag time is made up by the time it takes a check written on your money market fund account to be deducted from your fund account. Should you be dealing with large sums of money, deposits can be made by wire transfer to decrease the lag time. Another alternative is to deal with a mutual fund family like Fidelity or a brokerage firm like Charles Schwab that has local offices and can get funds immediately deposited and earning interest. This one extra step could earn you hundreds or even thousands of dollars of extra interest every year.

DEFENSE #98

Never fall into the bank-provided automobile insurance trap.

When you get an automobile or boat loan from your bank or any other financial institution, your contract states that you must carry insurance on that automobile (or boat) at all times. If your insurance should lapse, even for a day, that innocent-looking clause also says that the bank will automatically provide insurance. If for any reason that clause goes into effect, it will be one of the most painful financial lessons you'll ever learn. Your bank has purchased a blanket auto policy from an insurance company and can instantly write auto insurance on you or any borrower at astronomical rates and with equally huge commissions.

Your bank attaches auto insurance to your loan any time and every time your insurance company sends your bank a notice that your coverage has lapsed. Your insurance company is required by law to notify your bank because the bank is listed as an additional "loss payee" on your auto policy.

What triggers the notification? Anything that causes your policy to lapse, like changing insurance companies and having even one or two days between the time one policy was canceled and the other went into effect. If you are late with a payment after the grace period on your policy, even though your insurance company immediately reinstates you when your premium is received, you just bought bank-issued auto insurance. The insurance is also slapped on your loan if you decide to garage your car for a period of time and feel you don't need any insurance.

The monthly premiums through your bank are on the average six times what you are paying per month on a regular auto insurance policy. That means for 30 days of auto insurance through your bank, you will pay premiums equal to six months of regular auto insurance.

The bank is not required to notify you that the insurance is in force. To make matters worse, the bank will advance the money for the insurance, tack on the amount to the principal of your car loan and charge you interest on the insurance amount every month until your loan is paid off, not at your auto loan interest rate, but usually at 18 percent per year! Read your automobile loan contract. You can end up paying $400 for auto insurance the bank provided for just one day to one month. This auto insurance does not protect you, only your bank or finance company, and is called a single interest policy. The only thing covered is any loss the bank might suffer due to damage to your car.

Often you won't discover what is happening until you think you have paid your last car payment and the bank tells you in a late notice that it has added one or two extra payments to your loan, or if you ask for a payoff on your loan and find that the balance the bank shows is greater than the one shown in your records. Thousands of borrowers trade in their cars, letting auto dealers and the bank work out the details, and they never see the few hundred extra dollars charged for temporary insurance, which is then added to the amount financed for the new car on which another three to five years of interest is charged. Unbelievable? It is now standard business practice for banks and other lending institutions. Ask any loan officer.

Opposite is a copy of an actual bank insurance policy written when the insured changed auto insurance companies and was not insured for a total of three days. The $1,260 policy was written for one year and added to the loan, plus interest of $1,039.50, for a total of $2,299.50. The car owner was never contacted and only discovered something was wrong two years later when trying to sell the car and pay it off. It took over two months of correspondence even to ascertain what the extra charges were for. The charges were finally reduced to $221.39 for the actual three days of insurance. This transaction was created not by some off-the-wall finance company, but by one of the three biggest banks in the state of Florida.

FROM:

REFERENCE NUMBER	COLLATERAL
18420-0001	87CHEV 4721

ACCOUNT NUMBER: 709933280186

NOTICE DATE: DUPLICATE COPY

POLICY PERIOD	POLICY NUMBER
01/13/87 to 01/13/88	VE769A

PREMIUM	INTEREST	TOTAL CHARGED
$ 1260.00	$ 1039.50	$ 2299.50

RIB-3 (Rev 3/87)

Dear Customer:
As of this date we have not received evidence that the collateral on your loan is properly insured. **The insurance we applied for has been purchased. The premium has been added to your loan plus interest as shown, or if no rate is shown, at the rate of your contract.** You may pay this premium now to avoid the interest charge. If you provide us with evidence of insurance for the period above, this policy will be cancelled at no cost to you. If you purchase your own insurance this coverage will be cancelled but you will be charged for the time it was in force. If you or your agent have any questions, **please call us at the telephone number shown above.** The items checked indicate the condition that applies to your loan:

- [XX] We need a copy of the insurance policy on your loan opened on
- [XX] Your policy with was cancelled on
- [XX] Your policy with expired
- [XX] An audit of your loan indicates we do not have evidence of insurance covering your collateral.
- [ ] The policy received does not list us as a lienholder.
- [ ] The policy received does not provide collision insurance.
- [ ] The policy received does not list the collateral shown above.
- [ ] The insurance we purchased for your loan last year has expired.

THIS SINGLE INTEREST POLICY DOES NOT COVER OR INSURE ANY INTEREST OF YOURS.

Sincerely, Insurance Department

TO:

REQUIRED

1. **Policy lists us as lienholder or mortgagee, at the above address.**
2. **Vehicles require Comprehensive & Collision Insurance.**
3. **Mobile Homes & Dwellings require Fire & Extended Coverage.**
4. **Boats, Equipment, etc. require Physical Damage Insurance.**

The bottom line: Make sure your own insurance is paid up and in effect at all times.

ATTACK #99

Expect to be turned down when borrowing money, but never be denied.

Borrowing money and rejection seem to go hand in hand. When getting a car loan, a mortgage on that dream home or a loan to start a business, expect to be turned down every now and then. A lender scores your credit profile by a point system particular to that institution, and a rejection from one potential lender may mean an approval from another that uses different criteria. Sometimes even borrowers with good credit get turned down.

Let me share with you one of my experiences. After I owned 60 rental properties, I was buying a new home for myself. No problem, I thought, I do this every day. Thirty days later I got a rejection notice. Upon checking, I found that my success at real estate had created the problem. This particular mortgage company's rules required that every mortgage of mine be checked to determine if payments were current. However, a federal law says that the mortgage company has only 30 days to accept or reject an application. Because the mortgage company could not get responses from 60 other mortgage companies within the required 30 days, it automatically rejected my application at the end of the period. Once I discovered what was happening, I applied to another mortgage company and showed all the properties as part of partnerships but using the same financial figures. The mortgage company didn't require the checking of partnership properties, and the loan sailed through.

No matter what kind of loan you are after, there are always alternatives. If you are turned down for a home mortgage, apply with another mortgage lender. All have slightly different approval conditions, and their rules become less stringent the more money they have to lend. If you still have trouble, apply for a mortgage through a mortgage broker or assume a nonqualifying mortgage. (See Chapter 15.)

If you are turned down for a credit card, that doesn't mean you can't get one. MasterCard and Visa are franchises granted to different banks, and there are over 100 franchises in existence. The first four digits on a MasterCard or Visa represent the franchise number. If one franchisee turns you down, simply apply to another. Use the "best credit cards" list in Chapter 14, "High-Powered Credit Card Strategies."

Most people feel intimidated by the process of applying for a loan, as if they are asking for something they don't deserve. You may sometimes feel, I really need this money, but the bank doesn't need me. Wrong. The bank *does* need you. Banks are in business to make loans, large and small. That's where the profits come from. When you're applying for a loan, don't look at yourself as a beggar, but as a good investment opportunity for the bank. If one bank doesn't happen to agree, find another one that does. Make borrowing money a game that you intend to win. Say to yourself, "I will not be denied."

DEFENSE #100

Determine the true interest rate before signing a loan agreement.

One of the biggest deceptions for 50 years in the banking and loan business has been the misquoting of interest rates. Banks and other lenders have developed slick formulas that allow them to legally quote a low or reasonable interest rate on an automobile, personal or business loan, then hit you with an actual interest rate of 50 to 100 percent higher.

Because interest rate manipulation became so commonplace, the federal government stepped in more than 15 years ago to require that a financing statement be provided to all borrowers showing the interest rate stated as an APR, annual percentage rate. The APR formula converts the interest rate quoted to a true effective rate, as well as adding in all hidden interest, like points and finance charges. The problem, as always, is that the law neglected to require that a borrower be told what the APR means or how it compares with any other interest rate quoted. Most people never read or understand the financing statement.

There are six basic types of interest rates and methods of charging interest, and an understanding of each will give you the ability to compare the true cost of different loans, as well as the ability to save thousands in unnecessary interest over your lifetime. These six interest rate calculation methods are simple interest, effective interest, compound or nominal interest, add-on interest, discounted interest and APR (annual percentage rate).

Simple Interest Rate

Simple interest is the easiest rate to calculate and understand, and maybe that's why you will never see it used on any of your loans except money you borrow from or lend to a friend or relative. Simple interest means multiplying the amount of the loan by the interest rate and having the interest paid at the end of each year in a lump sum.

For example, you borrow $1,000 at 12 percent interest for one year. At the end of the year you pay back the $1,000 principal and $120 interest for a total of $1,120. You had 100 percent of the principal for the entire year and did not prepay any of the interest.

Nothing complicated here, but, of course, loans don't work that way anymore.

Effective Interest Rate

When you convert compounded, discounted or add-on interest rates for a loan to their simple interest rate equivalent, you have determined the effective rate. Any type of interest rate can be converted into an effective rate. You determine the effective rate by totaling the amount of interest that would be paid during the year or term of the loan and solve for what simple interest rate would produce the same amount of interest.

For instance, a loan with 15 percent interest compounded monthly will cost more than a 15 percent simple interest rate loan. What is the true effective rate when the 15 percent is compounded monthly? A $1,000 loan at a 15 percent simple interest rate means that $150 interest would be paid at the end of one year, but if the interest is compounded monthly the amount of interest owing at the end of the year would be $160.75. The effective rate of the loan, therefore, would be 16.07 percent. You can use any financial calculator to determine the effective interest rate.

From now on your objective is to convert every rate you are quoted into its effective interest rate for the simple reason that it is the true rate you will have to pay.

Compounded Interest

Somewhere along in the development of the banking system, someone figured out that if interest is being earned on a loan all year long but is not paid until the end of the year, the lender is losing money. For example, if $1,000 is lent at 12 percent interest, the interest rate is the equivalent of 1 percent per month. After one month the borrower owes the lender $10 in interest, but the lender won't receive the money until the end of the year. Shouldn't that $10 become part of the principal of the loan at that point, and the borrower pay interest on the interest due for the rest of the year? If the answer is yes, the interest paid then becomes compounded interest, and the total interest paid by the borrower in real dollars will be more than would be produced by the simple interest rate. Here is how monthly compounded interest works using the terms in the example above.

$1,000 @ 12% COMPOUNDED MONTHLY

MONTH	A BALANCE AT BEGINNING OF MONTH	B MONTHLY INTEREST RATE	C INTEREST EARNED DURING MONTH	D BALANCE OWED AT END OF MONTH (A+C)
1	$1,000.00	×1%	=$10.00	$1,010.00
2	1,010.00	×1%	= 10.10	1,020.10
3	1,020.10	×1%	= 10.20	1,030.30
4	1,030.30	×1%	= 10.30	1,040.60
5	1,040.60	×1%	= 10.41	1,051.01
6	1,051.01	×1%	= 10.51	1,061.52
7	1,061.52	×1%	= 10.62	1,072.14
8	1,072.14	×1%	= 10.72	1,082.86
9	1,082.86	×1%	= 10.83	1,093.69
10	1,093.69	×1%	= 10.94	1,104.62
11	1,104.62	×1%	= 11.05	1,115.67
12	1,115.67	×1%	= 11.16	1,126.83

Note from the table above that although the interest rate remains the same, each month's interest is computed on a slightly larger amount, which includes the original loan amount of $1,000 plus the interest accrued or earned to that point. Any term for compounding can be chosen, including yearly, semiannually, monthly (as in our example), daily, hourly, every second or perpetually. With every reduction in the compounding period, the total amount of interest due increases, but by an even smaller and smaller percentage. Note in our example that by compounding monthly at 12 percent interest, the total amount of interest paid at the end of the year is $126.83, or $6.83 more than the simple interest of $120. The same dollar amount of interest, if converted to an effective rate, would amount to 12.68 percent ($126.83 ÷ $1,000). You may wonder if monthly compounding *always* adds .68 percent to the yearly interest rate. Yes, if the interest rate is 12 percent, but there is a different fixed percentage if the interest rate is higher or lower than 12 percent.

Look at the table below, Effective Interest Rate, and you will see the effective or simple interest rate equivalent for interest rates of 9 to 18 percent compounded monthly or daily.

EFFECTIVE INTEREST RATE (%)

NO COMPOUNDING	COMPOUNDING MONTHLY	DAILY
9	9.38	9.42
10	10.47	10.52
11	11.57	11.63
12	12.68	12.75
13	13.80	13.88
14	14.93	15.02
15	16.08	16.18
16	17.28	17.35
17	18.39	18.53
18	19.56	19.72

Notice the biggest increase occurs when a loan is compounded monthly instead of no compounding at all. This allows the bank or finance company to charge an additional ½ to 1½ percent interest while quoting you the lower interest rate. All credit card, mortgage, automobile, personal and business loans with monthly payments have monthly compounding, but the interest is paid at the end of the month.

Notice that if we compound daily, 30 more times per month, the increase is not significant. If the compounding is done every second or every 1/100 of a second, the interest rate increases only a few thousandths of a percent over the daily rates. Banks have long used the "compounding every second" advertising gimmick to attract deposits, when in reality the extra compounding would add only a few cents per year to the real return on a normal account.

Discounted Interest

One method used for years by banks to increase the actual interest rate above the quoted rate is the discounted interest method. The total amount of interest is deducted from the loan proceeds in advance. If, as in our example, you borrowed $1,000 at 12 percent but with discounted interest, you would receive only $880 from the loan. The bank would keep the other $120 as prepaid interest. Since you are actually only getting $880, the interest rate is 13.64 percent ($120 ÷ $880), not at all the 12 percent quoted. Compounded interest can also be deducted using the discounted interest method. In our example of 12 percent compounded monthly, the interest was $126.83, which would make the net proceeds of the loan $873.17 and the effective interest rate 14.53 percent ($126.83 ÷ $873.17).

Because the law requires that all interest, including discounted loan interest, be stated as an annual percentage rate (APR), this deceitful practice is not used as often as it once was, although it is still common with second and third mortgages and business loans.

Add-On Interest

One of the worst abuses committed by banks, car dealers and other sources of financing is the add-on interest method. This deceptive interest quotation is normally used with automobile, boat, personal and other amortized loans with equal monthly payments to make the interest rate sound far less than it really is. Using the add-on method, the interest is computed on the principal as if the borrower were going to have use of the borrowed money for the full year. On an amortized or equal monthly payment loan, however, the borrower is constantly paying back a portion of the principal until the loan is paid off. The first month is the only time the borrower has use of the entire amount of the loan proceeds. Each succeeding month the amount or balance actually owed is less.

Here is how the add-on interest scheme works on our $1,000, 12 percent loan. "The interest rate," says the salesperson, "is just 12 percent add-on." And he computes your payments over 12 months as follows:

$1,000 × 12% = $120 interest + $1,000 amount borrowed = $1,120 to be paid back over 12 months at $93.33 per month ($1,120 ÷ 12).

Sound reasonable and logical? When you discover the true interest rate, you'll find out what a rip-off this really is. With a payment of $93.33 for 12 months on a $1,000 loan and a total interest paid of $120, the actual interest rate is 21.45 percent! And if the monthly compounding method was used in calculating the add-on interest rate, the total interest paid will be $125.83, the monthly payment $93.90 and the actual interest rate 22.63 percent. Let me put it another way. The last month, the balance of your loan including principal and interest is only

$93.33, but you are paying interest as if you still owed the full $1,000 original principal.

Annual Percentage Rate (APR) Interest

Even though on the financing statement the true annual percentage rate (APR) and not the add-on rate is shown, almost no one reads or comprehends what it means.

The APR is the federal government's attempt to make all interest rate comparable, no matter which of the interest rates a lender quotes. On the financing statement the interest rate must be shown as an APR. All points and finance charges, but not all loan costs, must be added as interest in determining the APR. If credit life or disability insurance is required, it must also be treated as finance charges and added to the interest to determine the true annual percentage rate.

For example, you borrow $10,000 to buy a car. You are quoted a 12 percent interest rate, but the finance charges and loan origination fees are $435, which are added to the loan amount. What is your APR rate if the loan is to be paid up in two years and payments made monthly? To calculate, you first add the $435 to the $10,000 principal. You will actually be paying back $10,435 plus interest. Your payment will be $491.21 per month for a total payback of $11,789 including the interest. The question is, if you pay back $1,789 extra on a $10,000 loan over two years, what is the real interest rate or APR? The APR, when the $435 finance charge and fees are figured in, is 16.33 percent, not 12 percent!

Always have a financing statement prepared *before* you make your decisions on a loan or mortgage. You will then know what rate you are truly paying for the loan.

When calculating the APR for a mortgage or loan with fees or points paid in advance, you deduct the fees from the original principal amount because, in essence, you are receiving less money.

For example, you borrow $60,000 for 30 years at 12 percent interest. If your loan has no fees or points and you are paying all interest due with your monthly payment in the month it is earned, your payment is $617.17 for principal and interest and your APR is also 12 percent.

The APR formula is based on the actual rate of interest paid monthly, times the number of payments made each year, in this case 12: for example, 1.5 percent per month equals 18 percent per year. Since the interest is paid monthly and not in one lump sum at the end of the year, your true effective rate based on our earlier definition of simple interest is 12.68 percent. The APR regulations *do not* require that the higher effective rate be shown, but only the nominal rate before compounding.

Now let's look at the same example with points and fees. You borrow the same $60,000 at 12 percent, but the bank is charging you 3 points or $1,800 (3% × $60,000), plus a loan origination fee of $300, for a total of $2,100, which you are required to pay in advance. The actual amount you are receiving is now only $57,900 ($60,000 − $2,100), since you paid $2,100 out of your pocket. However, you are still making payments on the full $60,000. Your true interest rate or APR is 12.48 percent, or almost ½ percent higher than the rate you were quoted. When this compounded rate is refigured to an effective rate equivalent, you are actually paying 13.22 percent! Reason? Your interest is being compounded monthly, not reflected in APR. In Canada, although payments are made monthly, the interest is compounded only every six months, making a 12 percent Canadian mortgage a better deal with an effective rate of 12.87 instead of 13.22 percent.

What do you do? When comparing loans or mortgages, take into consideration *all* required fees and charges. Over the full 360 months of a 30-year $60,000 mortgage, a 1.22 percent increase in the interest rate (13.22% − 12%) will cost you an extra $20,479!

Believe it or not, as good an idea as the APR originally was, it still does not reflect the true cost of borrowing money, especially mortgage money. In an effort to appease the big-spending banking lobby, the "Truth in Lending Act" does *not* require the following high-cost expenses of obtaining a mortgage to be included in calculating the APR:

Title examination fees
Title abstract fees
Title insurance fees
Surveys
Fees for preparation of deeds and mortgages
Notary fees
Credit report fees
Application fees, if charged to *all* customers
Credit life and disability insurance premiums if *not required* by the bank but taken voluntarily

The above costs of a mortgage for the most part are not optional and, therefore, should be included in calculating the true APR. When you are obtaining mortgage money or comparing mortgages, add the above items to the mortgage or loan amount shown on the financing or estimate of closing costs statement and then calculate your own APR using a financial calculator.

Remember, to determine your real principal (the amount you are actually borrowing) subtract from the original principal all fees and charges that are paid in advance or deducted from the loan, but add to the principal all fees and charges that are financed. Then solve for the true APR. The effective APR may be much higher than the APR given to you by your bank or mortgage company on the financing statement.

DEFENSE #101

Never sign a car or equipment lease without knowing the annual percentage rate.

One of the great financing deceptions you'll find when leasing a car or other equipment is that no one seems to be able to or want to tell you the true interest rate. Because the monthly payments are lower on a lease since only part of the principal is paid during the term, the interest rate can be much higher and still be disguised by the lesser payments. Most people are savvy enough at least to ask about the interest rate and are met with the statement, "Leases don't have interest rates, just leasing factors." That is a financial lie. The factor, which determines the monthly payment, is a derivative of the interest rate.

In a lease, the equivalent of the annual percentage rate (APR) interest rate (See Defense #100) is called the implicit interest or yield rate. The mathematical formula is the same as for an amortized car loan except that the lease has a residual value. You can easily find the APR on a lease contract with a financial calculator—yours or the leasing agent's. You will use the following keys:

Enter:

(PV), the present value or total cost you are putting on the lease.

(FV), the future value, which in this case will be the amount the car will cost you at the end of the term if you choose to buy it.

(PMT), the monthly payment you are quoted after the leasing agent applies the "lease factor."
(N), the term of the lease in months, i.e., a three-year lease is 36 months, a five-year lease is 60 months.

Compute:

(i), the monthly interest rate, which the calculator will determine. Multiply by 12 to get the true yearly interest rate.

Most calculators have a begin/end function to choose depending on whether the first payment is due in advance or at the end of the period. The first payment on a lease is almost always due in advance so use the begin function, which actually increases the interest rate slightly. On a car loan the first payment is usually not due for 30 days or at the *end* of the first period.

Here's an example. You are offered a car lease on a BMW for five years. The lease amount is $32,000, the residual value is $16,000 and the payments are $632 per month with the first payment due in advance. What is the real interest rate?

PV = 32,000
FV = 16,000
PMT = 632
N = 60

Solve for (i) and you get an interest rate of 1.48 percent per month. Multiply by 12 and you discover that the true interest rate you are paying is 17.8 percent. No wonder the salesperson wouldn't tell you. If the lease rate is more than about 2 percent above the prime rate, you are paying too much. If the prime rate is 6½ percent, your lease should have an APR of no more than 8½ percent. I have seen leases thrown at unsuspecting buyers with an interest rate of over 20 percent! It pays to do your arithmetic.

DEFENSE #102

Don't fall for the "no down payment" pitch on a car or equipment lease.

There is, of course, a cash down payment when you buy a car with the balance of the sale price covered by a loan. If you can't make the down payment, you can't buy the car. That's why many people fall for the "no down payment" promise in a car leasing company's sales pitch. When you sign the lease, say, for $400 a month, you find that you are required to pay $1,200 up front. The salesperson gets around calling the amount you pay up front a down payment by calling it a payment for the first and the last two months of the lease. In fact, it's a down payment since your first payment on a regular car loan normally wouldn't be due until 30 days after you drive away the car. If you are required to pay any money up front, treat it as a down payment when computing the interest and subtract the amount of the payment from the total loan.

For instance, in our previous example, Defense #101, if you had to make the first and last two payments in advance, you would have to write a check up front for $1,896. The total amount to be financed at $632 per month was $32,000; but since you are required to pay $1,896 in advance, that means you have just $30,104 left to pay ($32,000 − $1,896 = $30,104). Substituting $30,104 for the present value (PV) or the amount of lease for the $32,000 in our calculator formula, the interest rate is now 19.6 percent. Those payments up front make a big difference. Use the "end" mode when treating the three payments as paid in advance by reducing the total amount of the lease.

In dealing with banks or leasing companies, as with any other business that makes money by taking your money, your best financial defense is knowledge. Never sign any loan agreement or leasing contract without knowing exactly what it is going to cost you. Then you may be able to save money by shopping around for a better deal. Or, at the very least, you won't leave yourself open to an unpleasant financial aftershock.

CHAPTER 13

Keeping Your Credit Under Control

Controlling Your Credit File

There are some consumer laws that actually work *for* the consumer, laws that are so powerful they enable you to combat successfully both nuisance and real problems heaped on you by financial institutions. One such group of rules and regulations, called the Fair Credit Reporting Act, enables you to deal effectively with your dreaded credit report.

Nothing can slow you down faster financially than derogatory information that finds its way into a credit bureau file. Sometimes the information is true; other times it is deceiving or even totally wrong. In *More Wealth Without Risk*, I gave you the basic strategies for taking control of your credit bureau report, but when you take control of your financial life, not everyone is going to agree with your right to be in control. Many readers wrote me that while trying to exercise their rights granted under federal law, they actually encountered people at credit bureaus and creditors who didn't understand the rules. Some were even told they couldn't do what it was their legal right to do.

So, for those who have not yet gotten control of their credit bureau file, for those who are still trying to educate creditors and credit bureau people, and for those of you about to take the first step in controlling credit information, let me tell you about your astounding rights under public law 91-508, also known as the Fair Credit Reporting Act (FCRA). These federal rules and regulations regarding consumer credit reporting and credit reporting agencies were in the form of an amendment tacked on to the end of the Consumer Credit Protection Act.

Investigations in both houses of Congress found that consumers were constantly being damaged financially, emotionally and unfairly by the practices of creditors and by what we know as credit bureaus. In its findings, Congress stated:

> Unfair credit reporting methods undermine the public confidence which is essential to the continued functioning of the banking system. An elaborate mechanism has been developed for investigating and evaluating the creditworthiness, credit standing, credit capacity, character and general reputation of consumers. There is a need to insure that consumer reporting agencies exercise their grave responsibilities with fairness, impartiality and a respect for the consumers' right to privacy. It is the purpose of this [law] to require that consumer reporting agencies adopt reasonable procedures which are fair and equitable to the consumer with regard to the confidentiality, accuracy, relevancy and proper utilization of such information.

The laws that Congress enacted have given you both instant access to the information that credit bureaus gather about you and the opportunity to correct inaccurate or deceiving information. Look at Your Credit Bureau Bill of Rights on page 270. Understanding your rights under the FCRA is your first line of defense against unfair credit practices or inaccurate information about you that finds its way into your credit file.

Credit information about you is compiled by a so-called credit bureau, the generic name given to credit data gathering and reporting agencies. The three largest in the nation are TRW, TransUnion and Equifax, all of which have nationwide computer systems. They can follow you anywhere—great if your credit is good, a nemesis and a nuisance if you've had credit problems.

Credit bureaus are financed by "members," which include local companies, stores, banks, finance and mortgage companies and other issuers of credit. Members pay a yearly membership fee plus about $3 or more for each inquiry. Only members can pull your credit file, although almost anyone with a legitimate business can become a member. I became a member of a credit bureau once in the seventies solely to check on the references of prospective rental property tenants.

The credit bureau is the first place your potential creditors and employers will check to find out who you are, how you run your financial life and if you told the truth in completing an application for credit or even a job. Others who have the right to and will delve into your personal and credit history are insurance companies, potential landlords and government agencies if you are applying for state or federally regulated licenses.

The most important principle in dealing with credit bureaus is to realize that a complete, correct, up-to-date credit file is *your* responsibility and not that of the credit bureau. An accurate credit file is something you create through your knowledge of the Fair Credit Reporting Act. The credit bureau simply gathers all information about you from its members, incuding account information and payment habits, and records them in your file. If a creditor gives the bureau incorrect information, it goes into your file as is. No one checks. A credit bureau does not evaluate your creditworthiness or approve or disapprove you for loans. It simply sends a copy of all data in your file to members who request it.

Prior to the Fair Credit Reporting Act of 1970, no one had any legal right to know what was in his credit file or was able to correct any wrong information. Now you have those rights. With the FCRA laws you have tremendous clout, but only if you know how to use it. The FCRA doesn't give you the power to get accurate information about late payments, repossessions, tax liens or to remove judgments from your credit file, but it does give you the power to make their impact on your credit less devastating. Let me show you how to turn your rights under the Fair Credit Reporting Act into power strategies that can solve most of the frustrating problems you'll run into with a credit bureau and with your credit rating.

Let's go through your rights under the FCRA one by one, and I will show you how you can use them to get control of your credit. I will be referring to specific sections of the FCRA in the discussion that follows. If you would like a copy of the entire act, you can usually obtain one from your local credit bureau.

Right #1: To obtain from any credit bureau a complete report of the information in your credit file.

Should any consumer reporting agency ever give you a hassle about inquiring into your file, including getting all of the information that is given to potential creditors or potential employ-

Your Credit Bureau Bill of Rights

According to the federal Fair Credit Reporting Act, you have the following rights:

1. To obtain from any credit bureau a complete report of the information in your credit file.
2. To dispute any information in your file or to get missing data added to your file.
3. To have all potential creditors and employers who have inquired into your file during the past two years notified of errors that have been corrected.
4. To put your side of the story in your credit file.
5. To have detrimental credit information removed from your file after seven years and bankruptcy information after 10 years.
6. To keep private the information in your file from anyone other than legitimate members or users of the credit reporting agency.
7. To know exactly why you were refused credit.

The following are not covered in the FCRA, but are your rights under other laws or rulings:

8. To receive the same good credit rating as a former spouse.
9. To have your credit report transferred from one city to another anytime you move.
10. To use small claims court to resolve any disputes with the credit bureau about incorrect, inaccurate information in your file.
11. To remain silent about poor credit information that does not currently appear in your file.

ers, simply refer the agency to the FCRA, *Section 609, Disclosures to Consumers*. Section 609 states specifically what information the credit bureau must furnish you—basically, all of the information contained in your file except, for some reason, medical information. You also have a right to know the source of the information except if it was acquired while preparing an extensive investigative consumer report on you. Investigative consumer reports occur when someone, like a life insurance company, wants to check your lifestyle and habits and may request that a report be prepared by the credit bureau that would include interviews with your neighbors, friends and people with whom you work. A prospective employer might also request such an in-depth report.

The credit bureau, by law, must also tell you who has inquired into your file. You will be given, or can demand, a list of all of the prospective employers who have checked your credit file within the past two years, plus anyone who has checked on your credit history during the previous six months.

You may be interested to know that no one may request an in-depth investigative consumer report about you unless it is disclosed to you in writing that such a report is being prepared. If you receive such a notice, you have the right, upon written request, to a complete and accurate disclosure of the nature and scope of the investigation being prepared about you. This disclosure must be returned to you in writing within five days after your request for the information. The only exception to the disclosure rule seems to be if a prospective employer is doing an investigative report on you for a potential job for which you have not actually applied.

Section 610, Conditions of Disclosures to Consumers, lists the conditions under which the credit reporting agency is required to give you the information. If you show up in person at the credit bureau with proper identification, you must be given the information, or, after you've made a written request with proper identification, you can even get the information by telephone. The law also requires that the consumer reporting agency provide trained personnel to explain your credit file and the codes used. You have the right to bring one other person with you to the credit bureau, whether it be a friend, relative or someone to advise you.

Right #2: To dispute any information in your file or to get missing data added to your file.

Once you see your credit report, you will be shocked at the inaccuracies you will find. You may find your report showing late payments that weren't actually late or a tremendous amount of positive data that is missing. For instance, some credit card companies, like American Express, don't automatically report to credit bureaus on their customers, whether the information is good or bad. You always want to have positive information added to your file.

I've received letters from people who wanted the credit bureaus to correct data and were told that they had no right to request changes. *Section 611, Procedure in Case of Disputed Accuracy,* gives you the right to question information in your file and have it corrected within a reasonable amount of time if, upon investigation, it is found to be inaccurate or can no longer be verified. What's a reasonable period of time for the credit reporting agency to investigate the information and make any corrections? The standard is now about three weeks.

The best way to correct information in your credit file is to fill out a consumer dispute form, available at any consumer reporting agency. You'll see an example of a completed form at the end of this chapter, on page 279. If, after you have filed the consumer dispute form with the credit bureau, you don't hear from the agency, check your credit file again in 30 days to see if corrections have been made.

Right #3: To have all potential creditors and employers who have inquired into your file during the past two years notified of errors that have been corrected.

It's bad enough when prospective creditors and employers receive incorrect information from your credit file, but it's worse when you try to tell them that the information is not true. The attitude is always, "Ho-hum, I understand, but we've heard that one before." Part (d) of Section 611 instructs the consumer reporting agency, at your request, to notify all those who have received incorrect or disputed information of the corrections. It's the law.

Right # 4: To put your side of the story in your credit file.

There are two situations in which you will want to add your own information to your credit bureau file:

1. When the information in your file is accurate but does not tell the whole story. For instance, a reasonable or unavoidable circumstance made your payments late or extremely high medical bills made it temporarily impossible to keep all of your accounts current.
2. When the information in your file is inaccurate but resolving the dispute is taking some time. For instance, one of your creditors reported that your account is not current but

you believe the creditor must have misplaced or misrecorded a payment that you actually sent in. While the matter is being resolved, you will want to have entered into your credit file that you believe the creditor to be incorrect and that the matter is under dispute and being resolved. Until you can resolve the dispute, you have the absolute right, under Section 611 part (b), to put in your file a brief statement that summarizes factors that are not currently part of your file, including the fact that you believe the information to be totally incorrect. The credit bureau is even obligated to help you write a clear summary of the dispute and provide that information to anyone looking at your credit report.

Some credit reporting agencies will simply try to put a code into your file that says "disputed by consumer" without telling your side of the story. If that should happen, refer the agency to the Fair Credit Reporting Act and say that you want the actual statement added, not just a code.

One failure of the credit reporting system is that your file often shows how many times you have been 30, 60, or 90 days late in paying on an account, but it does not show how long ago the late payments occurred. You have a right to add that additional information to your file. Note the fact that all late payments were prior to a certain date, why they were late and that payments are now current and have been for some time. Your side of the story can make a difference to your potential creditors and employers in deciding whether to approve a loan or even give you a job.

Right #5: To have detrimental credit information removed from your file after seven years, bankruptcy information after 10 years.

Don't expect the credit bureau to remove derogatory information automatically from your file after the statute of limitations period has expired. Take it upon yourself to keep track of what's in your credit file and note when the information has passed the federal statute date. Use the consumer dispute form to request that the unwanted information be removed. Of course, if the information in your file is all positive, you needn't be in such a hurry.

Section 605, Obsolete Information, states how and when it is determined that detrimental information is past the statute limit and that it must be removed. All late payments and personal data must be removed after seven years and bankruptcy information after 10 years. There are three exceptions to the statute of limitations in the law:

1. If you're borrowing $50,000 or more,
2. If you're applying for an insurance policy of $50,000 or more,
3. If you're applying for a job with an annual salary equal to $20,000 or more.

In these cases, technically the consumer reporting agency could report on information older than the normal statute limit, but it normally doesn't.

Right #6: To keep private the information in your file from anyone other than legitimate members or users of the credit reporting agency.

Not just anyone can get the personal and credit data from your credit bureau file, including your friends or enemies. *Section 604, Permissible Purposes of Reports,* lists the specific and legitimate purposes for which a consumer reporting agency may give out the information in your file. *Section 607, Compliance Procedure,* obligates the consumer reporting agencies to make sure that only valid members and users receive information on you.

Right #7: To know exactly why you were refused credit.

Part of the FCRA requires that upon your written request all those who have turned you down for credit, insurance or employment based on information they obtained from your credit file must supply to you the name and address of the consumer reporting agency from which they obtained the report. This rule also applies if the interest rate for credit or the premium for insurance is increased because of the information in your file. If the information is obtained from some source other than a credit bureau, upon your written request, they must disclose the nature of the information that has been obtained. By law, if you are denied credit or employment or the rates are changed on transactions in which you are involved, the user of the information from your credit file is also required to inform you in writing of your rights to inquire about the reason. They often don't. But now that you know you have that right, always inquire about the source of any adverse credit information from a credit bureau and the nature of any adverse financial or personal information from any other source.

If the consumer reporting agencies willfully fail to comply with the laws, rules and regulations in the FCRA, are they liable? Can you sue them for damages? You bet! *Section 616, Civil Liability for Willful Non-Compliance,* states that there is liability on the part of the credit reporting agency, and *section 617, Civil Liability for Negligent Non-Compliance,* gives the penalty of actual damages plus court costs and attorney's fees.

Don't be intimidated by credit bureaus. Your credit is one of your most important financial assets, and when you are trying to protect it, the law is on your side.

DEFENSE #103

Check and correct your credit bureau file now and at least once a year.

The truth is that 24 out of 25 credit bureau files on individuals and businesses have major errors. Because of the volume of data given to credit bureaus, there are bound to be errors—and are there ever. Wrong information can easily get into your file. Great if the errors are positive, but, of course, they're usually not. Don't wait until a bank or mortgage company turns you down for credit based on incorrect information in your file. Check your file at least once a year, correct the errors and have any adverse information past the statute of limitations removed.

You will often find personal errors about your address, your income, your home and previous addresses and employment. The same holds true for information about your spouse. Whatever the error, you should correct it by filing a consumer dispute form with the credit bureau requesting that the corrections be made.

Request a copy of your credit file now and again next year at this time. You may have a file in several credit bureaus. Find their numbers in the Yellow Pages under Credit Reporting Agencies and request to see your file in person or in writing, or to review it over the phone.

Depending on the agency, a copy of your credit report will cost about $8. The law states, however, that if you have been turned down for credit during the past 30 days, you have the right to receive a copy of your credit file free. An interesting strategy enabling you to get a free report might be to apply for a $1 million loan at a local bank. Only one of two things can happen. Either you get the $1 million loan, which you can use to invest or start a business, or you will get turned down and thereby qualify for a free credit report and save $8. If you have been turned down for credit, all you need do is show the rejection letter to the credit bureau to get your credit file information without charge.

Check your credit report to learn:

1. Who has inquired into your file. The list will include all potential lenders and employers. These entries generally appear in your file a few days after you have completed a credit or employment application.
2. Which creditors have reported about you to the agency, including:
   a. your credit limit
   b. balance owing on your account
   c. your payment history—(1) means you are always on time, (9) is bankruptcy
   d. whether the account is revolving (R) or installment (I)
   e. the number of times you have been 30, 60 or 90 days late with your payments
3. If all of the personal data in your file, such as spouse, employers, residences and income, is correct.

If you don't understand anything on the report, ask for an explanation. If there are errors, request that they be corrected by filing a consumer dispute form, then check your credit file again to see that the corrections have been made.

DEFENSE #104

Use small claims court, consumer reporters and state agencies to resolve credit disputes.

What if you follow all these procedures but can't seem to get a creditor to supply correct information to the credit bureau? Take 'em to court—small claims court, that is. For a small filing fee and without an attorney, you can, in most states, file a suit claiming damages from the incorrect information. You probably won't have to go to court since it would be far less expensive for the creditor to straighten out the error than to pay an attorney to fight your claim. Name both the lender and the credit bureau in the suit, and you will get immediate results.

To file a suit you must claim damages, but you only need to prove damages if your case actually goes to trial. Of course, if incorrect data caused you to be turned down for a loan or job, you actually have a good case for collecting damages. To get action from a creditor, follow these procedures.

Notify the creditor in writing using the sample letter that follows, stating that if wrong information is not corrected in seven days, you will:

1. File a suit for damages in small claims court,
2. Contact the consumer reporters of your local newspaper and television stations,
3. Contact the Better Business Bureau,
4. Contact your state Trade Commission and state Consumer Affairs Office.

If the change is not made in the requested time, follow through on your promises.

Send your letter certified mail—return receipt requested. You will not believe how quickly you receive a response. Don't be intimidated if you get a call from an attorney. Just repeat what you said in the letter.

DEFENSE #105

Exercise your right to the same good credit as your spouse or former spouse.

The Equal Opportunity Act of 1975 prohibits credit discrimination on the basis of gender, marital status, race, religion, age and national origin. It also requires that, for married couples, credit be reported in both spouses' names if they request it.

If all credit is in the name of one spouse, don't think that leaves the other spouse out in the cold. If this is your situation, immediately complete a consumer dispute form requesting that the credit file be in both names. Having a mutual credit file is the least expensive form of insurance and is in the best interest of both spouses.

If something were to happen to one spouse, the mutual credit file prevents the other spouse from having to establish credit. If you are separated or divorced and all the credit was in your former spouse's name, you may have already had the unpleasant experience of applying for credit only to be told that you don't

Sample Letter

To: ______________________ *From:* ______________________

______________________ ______________________

______________________ ______________________

______________________ *Date:* ______________________

Recently I applied for credit and was turned down due to erroneous information in my credit file attributed to you. I have attempted to get your company to correct the incorrect data, but with no results. The incorrect information stated: ___________ . This is the correct information: ___________ . As required by law, you must submit the correct information. If you have not done so within seven days, I will file suit for damages against you in small claims court, contact the consumer reporters of our newspaper and television stations, contact the Better Business Bureau and contact both the state Trade Commission and the Consumer Affairs Office.

Thank you for your prompt action on this matter.

exist, that you are a nonperson. That's easy to change. According to the Equal Opportunity Act, you may have a separate file created under your name with the same information as in your spouse's or former spouse's file, which is a great strategy as long as your former spouse's credit file is positive.

DEFENSE #106

File Chapter 13 instead of personal bankruptcy when your debts far outweigh your ability to pay.

When you are in debt over your head and your monthly outgo is more than your monthly income, bankruptcy often seems like an easy, painless way to eliminate all the hassle, threatening phone calls and letters from creditors. In truth, the short-term

CONSUMER DISPUTE FORM

Personal Identification (Please Print or Type)

Name Drum (Last) Robert (First) J. (Middle Initial) Suffix (Jr., Sr. Etc.)

Present Address 962 Fenworth (Street) Boston (City) Mass. (State) 02115 (Zip)

Former Address (Street) (City) (State) (Zip)

Date of Birth 2 (Month) 5 (Day) 47 (Year) Social Security Number 388-04-6290

I recently received a copy of the report containing my credit history, and I disagree with the following information:

Credit History

Name of Business	Account Number	Specific Nature of Disagreement
MasterCard	3314-6279-2206	Report shows two payments
		late during the past year. No
		payments have been late.
Sears	4786993	I have never had an
		account at Sears.

Public Record and Other Information Court of Business	Case Number	Nature of Disagreement
Tax Lien on 131 Devon Lane	02-769978	Lien was paid two
		years ago.

Other: (i.e. information from other credit bureaus, etc.)	Item	Nature of Disagreement

I understand that the information I have disputed will be rechecked when necessary at the source, and I will be notified of the results of this recheck.

Robert Drum (Signature) 11-19-93 (Date)

gain will inflict too much long-term pain. Unlike bad credit, which has a credit file life of seven years, a bankruptcy stays in your credit file by federal law for 10 years. Chapter 13 is a part of the bankruptcy act that allows you to pay off your personal creditors without being forced into bankruptcy.

You will have to go to court to file Chapter 13, but you can do so without the expense of an attorney, although court rules allow you to have one if you wish. After you have completed the necessary application forms, including a detailed plan for how you intend to repay your creditors, file the papers with the court. A judge will review and rule on your application.

To get your plan approved by the judge, follow these guidelines:

- Allocate no more than 25 percent of your weekly or monthly salary to the repayment of your debts. Sometimes more is not better.
- Be certain to list all your debts. Your plan can later be canceled if it is found you were not totally honest.

If your creditors will all be paid off in about 36 months with your plan, it stands a good chance of approval. If your repayment plan is approved:

- You will begin making your payments directly to the court, which will disburse the money proportionately to your creditors
- Your creditors will be barred by the court from writing, phoning or contacting you
- You will not be charged extra interest for the time the repayment is extended

Because Chapter 13 is a court action, there is an 80 percent chance that the information will find its way into your credit file. During the repayment period, it is unlikely that anyone will be willing to extend you new credit. After you have paid off your creditors, however, immediately begin rehabilitating your credit using secured credit cards. See Chapter 14, High-Powered Credit Card Strategies. Unlike the case with bankruptcy, you have paid off your creditors in good faith even though it took a longer time. Chapter 13, although not a plus in your credit file, certainly looks better to potential lenders than a regular bankruptcy.

CHAPTER 14

High-Powered Credit Card Strategies

Believe it or not, there are people with credit cards who are under credit control, 35 percent of them, as a matter of fact. These people actually pay off their entire MasterCard or Visa balance every month, staying out of high-interest debt.

Obviously, paying off your credit card balance every month is the ideal strategy. You then have a record of your purchases and yet are not constantly going deeper in debt or fighting the battle to make monthly payments. In today's financial world where you can pay for most everything with plastic, that's not always easy to do.

According to a study done by RAM (Ram Research's Bankcard Update), the average interest paid on a MasterCard or Visa nationwide is 19.42 percent. Outrageous? You bet, especially if you begin letting your average monthly balance get larger and larger by opting to make a few minimum monthly payments instead of paying off the balance. Banks began getting away with high-interest credit cards 25 years ago because people were willing to pay for the convenience, never knowing there was an alternative—and after all, credit card interest used to be deductible. The interest deduction meant that a person in the 33 percent tax bracket paying 18 percent credit card interest was effectively paying 12 percent. Now that consumer interest is no longer deductible, the effective interest rate is the same as the actual interest rate, and it is more important than ever to cut the cost of borrowing money.

The average credit card debt for families who use credit cards is estimated to be around $5,000 with all too many stuck in the $7,000 to $15,000 range. Stuck is the right word. Have you noticed that the minimum payment on a credit card account is calculated to insure that you will never get out of debt? Yet with a few simple strategies you can make credit cards work to your advantage whether you are deep in debt or pay off your balance every month.

Are credit cards a blessing or a curse? That depends on whether you work for them or make them work for you. In *More Wealth Without Risk*, I discuss a number of powerful strategies for keeping your credit card debts under control. In this chapter, I will show you strategies for cutting credit card interest rates and fees in half, how to determine mathematically which are the best credit cards for you and how to use credit cards as a line of credit or even to reestablish credit. You'll learn how to save hundreds on your current credit card debt and even how to pay it off in half the time without additional financial strain. With these and the other strategies in this chapter, you will maximize your credit card control at minimum cost to you.

ATTACK #107

Cut the cost of your credit card accounts by 50 percent with no-fee and low-interest-rate cards.

Your first objective in mastering credit card management is to cut the total cost of your cards to a minimum. There are seven potential costs of a credit card that can add up to hundreds of dollars per year.

1. Interest rate
2. Yearly fee
3. Chargegard or credit life disability insurance
4. Late charge
5. Over-the-limit charge
6. Returned check fees
7. Cash advance fees

As you learned in Chapter 7, any form of credit life and disability insurance is a rip-off, and Chargegard, which can be added to your credit card account for $.66 per hundred per month, can actually add the equivalent of about 8 percent extra interest per year. Never take the insurance on a credit card account.

Four major charges that can easily be eliminated are late charges, over-the-limit charges, returned check fees and cash advance fees. How? By not getting caught in the traps that trigger these fees. The average for these charges is $15 or more each and the amounts must now by law be disclosed in the applications. These four extra, seemingly innocent costs can add up to 10 percent to the actual interest rate you are paying.

Here is a typical scenario that would cost you an extra $65. You get an anxious note from your credit card company saying you are over your credit limit by $50: charge $15. You quickly write a check right before the due date for the monthly payment plus a few dollars extra to get your balance below the limit. Unfortunately, the credit card payment check gets to your bank before your next paycheck and is stamped NSF (nonsufficient funds) by the bank and returned to the credit card company. Your bank charges you $20, the returned check to the credit card company costs you an added $15, and by the time you clear up the mess your credit card payment originally made on time is now counted late. There goes another $15. Total cost, in addition to all the time and hassle, is approximately $65. If something similar happens three times during the year, you have spent an extra $195 in fees. If your average monthly balance is $2,000 the cost to you is the equivalent of another 10 percent interest on top of the 18 percent you may already be paying. To avoid throwing your hard-earned money away on late fees, over-the-limit fees and bad check fees, you must maintain control of all your accounts.

Choosing the Right Credit Card

The next and most important step is to determine if a low-interest credit card or no-fee credit card is best for you. By using the strategies and sources I am going to give you, you can cut the average interest rate on your MasterCard or Visa by 40 percent or cut your yearly credit card fee to zero, but not both. Which kind of card, low-interest or no-fee, will save you the most money is determined by the average balance you keep in your account and the yearly fee on the available low-interest credit cards.

Use the formula that follows to make this important credit card decision.

Computing Your Average Monthly Credit Card Balance

	AVERAGE MONTHLY BALANCE		INTEREST RATE		YEARLY INTEREST
Card 1	$	×	%	=	$
Card 2	$	×	%	=	$
Card 3	$	×	%	=	$
Card 4	$	×	%	=	$
Total (all cards)	$		%	=	$

To compute the average monthly balance on any one of your credit cards, total the monthly balances on your statements for the past 6 to 12 months. If you use 6 months of statements, divide the total by 6; if you total 12 statement balances, divide by 12 to find your average monthly balance.

For example, your Visa account balances, shown as "new balance" on your statements for the past 6 months, are as follows:

April	$ 1,826
May	1,910
June	1,880
July	2,066
August	2,250
September	2,175
Six-month total	$12,107 ÷ 6 months = $2,017 average monthly balance

Enter the average monthly balance for all your MasterCard, Visa and Discover cards in the spaces on the chart marked Card 1 through Card 4. Enter the yearly interest rate for each card shown on your monthly statement. Now add the average monthly balances of all your credit cards to determine the total average monthly credit card debt you are carrying. Do not include credit card accounts you pay off every month. To determine the total amount of interest you are paying—and losing—each year, multiply the average monthly balance for each card by the yearly interest rate (18% = .18), enter the figure in the last column labeled Yearly Interest, and then total the entries in that column.

If you want to know the average interest rate you are paying on all your credit cards, total the interest rate on your cards and divide by the number of cards. The true overall rate you end up paying, of course, will be determined by how big the average balance was during the year on each card.

Once you know your average monthly balance and your average interest rate, you are in a position to make your most important credit card decision: which credit card will work best for you. Typically, you will have to pay a higher annual fee for a low-interest credit card, while you will be charged a higher rate of interest for a no-fee credit card. So in determining which is the least expensive for you, the only question becomes, "Will I save enough money with a lower interest rate to more than cover the yearly fee?" If the answer is "no," get a low- or no-fee card.

Look at the next table, Yearly Interest Saved by Low-Interest Credit Cards (page 287), and you can compare the true interest costs. Let's say your average monthly balance is $3,500 and the average rate on your credit card(s) is 18 percent. You are currently paying $630 a year or $52.50 a month just for interest. If you could get a low-interest credit card at 7.95 percent, reading across the $3,500 row in the chart you will see that your total yearly interest will drop to $278, which, as you can see from the 7.95 percent versus 18 percent column, will save you $352 a year in interest. Would you be better off with a no-fee credit card at 18 percent or a 7.95 percent credit card with a $35 annual fee? The low-interest card, of course, because the net automatic savings would be $317 per year even with a $35 fee (352 − 35 = 317).

If the 18 percent card you have now has a $20 annual fee versus $35, you would save $337 by switching cards. Look at the list of no-annual-fee credit cards on page 302 and you will see the low-interest-rate cards in the country that have no annual fees. The interest rates range from 6.75 percent on the Wachovia card to 9.65 on the AFBA Industrial Bank Card.

At some point those people who keep a smaller average monthly balance will do better with a no-fee or low-fee card than they will with a low-interest card. If you pay off your credit card balance every month, there is no question that a no-fee credit card is cheaper because you never pay interest anyway, no matter how high or low the rate. To compute the average monthly balance below which the no-fee or lower-fee card will save you more money than a difference in interest rates, use the following formula.

$$\text{Break-even balance} = \frac{\text{Card A Fee} - \text{Card B Fee}}{\text{Card A Interest Rate} - \text{Card B Interest Rate}}$$

Example:

$$\text{Break-even balance} = \frac{\$35 - \$15}{16\% - 12\%} = \frac{\$20}{.04} = \$500$$

Using this formula you can find the amount of average monthly balance at which a lower interest rate would exactly pay for the difference in fees by dividing the difference in fees by the difference in interest rates. For instance, if the difference in annual fees of two cards you are comparing is $20 and the difference in interest rates is 4 percent, then the break-even average monthly balance would be $500 ($20/4% = $500). If your average monthly balance is less than $500, you will save money with the lower-fee card; if your average balance is over $500, you will save more money with the lower-interest-rate credit card.

Another way of determining your *real* cost of credit is to convert your yearly fee to an equivalent interest rate. The formula is simple. You must know or estimate only your average monthly balance. The yearly fee divided by your average balance equals the amount of interest to add to the actual interest rate charged on your account to determine the *real* interest cost. The less your balance the higher the equivalent interest the fee represents.

Example: 18% card, $30 yearly fee, $4,000 average balance—$30 ÷ $4,000 = .75%, .75% + 18% = 18.75%

Example: 18% card, $30 yearly fee, $500 average balance—$30 ÷ $500 = 6% + 18% = 24%

You can also use this calculation to determine if you would save money with either a low-interest or a no-fee credit card. To help you make that determination, refer to the lists of low-interest-rate and no-annual-fee credit cards on pages 289 and 290. As of the writing of this book, they are the best cards in each category available on a nationwide basis. However, you should expect change.

YEARLY INTEREST SAVED BY LOW-INTEREST CREDIT CARDS

	Yearly Interest				Amount Saved	
AVERAGE MONTHLY PAYMENT	18%	16%	13.9%	7.95%	7.95% versus 18%	7.95% versus 13.9%
100	$ 18	$ 16	$ 14	$ 8	$ 10	$ 6
200	36	32	28	16	20	12
300	54	48	42	24	30	18
400	72	64	56	32	40	24
500	90	80	70	40	50	30
600	108	96	83	48	60	35
700	126	112	97	56	70	41
800	144	128	111	64	80	47
900	162	144	125	72	90	53
1,000	180	160	139	80	100	59
1,500	270	240	209	119	151	90
2,000	360	320	278	159	201	119
2,500	450	400	348	199	251	149
3,000	540	480	417	239	301	178
3,500	630	560	487	278	352	209
4,000	720	640	556	318	402	238
4,500	810	720	626	358	452	268
5,000	900	800	695	398	502	297
5,500	990	880	765	437	553	328
6,000	1,080	960	834	477	603	357
6,500	1,170	1,040	904	517	653	387
7,000	1,260	1,120	973	557	703	416
7,500	1,350	1,200	1,043	596	754	447
8,000	1,440	1,280	1,112	636	804	476

ATTACK #108

Capitalize on your credit card options. Get the CJGO Credit Card for the opportunity to get back, in cash, up to 100% of the interest you pay in.

The Charles J. Givens Organization has joined forces with powerhouse Mellon Bank of Wilmington, DE, to offer an exciting new credit card—the only credit card in the country that can pay back up to 100% of the interest you pay in.

The Organization also offers standard and gold cards, as well as a low-interest credit card for those who qualify.

The Givens Organization credit card provides the best of both worlds in the credit card industry: no annual fee plus interest back.

Simply pay off your monthly charges regularly and you get all the convenience of a credit card free, year after year.

If you find you must carry over a balance, all the interest you pay in eventually can come right back to you.

Here's how it works: You use the card and either pay off the balance each month or make minimum monthly payments and incur interest. You are eligible to receive a 10% interest rebate after the first two years, and an additional 5% rebate each year up to the 20th year, for a total of up to 100%.

When you use your card for 20 years you could receive up to 100% of your interest back, in cash. Once you receive a rebate, your interest automatically starts accumulating for your next rebate. To apply for the CJGO credit card, call 1-800-284-4082.

The list opposite represents the lowest-rate credit cards available on a nationwide basis as of the writing of this book. Expect changes.

LOW-RATE CREDIT CARDS

APR	TYPE	ANNUAL FEE	AREA	STATE	ISSUER NAME	ADDRESS	PHONE	OUT OF STATE	GRACE PERIOD
6.75	V/MC	$18	worldwide	Georgia	Wachovia Bank	P.O. Box 16989 Atlanta, GA 30321	1-800-842-3262	yes	25 days
8.5	V/MC	in-state 25 out-of-state 35	nationwide	Arkansas	Simmons First National	P.O. Box 6609 Pine Bluff, AK 71611	1-501-541-1000	yes	25 days
9.25	V/MC	$29	nationwide	North Carolina	Central Carolina Bank	P.O. Box 1846 Durham, NC 27702	1-800-577-1680	yes	25 days
9.25	V/MC	$35	worldwide	South Carolina	AFBA Industrial Bank	Attn. card service P.O. Box 100152 Columbia, SC 29202-9575	1-800-776-2265	yes	25 days
9.65	V/MC	—	worldwide	South Carolina	AFBA Industrial Bank	Attn. card service P.O. Box 100152 Columbia, SC 29202-9575	1-800-776-2265	yes	25 days
9.0	MC	$37	nationwide	Illinois	Amalgamated Trust Bank	P.O. Box A3979 Chicago, IL 60690	1-800-365-6464	yes	25 days

NO-ANNUAL-FEE CREDIT CARDS

APR	TYPE	ANNUAL FEE	AREA	STATE	ISSUER NAME	ADDRESS	PHONE	OUT OF STATE	GRACE PERIOD
9.65	V/MC	—	worldwide	South Carolina	AFBA Industrial Bank	Attn. card service P.O. Box 100152 Columbia, SC 29202-9575	1-800-776-2265	yes	25 days
11.24	V/MC	—	nationwide	Pennsylvania	PNC National Bank	PNC Service Corp. 300 Bellevue Pkwy. No. 200 Wilmington, DE 19809	1-800-762-2273	yes	no grace
11.40	MC	—	nationwide	Connecticut	Great Country Bank	Great Country Bank 200 Main St. Ansonia, CT 06401	1-800-204-7328	yes	25 days
12.25 Standard	MC	—	nationwide	Illinois	Amalgamated Trust Bank	P.O. Box A3979 Chicago, IL 60690	1-800-365-6464	yes	25 days
10.75 Gold	MC								
16.5	V/MC	—	nationwide	Tennessee	Union Planters Bank	P.O. Box 1165 Memphis, TN 38101	1-800-628-8946	yes	no grace
12.65 14.65 C/A	V/MC	—	nationwide	New York	Bank of NY Consumer's Edge	Bank of NY/Delaware P.O. Box 6998 Newark, DE 19725-9509	1-800-235-3343	yes	no grace
11.9 plus Prime	MC	—	nationwide*	Delaware	CJGO Bank Card	Card Services Wilmington, DE	1-800-284-4082	yes	25 days

DEFENSE #109

To save time and money in paying off your credit card debt, use debt shifting.

How would you like to be out of credit card debt in half the time without spending an extra dollar a month? You can, using the strategy I call "debt shifting." Debt shifting is a process of shifting all or part of your balance from a high-interest-rate credit card to a low-interest-rate credit card. There are 5,000 banks that issue MasterCard and Visa cards, and all of them have the option of making up their own rules, including what interest rate they charge unless regulated by state laws. Your strategy is to apply for and receive the lowest-interest-rate credit card you can and shift your high-interest credit card debt to the lower-interest-rate card up to the maximum limit on your low-interest account.

For instance, let's say you apply for and get a low-interest credit card with transfer checks. When you receive your card, make a list of all the current balances on your other high-interest credit cards and charge accounts. Use your transfer checks to transfer balances from higher-interest-rate accounts—up to the maximum credit limit available if necessary—and pay off all, or as much as possible, of those balances. On cash advances there may be a 2.5 percent fee (minimum charge $2.50). Of course, you will now owe exactly the same amount on your new card, but at a much *lower* rate of interest—from as much as 17 to 21 percent down to as little as 8.25 percent. And you'll find that your minimum monthly payment on your new card will drop by as much as 35 percent because of the lower interest rate. You can continue to make the same payment as you did with the higher-interest-rate card, but you will pay off your debt in half the time. The debt-shifting strategy not only will save you a lot of time in keeping track of your combined debts, but will also save you a lot of time and money in paying them off.

DEFENSE #110

Use a low-interest card as an automatic, low-cost line of credit.

Even if you pay off your normal credit card balance every month, it may still make sense to have a low-interest card in reserve. For instance, if you decide to buy an $800 VCR but don't have or don't want to spend the cash, you can instantly finance all or part of the $800 for as low as 8 percent interest with no additional paperwork, no credit check and no loan processing fees to penalize you. Using this strategy will also keep your loans for the purchase of assets separate from your regular charges for perishables. But instead of making the minimum monthly payment and paying for your VCR over the next three years, pay enough each month to get your credit card balance paid off in just one year. That strategy alone will save you hundreds of dollars in unnecessary interest payments.

ATTACK #111

Add long float to your no-fee credit card requirements.

There is an additional feature of several no-fee credit cards that can actually make you extra money—the long-float feature. From the time you make your purchase, it's usually about 30 days before you receive the statement containing the charge. Your statement may show that you have another 25 days to pay off the balance of your bill before any interest will be charged. This no-interest period is called float time. By mailing the check to pay off the balance on the last possible day, so that your payment is received the day before the due date, your charges are interest-free. You also have another few days of float time before the money is actually deducted from your checking account. With the statement delay time and the bank's additional 25-day float time, you can get about a 60-day window during which you are actually using the bank's money free. Some credit cards have a zero float time, and interest is charged from the date of purchase or statement. Other cards have a long float time of 25 days.

Obviously, you should choose the card with the longest float time. (See the Lowest-Interest No-Annual-Fee Credit Cards chart on page 302.)

Think about it. You charge $200 for clothes which you can wear immediately, but the check you will write to pay the charge won't actually clear until about 60 days after your visit to the clothing store. Let's turn float time into a strategy.

Charge everything on a no-fee, long-float MasterCard or Visa, even things for which you would normally have written a check or paid cash. During the 60-day float time, keep the money you haven't spent in a money market mutual fund. (See Chapter 12.) Remember, a money market mutual fund is not the same as a money market account at a bank. Over the past couple of years, money market mutual funds have averaged 9 percent interest per year, or about .75 percent per month, whereas money market accounts at banks have averaged an annual 5 percent, or only .4 percent per month. During the 60 days you have your money in a money market fund earning .75 percent per month, you have actually earned an average of 1.5 percent on money you've already spent. If you charge $2,000 a month on your credit cards, that 1.5 percent interest will equal $30 a month or an extra $360 per year in your pocket and an interest rate earned of 18 percent on your average balance.

Remember, you have not gone into debt when using this strategy even though you received a bill for the sum total of your credit card charges. The money to pay the bill is sitting safely in a money market mutual fund earning interest. Okay, so $300 or $400 a year won't make you rich, but it will make you a little richer, earning you $3,000 or $4,000 every 10 years and, best of all, there is absolutely no risk.

Legal float is not a new concept in money-making. Huge companies, such as American Express and Barclay's Bank, have made hundreds of millions using the same strategy. How? By selling phony money called traveler's checks. Ever think what happens when you walk into a bank and buy traveler's checks? You give the bank your real money, and it gives you "funny" money in return, which it may take you weeks or even months to spend. Some people hold onto traveler's checks continually as a safer way of carrying cash. Meanwhile, the bank has interest-free use of your money. Every day traveler's check companies and banks raise hundreds of millions of dollars at no interest. They then put the money in high-return, low-risk investments earning money with your money.

Legal float is the reason that traveler's checks have become one of the biggest financial businesses in the country. The insult? You are actually charged for the privilege of loaning your money interest-free. The normal charge for traveler's checks is $1 per $100, or 1 percent. Since people usually carry traveler's checks when they travel, their usefulness is only about two to four weeks. If your traveler's checks are gone in two weeks, that 1 percent charge in two weeks is the equivalent of 2 percent a month, or about 25 percent interest on an annualized basis. That's a pretty steep price to pay for so-called financial protection. A better alternative when you travel is certainly a no-fee, long-float credit card.

ATTACK #112

Pull out your credit card and offer a discounted cash price for a purchase.

An understanding of how the credit card system works can give you an average 4 percent discount on everything you buy. Let's say you're buying a stereo for $500. What if instead of putting the charge on your credit card you were to, with your credit card on the counter, say, "Look, let me save you the time of having to go through the credit card process and having the bank discount the amount you get by 4 percent. Let me just write you a check for $480. You'll get the same amount and you'll be helping me buy the stereo at a lower price."

One out of two salespeople will say yes after talking to the manager or the storeowner. Even if you have to spend a couple of extra minutes explaining the process to the manager, $20 for a few minutes' effort on a $500 purchase is well worth it. Think of it this way: the 4 percent that you are saving by writing the check will offset a large percentage of the sales tax that the merchant is about to add onto your purchase. Over the course of a year, if you spend $10,000 on large purchases, you can save an easy $400. Of course, you only make your offer after you have gotten the merchant down to the rock-bottom price.

DEFENSE #113

Never leave home without a back-up credit card.

Because MasterCard and Visa cards always come with credit limits, when you are shopping or traveling on business or on vacation, you may sooner or later end up being denied credit when your purchase amount is verified by telephone. Why? Not because you are a deadbeat or have overcharged on your credit card. You have simply overcommitted.

Sometimes your credit limit is exceeded by things you never charged. When you check into a hotel or rent a car using a credit card, the hotel or car rental company puts a hold on a portion of your credit limit by calling in the amount they think you will eventually end up owing. Since it doesn't cost the hotel or car rental company anything and the hold on the credit limit guarantees they will be paid, a hold is put on your account for the maximum possible charge. When you travel for a few days, hundreds or even thousands of dollars of your line of credit can be tied up even though you have not actually charged or used that amount. A hold is treated as if the money has actually been charged, and the full amount is deducted from your remaining available credit. Once your credit limit is exceeded, your card stops working, and you are left high and dry at the next counter with egg on your face. The hold stays on your account for up to 10 days or until a credit card draft comes in with the amount you have actually charged.

Your strategy is to carry a second, back-up MasterCard or Visa to use anytime one card is refused for any reason. An alternative is to carry an American Express or Diner's Club card, which has no limit but must be paid off monthly. Of course, you can also increase the credit limit on your MasterCard or Visa card if you qualify.

It does virtually no good to call the credit card company to try to get even an unused hold on your line of credit removed. You will simply be told that it expires automatically in 10 days. You can speed up that process, however. Once you have settled your final bill at a hotel or rental car counter, ask the clerk to call the credit card company with the actual charges and release the hold.

There's another way to avoid the problem. If you are planning to keep a hotel room or rental car for a week to 10 days, simply tell the car rental company or the hotel that you are going to use the car or the room for only a couple of days and you will notify them if you need it longer. In most cases, you will hear a simple, "No problem, just let us know." They will put a hold on your account for just a small amount of money not a larger amount that might exceed your credit limit.

ATTACK #114

Upgrade to a gold card for golden opportunities.

The latest wrinkle in the credit card wars is the attempt to attract affluent and upwardly mobile big spenders. MasterCard, Visa and American Express are all competing by adding services to their gold cards. Some of these services are amazing and will actually help you financially.

There are currently about 15 million each of MasterCard and Visa gold card holders. American Express has 7 million. Gold cards now number about 14 percent of the total 250 million bank credit cards issued in the United States. With 90 million families in America, that means each family has on the average about two and one-half bank credit cards. Gold card marketers target 35- to 55-year-old homeowners with one or two wage earners, with a total income in excess of $40,000. In the credit card business, they are known as the "twice the profit, half the risk" group.

To qualify for a gold card, depending on the issuer, your income must be at least between $25,000 and $50,000 per year with the average gold card holder having an income of $35,000 a year. Normally, you will also have to furnish a financial statement.

Is a gold card worth the extra trouble and the few extra dollars you might pay in annual fees? You bet it is. The minimum credit limit on a gold card is $5,000, making a gold card, or gold card and a back-up card, the only credit cards that most people will ever need. The six greatest benefits of the gold card are:

1. Rental car deductible insurance
2. Loss, theft or damage insurance on purchases
3. Automatic extended warranties on purchases

4. Medical assistance
5. Card replacement
6. Legal assistance

None of the insurance services would be worth much if you had to pay the going rate for them on a personal insurance policy, but as freebies they are worth a lot. In addition, some gold card issuers also provide one or more of the following extra services:

- A summarized charge record at the end of the year, which simplifies your recordkeeping system
- Free traveler's checks
- Your choice of billing date
- Free cards for other family members
- The skip-a-payment option (but you can't skip the monthly interest charge)

Rental Car Deductible Insurance

If you've ever rented a car, you know the most intimidating moment is when the clerk tries to hit you up for an extra $10 to $20 per day for the various kinds of insurance. The only one of the five coverages offered that could affect your pocketbook is the collision damage waiver. That's the amount of deductible you would have to pay before the rental car company's insurance kicks in should you have an accident. Over the past few years, auto rental companies have been dramatically raising the deductible, so that the average is now from $3,000 up to the full value of the car. The cost of this insurance is about $12 a day. Although your own automobile insurance policy covers you when you're driving someone else's car, even a rental car, when you're standing at the rental desk, you're never quite sure.

You *can* be sure with the gold card. On all gold cards—Visa, MasterCard and American Express—the collision damage waiver is covered. Should you smash up the car, the deductible of $3,000 or more is covered by the free insurance that comes with your gold card, provided you charged the rental on your card. The rental car company's insurance covers any balance. If you drive on business or vacation, it pays to use your gold card. The coverage is automatic. There are no extra forms to fill out. Just make sure that you keep a copy of your credit card receipt and rental papers for any potential claims.

If the company you work for gives you a Hertz, Budget or Avis rental car charge card, you may want to ask instead for a company gold card that would cover the deductible. Since so many of my employees travel, the Givens Organization rents at least 20 cars a week, and inevitably there have been some accidents. Although no one has ever been hurt, over the years about a dozen rental cars have been damaged in one way or the other. It is our company policy now to make sure that all car rentals are charged on credit cards that cover the collision damage waiver. Why not? It's a free service that has paid hundreds of dollars in damages, and saved even more in insurance costs.

Loss, Theft or Damage Insurance on Purchases

With a gold card you have free 90-day automatic insurance coverage on purchases made around the world. Anything you purchase with the card is insured against loss, theft, fire or accidental damage up to $50,000. It is known as secondary coverage and kicks in only after your homeowner's or automobile insurance policy has paid off. MasterCard and Visa have also expanded the coverage to include gifts, even after you've given them.

Purchase insurance is the greatest coverage a world traveler could have. When you're traveling abroad and buy jewelry, art or handcrafted items, invariably something is going to get lost, stolen or broken. Years ago on a trip abroad, I bought a beautiful diamond and 18K gold bracelet which somehow came off my wrist and was lost after only a couple of weeks. The loss occurred within the 90-day protection period, so American Express, without a whimper, reimbursed the almost $2,000 cost. On our last trip to Greece, my wife and I, as we often do, bought some beautiful Greek art, which was damaged in shipping. The retail store we purchased it from had gone out of business, and this time a gold card came to the rescue.

Automatic Extended Warranties on Purchases

When you're buying things that tend to break down, like appliances, TVs, stereos and car radios, gold card automatic warranties double the warranty period for up to one year. If the original warranty is 90 days, the extended warranty protection doubles the coverage to six months. If the original warranty is a year, you get two years of protection. Although purchasing extended warranties, as I said in Chapter 7, is a poor use of your money, doubled warranties that are free because the item is charged on a gold card are a great benefit.

If the manufacturer's warranty has run out, have the item repaired and submit the bill to your gold card company along with the original purchase documentation. If the gold card extended warranty is still in effect, your credit card company will pay the bill. Always keep good records of both your credit card purchase and any extended warranties that may apply.

Medical Assistance

Credit card companies have also gotten into the medical assistance business. If you carry a gold card, the company provides a telephone number you can call for medical assistance. When you're more than 100 miles away from home and you become ill, call your credit card company and you will get help with local doctors, emergency evacuation, information on prescriptions from your local pharmacy, notification of family members and pretty much any other emergency medical assistance you may need. Although you might seldom if ever need this kind of assistance, when you or someone in your family does have a medical emergency while you are traveling, it is well worth the protection. Besides, it's free.

Card Replacement

Having your credit cards or cash stolen is scary enough. What's worse is being away from home without credit cards or cash. If your gold card is lost or stolen, the card replacement service of the company will give you a replacement credit card within 48 hours, plus up to $5,000 in cash or the difference between your balance and your credit limit, whichever is less. This service will also help you in replacing a passport or airplane tickets that were lost or stolen. You may only need this service once, but that one time it will be worth much more than you spend on annual fees for your gold card.

Legal Assistance

One of the most highly touted benefits of the gold card, and the one that you will use the least, is legal assistance. This service provides attorney referrals or names of people at consulates and embassies to contact should you get in trouble. The only real value of this service is if you're traveling abroad and find yourself in legal difficulties with the police or some other authority.

These six major benefits should put a gold card (or the American Express platinum card) high on your list of financial friends. Check the following list to find the trade names under which these services are offered. Even if the annual fee on your gold card is $10 to $20 higher than the fee on regular card, these services are worth it. Even the less important services can be useful. If you qualify for a gold card, apply for one now and count yourself among a group that can enjoy the special benefits. Memorize or carry a list of the services in your wallet or purse with any necessary phone numbers.

GOLD CARD SERVICES AND TRADE NAMES

	VISA	MASTERCARD	AMEX
1. Rental Car Insurance	CDW Insurance	Master Rental	CDW Insurance
2. Purchase Insurance	Purchase Security	Purchase Assurance	Purchase Protection
3. Extended Warranties	Extended Protection	Extended Warranty	Buyer's Assurance
4. Medical Assistance	Emergency Medical/Medic	Master Assist	Global Assistance
5. Card Replacement	Emergency Card Replacement	Master Trip	Global Assistance
6. Legal Assistance	Legal Assistance	Master Legal	Global Assistance

The following lists show you the best gold cards to carry depending on how you use them. The no-fee cards are best if you pay off your balance every month. In developing these ratings, I took into consideration the annual fee versus the amount of money you save with lower interest rates on your balance. You can apply for these cards by calling the listed telephone numbers.

GOLD LOW-RATE SURVEY†

APR	TYPE	ANNUAL FEE	AREA	STATE	ISSUER NAME	ADDRESS	PHONE	OUT OF STATE	GRACE PERIOD
6.75	V/MC	$28	worldwide	Georgia	Wachovia Bank	P.O. Box 16989 Atlanta, GA 30321	1-800-842-3262	yes	25 days
8.75	MC	$45	nationwide	Illinois	Amalgamated Trust Bank	P.O. Box A3979 Chicago, IL 60690	1-800-365-6464	yes	25 days

†dated information, subject to change

GOLD NO-ANNUAL-FEE SURVEY†

APR	TYPE	ANNUAL FEE	AREA	STATE	ISSUER NAME	ADDRESS	PHONE	OUT OF STATE	GRACE PERIOD
9.65	V/MC	—	worldwide	South Carolina	AFBA Industrial	Attn. card services P.O. Box 100152 Columbia, SC 29202-9575	1-800-776-2265	yes	25 days
10.35	MC	—	nationwide	Illinois	Amalgamated Trust Bank	P.O. Box A3979 Chicago, IL 60690	1-800-365-6464	yes	25 days
12.5	V/MC	—	nationwide	Texas	USAA FSB	USA Fed. S.F. 10750 McDermott Freeway, San Antonio, TX 78288	1-800-922-9092	yes	25 days
9.8	V/MC	—	nationwide	Michigan	First Bank of America	P.O. Box 2349 Kalamazoo, MI 49003	1-800-423-3883	yes	25 days
6.9	V/MC	—	nationwide	Delaware	First USA Bank	P.O. Box 740115 Atlanta, GA 30374	1-800-537-6954	yes	25 days
13.65	V/MC	—	nationwide	Delaware	Bank of NY/Del. Consumer's Edge	P.O. Box 6999 Newark, DE 19714-6999	1-800-235-3343	yes	25 days
14.15	MC	—*	nationwide	Illinois	Oak Brook Bank	P.O. Box 5033 Oak Brook, IL 60522	1-800-666-1011	yes	25 days

*no fee for first year only
†dated information, subject to change

ATTACK #115

Begin a credit rehabilitation program with a secured credit card.

The main problem with trying to rehabilitate bad credit is finding someone to give you credit again. If you could just find a substantial lender like a bank to give you some credit, then you could prove your financial situation has changed, you could make your payments on time and everyone would be happy. The Catch-22 is no one wants to be first. Most financial sources would not mind being second or third but not first.

I have found several banks that will give you a MasterCard or Visa to help you reestablish your credit, no matter what your credit problems have been: late payments, no payments, even bankruptcy. How can they afford to take the chance? Because they minimize the risk by giving you a secured credit card.

To get a secured MasterCard or Visa, which looks like any other credit card, the bank will ask you to put up a deposit, often in an interest-bearing account. The minimum deposit is usually about $300 with a maximum of $3,000 to $5,000. The amount is chosen by you. The bank will then issue you a MasterCard or Visa with 75 percent to 100 percent of the amount you deposited as your credit line. When you get the card, go straight to your local credit bureau and have this new, good credit source put in your credit bureau file. And after 30 days check your credit file to be certain it has been updated. Although secured cards often have slightly higher than average annual fees or higher than average interest rates, reestablishing your credit is certainly worth the extra cost.

Your secured card, when you get it, is not to be used to put you further in debt with higher and higher payments. Use your secured card only to reestablish your credit. It can do more for you with 30 minutes of effort than you can possibly do in the next few years without it. Remember, if you have a bad credit record, it can take seven to ten years before you can get the derogatory information removed from your credit file. But with one or two secured cards, you can be well on your way to credit recovery in as little as 60 days. Once you have gotten your secured card and had the positive information entered into your credit file, you will find that others will now consider giving you automobile loans and even mortgages; that is, provided all of your other payments due are up-to-date. The secured credit card process won't suddenly give you perfect credit, but it will give you solid footing on which to stand.

Ninety-five percent of all applications for secured credit cards are approved. The exceptions are usually for those who have committed credit card fraud or are currently way behind in payments.

Because most banks are very poor at marketing, particularly if they are trying to sell a good idea nationally, few people realize that secured credit cards exist. That lack of general information paved the way for one of the biggest scams I've seen in recent years. The process is simple and profitable. A company is formed that buys thousands of one-minute advertisements on network and cable television that appeal specifically to the problems of people with poor or no credit. "No Credit Problem Too Big," the ads proclaim. "We'll repair your credit immediately. Simply call this 900 number." Down at the bottom of the screen, in tiny print, right where the picture tends to get fuzzy, it says that $45 will automatically be charged on your telephone bill when you make the call. One of two things happens if you do call. You may be sent a secured credit card application from a bank, which the marketing company got free from the bank and for which you just paid $45, or you may be sent an entire package of additional forms to fill out with brochures that promise to handle your total credit problem for charges ranging from $200 to $2,500. Whatever the amount, say "no thanks" to all these extra services. All you need is a secured card application that you can get free.

Following is a list of the best sources for secured MasterCard and Visa cards, including the annual fees. You'll be glad to know that after you have made your payments on time for about six months, the bank will return your deposit and allow you to keep the card. Or, if you request it, the bank will increase your credit limit above your deposit.

Be careful of the temptation to overuse your secured card. That's probably the kind of thinking that got you into trouble in the first place. Also be careful of charging anything on a secured card that has an interest rate of 17 percent to 23 percent.

SECURED CREDIT CARD SOURCES†

APR	TYPE	ANNUAL FEE	MIN. DEPOSIT	STATE	ISSUER NAME	PHONE	OUT OF STATE	GRACE PERIOD
18.9	VISA	$35	$400	Oregon	American Pacific Bank	1-800-879-8745	yes	30 days
19.8	MC	$45	$250	Texas	Associates National Bank	1-214-281-4955	yes	25 days
17.15	V/MC	$35	$500	Indiana	Bank One Lafayette	1-800-395-2555	yes	25 days
9.9	VISA	$49	$600	Colorado	Best Bank	1-303-450-9074	yes	no grace period

†dated information, subject to change

DEFENSE #116

Make your secured credit card deposit, then borrow the money back.

One reason why more people don't get secured credit cards to reestablish their credit is that they may be operating so close to the wire that it is difficult to leave even as little as $300 on deposit for any length of time. If that's your problem, here's your strategy: Make your deposit, let's say $500, in an interest-bearing account at the bank that issues your secured credit card, and when you get the card go to any MasterCard or Visa bank and borrow back the money up to your limit. When you have a $500 deposit at a secured credit card bank, which has given you a $500 credit limit, you can borrow back the entire amount. Therefore, your $500 is tied up for only a month or so. The real interest you pay for the loan is only the difference between what you're being charged in interest by the bank and what you're being paid in interest for your deposit, minus any small cash advance charge.

CHAPTER 15

Harness the Power of a Home Mortgage

Some of the most important and expensive decisions you'll ever make are about mortgages.

Mortgage payments are your second biggest financial expense, second only to the income and other taxes you'll pay during your lifetime. An average American family will pay $1,000 per month for 40 years and own three or more homes. Almost $500,000 or over 25 percent of your income will be spent on mortgage payments alone, over half of it wasted because of what you haven't been taught. No one escapes mortgage payments. When you rent you are still making a mortgage payment—your landlord's, for which you get no tax or appreciation benefits.

Nowhere in your financial life will some basic knowledge and the right strategies save you more money for the time involved than with mortgages.

Here are the questions for which you must have the correct answers and strategies in order to win the mortgage game:

1. What is the maximum price of home I can afford?
2. How can I determine the best mortgage when each has a different combination of interest rates and points?
3. Which is better and when, a fixed-rate mortgage (FRM) or an adjustable-rate mortgage (ARM)?
4. How long a term should I get on my mortgage—15, 20, 25 or 30 years? Is it a good idea to get the longest term possible to keep my monthly payment as low as possible?

5. What kind of mortgage should I look for—FHA, VA, conventional or first-time home buyer?
6. Where do I go if a mortgage company or S&L turns me down?
7. How do I buy a home if I have poor credit?
8. What should I watch out for when signing a mortgage contract?
9. What can I do now to make the mortgage that I already have a super deal?
10. Should I ever convert my adjustable-rate mortgage to a fixed rate?
11. How do I know when refinancing is in my best interest, if ever?

The answers to these questions are contained in simple mathematical formulas and strategies that I have developed for you, all of which we will cover in this chapter. With this knowledge you will, from today forward, be putting mortgage power on your side of the balance sheet.

DEFENSE #117

Buy a home with a mortgage whose annual payments do not exceed 30 percent of your total annual income.

How much in monthly payments on a mortgage can you really afford? How much house will that buy? Well, that depends on the rest of your lifestyle. But in order to make mortgage and house hunting practical, we've got to choose a rule to begin with. The old rule of thumb, up until the seventies, was that a family could afford to spend on housing no more than 25 percent of its gross annual income. Great idea when the average mortgage interest rate was 6 to 8 percent and the cost of housing was relatively modest. Today, inflation and higher interest rates have changed the rules of the game.

A good rule of thumb now is that you want to spend no more than 30 percent of your gross annual income on mortgage payments. Greater than 30 percent on a mortgage means fewer movies, fewer dinners out, less vacation money and less fun. Becoming a prisoner to your own home is not what life and successful living are all about. In fact, your gross annual income is probably the first figure a lender will look at when you apply for a mortgage, the second is the total amount of your monthly payments, and the third is your credit history.

Before you go shopping for a home, you must determine the maximum amount of mortgage payment that you can afford. Using the Maximum Mortgage Planning Chart on page 310, find your total annual income in column A. The figure in column B approximates your total income per month. After applying the 30 percent affordable mortgage factor in column C, column D then shows the maximum monthly home mortgage payment you can probably afford. Since your payment includes principal, interest, taxes and insurance, but the maximum mortgage amount is based on principal and interest only, column E allocates 90 percent for principal and interest and leaves the other 10 percent for taxes and insurance.

The next columns, F through I, show at interest rates from 10 to 13 percent how much total home mortgage or home price you can afford if you made no down payment, based on the monthly payment in column E. Add any down payment you intend to make to the maximum mortgage amounts shown, and the result will be the maximum price range of home you can afford.

I have included on the chart the maximum mortgage that you can afford with both 15-year and 30-year financing. Immediately you may say, "Well, I can afford a bigger mortgage with 30-year financing." No one, as you will soon see, can ever afford a 30-year mortgage.

Notice on the chart how the total amount of mortgage you can afford is influenced by the interest rates. If your family income is $60,000 for instance, the chart says that you can afford payments on a $126,000 mortgage for 15 years at 10 percent interest, but only a $107,000 mortgage if the interest rate is at 13 percent. Another way to look at it is that you can buy 20 percent more home when interest rates are lower simply because of the difference in the monthly payment.

All mortgage companies have their own rules for the maximum mortgage they will make based on your income and debt. This planning chart will tell you what you really can afford financially, rather than the size of the loan for which you will qualify. Use the chart every time you are thinking about buying a new home or upgrading to a more expensive home. As your income increases over time, naturally so will the maximum mortgage amount and price of home that you can afford.

MAXIMUM MORTGAGE PLANNING CHART

(A) GROSS ANNUAL INCOME	(B) APPROX. MONTHLY INCOME	(C) MAXIMUM MORTGAGE FACTOR	(D) AFFORDABLE MONTHLY PAYMENT AMOUNT	(E) 90% FOR PRINCIPAL AND INTEREST	MAXIMUM MORTGAGE YOU CAN AFFORD (F) 10%		(G) 11%		(H) 12%		(I) 13%	
					15 YR.	30 YR.	15 YR.	30 YR.	15 YR.	30 YR.	15 YR.	30 YR.
$20,000	$1,700	×.30	$500	$450	$42,000	$51,000	$40,000	$47,000	$38,000	$44,000	$36,000	$41,000
$25,000	$2,100	×.30	$625	$560	$52,000	$64,000	$49,000	$59,000	$47,000	$54,000	$44,000	$50,000
$30,000	$2,500	×.30	$750	$670	$63,000	$77,000	$59,000	$70,000	$56,000	$65,000	$53,000	$60,000
$35,000	$2,900	×.30	$875	$790	$74,000	$90,000	$69,000	$84,000	$66,000	$77,000	$63,000	$72,000
$40,000	$3,300	×.30	$1,000	$900	$84,000	$102,000	$79,000	$95,000	$75,000	$87,000	$72,000	$81,000
$50,000	$4,200	×.30	$1,250	$1,120	$104,000	$128,000	$99,000	$118,000	$93,000	$109,000	$88,000	$101,000
$60,000	$5,000	×.30	$1,500	$1,350	$126,000	$154,000	$119,000	$142,000	$112,000	$131,000	$107,000	$122,000
$70,000	$5,800	×.30	$1,750	$1,575	$147,000	$180,000	$140,000	$165,000	$131,000	$153,000	$125,000	$142,000
$80,000	$6,700	×.30	$2,000	$1,800	$168,000	$205,000	$158,000	$189,000	$150,000	$175,000	$142,000	$163,000
$100,000	$8,300	×.30	$2,500	$2,250	$233,000	$285,000	$220,000	$263,000	$208,000	$243,000	$197,000	$226,000
$150,000	$12,500	×.30	$3,750	$3,375	$350,000	$430,000	$332,000	$396,000	$314,000	$366,000	$297,000	$341,000
$200,000	$17,000	×.30	$5,000	$4,500	$419,000	$512,000	$398,000	$473,000	$375,000	$437,000	$357,000	$407,000
$300,000	$25,000	×.30	$7,500	$6,750	$628,000	$769,000	$594,000	$709,000	$563,000	$656,000	$534,000	$610,000

DEFENSE #118

Convert points to their interest rate equivalent in order to compare mortgage rates.

Points are the mortgage lender's method of getting thousands in extra interest from you while making you think you are getting a lower interest rate. One point is 1 percent of the amount you are borrowing, and points charged on a mortgage these days range from zero to eight. Five points on a $100,000 conventional mortgage is an extra $5,000, which can be paid in cash at closing or, as is usually the case, added to your mortgage amount. If you finance the $5,000 and the mortgage interest rate is 11 percent, you would pay a total of $10,229 for the extra $5,000 on a 15-year mortgage, or $17,143 for your five points over 30 years. Points will cost two to three times the original amount when financed into the mortgage, which means you are paying, in effect, a higher interest rate than the one you are quoted. Points are therefore an important factor to consider when you are applying for a mortgage.

The confusion about points comes because there are so many lenders charging different combinations of points, interest rates and mortgage terms. Even the same lender may ask you, "Do you want the 9¾ percent mortgage with six points or the 10 percent mortgage with two points?" How do you choose your best deal? If you've ever asked a real estate broker or mortgage lender, you got an answer that sounded as if it came from Mumbles in the Dick Tracy movie. For some reason no one seems to know the formula.

To compute the true interest rate, you must first convert points to their equivalent mortgage interest rate. You then add that equivalent interest rate to the mortgage interest rate you are quoted, to compare your mortgage options accurately. Here is an example, assuming you intend to finance the points.

Mortgage Amount:	$100,000
Interest Rate:	11%
Term:	15 or 30 years
Points:	5 points or $5,000
Amount Actually Financed:	$105,000 ($100,000 mortgage + $5,000 points)

To determine the true interest percentage you are paying when points are included, determine the total amount you will pay over the 30 years on the $105,000 you are financing. The total on a 15-year mortgage is $214,817 as shown in the table that follows. That means based on the fact that the amount you borrowed was only $100,000, you are paying $114,817 in interest. Using a financial calculator, you can determine, as shown in the chart, that your actual interest rate is 11.90 percent instead of the 11 percent quoted. Five points financed on a $100,000, 15-year mortgage at 11 percent adds the equivalent of .90 percent interest.

THE EFFECT OF FIVE POINTS ON YOUR INTEREST RATE

INTEREST RATE	MORTGAGE AMOUNT	YEARS	MONTHLY PAYMENT	TOTAL
	WITHOUT POINTS			
11%	$100,000	15	$1,136.60	$204,588
		30	952.33	342,839
	WITH POINTS			
11%	$105,000	15	$1,193.43	$214,817
		30	999.95	359,982

QUOTED RATE VS. ACTUAL RATE	YEARS	QUOTED RATE	ACTUAL RATE	EXTRA INTEREST FOR 5 POINTS	EXTRA INTEREST FOR 1 POINT
	15	11%	11.90%	.90%	.18%
	30	11%	11.75%	.63%	.13%

The greater the number of points, the higher the interest rate. Here is the true interest on an 11 percent, 15-year mortgage when you add from one to eight points.

15-YEAR MORTGAGE

POINTS	TRUE INTEREST	POINTS	TRUE INTEREST
0	11.00%	5	11.90%
1	11.18%	6	12.07%
2	11.36%	7	12.25%
3	11.54%	8	12.42%
4	11.72%		

Now let's look at points if financed for 30 years at the same interest rate of 11 percent. Using the same $100,000 mortgage with five points, or $5,000, added, you will pay an additional $17,143 and the true interest rate will be 11.63 percent.

11.00%	Quoted Rate
.63%	Interest Equivalent of 5 Points
11.63%	True Rate

On the 30-year mortgage at 11 percent, one point is therefore the equivalent of about .13 percent interest.

Here is the true interest on an 11 percent, 30-year mortgage when you add one to eight points:

30-YEAR MORTGAGE

POINTS	TRUE INTEREST	POINTS	TRUE INTEREST
0	11.00%	5	11.63%
1	11.13%	6	11.78%
2	11.25%	7	11.91%
3	11.38%	8	12.04%
4	11.50%		

Use these formulas to determine interest rate equivalents when comparing mortgages in order to find your best option. At a quoted rate of 10 percent or 12 percent, the equivalent is only slightly different from what it is at 11 percent, so you can use the tables above as your rule of thumb to compare mortgages at any interest rate. If you want to be even more accurate, use the table below, The Interest Equivalent of Points.

THE INTEREST EQUIVALENT OF POINTS

QUOTED INTEREST RATE	*Amount to Add for Each Point Charged*	
	15 YRS.	30 YRS.
9%	.170	.112
10%	.175	.119
11%	.181	.126
12%	.186	.134

The table shows the percentage of interest to add for each extra point charged by your mortgage lender for interest rates of

9 percent to 12 percent on 15- and 30-year mortgages. For instance, an 11 percent mortgage with one point for 30 years is really a rate of 11.126 percent. With two points the rate increases to 11.252 percent or over ¼ percent higher than you were quoted. Your mortgage lender would probably rather you didn't take the time to figure out these interest equivalents, but if you do, you can save yourself a lot of money.

Now let's go back to the question asked earlier in this strategy. Would you be better off with a 9¾ percent, 30-year mortgage with six points or a 10 percent mortgage with two points if you include the points in the financing? To answer that question, first convert the points in both cases to an extra percentage and then compare the true interest rates.

From The Interest Equivalent of Points table, one point at either 9¾ percent or 10 percent equals an extra .12 percent interest when rounded. Six points therefore equal about an extra .72 percent interest and two points add about .24 percent interest.

9.75%	Quoted Interest Rate	10.00%	Quoted Interest Rate
+.72%	Added Equivalent Interest from 6 Points	+.24%	Added Equivalent Interest from 2 Points
10.47%	True Interest Rate	10.24%	True Interest Rate

In this case the 10 percent mortgage is the better value, since the true interest rate is 10.24 percent versus 10.47 percent for the 9¾ percent mortgage.

DEFENSE #119

Choose an FRM or ARM based on total potential payments, not monthly payments.

One question you will always face when getting a mortgage is whether the fixed-rate or the adjustable-rate mortgage is the best choice. Fixed-rate mortgages have interest rates and monthly payments that remain constant during the entire term of the mortgage. Adjustable-rate mortgages, also called variable-rate mortgages, have interest rates that fluctuate during the term of the mortgage. Emotionally, the fixed rate feels better because the payment remains constant; there is a sense of security in knowing what to expect. Financially, however, the fixed-rate mortgage is not always your best bet.

Your objective is to pay the least amount of total interest during the years you own the home. If the average interest rate during the years you own your home is less with an ARM mortgage than with an FRM, you will pay less interest with the ARM. Although mortgage rates on new ARM or FRM mortgages fluctuate from 8 to 16 percent over the years, the average mortgage rate is about 10 percent. If you got a 10 percent FRM, you would pay about the same total amount over the 15- to 30-year term of your mortgage as you would with an ARM except for one difference—the first two years' ARM discount.

To entice borrowers to take the ARM, mortgage lenders have offered the first two years of ARM interest rates at about 2 percent less than the new FRM rate available at the same time. On a 10 percent, $100,000 mortgage, the 2 percent two-year discount saves you $2,000 each year, or $4,000 total interest. That same $4,000 in an investment earning only 10 percent over the term of a 15-year mortgage would grow to a respectable $12,000. That's what the first two years' discount of an ARM can mean to you.

The break-even interest rate when comparing new ARMs and FRMs, because of the ARM discount, is about 9¾ percent instead of 10 percent. If the FRM interest rate at the time you are shopping is over 9¾ percent, always opt for the ARM. If, on the other hand, FRM interest is 9¾ percent of less, take the FRM. Simple enough. Remember to adjust the quoted interest rates by the interest equivalent of the points to find the true interest rate. See Defense #118. Ask what the ARM interest rate would be now if not discounted and use the regular ARM rate to compare with the FRM or another ARM.

Check at least five mortgage lenders in your area to determine the best rates available, and convert points, if any, to their interest percentage equivalent. The chart below will help you make the comparison.

LENDER'S NAME	MORTGAGE TERM/YEARS	FRM INTEREST	FRM POINTS	TRUE FRM RATE	ARM INTEREST	ARM POINTS	TRUE ARM RATE
1.							
2.							
3.							
4.							
5.							

STRATEGY:

If true FRM rate is 9¾ percent or less, take the FRM mortgage.
If true FRM rate is over 9¾ percent, take the ARM mortgage.

ATTACK #120

Ask for a 15-year mortgage instead of a 30-year mortgage to triple your wealth-building power.

You can save tens of thousands of mortgage interest dollars by putting the time value of money on your side. The mortgage company will automatically give you a 30-year term if you don't object. Why? Because 30-year mortgages make mortgage companies rich.

For every $100,000 you borrow at 10 percent interest for 30 years, your principal and interest will be $877.57 a month. At the end of five years (60 payments), you will have paid $52,650 to the mortgage company but reduced your principal balance by only $3,425, less than 3½ percent. After 10 years (120 payments) on the same mortgage, you have sent the mortgage company $105,308—more than the original mortgage amount—but have paid off only $9,000, or 9 percent, of the principal.

Let's say you get a 15-year instead of the 30-year mortgage for the same $100,000 at 10 percent. Your monthly payments go up $197.04 to $1,074.61 per month, but you will save $122,500 in total interest over the 15 years. Your equity is always growing much faster with a 15-year mortgage. With a 15-year mortgage at the end of five years (60 payments), you have reduced your principal by $18,684 instead of $3,425, and at the end of 10 years (120 payments) your principal balance has been cut by $49,424 instead of just $9,000. What a difference!

Let's compare a 15-year and a 30-year mortgage every year for the first 15 years. We'll use 10 percent as the interest rate. Look at the table that follows, The Wealth-Building Power of a 15-Year Mortgage.

THE WEALTH-BUILDING POWER OF A 15-YEAR MORTGAGE

Interest Rate 10%

	A *Mortgage Balance (% of Original Loan Still Owed)*		B *Your Equity*	
AGE OF MORTGAGE (YEARS)	15-YEAR MORTGAGE	30-YEAR MORTGAGE	15-YEAR MORTGAGE	30-YEAR MORTGAGE
1	97%	99%	3%	1%
2	94	99	6	1
3	90	98	10	2
4	86	97	14	3
5	81	97	19	3
6	76	96	24	4
7	71	95	29	5
8	65	94	35	6
9	58	92	42	8
10	51	91	49	9
11	42	89	58	11
12	33	88	67	12
13	23	86	77	14
14	12	84	88	16
15	0	82	0	18

The figures in section A show the mortgage balance percent or percentage of your original loan you still owe after each year, 1 through 15, on 15-year and 30-year mortgages at 10 percent interest. The figures in section B show the percentage of your original mortgage you have paid off after each year, 1 through 15, on the same 15- and 30-year mortgages. There is no question that a 15-year mortgage will build your wealth at a much faster pace, and all for just a few extra dollars a month.

If you are buying your first home or barely qualify for a 30-year mortgage, you may not qualify for a 15-year mortgage because of the difference in monthly payments. In that case, you may accomplish nearly the same savings by accepting the 30-year mortgage and immediately making extra principal payments. See Attack #128. During the first few years of a 30-year mortgage, the extra principal payment required each month will be less than the difference in the monthly payment between a

15-year and a 30-year mortgage, giving you some slack now when you need it most. During the last few years of the mortgage term, as the monthly principal becomes the larger part of your payment, the extra principal required will exceed the difference in payments on the 15-year and 30-year mortgages.

After 15 years of payments on a 15-year mortgage, your mortgage balance is zero. But notice after 15 years on the 30-year mortgage, you still owe 82 percent of the amount you originally borrowed! Could that be possible! You bet it is. All those huge payments for 15 years, and you have paid off only 18 percent of the original amount of your loan. If your 30-year loan was originally for $100,000, after 15 years you have paid off only $18,000 and still owe $82,000. No one, under any circumstances, can afford a 30-year mortgage. Think of it this way. On the 15-year, 10 percent mortgage, you paid only 20 percent more a month, but at the end of 15 years the whole $100,000 original mortgaged amount of your home belongs to you. Even if you sell your home after just three, five or 10 years, you have still saved thousands with the 15-year mortgage.

For instance, let's say that you intend to sell your home in five years. Refer back to the Wealth-Building Power of a 15-Year Mortgage table on page 317. Let's see what the balance would be on both a 15- and a 30-year loan. Reading down the "Age of Mortgage" column to five years and then going horizontally to the 15-year column, you will notice that after five years you have paid off 19 percent of your 15-year loan, still owing 81 percent, but after five years on your 30-year loan, you owe a whopping 97 percent. Five years of big payments and you paid off only 3 percent of the principal! As you can see, the 15-year mortgage makes sense, no matter how long you intend to keep your home. If you own between three and five homes over a 15-year period and get a 15-year mortgage instead of a 30-year mortgage on each, you will still end up after 15 years with close to total ownership of your current home.

Surprisingly enough, the purpose of a 15-year mortgage is not to end up with a paid-off home. The purpose is to be paying yourself, contributing to your equity account instead of overpaying interest to your mortgage company, a process that is totally worthless to you unless you also happen to own the mortgage company.

One question probably on your mind is, "If a 15-year mortgage is great, is a 10-year or seven-year mortgage even better?" Absolutely. However, the shorter the term, the more the payments increase relative to the savings, so the law of diminishing returns begins to take effect. To help understand the big picture, I developed the table that follows, which will show you in five-year increments how many dollars and months you will save with shorter mortgage terms and how much your payments will increase in the process.

Increasing Benefits of Decreasing the Mortgage Term

For our table we'll use a $100,000 mortgage at 11 percent interest and compare the monthly payment increases with the total payment decreases as the mortgage term gets shorter.

$100,000 MORTGAGE, 11% INTEREST

					COMPARED WITH 30-YEAR MORTGAGE			
MORTGAGE TERM—YEARS	NUMBER OF MONTHS	MONTHLY PAYMENT	TOTAL AMOUNT PAID OVER TERM	TOTAL INTEREST PAID	% INCREASE IN PAYMENT	PAYMENT INCREASE PER $100,000	AMOUNT OF INTEREST SAVED	# OF MONTHS SAVED
30	360	$ 952	$342,836	$242,836	—	$ —	$ —	—
25	300	980	294,034	194,034	3%	28	48,802	60
20	240	1,032	247,725	147,725	8%	80	95,111	120
15	180	1,136	204,587	104,587	19%	184	138,249	180
10	120	1,377	165,300	65,300	45%	425	177,536	240
5	60	2,174	130,455	30,455	128%	1,220	212,381	300

Notice from the last two columns in the table that the amount of interest and number of months saved increase dramatically as you shorten the term. However, the percentage increase in payments is dramatic for a mortgage term shorter than 15 years. To pay off your mortgage in 10 years instead of 15, for instance, you would have to increase your payments to $1,377, up 45 percent from the 30-year mortgage payment instead of only a 19 percent increase to $1,136 for the 15-year mortgage. Great if you can afford it, but that big an increase may not be practical if you have not yet applied all of the strategies in this book.

Now that you know how to evaluate and compare mortgages and terms, it is time to learn the best types of mortgages available and where to find them.

ATTACK #121

If you qualify for a state or county first-time-buyer mortgage, take it.

One of the best mortgage alternatives is state or county mortgages for first-time home buyers. Many states and counties have raised mortgage money through bond issues to make it easier for individuals or couples to buy their first home. Bonds are sold to investors by the local government, and the money is used to make low-interest home loans. Qualifications for these mortgages are less stringent than for FHA or conventional mortgages. The maximum amount you can borrow, however, is limited to the cost of an average-priced home or less in the area in which you live.

First-time-home-buyer mortgages are usually offered at an exceedingly low interest rate and are the right alternative if you qualify. If either you or your spouse have owned property before, you will not qualify for first-time-buyer mortgage money. The only drawback to these mortgages is that they are not automatically assumable by the new buyer when you sell the property. However, if the new buyer is a first-time home buyer, the mortgage can be assumed if the buyer qualifies.

ATTACK #122

Choose a new FHA or VA mortgage to finance your home purchase.

Federal Housing Authority (FHA) and Veterans Administration (VA) mortgages are your best bet for new mortgages other than first-time home-buyer bond money because qualification is easier than for a conventional mortgage, and a smaller down payment is required. FHA new mortgages require only 2.75 percent down payment plus closing costs, and VA mortgages, made only to veterans, require no down payment at all, although closing costs may run as high as $2,000. Only those who have served 12 months of active duty in the armed services and certain widows of servicemen qualify for a VA mortgage. The U.S. government sets the interest rate and qualification requirements on FHA and

VA mortgages, and rates change over time along with conventional mortgage rates.

FHA- and VA-approved mortgages come with a form of government insurance that allows a home buyer to make less than the normal 20 percent down payment. The insurance pays the lender's loss between the sale price of a home and the mortgage balance if the mortgagor defaults and the house is sold for less than the mortgage balance. The maximum the government insurance will pay, however, is 20 percent of the original mortgage amount.

There are limits to the maximum amount of money you can borrow with these mortgages. Anyone may apply for a new FHA mortgage, but the maximum limit for the mortgage in the most expensive metropolitan areas in the country is approximately $125,000. In other areas of the country where property prices are lower, the maximum FHA mortgage may be limited to an amount as low as $70,000. You can call any local real estate agent to find out the limits for your area. With an FHA mortgage you pay approximately one half percent extra for the privilege of making less than a 20 percent down payment.

Within the last year the VA raised its entitlement to a maximum loan amount of $144,000. However, veterans who have already used their benefit, regardless of whether or not the loan has been paid in full, have a maximum loan available of $144,000 minus any outstanding VA loans. This figure includes any VA loans that have been assumed by a new buyer. Veterans who have never used their VA benefits prior to the change in the entitlement amount are eligible for the maximum loan amount of $144,000. Unfortunately, at this time there are very few lenders who will make a $144,000 VA loan with no down payment, even to a veteran.

There is no limit to the purchase price of the property on which you can place an FHA or VA mortgage, but the maximum amount you can borrow on the first mortgage is limited by the current FHA or VA rules. Any difference would have to be paid in cash or with a second mortgage.

When applying for a new FHA or VA mortgage, you must sign a statement that confirms that your intent is to live in the property. The occupancy statement, however, does not require that you live in your property for any specific length of time before you can move out and turn it into rental property.

Most banks, savings and loans and mortgage companies will make FHA- or VA-approved loans. Both the FHA and the VA set the mortgage interest rates, but different lenders may have different closing costs. The seller is required by law to pay the points (prepaid interest) for the buyer on a new FHA or VA mortgage.

Another great financial benefit of an FHA or VA loan is that it makes your house worth more when the property is sold. FHA and VA mortgages are assumable by the buyer when the property is sold (see Attack #127 for limitations). If your home is worth $100,000 and has a $70,000 FHA or VA mortgage, the buyer may be able to assume your mortgage without the long, tedious process of qualifying and without paying points or appraisal fees. Because your home comes with a built-in mortgage, you can expect to ask for and get an extra $5,000 when you sell, or about 5 percent more than a home that must be purchased with a new mortgage.

ATTACK #123

Apply for a conventional mortgage when you do not qualify for an FHA or VA loan.

The term "conventional mortgage" has come to mean simply any mortgage that is not an FHA or VA. That doesn't mean, however, that conventional loans are not associated with the government. The government-chartered Federal Home Loan Mortgage Corporation (FHLMC) was authorized by Congress to purchase conventional mortgages from mortgage companies, S&Ls and other mortgage lenders to keep money available for new home loans. The FHLMC has popularly become known as "Freddie Mac" and raises billions of dollars through the sale by brokerage firms of participation certificates similar to bonds and secured by specific groups of conventional mortgages. When the FHLMC buys a $100,000 mortgage from an S&L, for instance, the S&L now has the $100,000 to loan again to someone else. The S&L makes money on the mortgages it writes by selling the mortgage to the FHLMC at a discount and charging a fee for "servicing" the mortgage, which means collecting the payments. Freddie Mac only buys mortgages that fit a specific group of rules, including the credit and income profile of the borrower. Most conventional mortgage lenders therefore require that you qualify for a new mortgage under the Freddie Mac guidelines.

Anyone is eligible to apply for a conventional mortgage. The maximum mortgage amount that FHLMC will buy is now about $202,350 for a single-family home, $240,000 for a two-family unit, $290,000 for a three-family unit and $360,000 for a four-family dwelling. If you are buying a home that is more expensive than the FHLMC guidelines allow, your mortgage will be called a jumbo loan, and you will find that only a few lenders make such loans because they cannot be sold to the FHLMC.

Conventional mortgage interest rates are not set by the government and fluctuate freely. Different lenders in the same area on the same day will charge different interest rates and points, so it is important to shop for the best conventional mortgage rates.

Conventional mortgages can have graduated payments, a growing equity provision or negative amortization. See *More Wealth Without Risk* for an explanation and strategies relating to these features.

Your basic strategy with a new conventional mortgage is to make the least possible down payment unless you are equity shifting (see Attack #136). the standard down payment choices for a conventional mortgage are 5 percent, 10 percent and 20 percent. If you pay 20 percent or more down, you are not required to purchase private mortgage insurance, commonly referred to as PMI, which protects the lender in case you default. If you want to make a 5 or 10 percent down payment, lenders will require you to purchase private mortgage insurance. There are about a dozen different private mortgage insurers for lenders to choose from, and all have slightly different rates and terms.

If you make only a 10 percent down payment, you could be charged with an extra .65 percent of the loan amount, or $650 per $100,000 mortgage, plus one-quarter of 1 percent added to the interest rate. The premiums are about double if you want to pay only 5 percent down. If the quoted interest rate is 10 percent, you will end up paying 10.25 percent with a 10 percent down payment and 10.50 percent if you pay only 5 percent down. On a $100,000 mortgage an extra .25 percent will cost you about $250 per year. The PMI premiums you pay don't insure you but insure the lender's top 20 to 25 percent of the loan in case you default. If the lender has to sell your property at a quick sale below the mortgage amount, the PMI insurance will pay the difference or loss to the lender up to the insured amount just like FHA or VA insurance.

Your strategy is to limit your down payment to no more than 5 to 10 percent even if you can afford more. If you have extra money, invest it at a return higher than your mortgage rate, for instance in mutual funds.

You may logically think, once your home has appreciated, maybe doubled in value, that you could stop paying the PMI premiums since based on the market value of your home, the lender has no risk, not even from a quick sale. Well, money doesn't work logically, and in this case you will be required to continue the payments until you have paid off at least 20 percent of your original mortgage no matter what the value of your home. Your PMI company loves to receive your premiums to insure virtually no risk.

Can you ever get the PMI payments removed? Yes, you can. Once your loan is paid down to 80 percent of its initial amount, most lenders will quickly remove the required PMI insurance if you request it in writing, particularly if your payments have been kept current. The insurance is no longer protecting the mortgage company anyway. Don't expect your mortgage lender to volunteer that information unless you live in California, where a law was passed in 1988 requiring notification of when PMI can be canceled.

The only discouraging note about getting the PMI removed from your loan is that on a 30-year mortgage at 10 percent, it takes over 15 years of payments before you have paid off the required 20 percent of the original mortgage amount. However, on a 15-year mortgage you can have the PMI canceled in just five years. See Wealth-Building Power of a 15-Year Mortgage, page 317.

ATTACK #124

If you are turned down for a new mortgage, or have an unusual mortgage situation, contact a mortgage broker.

The mortgage business is set up like the insurance business. With insurance, you can do business with the issuing company directly or you can work with an independent agent who represents many companies. The independent agent often has many more alternatives and better rates. The same is true in the mortgage business, in which the mortgage company is called a *mortgage banker* and independent mortgage agents are called *mortgage brokers*. Both are listed in your Yellow Pages.

Mortgage bankers include banks, savings and loans, mortgage companies and other financial institutions that make loans using real estate as collateral. Most people when looking for a mortgage go to a mortgage banker, which is great if you're approved. If not, contact a mortgage broker. Experienced mortgage brokers represent many mortgage sources, including mortgage bankers and private lenders with less stringent approval rules. A mortgage broker is a one-stop shopping center for your mortgage situation. The mortgage source pays the commission to the mortgage broker, ranging from ⅛ to ½ percent. The cost, of course, is added to your cost for the loan.

Many years ago I needed about $750,000 cash to make a down payment on a radio station. The biggest obstacle was that I needed the money within a week. The best way to get the money quickly was to use the combined equity of two of my real estate properties as collateral. No mortgage banker that I or my staff knew could respond that quickly or could make such an unusual loan. Then we found a mortgage broker who felt he could handle the transaction, and he did. Working with the lenders and the appraisers and actually walking the papers through the tedious bureaucratic process, we were able to have the closing and get the check within a week. Persistence and creative thinking can always work miracles for you.

DEFENSE #125

Don't sign a mortgage agreement that contains a prepayment penalty lasting over five years.

Conventional mortgages usually have a prepayment penalty, but FHA and VA mortgages usually do not. The penalty is nothing more than a scheme that puts extra money into the lender's pocket if you decide to pay off your mortgage early. The prepayment penalty can be triggered if someone else buys your home with a new mortgage that pays off your old mortgage or if you come into a large sum of cash and decide to pay off your mortgage early.

On many older mortgages the prepayment penalty applies for the life of the mortgage, but on many newer mortgages the lender will impose the penalty only for the first five years of the mortgage. After five years of making payments there is no penalty for an early payoff.

Mortgage lenders will tell you that the purpose of the penalty is to help them recover the costs and paperwork involved in issuing the mortgage if the mortgage is paid off before the end of the original term. Don't be fooled. Between the add-on costs of points, appraisals and the seemingly endless list of up-front fees, the lender makes out quite well without the penalty.

Before completing a mortgage application, ask if there is a prepayment penalty. If so, and if the lender won't remove it, look for a lender with better terms. If you have already applied for a mortgage, read the mortgage agreement to ascertain if there is a prepayment penalty after five years. Ask to have the prepayment penalty changed or stricken from the agreement. You may have to speak to someone higher up than a mortgage loan officer. If the lender wants your business, he will agree.

ATTACK #126

To save time, locate a mortgage lender who uses the "low-doc" mortgage approval program.

It has been said that the process of getting a mortgage is about as quick and as fun as watching grass grow. Because of the high-tech computer interfaces that are available to mortgage lenders, appraisers and credit bureaus, you now have the opportunity to cut the mortgage approval process from two months to less than two weeks.

Low-doc is a mortgage term for loans that require less documentation and inquiry into the borrower's credit history and financial situation. Although the credit requirements for getting a mortgage don't change, the time required does.

Under the old system, which is still in use by most lenders, you are required to complete and sign about 30 pages of mortgage application forms that allow the lender to get written verification of your job history, your credit history and your mortgage history. The more properties you own, the longer the verification process takes. It could take an additional 10 days just to get a computer printout on your credit history from the credit bureau. If your mortgage company, landlord or employer is slow in responding to the lender's request, which is usually the case, weeks are added to the approval process, making you pace the floor, feeling as though you must have already been denied.

The low-doc process can actually take as little as 15 minutes to gather all the necessary data for a mortgage application, although the appraisal and title search will usually take one to three weeks. Since Freddie Mac and Fannie Mae, the quasigovernmental institution that buys FHA and VA loans from mortgage lenders, have issued guidelines for quick mortgage approval, you will over the next few years see almost the entire mortgage industry going to the low-doc plan.

In the meantime, your goal is to work with mortgage lenders who can get you through the process quickly. How do you find out? Just ask. Look at the illustrations on pages 328–29, and you will see a comparison between old and new methods of approving mortgage loans and how the new process speeds you on the way to occupying your home.

You will first notice the difference in the amount of paperwork and time the old and new mortgage processing systems require. Under the old system, the lender relies on documents furnished by people and institutions other than the borrower, including employers, mortgage companies, banks and landlords. Under the new system, the lender relies on documents furnished by the borrower, which include W-2 forms, bank statements, pay stubs, charge accounts and, in some instances, one year's worth of mortgage or rent payment check stubs.

Under the low-doc system, if you make a minimum 30 percent down payment on a home, which few people do, you need to furnish even less documentation since the lender will rely on the equity in the property for security. If you are refinancing or getting a new mortgage with a lender you have used before, your previous payment history with that institution may be all you need to furnish. If you're getting a conventional loan with the minimum 20 percent down payment, the low-doc process can take a week or so longer, as the lender will often want to do additional checking.

Of course, faster loan approvals also mean faster loan denials, but that works to your advantage because if you get turned down by one lender, that in no way means you will automatically get turned down by another. One of the most discouraging aspects of the old system is waiting an average of 45 days to hear from the lender only to find out you are not approved. You then have to start the process all over, or you lose the property because the time for mortgage approval under the purchase agreement has been exceeded.

THE OLD MORTGAGE APPROVAL PROCESS
45 Days

Step One

You fill out information about your job, credit history, and charge accounts at a mortgage interview.

Step Two

You sign reams of forms allowing lender to check with your bank, your mortgage company, your employer and the credit bureau.

Step Three

You wait while mortgage lender waits weeks for responses; sometimes issues second or third requests. Can't act until all are in.

Step Four

Lender arranges for appraisal and appraiser takes additional weeks to visit the property and prepare a complex written appraisal.

Step Five

Your application is approved.

THE "LOW-DOC" MORTGAGE APPROVAL ALTERNATIVE
Three Days to Two Weeks

Step One

You furnish to the lender: two years' W-2 forms or tax returns, three bank statements, one month's pay stubs, and a list of all your charge accounts.

Step Two

In 15 minutes the lender's computer has contacted the credit bureau's computer and gives you preliminary approval or denial of mortgage.

Step Three

Lender requests appraisal through computer link to the appraiser's office. In one day the appraiser does a computer-prepared appraisal using comparable property as guideline and a quick visit to the property to verify the condition. Your application is approved.

The newest addition to the quick-approval, low-doc program is a computer link to the appraiser's office. Instead of preparing an extended written report, which takes hours of effort and work, the appraiser simply pulls up on his or her computer the values of comparable properties in the same area and makes only a quick visit to your property to determine that it is still there and to verify its condition. This process takes as little as a day.

It's amazing how easy life becomes when communication between those involved in the mortgage approval process is adequate and the bureaucratic red tape is eliminated.

ATTACK #127

Find properties with existing FHA and VA mortgages, and avoid qualifying for a mortgage.

Thirty to 50 percent of the properties in any area have existing FHA or VA mortgages. FHA and VA mortgages for the most part are fully assumable by federal law with no qualifying and with a transfer fee of only $125. Any time you can buy a property with financing attached, you have saved yourself hours of effort and hassle, plus thousands in closing costs. No qualifying means that you have the right to assume the mortgage no matter how bad your credit rating and no matter how little your down payment or what terms you make for paying the balance owed to the seller. No credit check is done, nor is there any way you can be turned down even if you filed bankruptcy right before you bought the property.

Assuming an existing FHA or VA mortgage is an ideal method of buying and financing your first home or rental property with no qualifying. Any difference between the price of the home and the amount of the assumable mortgage you can handle with cash, a commercial second mortgage or, better still, a note or mortgage between you and the seller.

All FHA and VA mortgages used to be automatically assumable without qualifying. But in 1986 the FHA instituted new rules to protect itself from many defaults caused by quick investor turnovers of properties with fully assumable FHA mortgages. The new restrictions limit how quickly an FHA mortgage can be assumed without qualifying, but the restrictions will not affect your ability to find hundreds of properties with assumable mortgages.

Here are the assumability rules for all FHA mortgages based on the date they were originally issued.

Rule 1—All FHA mortgages closed prior to December 1, 1986, are still fully assumable with no qualifying with payment of a $125 transfer fee.

Rule 2—All FHA mortgages closed on or after December 1, 1986, require qualification of the buyer on the following basis:

Owner Occupant: If the original mortgagor is an owner-occupant, qualification is required for a new buyer only during the first twelve months of the existence of the mortgage. After the mortgage has been in place one year, no further qualification for assumption is required.

Investor: If the original FHA mortgage was granted to an investor, a new buyer must qualify during the first 24 months of the term of the mortgage. Subsequent buyers are not required to qualify to assume the mortgage.

Rule 3—After February 5, 1988, and applying to all mortgages closed on or after December 1, 1986, the original mortgagor remains liable for a five-year period after the assumption for the default of a buyer who assumes the loan, unless the new buyer qualifies for the mortgage and the FHA releases the original mortgagor from liability.

When you buy a property and assume an FHA mortgage, you will probably have to do some explaining to the seller. If the seller says, "But I will still be liable for five years," your answer is, "Yes, but the worst that can happen is after a couple of years you get the property back, make a few payments yourself, and then sell at a higher price than you sold to me." And remember, these rules apply only to FHA mortgage closed on or after December 1, 1986.

VA loans have slightly different rules. Any VA loan *approved* on or after March 1, 1988, is subject to the following restrictions on assumability. The loan repayment may be accelerated, which means the balance is immediately due in full if the property is sold without the loan being paid in full, unless:

1. the loan is current; and
2. purchaser assumes full liability for repayment of the loan; and
3. purchaser qualifies from a credit standpoint.

All VA mortgages approved or granted before March 1988 are still fully assumable with no qualifying.

Don't let these new restrictions deter you from looking for properties with FHA or VA mortgages. Normally, a mortgage on a property for which you are negotiating will be more than two or three years old and can be assumed without qualifying.

Creating a Mortgage Reduction Plan

Up until now we've talked about the strategies to use when you are looking for a new mortgage, but there are strategies just as powerful that can be applied to any mortgage you already have.

A standard mortgage is for 30 years, and, in fact, about 90 percent of new mortgages fit into this category. A typical 30-year mortgage is one of the most destructive decisions you can make in your wealth-building plan. During your lifetime, 30-year mortgages can eat up literally hundreds of thousands of dollars that could have paid for a two-week vacation every year or could have paid for all the cars you'll ever own or even completely funded your retirement plan. Thirty-year mortgages will keep you living in half the house you could eventually afford if you had just used any one of the following mortgage reduction plan strategies.

Because your home is the second biggest expense you'll ever encounter, home mortgages contain the biggest potential for giant savings. A mortgage reduction plan is a method of taking control of your mortgage and causing it to build wealth for you instead of only for the mortgage company. Your mortgage reduction plan will allow you to build equity in your home up to 10 times faster than with your current 30-year mortgage.

While your mortgage represents the amount of your home owned by your mortgage company, your equity is the part of your home that represents *your* wealth. Your strategy becomes apparent: increase the speed at which you reduce your mortgage balance, and you will increase the speed at which you build equity or wealth. This is exactly what the mortgage reduction strategies that follow will do for you.

One of these strategies is to make extra principal payments on your mortgage. Occasionally a mortgage company or an official-sounding but uninformed source may tell you that extra payments toward your principal are not a good idea because you get no benefit now and that the extra principal comes off the "back end." Or you may even be told you will lose the tax deductions for mortgage interest. Both beliefs are totally incorrect, as you will soon see.

Extra principal payments can be made on any mortgage or loan that does not, by contract, preclude the mortgagor's right to make such payments. Less than 3 percent of mortgages and loans contain such a clause. Two categories of mortgages contain clauses limiting the mortgagor's right to make extra principal payments:

- FHA 235 mortgages or other government-subsidized loans
- State or county first-time-home-buyer low-interest mortgages

In the first case, the government rightly feels that if you have money to make extra principal payments, why should the government be making part of your mortgage payment for you? In the second case, many of the bonds sold to investors to raise money to make low-interest mortgage loans to first-time home buyers contain a clause guaranteeing the investors that their money won't be paid back early unless the home is sold and the entire mortgage paid off.

You can even make extra principal payments on a private mortgage or a seller's purchase money mortgage (a second mortgage given to you by the seller when you bought your home). But sometimes it is difficult to convince individual mortgage lenders that you do have that right. They may have trouble understanding why they won't be getting the full amount of interest they calculated in advance. You will have to explain that any interest stated in the contract as a total amount applies only if payments are made over the full term of the mortgage, but you intend to reduce the term with your extra principal payments.

Don't let the thought of losing the mortgage interest deductions on your income tax deter you from making extra principal payments. You may think a bigger, longer mortgage is better because the interest is deductible. Absolutely not. Taking tax deductions for mortgage interest is a great additional benefit of owning a home instead of renting, but mortgage interest is not a tax shelter.

Here's why. Even if you are in the personal federal income tax bracket of 31 percent, you have to spend $1,000 cash for mortgage interest to get a $310 reduction in your taxes. Your net cost or money lost is $690. You can't make money by spending more than you can deduct from your tax bill. I have even heard and read advice from those who would tell you to buy a bigger house with a bigger mortgage just to get a bigger tax deduction. Now you know what mathematical nonsense that is. Buy a bigger house only if you want one. Don't double your loss just to double your tax deduction. Think of the interest deduction as simply lowering the interest rate on your mortgage. If your home mortgage interest rate is 10 percent and your tax bracket is 31 percent, the amount of your tax savings is equal to about one-third of the total interest you paid for the year. You paid a real interest rate of one-third less. Here is a table that shows your real interest rate on a home mortgage after you take the deduction based on your tax bracket.

YOUR REAL INTEREST RATE AFTER TAX DEDUCTIONS

MORTGAGE INTEREST RATE	Tax Bracket 0%	15%	28%	31%	40%*
8%	8%	6.8%	5.8%	5.5%	4.8%
9	9	7.7	6.4	6.2	5.4
10	10	8.5	7.2	6.9	6.0
11	11	9.4	7.9	7.6	6.6
12	12	10.2	8.6	8.3	7.2
13	13	11.0	9.4	9.0	7.8
14	14	11.9	10.1	9.7	8.4

*The 40% bracket is a combination of 36% federal bracket and 4% state taxes.

As you can see, the interest deduction neither eliminates the costs of a mortgage nor makes you a profit. The deduction simply reduces your real mortgage interest rate.

The real savings occur not only when you reduce your mortgage interest rate, but when you reduce the total amount you will pay on your mortgage. There are six different mortgage reduction plan strategies you can choose from. We will discuss each, but not all are always in your best interest.

MORTGAGE REDUCTION PLANS

- Fixed extra principal payments
- Double principal payments
- The biweekly mortgage
- Equity shifting
- Equity to mortgage income conversions
- Converting an ARM to an FRM
- Refinancing to a lower interest rate

The first three strategies above are extra principal payment strategies. All extra principal payment strategies are based on the same concept. You can reduce the total amount you will pay on any mortgage by making extra payments that will reduce your principal balance faster than shown on your amortization table. An amortization table is a schedule that contains one line for each monthly mortgage payment and breaks the payment into the amount collected for interest and the amount that reduces your prinicpal balance. On a fixed-rate mortgage your monthly payment remains the same during the entire term of your mortgage and is determined as the amount that will enable your mortgage to be completely paid off after your last payment. On an adjustable-rate mortgage the payment fluctuates with any change in interest rates, but the mortgage is still paid off in the same amount of time.

Get an amortization table for every mortgage you have, and be certain to request one whenever you are getting a new mortgage. Here are some sources for an amortization table for the mortgage(s) you already have:

1. Your personal mortgage file—50 percent of new mortgages come with an amortization table.
2. Your mortgage company—often your mortgage company may print you a table for a minimal charge.
3. A local real estate broker.

When you get a 30-year (360-month) mortgage, there are 360 lines on your amortization table, representing each monthly payment until you mortgage is completely paid off. On a 15-year mortgage there are 180 payments and, therefore, 180 lines on your amortization table.

Notice from the sample amortization table, below, that each month the amount applied to the principal balance increases by exactly the amount that the interest portion decreases. The interest is less each month because you owe less principal on which you are paying interest. Notice, also, that your new principal balance each month decreases by exactly the amount of your principal payment.

MORTGAGE AMORTIZATION TABLE.

Mortgage Amount	$100,000
Interest Rate	10%
Term	30 years
Monthly Payment	$877.57

PAYMENT NUMBER	INTEREST	PRINCIPAL	BALANCE
1	$833.33	$ 44.24	$99,955.76
2	832.96	44.61	99,911.15
3	832.59	44.98	99,866.17
4	832.22	45.35	99,820.82
5	831.84	45.73	99,775.09
6	831.46	46.11	99,728.98
7	831.07	46.50	99,682.48
8	830.69	46.88	99,635.60
9	830.30	47.27	99,588.33
10	829.90	47.67	99,540.66
11	829.51	48.06	99,492.60
12	829.10	48.47	99,444.13
13	828.70	48.87	99,395.26
14	828.29	49.28	99,345.98
15	827.88	49.69	99,296.29
16	827.47	50.10	99,246.19
17	827.05	50.52	99,195.67
18	826.63	50.94	99,144,73
19	826.21	51.36	99,093.37
20	825.78	51.79	99,041.58
↓	↓	↓	↓
358	21.61	855.96	1,736.79
359	14.47	863.10	873.69
360	7.28	873.69	0

Although a computer program or financial calculator is normally used to determine the breakdown of interest and principal on your amortization table, it is important that you understand how the monthly interest is determined in order to understand how the extra principal payments strategies work.

Most people assume, once you have agreed to the payment terms of a mortgage, that they are etched in stone. Not correct. The amount of interest and principal allocated per payment is only valid if you pay your monthly payments *exactly* as shown on your amortization table. Although you cannot stretch out your payments over a longer term without violating the terms of your contract, you have every right to pay off your mortgage in a shorter time.

Surprisingly, if you wanted to pay off your 30-year mortgage in half the time, you would not need to make two full payments each month instead of one. In fact, if you increased your monthly payment by less than 20 percent, you would pay off a 30-year mortgage in half the time. To understand why, we must look at how the interest on a mortgage is really calculated. Your mortgage company's computer actually charges you interest each month based on the principal balance you owe at the end of the previous month. Your monthly interest rate is your annual interest rate as shown in your mortgage agreement divided by 12 months. On a 12 percent mortgage, for instance, the monthly interest rate is exactly 1 percent of the principal balance; at 11 percent the monthly interest rate is .917 percent (11 percent divided by 12 months), and at 10 percent the monthly rate is .833 percent (10 percent divided by 12 months).

As shown in the example above, for example, the monthly payment necessary to amortize (pay off) a $100,000 mortgage at 10 percent in 30 years is $877.57. The balance at the end of the first month is the full $100,000 and multiplied by the monthly interest rate of .833 percent yields $833.33 as the amount to be applied to interest. That leaves only $44.24 out of the payment to be applied to principal. The next month the mortgage company computer looks up your account and sees that you now owe $99,955.76. Multiplying your new mortgage balance of $99,955.76 by the monthly rate of .833 percent, your interest for the second month is $832.96, leaving $44.61 to be applied to your mortgage balance. This month you paid a whole $.37 less in interest, which increased by $.37 the amount applied to paying off your mortgage balance. The same process continues every month for the entire term of your mortgage. The interest is calculated separately every month based on the balance you owe at the beginning of the previous month. Remember a mortgage is always paid in arrears. The interest you pay in February is based on the outstanding principal balance at the beginning of January.

What would happen if you were to walk into your mortgage company the second month of your mortgage with a $1,000 check and tell the manager, "I want to put this toward paying down the balance I owe on my mortgage"?

As long as your regular monthly payments are current, your request will be honored. At the end of the third month (remember interest is paid in arrears) when the computer looks up your account, it finds you owe only $98,511.15, instead of the $99,911.15 balance shown on your amortization table. The computer doesn't care about your amortization table. The schedule was prepared solely for your benefit. The computer only looks at your actual mortgage balance. At the beginning of the third month the computer will calculate your interest payment for the third month at $824.26 instead of the $832.59 as shown on your amortization schedule (a savings of $8.33, .833 percent times $1,000 additional principal payment). That means that the extra $8.33 can be used to reduce your principal even further.

Because of the $1,000 extra payment applied to the principal and the fact that your payment of $877.57 remains the same, you will pay off your mortgage in 340 payments instead of the originally scheduled 360 payments, saving you $17,000 in interest! Are there other ways you can accomplish the same thing with no financial strain? You bet—with periodic small extra principal payments that will create the same kind of mortgage reduction plan. We'll divide your mortgage reduction plan options into three strategies:

- Fixed monthly extra principal payments
- Doubling the principal payments
- The biweekly mortgage

Prepaying principal does not reduce your regular required monthly payment, but as you can see it does dramatically reduce your total payments.

ATTACK #128

Pay a fixed amount of extra principal every month to keep your total payments the same.

By choosing a fixed amount of extra principal to pay each month—$25, $50, $100 or $200, for example—you can fit the extra payment into your overall budget without strapping yourself financially. Fixed monthly extra principal payments will also allow you to predetermine how much money you will save and how many months early your mortgage will be completely paid off.

If your mortgage payment coupon has a box that is marked "enter amount extra principal here," you can combine your extra principal payment in one check with your regular payment. If not, it is a good idea to write two separate checks, one for your regular payment and another for the extra principal amount. In the space marked "for" on the second check, write, "Apply to principal only, loan # ____."

On pages 340 to 343 you will find tables that will show you for any amount of mortgage balance and for extra monthly principal payments of $25 to $200 how much money and how many months you will save. One table is to be used with 30-year mortgages, the other is for mortgages with an original term of 15 years.

For instance, look on the 30-year mortgage table for a $75,000 mortgage under 11 percent interest. The table shows that if you pay an extra $25 every month without fail, you will save $41,683 and cut 68 months off the term of the mortgage. If you pay an extra $100 each month, you will save a total of $91,144 and cut 156 months, or 43 percent, off the term of your mortgage. A small amount of extra money can go a long way in securing your financial future.

Let these tables inspire you to begin a mortgage reduction plan *now* and stick with it. A fixed-rate mortgage reduction plan will automatically make you wealthier.

DOLLARS AND MONTHS SAVED
FIXED EXTRA PRINCIPAL PAYMENTS
30-YEAR MORTGAGE

		Mortgage Interest Rate									
		9%		10%		11%		12%		13%	
MORTGAGE AMOUNTS	MONTHLY EXTRA PRINCIPAL PAYMENT	DOLLARS SAVED	MONTHS SAVED	DOLLARS SAVED	MONTHS SAVED	DOLLARS SAVED	MONTHS SAVED	DOLLARS SAVED	MONTHS SAVED	DOLLARS SAVED	MONTHS SAVED
$ 10,000	$ 25	$ 11,400	193	$ 13,300	198	$ 15,347	202	$ 17,451	206	$ 19,641	211
	50	14,032	245	16,177	248	18,409	250	20,718	253	23,093	255
	100	15,993	288	18,319	289	20,720	290	23,185	291	23,705	292
	200	17,287	318	19,737	318	22,256	319	24,833	319	27,459	320
25,000	25	18,948	123	22,627	129	26,644	135	30,987	141	35,634	148
	50	26,279	176	30,798	181	35,601	186	40,666	190	45,967	195
	100	33,140	229	38,325	232	43,741	235	49,363	239	55,165	242
	200	38,593	275	44,279	277	50,159	278	56,208	280	62,404	282
50,000	25	24,720	78	30,166	84	36,323	90	43,207	96	50,807	103
	50	37,897	123	45,254	129	53,289	135	61,975	141	71,268	148
	100	52,559	176	61,595	181	71,202	186	81,333	190	91,934	195
	200	66,282	229	76,651	232	87,841	235	98,726	239	110,330	242
75,000	25	27,564	58	34,164	63	41,683	68	50,274	74	59,969	80
	50	44,804	96	54,181	202	64,625	108	76,128	114	88,651	121
	100	65,907	144	78,047	250	91,144	156	105,140	161	119,960	167
	200	87,752	198	102,200	202	117,430	207	133,372	211	149,945	215

100,000	25	29,444	46	36,664	50	45,128	55	54,946	60	66,027	66
	50	49,439	78	60,331	84	76,648	90	86,411	96	101,614	103
	100	75,792	123	90,508	129	106,579	135	123,947	141	142,536	148
	200	105,117	176	123,190	181	142,405	186	162,663	190	183,868	195
125,000	25	30,652	38	38,382	42	47,538	46	58,284	51	70,671	56
	50	52,781	67	64,584	72	78,667	77	94,291	84	111,754	90
	100	83,463	108	100,354	113	118,995	120	139,342	126	161,325	133
	200	119,560	158	140,892	164	163,741	169	188,003	174	213,554	180
150,000	25	31,525	32	39,636	36	49,324	40	60,792	44	74,239	49
	50	55,308	58	68,328	63	83,366	68	100,546	74	119,941	80
	100	89,608	96	108,364	101	129,251	108	152,253	114	117,306	121
	200	131,814	144	158,096	150	182,289	156	210,278	161	239,923	167

DOLLARS AND MONTHS SAVED
FIXED EXTRA PRINCIPAL PAYMENTS
15-YEAR MORTGAGE

		Mortgage Interest Rate									
	MONTHLY EXTRA	9%		10%		11%		12%		13%	
MORTGAGE AMOUNT	PRINCIPAL PAYMENT	DOLLARS SAVED	MONTHS SAVED	DOLLARS SAVED	MONTHS SAVED	DOLLARS SAVED	MONTHS SAVED	DOLLARS SAVED	MONTHS SAVED	DOLLARS SAVED	MONTHS SAVED
25,000	$ 25	$ 3,959	30	$ 4,621	60	$ 5,341	31	$ 6,121	32	$ 6,966	33
	50	6,581	51	7,628	52	8,749	53	9,947	54	11,224	55
	100	9,884	78	11,387	79	12,932	80	14,581	81	16,312	82
	200	13,263	108	15,154	109	17,126	109	19,178	110	21,309	110
50,000	25	4,413	16	5,179	17	6,020	17	6,943	18	7,955	18
	50	7,918	30	9,243	31	10,682	31	12,243	32	13,933	33
	100	13,163	51	15,256	52	17,496	53	19,894	54	22,449	55
	200	19,768	78	22,734	79	25,865	80	29,162	81	32,625	82
75,000	25	4,590	11	5,339	11	6,290	12	7,273	12	8,357	13
	50	8,500	21	9,956	22	11,547	22	13,287	23	15,186	24
	100	14,826	38	17,259	38	19,887	39	22,721	40	25,771	41
	200	23,690	62	27,369	62	31,284	63	35,442	64	39,847	66
100,000	25	4,780	8	5,518	9	6,434	9	7,541	9	8,756	10
	50	8,827	16	10,358	17	12,040	17	13,885	18	15,911	18
	100	15,835	30	18,485	31	21,363	31	24,485	32	27,866	33
	200	26,325	51	30,512	52	34,996	53	39,778	54	44,899	55

125,000	25	4,744	7	5,588	7	6,525	7	7,564	7	8,713	8
	50	9,036	13	10,617	14	12,357	14	14,275	15	16,381	15
	100	16,513	25	19,313	25	22,366	26	25,693	27	29,313	28
	200	28,222	43	32,789	44	37,705	45	42,985	46	48,645	47
150,000	25	4,784	6	5,639	6	6,587	6	7,639	6	8,808	6
	50	9,181	11	10,797	11	12,579	12	14,456	12	16,714	13
	100	17,000	21	19,911	22	23,095	22	26,573	23	30,371	24
	200	29,653	38	34,518	38	39,774	39	45,441	40	51,542	41

Round $ off to nearest $100.

ATTACK #129

Double or triple your mortgage principal payment every month, and cut your mortgage term in half or by two-thirds.

There is a mortgage reduction strategy that will allow you to make smaller extra principal payments in the early years of your mortgage when you are least likely to have extra cash, and increase them slightly every month with the end result that your mortgage is paid off in half the number of years or less.

Let's begin with an example of a 30-year mortgage for $100,000 at 10 percent interest. If you total the 360 entries under the principal payment column on your amortization table, the total will equal the amount you originally borrowed, in this case $100,000. That makes sense because, during the term of your mortgage, you must pay back the entire amount you borrowed in order to end up owing nothing at the end of the 30-year term. The $100,000 borrowed amount is paid back in the 360 unequal principal reduction payments shown on an amortization table under the column marked Principal. The principal payment is very small at first, amounting, as you saw earlier, to only $44.24 the first month. The first principal amount increases every month, amounting to $100.60 the 100th month, $230.68 the 200th month, $357.33 the 300th month and $873.69 the final month, with all 360 payments totaling $100,000.

In order to pay off your mortgage in half the time, you must pay off the principal twice as fast. There's your strategy. Pay exactly double the principal amount shown for each payment along with the interest, and your mortgage will automatically be retired in about half the time. If your mortgage is new and has the full 30 years to run, it will now be retired in 15 years. If you have been paying on your 30-year mortgage for six years, it has 24 years to go, and this strategy will cut the term to 12 years.

Because you are paying double the principal, in essence you are jumping down your mortgage amortization table two months at a time. You are paying this month's and next month's principal in the same payment, totally eliminating the interest from the second month's payment.

If you have already made 14 payments when you begin this strategy, you would start by doubling the principal of payment 15, skip payment 16 and the next month double the principal of payment 17. If you wanted to be more exact you could, instead of doubling the principal for payment 15, add the principal shown for payment 16 to your regular payment for interest and principal on payment 15 of $877.57. Although the difference in the two methods may be less than $1 each month, this method will cut your mortgage term *exactly* in half.

Look at the mortgage amortization table below for a $100,000, 10 percent mortgage for 30 years. Let's say you have made 10 payments before beginning this strategy. For payment number 11 you make your regular payment of $877.57, which, notice from the table, includes $829.51 for interest and $48.06 for principal, to which you add payment number 12's principal of $48.47 for a total payment of $926.04. The following month you begin with payment 13, which has an interest portion of $828.70 and a principal portion of $48.87. Adding only the principal for payment 14, which is $49.28, your total payment is $926.85, which makes your new balance $99,345.98. Each succeeding month you follow the same procedure starting with month 15, then 17, then 19, to the end of the term.

If you wanted to pay off your mortgage with this strategy in one-third instead of one-half the time, you would simply include three successive principal portions in each payment and move down three payments on your amortization table each month. You can cut a 30-year mortgage to 10 years, or a 24-year

MORTGAGE AMORTIZATION TABLE

Payments 10–20

Mortgage Amount	$100,000	Term	30 Years
Interest Rate	10%	Monthly Payment	$877.57

PAYMENT NUMBER	INTEREST	PRINCIPAL	BALANCE
10	$829.90	$47.67	$99,540.66
11	829.51	48.06	99,492.60
12	829.10	48.47	99,444.13
13	828.70	48.87	99,395.26
14	828.29	49.28	99,345.98
15	827.88	49.69	99,296.29
16	827.47	50.10	99,246.19
17	827.05	50.52	99,195.67
18	826.63	50.94	99,144.73
19	826.21	51.36	99,093.37
20	825.78	51.79	99,041.58

mortgage to eight years with this method. The balance shown at the end of each group of three months would be your new principal balance.

With this mortgage reduction strategy you are always in control and know at any moment where you stand. One additional advantage to this strategy is that you can use your original amortization table even though the term is growing shorter with each extra principal payment.

DEFENSE #130

Check your mortgage company yearly for the correctness of your principal balance.

How do you know your mortgage lender is applying your extra principal payments correctly to your account? You can check your interest statement or account balance each January.

In order to determine accurately how the monthly interest and principal are split in your payment, your mortgage company must keep your current principal balance in the computer. Often your year-end principal balance will be sent to you in January noted on the interest statement from your mortgage company. Sixty percent of the mortgage companies send such statements automatically, 40 percent don't. If you don't get one, ask by phone or preferably in writing for your account information. Remember, if you have made any extra principal payments, your actual principal balance should be less than the one shown on your amortization table.

To determine what your balance figure should be, and beginning with the month you started making extra principal payments, make up your own amortization table for a 12-month period representing the current year. Use the beginning principal, interest and balance figures that are on your amortization table for the month prior to the month you began paying extra principal. Each month, multiply the balance on your loan by your monthly interest factor, which is your actual mortgage interest rate divided by 12. Subtract the interest from your monthly payment, and what's left is the amount of your regular payment that should be applied to your principal balance. Don't forget to first deduct the taxes and insurance included in the payment before splitting the rest of your payment into principal and interest. Add the extra principal you paid to the regular principal portion of your payment, and subtract from last month's balance to obtain your new balance. The next month begin the process again by applying your monthly interest factor to the new mortgage balance you determined.

Let's step through an example using the same $100,000 mortgage at 10 percent for 30 years. Although the total monthly payment when taxes and insurance are included is probably around $950, the amount applied to principal and interest each month for the entire term is $877.57 (see page 345).

Let's say you began making extra principal payments in January of $100 per month, six months after you originally took out your mortgage, and you want to determine the actual principal balance at the end of the following December. Look at the table on page 348, Creating a New Amortization Table. The table on the left is your original amortization table, while the one on the right is for the same mortgage after you begin making the extra $100-a-month principal payments. The balance shown on the new schedule for month 23 is $97,627.03, instead of the $98,883.60 shown on your original amortization schedule, and should, within a few cents, match the balance shown by your mortgage company on its records at the end of the year. If not, your mortgage company is computing your balance incorrectly or not giving you proper credit for your extra principal payments. The formula I have given you is in accordance with generally accepted accounting practices, so don't let your mortgage company give you any excuses.

If you use the double-your-principal-payment strategy (see Attack #129), your job is much easier since the principal balance shown on your original amortization table will approximately and continuously match your actual balance as you move down your amortization table two months at a time.

You can approximate your balance by simply subtracting the extra $1,200 you paid at $100 per month for 12 months from the month 23 balance of $98,883.60 shown on your original amortization table for December. The result would be $97,683.60, which is $56.57 more than your true balance. Why? Because you have actually saved an extra $56.57 in additional interest from the $100 per month reduction of your principal, and that $56.57 was applied to further reducing your balance. Whether you estimate or compute what your actual balance should be, check every year against your mortgage company's records. Don't assume it will be done correctly just because your mortgage lender is a big financial insitution.

CREATING A NEW AMORTIZATION TABLE

Payment for principal and interest = $877.57 Monthly

PAYMENT NO.	MONTH	ORIGINAL INTEREST	PRINCIPAL	BALANCE	INTEREST	NEW PRINCIPAL	EXTRA PRINCIPAL	BALANCE
6	July	831.46	46.11	99,728.98	831.46	46.11	0	99,728.98
7	August	831.07	46.50	99,682.48	831.07	46.50	0	99,682.48
8	September	830.69	46.88	99,635.60	830.69	46.88	0	99,635.60
9	October	830.30	47.27	99,588.33	830.30	47.27	0	99,588.33
10	November	829.90	47.67	99,540.66	829.90	47.67	0	99,540.66
11	December	829.51	48.06	99,492.60	829.51	48.06	0	99,492.60
12	January	829.10	48.47	99,444.13	829.10	48.47	100	99,344.13
13	February	828.70	48.87	99,395.26	827.87	49.70	100	99,194.43
14	March	828.29	49.28	99,345.98	826.62	50.95	100	99,043.48
15	April	827.88	49.69	99,296.29	825.36	52.21	100	98,891.27
16	May	827.47	50.10	99,246.19	824.09	53.48	100	98,737.79
17	June	827.05	50.52	99,195.67	822.81	54.76	100	98,583.03
18	July	826.63	50.94	99,144.73	821.53	56.04	100	98,426.99
19	August	826.21	51.36	99,093.37	820.22	57.35	100	98,269.64
20	September	825.78	51.79	99,041.58	818.91	58.66	100	98,110.98
21	October	825.35	52.22	98,989.36	817.59	59.98	100	97,951.00
22	November	824.91	52.66	98,936.70	816.26	61.31	100	97,789.69
23	December	824.47	53.10	98,883.60	814.91	62.66	100	97,627.03

DEFENSE #131

Stay away from biweekly mortgages as a mortgage reduction plan.

A biweekly mortgage is the process of paying one-half of your regular monthly mortgage payment every other week. During the course of the year, you would end up making 26 half-mortgage payments, or the equivalent of one extra full payment. Mathematically a biweekly mortgage will reduce a 30-year mortgage to a 22½-year mortgage.

The biweekly mortgage does have the advantage of smaller, more frequent payments, helping those who have trouble coming up with a monthly mortgage payment all at one time. For instance, if a regular mortgage payment is $800 per month, the mortgagor would pay instead $400 every two weeks, but that's where the advantages stop.

Most mortgage lenders will not give biweekly mortgages. Our research has found that only one in 20 lenders will set one up. The biweekly mortgage concept, because of its limited availability, has been turned into an expensive multilevel marketing scheme. You buy a plan set up by a company not associated with your mortgage company and pay an up-front fee ranging from $500 to $1,000. After you sign the contract, you may have to pay an additional 1 percent of your eventual savings, or $1,000 per $100,000 of savings, or a flat amount per month ranging from $10 to $20. If you should discontinue using the service, you've paid the money but gotten no benefit. Your biweekly mortgage payments are set up with an automatic withdrawal from your checking account, and there is often an extra charge of $2 to $3 every couple of weeks for the electronic transfer. Those who are managing your account do nothing more than put your biweekly payments in their own account and make your regular, normal mortgage payments once a month, supposedly on the due date. Once or twice a year, the extra amount that accumulates from your biweekly mortgage payments is sent to the bank as extra principal. Why in the world would you want to pay big dollars for something you can do free and much more easily by using any of the extra principal payments strategies in this chapter? Your strategy when using a bimonthly mortgage as a mortgage reduction plan is get one from your lender or don't get one at all.

DEFENSE #132

If you possess great discipline, invest your extra mortgage principal payments in a mutual fund instead.

Often I am asked, "Couldn't I do better by investing my money in a mutual fund earning 15 to 20 percent rather than making extra principal payments on my mortgage, which has an interest rate of only 10 percent?" The answer in theory is yes. The opportunity in the mutual fund is better, but that strategy is seldom used correctly. To generate the wealth-building power of extra principal payments on a mortgage using a mutual fund instead you must:

1. Set up a special mutual fund for your monthly deposits
2. Send an amount exactly equal to your extra principal payment to your special mutual fund on the first of each month
3. Allow all dividends and capital gains to be reinvested in the mutual fund
4. Never touch a dime of your investment until you would have used the extra equity you would have created in your home

Violate any of these four investment rules and you will drain the power from your plan. For almost everyone it is easier to add the extra principal payment every month to the mortgage check. However, if you are the exception, there is no doubt that you will do better in the mutual fund. One drawback of the mutual fund alternative investment plan is that you can be taxed on the dividends and capital gains each year. Even so you can still build more "equity" in your mutual fund than in your home mortgage.

There is another time when you would invest the amount of your extra principle payments in a mutual fund instead of into your mortgage—when the interest rate on your mortgage is 9 percent or less. Never pay off a low-interest mortgage early. You have already beaten the bank. Instead, invest the extra principal payment amount in a mutual fund for bigger profits.

DEFENSE #133

Don't make large, lump-sum extra principal payments on your mortgage.

If small extra principal payments are a good idea, aren't bigger ones better? Not necessarily. Paying off your mortgage in a lump sum or making a large one-time extra principal payment from a settlement or inheritance makes sense only if your home is worth less than 10 percent of your total net worth. Otherwise you will do better financially by investing your cash somewhere else.

Making small extra principal payments periodically is not a major financial decision, although the strategy produces major results. The small amount of the extra principal payments is pocket change, money you won't really miss. Larger sums do require you to make major financial decisions. A large lump sum is money for which you have alternatives, such as investing in a mutual fund and earning a return as much as 50 percent more than the interest rate on your mortgage. In fact, by investing a large lump sum in a higher-return investment, you can withdraw some or all of the investment income to help make the payments on your mortgage and still have the entire principal left in the investment.

DEFENSE #134

Don't make extra principal payments on rental property mortgages.

On your own home you make extra principal payments for the purpose of building your equity as quickly as possible. On your rental properties your goal is to improve your cash flow. Positive cash flow is accomplished, in part, by longer-term and even negative amortization mortgages. When buying a rental property, finance for as long as possible and don't make extra principal payments. Remember, on your home mortgage you make the payments, but on your rental properties your tenants are making the payments for you, and paying off a rental property early is not as important as having the cash to cover your rental property expenses.

DEFENSE #135

Don't let a prepayment penalty scare you out of paying off a mortgage early.

Mention the word "penalty" and most Americans tremble without analyzing what effect a penalty may have. For instance, cutting your mortgage term in half with extra principal payments will automatically cut an existing 30-year mortgage down to a 15-year mortgage, saving you tens of thousands of dollars in unnecessary payments and interest. But suppose the mortgage contract states that there will be a prepayment penalty of 1 percent of the amount paid off early? The penalty is not assessed against each extra principal payment as you make it but only charged 15 years later when the entire mortgage is paid off. If the original mortgage was $80,000 and the amount paid off early was $40,000, the prepayment penalty would amount to only $400, a small price to pay for saving tens of thousands of dollars. However, if you were really on your toes, you would never have signed a mortgage contract with a prepayment penalty lasting over five years (see Defense #125).

ATTACK #136

Use equity shifting to carry forward the benefits of your mortgage reduction plan.

One question I'm asked continuously when discussing mortgages is, "What if I plan to live in a home only three or four years? Does a mortgage reduction plan or extra principal payments still make sense?" Of course it does—especially if you use an equity-shifting strategy. Let's say you're using the one-extra-principal-payment-per-month mortgage reduction plan. Over the next three to five years, until you sell, you will pay an average extra principal payment of $55 a month. In three years you will have paid $1,980 in extra principal or, if you don't change homes for five years, your extra principal payments will amount to $3,300. When you sell your current home you will receive that extra $1,980 or $3,300 as cash from the buyer. By using the money as an additional down payment on your new home, you will have effectively reduced the amount of the mortgage on which you will be making payments. Let's say you own four homes during the 15-year period, and each time you sell one home and buy another, you shift the extra equity to the new home. The total mortgage reduction effect is the same as if you had made all the extra principal payments on just one home. You will have cut your total mortgage term almost in half, saving, by the end of the same 15 years, the same thousands of unnecessary extra dollars of mortgage payments.

ATTACK #137

Convert extra equity into high-interest income when you sell.

An alternative to equity shifting when you sell your home is to turn your equity into income. For example, let's say that when you sell, the extra equity you have built amounts to $3,000. You can take back an interest-only mortgage for $3,000 from the buyer at 12 percent for eight years, which will about double your money. On the $3,000 you have lent to the new buyer, you will receive $360 per year interest, or a total of $2,880 during the eight years. At the end of the eight years, the buyer or mortgagor will owe you the entire $3,000 principal in one lump sum. If you own four homes during a 15-year period and continue to convert your extra equity to income, you will have increased your ongoing monthly income, your net worth and your mortgage investments all at the same time. A strategy that began with just a few extra dollars per month in principal payments will be worth tens of thousands.

DEFENSE #138

Convert your ARM to an FRM only when the new FRM rate would be 10 percent or less.

When mortgage interest rates are rising, the 11 million American homeowners with adjustable-rate mortgages always begin to worry. For instance, from April 1988 through April 1989, homeowners with one-year ARMs saw their payments increase by $150 a month per $100,000 of mortgage. The natural emotional response is immediately to convert your ARM to an FRM. Your bank or mortgage company may even write you a letter encouraging you to do so.

Many ARMs now have a conversion feature that allows you to switch to a fixed rate from the thirteenth to the sixtieth month with no or only small additional closing costs. Knowing when and if to convert to a fixed-rate mortgage is an important decision that should never be made emotionally, but only when it is to your advantage mathematically.

In April 1989 an ARM could be converted to an 11.5 percent FRM. Your mortgage company knows that if you convert to a fixed rate at 11.5 percent, over the course of the next few years there is a 95 percent chance that you will pay more in total interest than you would have paid had you kept your ARM. Even though the interest rates on ARMs over short periods are sometimes higher, they will always be lower in a couple of years.

Don't let the fear of higher payments on your ARM overcome good financial sense. Even though the rates and payments go up periodically on an ARM, they don't stay high for long. Interest rates are low twice as often as they are high. Locking in a fixed high interest rate out of fear will cost you thousands in the long run. However, there is a correct time to convert your ARM to an FRM, and that is whenever you can lock in a fixed rate at 10 percent or less. In other words, always convert from an ARM to an FRM when interest rates have fallen to 10 percent or below, not when they are high and rising.

If you have a new $100,000, 30-year ARM and convert to an FRM at 11.5 percent, you will pay a total of $256,000 in interest during the 30 years, but if you wait until interest rates have dropped to 10 percent before you convert, the maximum interest you can pay is only $216,000—a total savings of $40,000 just for waiting a few months for a low-interest-rate cycle. If the interest-rate never drops to 10 percent (which is unlikely), stay with your ARM. You will pay less in the long run.

Never make the error that so many homeowners do of totally refinancing your current adjustable-rate mortgage with a new fixed-rate mortgage from a different lender and paying $3,000 to $8,000 in new closing costs.

Follow the steps in the checklist below to determine the right time to convert from an ARM to an FRM mortgage:

- Check your mortgage company for their current fixed-rate mortgage interest rate.
- Read your ARM contract to determine if, how and when you

may convert your mortgage to an FRM. Each mortgage lender has different rules.

- If FRM rates are currently 10 percent or less, call or write your mortgage company immediately, referring them to the conversion rules in your mortgage contract, and begin the conversion process.
- If FRM rates are currently above 10 percent, watch the mortgage rates on the financial pages of your newspaper and begin the conversion process when the fixed-rate mortgages do fall to 10 percent or less. Eventually they will.
- If your mortgage does not offer the conversion feature or your lender does not make fixed-rate mortgage loans, it will not pay you to refinance unless the difference between your current ARM interest rate and the new fixed interest rate is at least 2 percent and the fixed rate is 10 percent or less. Why? Because if you refinance instead of convert, you will more than likely pay huge closing costs that will eat up any potential savings.

DEFENSE #139

Never pay off a low-interest mortgage because the bank offers you a discount.

When mortgage interest rates get higher, banks and mortgage companies send letters to those who have low-interest mortgages, offering a discount of 5 to 25 percent for paying off their mortgages early in a lump sum. As you realize by now, anything your bank or mortgage company wants you to do is probably in their best interest, not yours. If you have an 8 percent or less fixed-rate mortgage and the current mortgage rates are 12 percent or higher, the bank can make money if you pay off your mortgage in a lump sum by loaning your money out again at a higher interest rate. The bank will earn thousands of dollars of extra interest over the next 30 years by giving the money to someone else at a higher rate and therefore can afford to give you a discount as an incentive for paying early. If you receive the discount letter from your mortgage company, trash it. The discount of 10 to 20 percent is never enough to offset the amount of interest dollars you are saving with your low-rate mortgage. In addition, the IRS has a special rule known as debt forgiveness. For instance, if your mortgage balance is $30,000 but your bank lets you pay it off for $25,000, the IRS considers the $5,000 debt forgiveness as income, which is taxable to you. Of course, the bank normally won't tell you that.

ATTACK #140

Save money when refinancing by choosing a lender that uses the new FNMA refinancing guidelines.

You can cut in half the hassle and the costs usually encountered when you refinance your home mortgage if you don't need more cash than the original amount of your mortgage. The Federal National Mortgage Association, or Fannie Mae, which is the nation's biggest investor in home mortgages, has streamlined its requirements for refinancing your home, if you refinance with your current mortgage lender. The FNMA refinancing program is similar to the low-doc program for new mortgages. Up until 1989, even if you refinanced with your current mortgage company, your closing costs were 3 to 5 percent of the refinanced amount or $2,100 to $3,500 extra on a $70,000 mortgage, pure gravy for the mortgage company. The refinancing would often take as long as 60 days. The rules cut closing costs to about $300 and allow the refinancing process to be completed in one to two weeks. Most lenders have changed their policies to conform to the Fannie Mae guidelines.

Here are some of the time and money savers when you refinance with the same lender under the Fannie Mae guidelines:

- You won't need a new appraisal on your home. The lender will simply be required to state in writing that your property hasn't declined in value since you obtained the original loan. If your LTV is in line (80 percent) your lender may not require a full appraisal.
- Your mortgage company won't require a total credit report, verification from your employer or tax returns. The lender will simply pull a copy of your credit report by computer from the credit bureau. The lender, of course, will check your mortgage payment record, which must be reasonably good—no late payments within the last 12 months—but need not be perfect.
- Up to 1 percent of the cost of refinancing can be added to the loan amount.

- There is no minimum waiting period from the time you got your original loan until you decide to refinance.

The maximum loan cannot be more than 90 percent of your home's value on a first home or 70 percent on a second home, and you cannot use the new streamlined rules if you want to take out more than 1 percent above your original mortgage amount as additional cash.

PART V

Put the Tax System on Your Side

CHAPTER 16

Smart Taxpayer Tactics

Taxes are the single biggest expense you'll ever face in life. The taxes you will pay are much greater than home mortgages and your children's college educations combined, and yet in any financial plan, taxes are the most overlooked financial drain.

It has been my experience that no individual or family in America can build and keep much wealth until they first get their tax life under control. Control means putting together an income tax plan, a plan that creates thousands of dollars of deductions every year where you had none before. Tax deductions can be created through tax strategies in the same way that other money strategies can save you thousands on insurance, mortgages, interest, automobiles and other necessary expenses. Income taxes are an expense as are groceries, car payments or your telephone bills. The difference is that taxes can eat up to half of your total income. To save lots of money on groceries, car payments or your telephone, you might have to change your lifestyle, settling for less. Saving money on taxes requires no sacrifice, just a few hours a year of your time. The tax money you save can then be used to upgrade your lifestyle.

When I was 19, I discovered an indisputable fact about taxes that inspired me to learn the tax system inside and out, which, in turn, has enabled me to save millions of tax dollars. *The percentage of your income you are required to pay in income taxes has little to do with the amount of money you make and has everything to do with how well you have created your tax plan.* Without a tax plan and tax control, taxes will eat up 50 percent of every dollar you'll ever earn. You heard it right, 50 percent! Look at the following table and you will see how.

HOW TAXES EAT UP YOUR WEALTH

Federal income tax	28%
Social Security tax	7%
State income tax	7%
Sales tax	7%
Property tax	3%
Total	52%

In addition, you are often paying hidden, unexpected taxes such as:

Real estate transfer tax	Recording fees
License tax	Inheritance tax
Gift tax	Airport departure tax
Customs fees/duty	Corporate income tax[1]
Excise tax	Entertainment tax
Personal property tax	Transportation tax[2]

[1] Consumers, not corporations, pay corporate income tax, through higher prices for goods and services.

[2] Fees paid by taxi companies, airlines and other providers of transportation, are added to your costs for their services.

Beating the high cost of taxes is one of your greatest financial challenges and lasts an entire lifetime. It can be done only with very careful planning. There are three magic words when it comes to your tax plan: *income, assets* and *expenses.* In each of these categories, you can create thousands of new deductions by planning your activities correctly. It's easy. At first you will have to think about how to connect your activities to potential deductions, but soon, through practice and experience, almost everything in your life will become deductible. Here are examples of your income, assets and expenses, all of which can be made deductible with the right strategies:

THE THREE MAGIC WORDS IN TAX PLANNING
Items That Can Be Made Directly or Indirectly Deductible

INCOME	ASSETS	EXPENSES
Salary	Home	Interest
Commissions	Addition to your home	Home mortgage
Income from small business	Automobiles	Second home
Investment income	Video tape recorder	Credit card
Retirement income	Video camera	Personal (consumer)
	Home computer	Spouse
	Tools and equipment	Children
	Investment assets	Entertainment
	Boat	Travel/vacations
	Airplane	Automobile insurance
		Homeowner's insurance
		Medical insurance
		Capital losses

Creating Your Tax Plan

The objective of your tax plan is to create as many deductions as possible for your income, assets and expenses. Is it worth the trouble? You bet it is, because tax deductions convert to spendable dollars. For every one dollar of tax deductions you create and claim, the IRS will let you keep the amount of tax it was going to charge you on that dollar.

The amount of cash savings you can create through tax deductions is easy to determine. Let's do a simple calculation to see how it works. You have an income of $50,000 a year, and at a combined rate of 35 percent, you are paying about $17,500 in state and federal income taxes. If you can make half of your income dollars tax deductible, you will pay only half of $17,500, or $8,750. You have saved $8,750 and your spendable income has increased by the same amount. That's quite a difference!

But just how do you make your income dollars tax deductible?

Tax deductions are not something you find at your tax preparer's office in April. Tax deductions must be created, not found. The traditional approach to taxes is to wait until the end of the year and while doing your taxes yourself or working with your tax preparer, you look for little-known tax rules that might make a few extra dollars of your income and expenses deductible. This traditional approach is not only nonsense, but it in no way creates a tax plan.

A tax plan is a set of strategies used during the entire tax year to create deductions. The same income, assets or expenses can be deductible or nondeductible, depending solely on how you conduct your activities during the year. To give a clear picture of how your activities determine the deductibility of your income, assets or expenses, look at the next list, entitled Making Your Activities Deductible. The 9 items in this list will give you a clear picture of how your regular activities can generate extra tax deductible dollars.

Almost any form of income, assets or expenses can be made deductible. Your job is to plan your activities so that they become deductible, but without spending so much extra time that you must change your lifestyle. Is it possible? Not only is it possible, it is the well-kept secret that all multimillionaires and supersuccessful entrepreneurs have used to legally reduce their taxes for the past 75 years.

One question. Do you believe the rumor we all heard growing up that multimillionaires pay far less in taxes as a percentage of their income than families earning $20,000 to $100,000 a year? That rumor is fact. Tax damage control is one of the processes that most all American supersuccesses have used to build and keep wealth. It is not that the wealthy are treated more favorably under the tax code; in fact, tax brackets for higher-income people are higher than for those with lower incomes. The difference is the application of "tax smarts," learning to turn life's everyday expenses into tax deductions.

I discussed dozens of these tax-saving strategies in *More Wealth Without Risk*. Combining the tax strategies that follow with those in *More Wealth Without Risk*, you will become a master at tax reduction. My focus in this chapter is how to deal one-on-one with the IRS. Most people are intimidated by the IRS and approach taxes with a four-letter word—fear. Only if you refuse to pay your taxes or deliberately violate tax laws do you have cause for concern. Actually, the IRS stands ready to help you with many taxpayer services and scores of free publications, but almost no one knows about or uses them. If you do understand the tax system, the IRS may challenge your interpretation of a tax law, but only if you attempt to cheat the system is any legal action taken or are fines and punishments imposed. Unlike some insurance salespeople, mortgage lenders and car dealers, the IRS is not out to get you—it is lack of a plan and lack of knowledge that will do you in financially.

MAKING YOUR ACTIVITIES DEDUCTIBLE

This list shows how nondeductible activities are easily converted into tax deductible activities. These strategies are explained in detail in *More Wealth Without Risk*.

CURRENT NONDEDUCTIBLE ACTIVITY	TAX DEDUCTIBLE ACTIVITY
1. You rent.	Buy a home. Your mortgage interest and property taxes become deductible.
2. You use your VCR and/or home computer only personally.	Use your VCR and/or home computer in your small business and for your personal tax and financial plan.
3. You love to travel and vacation but get no tax deductions.	Plan your travel around conventions or job interviews, or create a small importing company.
4. You give your children allowances, cash gifts and handouts.	Pay your children a salary for working in your small business.
5. You give your kids or parents money to buy a home.	Buy a home with your kids or parents and you own half, allowing you to deduct part of the depreciation and other expenses.
6. You take money out of your paycheck to invest or save.	Have the same amount of money put into your company retirement plan or an IRA and take a deduction for every dime you contribute.
7. You use your recreational vehicle or boat only personally.	Use your RV or boat in a small business, lease it out as a small business activity or "quarter share" it.
8. You pay nondeductible interest on your credit cards and automobile loan.	Pay off your credit cards and automobile loan with a home equity loan. The interest becomes deductible.
9. You invest in stocks, bonds, mutual funds, CDs or savings accounts but get no deduction.	Move some of your investment capital into rental properties, tax-sheltered partnerships and self-directed annuities to create deductions.

ATTACK #141

When you're wondering about your refund, call the IRS Tele-Tax service line.

Most taxpayers have their refunds spent before the IRS sends the money. Once you file for a refund, it can take up to eight weeks, sometimes more, before the check is mailed, depending on how busy the IRS is at the time. All refund information is now put on computer by the IRS and you can find out your current refund status with a simple phone call, and it's toll-free! You can call the IRS Tele-Tax service line Monday through Friday, 7 A.M. to 11 P.M., from any push-button telephone, or Monday through Friday, 8 A.M. to 5 P.M., if you are using a rotary dial phone. When you call the IRS, have your tax return in front of you. You will need to give the first Social Security number shown on your return, whether yours or your spouse's, and the exact amount of the refund from line 65 on page 2 of your 1040 form, line 8 of your 1040EZ or line 27 of Form 1040A, depending on which of the three forms you filed. Use the Tele-Tax service phone numbers listed at the end of this chapter.

ATTACK #142

Use the IRS Tele-Tax service to get prerecorded instant answers to puzzling tax questions.

When you're completing your tax return or are working on a strategy to create additional tax deductions, often you need instant answers on different subjects, such as depreciation, capital gains or recordkeeping for a small business. If you have the right tax publications (see list in Chapter 17), you're in great shape. If you don't, there is another alternative, the recorded tax information provided by the IRS Tele-Tax service. The IRS has taken the answers to the most often asked questions, combined them with the most important rules you must know on each subject, and recorded the information in the sweetest voice possible. This service is excellent but few are aware that it exists and fewer still take advantage of it.

At the end of this chapter you will see a list of tax topics and their three-digit code numbers for which the IRS has prerecorded information. You can find lots of answers by simply calling the Tele-Tax number for your area and then, from your touch-tone phone, punching in the three-digit code number of the recording you want to hear. With a push-button phone you can call anytime, 24 hours a day, 7 days a week. If you have a rotary dial, you must first get an operator, who will then switch you to the appropriate recording. Use the telephone numbers listed for your area at the end of this chapter to call the Tele-Tax service. A recorded voice will give you any additional instructions that you may need.

ATTACK #143

Call the IRS with your tax question but get a second opinion.

For many years the IRS has had people waiting by the phones ready to answer your tax questions. When preparing your return or creating your overall tax plan, a quick answer can be a big help. But there are two possible pitfalls. The first is that at tax time you will often get continuous busy signals. The second is that when you do get through you may end up with an incorrect answer. If you dial the Tele-Tax service for a prerecorded message, it is in all likelihood 100 percent accurate. But if you are looking for an answer to a very specific and personal question and are speaking with an IRS representative, you may or may not get the correct information.

Every year *Money* magazine does a study in which a group of tax professionals armed with 10 tax questions each ask for IRS phone help. It was found that the IRS answered up to 40 percent of the questions incorrectly.

If you do get an incorrect answer from the IRS and that answer causes you to pay more in income tax, you will not be liable for the additional tax. But to prove the IRS was at fault, you must have the name of the IRS representative you spoke with and the date and time of your call.

Because of the problem of incorrect answers, the IRS has now put some experts on the phone to handle tax questions in more complicated areas of tax law, including retirement plans. The service includes 401(k), 403(b), SEP, IRA and Keogh questions. Call 202-566-6783, Monday through Thursday, 1:30 P.M. to 4 P.M. EST. You pay for the call; the information is free.

For your personal questions on other subjects, use the telephone numbers listed for the IRS in your local telephone directory or on the tax forms. Tax question telephone numbers are also listed at the end of this chapter. Because of the complicated and often individual nature of the questions, the regular IRS telephone staff sometimes makes mistakes. Always ask IRS representatives for their names and for the appropriate tax publications from which they are getting their answers. Read the publication yourself as a double check and seek a second opinion. The IRS does not trace your call or ask for your name and Social Security number, so you can be frank with your questions.

ATTACK #144

File Form 1040X to get back refund money you missed from previous years' returns.

The smarter you get about taxes, the more refund opportunities you will find. About one out of three people who read *More Wealth Without Risk* or have become members of the Charles J. Givens Organization find that they have missed legitimate tax deductions and should have gotten a bigger refund for years gone by.

What do you do? File Form 1040X, the Amended U.S. Individual Income Tax Return. Form 1040X allows you to claim a tax refund for up to three years from the date your return was due or filed, or within two years of the date you paid your taxes, whichever is later. If the refund is from a public limited partnership investment, the refund period is extended to four years. If you find that you have an unused investment tax credit or a business loss carry-back which you could use personally, Form 1040X is also your ticket to a refund. If a stock you own or a loan you made becomes worthless, you must take the deduction in a prior year, and Form 1040X is used. When you find additional federal tax deductions, you may also have reduced your state tax liability. Be sure you file the corresponding form for state taxes you may have overpaid. Of course, if you find income that you should have reported but missed, you also use Form 1040X to report the additional taxes you owe.

Here is a typical example of how to use Form 1040X to claim missed deductions. Let's say that your tax preparer told you not to claim deductions for a small business that you created because it might "flag" your return for audit. That kind of advice is bad advice and the most painful part is that you actually had to pay for it. You would use Form 1040X to claim the deductions you should have received.

So many times at my lectures people have come up and said, "My tax preparer told me not to claim those deductions, even though they are legitimate." If that happens to you, that's a tax preparer who should be on your "firing list." File Form 1040X to get your money back; after all, it is your money, not the IRS's or your tax preparer's. When it comes to legitimate tax deductions, you deserve to take all you can. The IRS is required to allow you to take legitimate deductions. It's not up for a vote.

The example of Form 1040X that follows will give you an idea of how to claim deductions you may have missed. In this example, Bob and Eileen Ventro had a small business, but as all too often happens, their tax preparer incorrectly advised them to report the income but not the expenses. After becoming members of the Givens Organization, they realized they had unnecessarily overpaid their taxes. By computing their $3,120 deductions on a Schedule C (not shown) and entering the total on Form 1040X (shown) in line 1-B, they will receive a refund of $472, as indicated on line 24, plus interest.

Many people who are due extra refunds or deductions don't file Form 1040X because they have a feeling they will automatically be flagged for audit. Not true. The IRS audit department does not process your 1040X unless it appears that the deductions you claim may not be owed to you. Filing Form 1040X does allow the statute of limitations to keep your return open for audit for three years from the time you filed the amended return, but as long as you feel your return is otherwise correct, the additional time limit is no problem.

If you filed an incorrect return *before* April 15 or an extension date and then realized your mistake, don't use 1040X; simply file a corrected 1040 form before the due date. If you do file a Form 1040X, make sure you mail it to the same IRS service center where you sent your original return, or the chances of the IRS making the connection are practically nil.

ATTACK #145

Get Package X each year and have all your blank tax forms in one place.

Package X was originally designed for tax preparers, but anyone, with a little effort, can get a copy. Package X is two volumes, each about ¾″ thick, and contains almost every IRS form, including personal, business and supplemental schedules. If you're like most, when doing your taxes, you discover at the last minute that you need that one form or schedule you forgot during your last trip to the IRS, or the one that wasn't available at the post office. Not only will Package X solve the problem, but it will also give you an overview of how the entire tax process and tax form system fit together.

If you have a copying machine at the office or near your home, make copies of the forms in Package X rather than tearing out the sheets. It is not a violation of copyright laws to photocopy any IRS form or publication, so feel free to copy whatever you need. You can also make copies of all tax forms at any library. If you need a special tax form, stop by the library and copy the form on the library's copy machine. The $.25 you pay per page is deductible as a tax preparation expense.

ATTACK #146

When you can't find your tax return, get a copy from the IRS or check your tax account.

Copies of tax returns often get misplaced when you move, or occasionally you may, in your haste to get your return filed, forget to keep a copy. You can obtain a copy of any prior year's tax return by filling out Form 4506, Request for Copy of Tax Form. There is a Form 4506 in Package X, or you can get one from your nearest IRS office by calling the IRS forms telephone number.

Mail Form 4506 to the same IRS service center where you file your tax returns. The addresses are listed on the back of the form. Send in $4.25 for each year's return that you want, no

Form **1040X** (Rev. October 1992)

Department of the Treasury—Internal Revenue Service

Amended U.S. Individual Income Tax Return

▶ See separate instructions.

OMB No. 1545-0091
Expires 10-31-94

This return is for calendar year ▶ 19 , OR fiscal year ended ▶ , 19

Please print or type

Your first name and initial	Last name	**Your social security number**
If a joint return, spouse's first name and initial	Last name	**Spouse's social security number**
Home address (number and street). If you have a P.O. box, see instructions.	Apt. no.	Telephone number (optional) ( )
City, town or post office, state, and ZIP code. If you have a foreign address, see instructions.		**For Paperwork Reduction Act Notice, see page 1 of separate instructions.**

Enter name and address as shown on original return. If same as above, write "Same." If changing from separate to joint return, enter names and addresses from original returns.

A Service center where original return was filed

B Has original return been changed or audited by the IRS? ☐ Yes ☐ No
If "No," have you been notified that it will be? . . . . . ☐ Yes ☐ No
If "Yes," identify the IRS office ▶

C Are you amending your return to include any item (loss, credit, deduction, other tax benefit, or income) relating to a tax shelter required to be registered? . . . . . ☐ Yes ☐ No
If "Yes," you must attach **Form 8271,** Investor Reporting of Tax Shelter Registration Number.

D Filing status claimed. **Note:** *You cannot change from joint to separate returns after the due date has passed.*

On original return ▶ ☐ Single ☐ Married filing joint return ☐ Married filing separate return ☐ Head of household ☐ Qualifying widow(er)
On this return ▶ ☐ Single ☐ Married filing joint return ☐ Married filing separate return ☐ Head of household ☐ Qualifying widow(er)

Income and Deductions (see instructions) **Caution:** *Be sure to complete Part II on page 2.*		**A.** As originally reported or as adjusted (see instructions)	**B.** Net change—Increase or (Decrease)—explain on page 2	**C.** Correct amount
1 Total income	1			
2 Adjustments to income	2			
3 Adjusted gross income. Subtract line 2 from line 1	3			
4 Itemized deductions or standard deduction	4			
5 Subtract line 4 from line 3	5			
6 Exemptions. If changing, fill in Parts I and II on page 2	6			
7 Taxable income. Subtract line 6 from line 5	7			
Tax Liability				
8 Tax (see instructions). Method used in col. C ______	8			
9 Credits (see instructions)	9			
10 Subtract line 9 from line 8. Enter the result but not less than zero	10			
11 Other taxes (such as self-employment tax, alternative minimum tax, etc.)	11			
12 Total tax. Add lines 10 and 11	12			
Payments				
13 Federal income tax withheld and excess social security, Medicare, and RRTA taxes withheld. If changing, see instructions	13			
14 Estimated tax payments	14			
15 Earned income credit	15			
16 Credits for Federal tax paid on fuels, regulated investment company, etc.	16			
17 Amount paid with Form 4868, Form 2688, or Form 2350 (application for extension of time to file)			17	
18 Amount paid with original return plus additional tax paid after it was filed			18	
19 Add lines 13 through 18 in column C			19	
Refund or Amount You Owe				
20 Overpayment, if any, as shown on original return or as previously adjusted by the IRS			20	
21 Subtract line 20 from line 19 (see instructions)			21	
22 **AMOUNT YOU OWE.** If line 12, column C, is more than line 21, enter the difference and see instructions			22	
23 **REFUND** to be received. If line 12, column C, is less than line 21, enter the difference			23	

Sign Here
Keep a copy of this return for your records.

Under penalties of perjury, I declare that I have filed an original return and that I have examined this amended return, including accompanying schedules and statements, and to the best of my knowledge and belief, this amended return is true, correct, and complete. Declaration of preparer (other than taxpayer) is based on all information of which the preparer has any knowledge.

▶ Your signature Date ▶ Spouse's signature. If a joint return, BOTH must sign. Date

Paid Preparer's Use Only

Preparer's signature ▶	Date	Check if self-employed ☐	Preparer's social security no.
Firm's name (or yours if self-employed) and address ▶		E.I. No.	
		ZIP code	

Cat. No. 11360L

Form **1040X** (Rev. 10-92)

Form 1040X (Rev. 10-92) Page 2

Part I **Exemptions.** See Form 1040 or Form 1040A instructions.

If you are not changing your exemptions, do not complete this part.
If claiming more exemptions, complete lines 24–30 and, if applicable, line 31.
If claiming fewer exemptions, complete lines 24–29.

			A. Number originally reported	B. Net change	C. Correct number
24	Yourself and spouse	24			
	Caution: *If your parents (or someone else) can claim you as a dependent (even if they chose not to), you cannot claim an exemption for yourself.*				
25	Your dependent children who lived with you	25			
26	Your dependent children who did not live with you due to divorce or separation	26			
27	Other dependents	27			
28	Total number of exemptions. Add lines 24 through 27	28			
29	**For tax year 1992,** if the amount on page 1, line 3, is more than $78,950, see the instructions. Otherwise, multiply $2,300 by the number of exemptions claimed on line 28. **For tax year 1991,** if the amount on page 1, line 3, is more than $75,000, see the instructions. Otherwise, multiply $2,150 by the number of exemptions claimed on line 28. **For tax year 1990,** use $2,050; **for tax year 1989,** use $2,000. Enter the result here and on page 1, line 6	29			

30 Dependents (children and other) not claimed on original return:

(a) Dependent's name (first, initial, and last name)	(b) Check if under age 1 (under age 2 if a 1989 or 1990 return)	(c) If age 1 or older (age 2 or older if a 1989 or 1990 return), enter dependent's social security number	(d) Dependent's relationship to you	(e) No. of months lived in your home

No. of your children on line 30 who lived with you ▶ ☐

No. of your children on line 30 who **didn't** live with you due to divorce or separation (see instructions) ▶ ☐

No. of other dependents listed on line 30 ▶ ☐

31 If your child listed on line 30 didn't live with you but is claimed as your dependent under a pre-1985 agreement, check here ▶ ☐

Part II **Explanation of Changes to Income, Deductions, and Credits**

Enter the line number from page 1 for each item you are changing and give the reason for each change. Attach all supporting forms and schedules for items changed. If you don't, your Form 1040X may be returned. Be sure to include your name and social security number on any attachments.

If the change pertains to a net operating loss carryback or a general business credit carryback, attach the schedule or form that shows the year in which the loss or credit occurred. See instructions. Also, check here ▶ ☐

Part III **Presidential Election Campaign Fund**

Checking below will not increase your tax or reduce your refund.

If you did not previously want to have $1 go to the fund but now want to, check here ▶ ☐

If a joint return and your spouse did not previously want to have $1 go to the fund but now wants to, check here ▶ ☐

*U.S. Government Printing Office: 1992 — 315-204

matter how many or how few pages. It takes about a month and a half to receive the copies you requested.

At the IRS you also have your own tax account, which includes your name, Social Security number, marital status, the type of return you filed, the amount of tax shown on the return, your adjusted gross income, your taxable income, any self-employment tax you paid and the number of exemptions you claimed. If this is the information you need, you can get it free by calling your local IRS office. Your tax account information will take about two weeks to reach you. As you learn more about taxes, you may wish to gather previous years' data together to measure the progress you are making with your tax plan, and having previous years' returns is a must.

DEFENSE #147

If you live abroad, contact your consulate for tax help.

When I am talking to people who live abroad, this question comes up time and time again: "Where do I get tax help? I can't call the IRS, as I can in the U.S." Yes, you can. The IRS keeps a permanent staff at 14 U.S. embassies and consulates around the world. There you can get tax forms, answers to questions and help with errors made by the IRS.

Here are the cities and local phone numbers:

Bonn, West Germany	339-2119
Caracas, Venezuela	285-3111, ext. 333
London, England	408-8076 or 408-8077
Manila, Philippines	521-7116, ext. 613 or 644
Mexico City, Mexico	(525) 211-0042, ext. 3559
Nassau, Bahamas	(809) 322-1181
Ottawa, Canada	(613) 238-5335
Paris, France	4296-1202
Riyadh, Saudi Arabia	488-3800, ext. 206
Rome, Italy	4674-2560
Sao Paulo, Brazil	881-6511, ext. 287
Singapore	338-0251, ext. 245
Sydney, Australia	261-9275
Tokyo, Japan	224-5466

From January 1 to June 15 each year, the IRS has a traveling band of tax helpers that visit an additional 139 cities in 72 countries. Check your nearest embassy or consulate to find the schedule of traveling tax helpers. Should you stump the IRS representatives abroad, you can still get an answer to your technical tax questions by writing to the Assistant Commissioner International, 950 L'Enfant Plaza S.W., Washington, D.C. 20024, USA.

If you have never lived abroad or considered it, maybe you should. One of the greatest tax exemptions in the tax code is for income earned abroad. Can you imagine getting a bonus of being able to earn $70,000 a year tax-free in addition to the opportunity to travel the world? That's right. Whether you work for an American company or foreign company abroad, or even start your own business overseas, your first $70,000 each year is exempt from U.S. taxes. (See IRS Publication 54.)

In addition to the foreign income exclusion, you will also be eligible for a deduction for housing costs and a foreign tax credit. If you are single, the foreign income exclusion can save you as much as $18,000 in taxes; if married filing jointly, your cash tax savings can be up to $15,500. That's the equivalent of getting $15,500 to $18,000 of free, tax-exempt cash for every year you work abroad.

To qualify you must meet either the foreign residency test or the physical presence test. Establishing foreign residency can be accomplished by renting an apartment or buying a home abroad rather than residing in a hotel, by taking your family with you or by changing your permanent mailing address. You must remain in the country as a resident for a full tax year, from January 1 to December 31. If you file an exemption statement with a foreign government denying you are a resident of that country to avoid paying its income tax, you have invalidated your residency requirement for the U.S. foreign income exclusion.

ATTACK #148

Learn how to behave in an audit.

It's important to mind your manners when you're being audited. But contrary to what many people believe, you can be aggressive and well-mannered at the same time. Here are the rules to follow:

- Say little; smile a lot. Never volunteer information.
- If you feel strongly about your position, let the auditor know. Often the auditor will let the point go in your favor.
- Provide as much documentation as possible for each point in an audit.
- Don't give up, even if you don't have all the documentation.
- Don't make too many concessions.
- Don't be rushed unless you feel hurrying will work in your favor.
- Don't complain about the tax system; the auditor pays taxes, too.
- Don't take your crumpled-up receipts in a brown paper bag. That old strategy won't work anymore. Auditors are trained to believe that if you keep your records in a disorganized manner, there must be an error in there somewhere.
- Don't take the Fifth Amendment. Tax protesting is a disaster. The jails and courts are full of people who believed such nonsense would work.
- Don't try to tape-record the conversation. The IRS found from experience that recording tended to fluster auditors. Recording once was a great way to get control of an audit, but now, you will have to go to court to get permission to record. Even if you win, it's not worth the trouble.
- Act with confidence that you're right. You probably are.

TELE-TAX PHONE NUMBERS

Use for refund status or recorded tax information

FOR THESE STATES CALL:
1-800-829-4477

ALABAMA
ALASKA
ARKANSAS
CONNECTICUT
DELAWARE
FLORIDA
HAWAII
IDAHO
KANSAS
KENTUCKY
LOUISIANA
MAINE
MISSISSIPPI
MONTANA
NEVADA
NEW HAMPSHIRE
NEW JERSEY
NEW MEXICO
N. CAROLINA
N. DAKOTA
OKLAHOMA
PUERTO RICO
RHODE ISLAND
S. CAROLINA
S. DAKOTA
UTAH
VERMONT
WEST VIRGINIA
WYOMING

ARIZONA
Phoenix
640-3933
Elsewhere
1-800-829-4477

CALIFORNIA
Counties of:
Alpine, Amador, Butte, Calaveras, Colusa, Contra Costa, Del Norte, El Dorado, Glenn, Humboldt, Lake, Lassen, Marin, Mendocino, Modoc, Napa, Nevada, Placer, Plumas, Sacramento, San Joaquin, Shasta, Sierra, Siskiyou, Solano, Sonoma, Sutter, Tehama, Trinity, Yolo, Yuba
1-800-829-4032
Oakland
839-4245
Elsewhere
1-800-829-4477

COLORADO
Denver
592-1118
Elsewhere
1-800-829-4477

DISTRICT OF COLUMBIA
628-2929

GEORGIA
Atlanta
331-6572
Elsewhere
1-800-829-4477

ILLINOIS
Chicago
886-9614
In area code 708
1-312-886-9614
Springfield
789-0489
Elsewhere
1-800-829-4477

INDIANA
Indianapolis
631-1010
Elsewhere
1-800-829-4477

IOWA
Des Moines
284-7454
Elsewhere
1-800-829-4477

MARYLAND
Baltimore
244-7306
Elsewhere
1-800-829-4477

MASSACHUSETTS
Boston
536-0709
Elsewhere
1-800-829-4477

MICHIGAN
Detroit
961-4282
Elsewhere
1-800-829-4477

MINNESOTA
St. Paul
644-7748
Elsewhere
1-800-829-4477

MISSOURI
St. Louis
241-4700
Elsewhere
1-800-829-4477

NEBRASKA
Omaha
221-3324

Elsewhere
1-800-829-4477

NEW YORK
Bronx, Brooklyn, Queens, and Staten Island
488-8432
Buffalo
685-5533
Manhattan
406-4080
Elsewhere
1-800-829-4477

OHIO
Cincinnati
421-0329
Cleveland
522-3037
Elsewhere
1-800-829-4477

OREGON
Portland
294-5363
Elsewhere
1-800-829-4477

PENNSYLVANIA
Philadelphia
627-1040
Pittsburgh
261-1040
Elsewhere
1-800-829-4477

TENNESSEE
Nashville
781-5040
Elsewhere
1-800-829-4477

TEXAS
Dallas
767-1792
Houston
541-0440
Elsewhere
1-800-829-4477

VIRGINIA
Richmond
783-1569
Elsewhere
1-800-829-4477

WASHINGTON
Seattle
343-7221
Elsewhere
1-800-829-4477

WISCONSIN
Milwaukee
273-8100
Elsewhere
1-800-829-4477

TELE-TAX SUBJECTS AND THREE-DIGIT TOPIC NUMBERS

TOPIC NO.	SUBJECT
	IRS Help Available
101	IRS services—Volunteer tax assistance, toll-free telephone, walk-in assistance, and outreach programs
102	Tax assistance for individuals with disabilities and the hearing impaired
103	Small Business Tax Education Program (STEP)—Tax help for small businesses
104	Problem Resolution Program—Help for problem situations
105	Public libraries—Tax information tapes and reproducible tax forms
911	Hardship assistance applications
	IRS Procedures
151	Your appeal rights
152	Refunds—How long they should take
153	What to do if you haven't filed your tax return (Nonfilers)
154	Form W-2—What to do if not received
155	Forms and Publications—How to order
156	Copy of your tax return—How to get one
157	Change of address—How to notify the IRS
	Collection
201	The collection process
202	What to do if you can't pay your tax
203	Failure to pay child support and other Federal obligations
204	Offers in compromise

Topic numbers are effective January 1, 1994.

TOPIC NO.	SUBJECT
	Alternative Filing Methods
251	1040PC tax return
252	Electronic filing
253	Substitute tax forms
254	How to choose a tax preparer
	General Information
301	When, where, and how to file
302	Highlights of 1993 tax changes
303	Checklist of common errors when preparing your tax return
304	Extensions of time to file your tax return
305	Recordkeeping
306	Penalty for underpayment of estimated tax
307	Backup withholding
308	Amended returns
309	Tax fraud—How to report
310	Tax-exempt status for organizations
311	How to apply for exempt status
312	Power of attorney information
999	Local information
	Filing Requirements, Filing Status, and Exemptions
351	Who must file?
352	Which form—1040, 1040A, or 1040EZ?
353	What is your filing status?
354	Dependents
355	Estimated tax
356	Decedents
	Types of Income
401	Wages and salaries
402	Tips
403	Interest received
404	Dividends
405	Refunds of state and local taxes
406	Alimony received
407	Business income
408	Sole proprietorship
409	Capital gains and losses
410	Pensions and annuities
411	Pensions—The general rule and the simplified general rule
412	Lump-sum distributions
413	Rollovers from retirement plans
414	Rental income and expenses
415	Renting vacation property and renting to relatives
416	Royalties
417	Farming and fishing income
418	Earnings for clergy
419	Unemployment compensation
420	Gambling income and expenses
421	Bartering income
422	Scholarship and fellowship grants
423	Nontaxable income
424	Social security and equivalent railroad retirement benefits
425	401(k) plans
426	Passive activities—Losses and credits
	Adjustments to Income
451	Individual retirement arrangements (IRAs)
452	Alimony paid
453	Bad debt deduction
454	Tax shelters
	Itemized Deductions
501	Should I itemize?
502	Medical and dental expenses
503	Deductible taxes
504	Moving expenses
505	Interest expense
506	Contributions
507	Casualty losses
508	Miscellaneous expenses
509	Business use of home
510	Business use of car
511	Business travel expenses
512	Business entertainment expenses
513	Educational expenses
514	Employee business expenses
515	Disaster area losses (including flood losses)

TOPIC NO.	SUBJECT
	Tax Computation
551	Standard deduction
552	Tax and credits figured by the IRS
553	Tax on a child's investment income
554	Self-employment tax
555	Five- or ten-year averaging for lump-sum distributions
556	Alternative minimum tax
557	Estate tax
558	Gift tax
	Tax Credits
601	Earned income credit (EIC)
602	Child and dependent care credit
603	Credit for the elderly or the disabled
604	Advance earned income credit
	IRS Notices and Letters
651	Notices—What to do
652	Notice of underreported income—CP 2000
653	IRS notices and bills and penalty and interest charges
	Basis of Assets, Depreciation, and Sale of Assets
701	Sale of your home—General
702	Sale of your home—How to report gain
703	Sale of your home—Exclusion of gain, age 55 and over
704	Basis of assets
705	Depreciation
706	Installment sales
	Employer Tax Information
751	Social Security and Medicare withholding rates
752	Form W-2—Where, when, and how to file
753	Form W-4—Employee's Withholding Allowance Certificate
754	Form W-5—Advance earned income credit
755	Employer identification number (EIN)—How to apply
756	Employment taxes for household employees
757	Form 941—Deposit requirements
758	Form 941—Employer's Quarterly Federal Tax Return
759	Form 940/940-EZ—Deposit requirements
760	Form 940/940-EZ—Employer's Annual Federal Unemployment Tax Return
761	Targeted jobs credit
762	Tips—Withholding and reporting
	Magnetic Media Filers—1099 Series and Related Information Returns (For electronic filing of individual returns, listen to topic 252.)
801	Who must file magnetically
802	Acceptable media and locating a third party to prepare your files
803	Applications, forms, and information
804	Waivers and extensions
805	Test files and combined Federal and state filing
806	Electronic filing of information returns
807	Information Returns Program Bulletin Board System
	Tax Information for Aliens and U.S. Citizens Living Abroad
851	Resident and nonresident aliens
852	Dual-status alien
853	Foreign earned income exclusion—General
854	Foreign earned income exclusion—Who qualifies?

TOPIC NO.	SUBJECT
855	Foreign earned income exclusion—What qualifies?
856	Foreign tax credit
	Tax Information for Puerto Rico Residents (in Spanish)
901	Who must file a U.S. income tax return in Puerto Rico
902	Deductions and credits for Puerto Rico filers
903	Federal employment taxes in Puerto Rico
904	Tax assistance for Puerto Rico residents
	Other Tele-Tax Topics in Spanish
951	IRS services—Volunteer tax assistance, toll-free telephone, walk-in assistance, and outreach programs
952	Refunds—How long they should take
953	Forms and publications—How to order
954	Highlights of 1993 tax changes
955	Who must file?
956	Which form to use?
957	What is your filing status?
958	Social security and equivalent railroad retirement benefits
959	Earned income credit (EIC)
960	Advance earned income credit
961	Alien tax clearance

TAX QUESTION TELEPHONE NUMBERS

Phone numbers for tax questions answered by IRS representatives. Use these numbers to talk to real people. Hours of operation: Monday through Friday during regular business hours.

ALABAMA
1-800-829-1040

ALASKA
Anchorage, 561-7484
Elsewhere
1-800-829-1040

ARIZONA
Phoenix, 640-3900
Elsewhere
1-800-829-1040

ARKANSAS
1-800-829-1040

CALIFORNIA
Oakland, 839-1040
Elsewhere
1-800-829-1040

COLORADO
Denver, 825-7041
Elsewhere
1-800-829-1040

CONNECTICUT
1-800-829-1040

DELAWARE
1-800-829-1040

DISTRICT OF COLUMBIA
1-800-829-1040

FLORIDA
Jacksonville, 354-1760
Elsewhere
1-800-829-1040

GEORGIA
Atlanta, 522-0050
Elsewhere
1-800-829-1040

HAWAII
Oahu, 541-1040
Elsewhere
1-800-829-1040

IDAHO
1-800-829-1040

ILLINOIS
Chicago, 435-1040
In area code 708
1-312-435-1040
Elsewhere
1-800-829-1040

INDIANA
Indianapolis, 226-5477
Elsewhere
1-800-829-1040

IOWA
Des Moines, 283-0523
Elsewhere
1-800-829-1040
KANSAS
1-800-829-1040
KENTUCKY
1-800-829-1040
LOUISIANA
1-800-829-1040
MAINE
1-800-829-1040
MARYLAND
Baltimore, 962-2590
Elsewhere
1-800-829-1040
MASSACHUSETTS
Boston, 536-1040
Elsewhere
1-800-829-1040
MICHIGAN
Detroit, 237-0800
Elsewhere
1-800-829-1040
MINNESOTA
Minneapolis and St. Paul, 644-7515
Elsewhere
1-800-829-1040
MISSISSIPPI
1-800-829-1040
MISSOURI
St. Louis, 342-1040
Elsewhere
1-800-829-1040
MONTANA
1-800-829-1040
NEBRASKA
Omaha, 422-1500
Elsewhere
1-800-829-1040
NEVADA
1-800-829-1040
NEW HAMPSHIRE
1-800-829-1040
NEW JERSEY
1-800-829-1040
NEW MEXICO
1-800-829-1040
NEW YORK
Bronx, Queens, Staten Island, and Brooklyn, 488-9150
Buffalo, 685-5432
Manhattan, 732-0100
Nassau, 222-1131
Suffolk, 724-5000
Elsewhere
1-800-829-1040
NORTH CAROLINA
1-800-829-1040
NORTH DAKOTA
1-800-829-1040
OHIO
Cincinnati, 621-6281
Cleveland, 522-3000
Elsewhere
1-800-829-1040
OKLAHOMA
1-800-829-1040
OREGON
Portland, 221-3960
Elsewhere
1-800-829-1040
PENNSYLVANIA
Philadelphia, 574-9900
Pittsburgh, 281-0112
Elsewhere
1-800-829-1040
PUERTO RICO
San Juan Metro Area
766-5040
Elsewhere
1-800-829-1040
RHODE ISLAND
1-800-829-1040
SOUTH CAROLINA
1-800-829-1040
SOUTH DAKOTA
1-800-829-1040
TENNESSEE
Nashville, 834-9005
Elsewhere
1-800-829-1040
TEXAS
Dallas, 742-2440
Houston, 541-0440
Elsewhere
1-800-829-1040
UTAH
1-800-829-1040
VERMONT
1-800-829-1040
VIRGINIA
Richmond, 649-2361
Elsewhere
1-800-829-1040
WASHINGTON
Seattle, 442-1040
Elsewhere
1-800-829-1040
WEST VIRGINIA
1-800-829-1040
WISCONSIN
Milwaukee, 271-3780
Elsewhere
1-800-829-1040
WYOMING
1-800-829-1040

Phone help for people with impaired hearing who have TDD Equipment: All areas in United States, including Alaska, Hawaii, Virgin Islands and Puerto Rico, 1-800-829-4059.

CHAPTER 17

How to Keep Records for Maximum Tax Deductions

Nowhere in your financial life can you measure the effect of good recordkeeping on dollars saved more than in records that produce tax deductions. Making an expense deductible is the same as an automatic 30 percent discount on the purchase. Every $100 of expenditures made tax deductible will return to you about $30 cash, or 30 percent. The tax savings can be as high as 49.6 percent when you combine the 39.6 percent maximum federal income tax bracket with the up to 10 percent state and local income tax.

The purpose of good tax records is to:

- trigger the memory of deductible expenses
- document the amount, date and purpose of the expenses
- substantiate the validity of deducting the expense in a tax audit.

There are a few simple recordkeeping strategies in the following pages that will ensure that you get the maximum tax deductions you deserve and put you in a position to prove your point in any dispute. I have compiled these recordkeeping strategies from my own experience, from IRS publications and from the IRS auditor's manual, which gives instructions to IRS auditors for which taxpayer records can be used to substantiate deductions. Keeping the right records always keeps you prepared. Remember, when you carry an umbrella, it seldom rains.

The way the tax code is written, it is your responsibility to be able to substantiate the amount and purpose of each of your tax deductions. You don't send in receipts with your tax return, but you will want them easily accessible and organized if you are ever audited. If your recordkeeping is poor you won't be in trouble with the IRS, but you may lose some of the deductions you really deserve. That's just like burning your money.

Whether you take deductions as an individual or on a joint return, run a part-time business from your home, operate a full-time business or are a professional or a salesperson, the same recordkeeping strategies apply.

DEFENSE #149

Keep all tax records at least seven years.

Although the statute of limitations for an IRS audit is three years, you may be required to produce older supporting records that apply to these years' tax returns, such as contracts or written agreements. Therefore, a good rule of thumb is to keep all tax records at least seven years.

Records that fall under the seven-year rule are:

- Contracts
- Agreements
- Receipts
- Canceled checks
- Tax returns
- Correspondence with the IRS

When you create your most recent tax file, throw away the file and all its contents that are now eight years old, unless you have a sentimental attachment to them. You may wish to keep your tax returns indefinitely so you can build a history of your financial progress over your lifetime. Records that apply to the purchase and sale of real estate assets and long-term investments should be kept indefinitely. Keep all your current tax records in a folder in the top drawer of your filing cabinet. Tax records for past years can be kept in the bottom drawer until it's time to throw them away.

DEFENSE #150

Keep a written record of all deductible expenses under $25. Keep receipts for all expenses over $25.

To keep track of all your expenses, buy a preprinted expense log. You can get one for a couple of dollars at any stationery or office supply store. (An example will follow.)

Your expense log makes it easy to record any deductible expenses you incur during the course of your business day, like lunches or cab fares, as well as those that you incur while you are away from home. These expenses can include:

- Gas, car repairs, tolls, parking
- Deductible meals and entertainment
- Office supplies
- Motel rooms and other travel expenses

Your log should fit easily into your pocket, briefcase or purse and allow you to keep running totals for all expenses. *Enter the expense in your book at the point of purchase.* Waiting until later, as you are often tempted to do, may mean you will miss hundreds of dollars in deductions by year's end. Think of your recordkeeping process as one that creates free money and saves you an average of 30 percent on every deductible purchase. You can't deduct what you don't document. Make it a game and not a chore.

There are also hand-held computers available no larger than an expense book in which you can keep your deductible expenses, like Sharp's Wizard or Casio's Digital Diary. Cost? About $100, which is tax deductible as a tax preparation expense.

Following is an example of a page from a typical expense book:

WEEK BEGINNING ____________

EXPENSE AND TAX RECORD

ITEMS		SUNDAY		MONDAY		TUESDAY	
BREAKFAST							
LUNCH							
DINNER							
HOTEL							
TIPS & MISC.							
LAUNDRY & VALET							
TEL. & POSTAGE							
AIR, TRAIN, BUS							
LOCAL TRANS.							
CAR RENTAL							
PARKING, TOLLS							
GAS, OIL, WASH, SVC.							
ENTERTAINMENT							
TOTALS							
MILEAGE	BUSINESS						
	PERSONAL						
CITY							
NAME OF HOTEL							

DATE	BUSINESS PURPOSE, CONTACT(S)

The IRS does not require a receipt for any tax deductible expense under $25, except for lodging. (Where can you get a hotel room for under $25?) All you need do is keep a record of the amount and purpose of small expenses in your expense log. Examples of deductible expenses under $25 could be taxi fares, tips, lunches, calculator tape, books, pens and blank audio or video tapes.

Also enter deductible expenses over $25 in your expense log, whether you pay by cash, check or credit card. And make sure you get—and keep—the receipts. Tuck them in your briefcase, pocket or purse; then when you return to your home or office, file them in your expense folder. With your expense log and filed receipts, it will be a snap to compile your monthly expense account for your employer or small business—and your yearly tax forms for Uncle Sam.

The IRS decided many years ago that your canceled checks alone are not necessarily proof of a tax deductible expenditure. Checks don't show why the expense should be deductible. So be certain you also keep the receipt or invoice that contains the address of the company and lists the deductible items or services purchased. You do not have to send in the receipts or checks when you file your return, but you may need those records someday to substantiate the deductibility of an expense. To cross-index your checks and corresponding receipts, write the check number on the receipt or invoice at the point of purchase. File the receipt in the appropriate folder as soon as you get home, and mark both checks and receipts for tax deductible expenses with a big "T" for easy retrieval at tax time.

DEFENSE #151

Use a credit or debit card for effective recordkeeping of deductible expenses.

Cash purchases are the most difficult deductible expenditures to document and remember. A credit or debit card receipt produces an immediate, acceptable tax record, because your statement shows the date, amount and name of company paid. All you need do is add in a few short words describing the deductible purpose of what you purchased.

A credit card creates a charge that is billed to you on a monthly statement. A debit card works like a check. Purchases are deducted from your checking account instead of billed to you at the end of the month. The advantage of a debit card is that it cannot get you in credit trouble and there is no interest on unpaid balances.

Write on each credit or debit card receipt at the point of purchase the deductible purpose: e.g., "lunch with Bob to discuss his products," or "office supplies," or "gasoline." Go through each credit or debit card folder at tax time and total your deductible expenses for each category of deduction. Deductible categories can include:

- Automobile expenses
- Entertainment expenses
- Travel expenses
- Food expenses
- Office supplies
- Advertising
- Product costs
- Salaries paid
- Services purchased
- Investment and tax advice

Each category goes in a separate space on your tax return. When you receive your statement each month, mark all tax deductible items with a "T" and personal expenses with a "P." For easier recordkeeping, get a separate credit or debit card to use just for tax deductible expenses. You will then have your deduction records all on one statement. Credit card or debit card fees are deductible as a business expense.

DEFENSE #152

To get the maximum tax deduction for your VCR, home computer or other assets, keep a 90-day "time use record."

Recordkeeping for tax deductions used to be very complicated and time consuming. Congress passed what it called the Adequate Contemporaneous Recordkeeping Rules, which required extensive documentation of every expense and every tax deductible business mile. But evidently members of Congress found the rules too difficult to follow themselves, so recordkeeping requirements have been greatly simplified, particularly in the cases of assets like cars, VCRs or home computers used part of the time for deductible business or financial planning purposes and the rest of the time for nondeductible personal purposes.

Amex Ref No.	Item No.		Listing of Charges and Credits	
835079–0				
835104–0				
563078–1				
195085–1	001	T	BILLBOARD PUBL INC NEW YORK NY (Tax Guides) INV # 653652	266.00
108086–1	002	P	TAYLOR RENTAL BOCA RATON FL INV # 049053	139.92
002101–1	003	T	SKYMASTER AIR TAXI GILFORD NH INV # 836936	1,290.80
028076–1	004	P	STEIN ERIKSEN RESTAURANT PARK CITY UT (Ski Trip) INV # 646343	39.21 •
111080–1	005	P	FREDDIE'S STK/SEAFOOD HSE FERN PARK FL (Birthday Party) INV # 474837	238.68 •
187081–1	006	P	SFUZZI / NEW YORK ACH NEW YORK NY INV # 684779	85.61 •
930081–1	007	T	FOUNTAINS SUITE HOTEL PHOENIX AZ INV # 089251	4.00
191083–1	008	T	BILLBOARD PUBL INC NEW YORK NY INV # 113618	55.00
147090–1	009	T	GRAND HYATT WASHINGTON WASHINGTON DC INV # 690293	18.11
147090–1	010	T	GRAND HYATT WASHINGTON WASHINGTON DC INV # 825997	651.24 •
003096–1	011	T	SHERATON LNCLN INN / WRCSTR WORCESTER MA INV # 798091	98.73
003096–1	012	T	SHERATON LNCLN INN / WRCSTR WORCESTER MA INV # 798086	700.00
950101–1	013	T	BANGOR HILTON INN BANGOR ME INV # 463549	15.75
			Page Total	3,603.05

Your assets used in a small business or for tax or investment recordkeeping *do* become tax deductible. But if you use a VCR or home computer for both tax deductible and nondeductible purposes, you must first determine the percentage of deductible use in order to earn the tax deduction. The simplest method of apportioning the deductible and non-deductible use is to keep a form similar to the one on page 390. For a period of 90 days enter the beginning and ending times for deductible use in the left column and the same information for nondeductible use in the right column. At the end of 90 days, divide the total deductible usage time by the total time the asset was used to determine your deductible percentage. Note that if you use your asset more than 50 percent of the time for a combination of business and financial managment, such as taxes and investing, you may be able to use the powerful asset expensing deduction method. See IRS Publication 334 for a complete description of asset expensing.

Deductible uses of a VCR or home computer include:

- Investment education and recordkeeping
- Tax education, recordkeeping and tax preparation
- Real estate education or recordkeeping for real estate investments
- Any use in your small business
- Financial planning

Nondeductible uses include:

- Personal use
- Entertainment
- Use by your children

Use this form to comply with the 90-day recordkeeping requirements for VCRs, computers or other items that are used for both deductible and nondeductible purposes. Use an automobile expense record book for calculating the deductible percentage of your automobile expenses.

Asset Usage Record

Item
__VCR
__Home Computer
__Other________

From ____ ____ ____ To ____ ____ ____
Month Day Year Month Day Year

DEDUCTIBLE			NONDEDUCTIBLE		
BEGIN TIME	END TIME	TOTAL TIME	BEGIN TIME	END TIME	TOTAL TIME
1					
2					
3					
4					
5					

Total Deductible Time ______ Total Nondeductible Time ______

$$\frac{\text{Total Deductible Time}}{\text{Total Time (Deductible and Nondeductible)}} = \text{Deductible} \_\_\_\_\_\_ \%$$

DEFENSE #153

Build a tax reference library with IRS publications and forms.

Building a tax library of IRS manuals and publications is one of the easiest, yet most important steps in maximizing your tax deductions. To use tax-reducing strategies successfully you must know both the IRS recordkeeping rules and the correct tax forms on which to take your deductions.

The two most important IRS publications to keep in your tax library are Publication 17, which will give you the IRS guidelines for your personal taxes, and Publication 334, which will help you with recordkeeping and tax rules for your small business.

Call the nearest office of the IRS to get all of the publications recommended below and put them together on a shelf in your records management area or in a folder in your filing system. You'll find the tax-forms telephone number listed in your local telephone directory under United States Government Offices,

Treasury Department, Internal Revenue Service, Federal Tax Forms. Replace these publications once each year when the new ones are available, usually each December. Keep the old ones three years in case you are ever questioned about an item on which you will need to recheck the rules.

If you prefer, you can obtain these publications in person from the IRS forms room at the federal building in your area (your mileage is deductible as a tax preparation expense).

From the list below, note the personal and small business forms, instructions and publications you need for your tax library. Call the IRS tax-forms number and ask that these publications be sent to you.

Personal

____ Pub. 1 federal taxes
____ Pub. 17 general income tax
____ Pub. 503 child care credit
____ Pub. 523 Sale of Personal Residence
____ Pub. 527 rental property
____ Pub. 534 depreciation
____ Pub. 545 interest on debt
____ Pub. 550 investments
____ Pub. 556 amended returns
____ Pub. 564 mutual fund gains

Small Business

____ Pub. 334 small business taxes
____ Pub. 463 car expenses
____ Pub. 534 depreciation
____ Pub. 535 business expenses
____ Pub. 538 inventories
____ Pub. 587 use of home

CHAPTER 18

Freelancing for Pleasure and Profit

Almost everyone I've ever talked to has a secret desire to be creative. Some see themselves as writers, others as photographers, and still others have that knack of creating beautiful artwork.

From 1982 to 1989, those who were freelancing in these fields were severely penalized under the tax rules. They could not treat themselves as small businesses and take all the related expense deductions in the current tax year. The hobby loss rules were applied, and freelancers could take tax deductions for travel, research, advertising and other expenses only up to their level of income from that activity. Any extra deductions had to be postponed to a year, if there was one, in which income exceeded expenses. If you had always dreamed of taking some beautiful pictures of your Grand Canyon trip and submitting them to *National Geographic* or writing that book on the best restaurants of southern California, you couldn't take any deductions unless you either got an advance from a publisher or made money by publishing and selling the work yourself.

Today freelancers can consider themselves legitimate small businesses, whether or not their activities generate immediate income. A freelancer is an individual or family who creates some type of work of art—whether written, photographed, drawn or sculpted—and attempts to sell it. As a freelancing business, you may deduct all the ordinary and necessary business expenses in the year incurred.

ATTACK #154

Become a tax-deductible freelance author, photographer or artist.

If you have dreamed of being more creative but have never taken the time to start, the benefits from tax rules and the tax deductions you can claim from freelancing will certainly give you encouragement. Artistic work that falls under the IRS's definition of freelancing includes:

- Photographs
- Paintings
- Sculpture
- Graphic designs
- Oils
- Lyrics
- Dance scores
- Literary manuscripts
- Original prints
- Cartoons
- Etchings
- Drawings
- Water colors
- Musical compositions
- Magazine articles
- Short stories

The work must be original and unique, and the IRS says that the item must have aesthetic value over utilitarian value. (How would it know?) If your goal, for instance, is to write a novel like James Michener's *Hawaii*, how could you do the research without spending considerable time in Hawaii? If you finish the manuscript and submit it for publication, the new rules say you may deduct the cost of your travel whether or not you have made any money. If your goal is to do a series of sketches or paintings of the French coastline at Le Havre, obviously you have to travel to the site. According to the tax code, that would be an ordinary and necessary business expense of producing the works.

There are some exclusions. You may not use these rules to freelance in the manufacture of furniture, jewelry, silverware or other items not deemed as art by the IRS. However, if you are manufacturing or selling these items, using the freelancing rules to produce deductions isn't necessary, since your activities would fall under the regular business tax deduction rules. Video tapes, motion picture films or photographic or printing plates do not qualify under these rules either, since these items were at one time used in the creation of phony tax shelters. However, the cost of producing them may be deducted. If you produce a video or a tape travelogue, for instance, instead of using the freelancing rules you could take the deductions under what have come to be called the IRS three-year safe harbor rules. To simplify their meaning, safe harbor rules allow you to deduct 50 percent of all production costs and promotional expenses in the year you spend the money and 25 percent in each of the next two years.

Freelancing can, of course, be deducted even if you have a full-time job or another business. You no longer need to starve to be artistic. Creating a business around freelancing may be just the thing for you. It will earn you tremendous amounts of tax deductions and, who knows, maybe even fame and fortune.

To treat yourself as a small freelancing business for tax purposes, complete a Schedule C each year and attach it to your personal tax return. Use Publication 334 as your guide.

CHAPTER 19

Build a Better IRA

Over the past few years there has been so much talk about IRAs (individual retirement accounts) that most people, even those who qualify, have become numb to the term. The truth is that a one-person $2,000 IRA, or a $4,000 IRA for two working people, provides one of the best opportunities you'll find to create hundreds of thousands of dollars of investment wealth for less than the cost of a monthly car payment. Tax-free compounding has always been the secret to maximum wealth building in the minimum time. When you combine the compounded tax-free earnings of an IRA with a tax deduction for every dollar invested, you have created a money machine. Taxes are paid only at withdrawal time and after the compounding.

Under our tax system, the only two opportunities for a dollar-for-dollar tax deduction for money you invest, plus the tax-deferred compounding of the investment earnings, are IRA accounts and your retirement plan at work. In *More Wealth Without Risk*, in Chapter 18, I gave you all the insider strategies for contributing to and choosing investments for your IRA and/or your 401(k) or other work-related retirement plan. Here, I want to concentrate on the least known of the IRA wealth-building strategies, including how you can get your money out of an IRA at any age with no penalties and while paying the least amount in taxes, by mathematically rigging the withdrawal system in your favor.

No matter how old you are now, eventually you will be withdrawing money from your IRA. Tax law requires you to begin withdrawing the year after you turn 70½ and applies a 10 percent penalty if you withdraw a lump sum before age 59½. The average IRA account in America today is $20,000, but there are thousands who have managed to create IRAs now worth $50,000 to $150,000. The sad fact is that billions are being lost each year by those who qualify for but don't invest in an IRA at all. Before the Tax Reform Act of 1986, 29 million people qualified to contribute money to IRAs. After tax reform, about 23 million people are still eligible for IRA contributions but less than 5 million Americans are actually taking advantage of this incredible wealth-building opportunity.

One reason is most people who do qualify falsely believe they don't. Another reason is the inability to scrape together the $2,000 or $4,000 when needed. The last excuse for not contributing is that most Americans have trouble planning beyond next month and are concerned about having money "stuck" in an IRA until age 59½, particularly if they are currently in their early 20s to early 40s.

In this chapter I will show you how to:

- Contribute to an IRA even if you thought you could not.
- Make your full deductible contribution to an IRA when you dream rich but are cash poor.
- Make withdrawals from your IRA anytime before age 59½ totally penalty-free.

Then there will be no more excuses for underusing an IRA.

The first step in harnessing the power of an IRA is to determine what kind of income or compensation qualifies for an IRA and what does not. Look at the Compensation Computation Chart for IRA Accounts that follows. Referring to this chart will clear up any questions you may have about what part of your income qualifies to be used in funding an IRA.

Your adjusted gross income is one factor that determines the maximum tax deductible contribution you can make to an IRA. Adjusted gross income is determined by subtracting six potential adjustments from your total income shown on line 23 of your 1040 form. (See Computing Adjusted Gross Income on page 399.) The maximum you or you and your spouse may contribute to an IRA can be limited by your adjusted gross income as shown on line 31 of your 1040 form.

COMPENSATION COMPUTATION CHART FOR IRA ACCOUNTS

Income that can or cannot be included in calculating your maximum yearly IRA contribution.

INCLUDED	NOT INCLUDED
Hourly wages	Rental property income
Salaries	Interest income
Commissions	Dividend income
Tips	Pension income
Bonuses	Annuity income
Fees	Amount contributed to a deferred compensation retirement plan, i.e., 401(k), 403(b)
Alimony received	Military retirement or federal retirement income
Separate maintenance income	Foreign income
	Income from the sale of:
	Investments
	Small business
	Personal assets

To contribute to an IRA, your adjusted gross income must be greater than the amount you want to contribute. You may contribute the full $2,000 maximum contribution no matter how large your total earned income, as long as neither you, your spouse nor your employers contribute to a retirement plan where you work. That's right, those with income of $80,000, even $200,000, per year can contribute to an IRA as long as they are not contributing to other retirement programs. Furthermore, you are not prevented from contributing to an IRA just because your company has a retirement plan. If you choose not to contribute and neither does your employer, you may take a deduction for your contributions to an IRA. So may your spouse if he or she works.

Even if you are covered by a retirement plan at work to which you or your employer contributes, you may still be eligible for deductible contributions to an IRA, as a majority of Americans are, if you meet the following conditions:

If you are married, filing jointly, and have an adjusted gross income (AGI) of less than $40,000 or are single with an AGI of less than $25,000, you can contribute the maximum to your

IRA and take a tax deduction for every dollar you invested, regardless of any company retirement plan to which you may or may not be contributing.

If your adjusted gross income is over $40,000 as a couple filing jointly or over $25,000 if you are single and you or your spouse contributes to a company retirement plan, your $2,000 per year maximum deductible contribution is reduced by $200 for every $1,000 of income above these amounts.

For example, you and your spouse file jointly and you contribute to a 401(k) plan where you work. After completing a tentative 1040 form for the year, you show an adjusted gross income on line 31 of $44,000. According to the IRA rules, you lose $200 of deductible IRA contributions for every $1,000 of income above $40,000. Therefore, your maximum deductible IRA contribution would be $1,200 each if both of you work, or $1,450 total if only one works. The contribution for two working spouses is computed as follows:

$$\frac{\$44{,}000 - \$40{,}000}{\$1{,}000} \times \$200 = \$800 \text{ contribution loss}$$

$$\$2{,}000 - \$800 = \$1{,}200 \text{ maximum IRA contribution}$$

The maximum contribution to a spousal account when one spouse works and the other does not is shown in the IRA Maximum Contribution chart on page 400. The maximum amount that can be contributed to an IRA by singles and two-wage-earner couples with other retirement plan contributions is also shown.

To compute your adjusted gross income see the chart and illustration from Form 1040 that follows. After you total your adjustments on line 30, you subtract line 30 from your total income shown on line 23. The result is entered on line 31 as your adjusted gross income, or AGI. Your AGI determines not only the maximum IRA deduction that can be taken for those who contribute to company retirement plans, but also what portion of your miscellaneous deductions on tax Schedule A are not deductible (2% of your AGI) and whether or not you qualify to take any deductions for medical expenses (7.5% of AGI is not deductible). The less your adjusted gross income, the more tax deductions and deductible IRA contributions for which you are likely to qualify.

Computing Adjusted Gross Income

FORM 1040 LINE			
23	Total income		$
24	Your IRA deduction	$	
25	Spouse's IRA deduction		
26	Self-employment health insurance deduction		
27	Keogh or SEP retirement plan deduction		
28	Penalty for early withdrawal of CDs or savings		
29	Alimony or separate income payments paid to former spouses		
30	Total adjustments to your income	–	
31	Your adjusted gross income (AGI)		$

This is how these adjustments to income look on the front of your 1040 form:

Adjustments to Income	**24a**	Your IRA deduction (see page 20)	24a	
	b	Spouse's IRA deduction (see page 20)	24b	
	25	One-half of self-employment tax (see page 21) . . .	25	
	26	Self-employed health insurance deduction (see page 22)	26	
	27	Keogh retirement plan and self-employed SEP deduction	27	
	28	Penalty on early withdrawal of savings	28	
	29	Alimony paid. Recipient's SSN ▶	29	
	30	Add lines 24a through 29. These are your **total adjustments** . . . . ▶		30
Adjusted Gross Income	**31**	Subtract line 30 from line 23. This is your **adjusted gross income.** *If this amount is less than $23,050 and a child lived with you, see page EIC-1 to find out if you can claim the "Earned Income Credit" on line 56* . . . . ▶		31

Compute your adjusted gross income for an average year, or simply refer to line 31 on the 1040 forms you filed with the IRA the last two or three years. Do you qualify to make a tax deductible contribution to an IRA account? If so, what is the amount? That is exactly the amount that you will be able to deduct from your taxes. And that's exactly the amount you can put to work for you compounding tax-free until you withdraw it. Unfortunately, you cannot make IRA contributions for prior years even if you qualified.

IRA MAXIMUM CONTRIBUTION FOR THOSE
WHO CONTRIBUTE TO ANOTHER RETIREMENT PLAN*

SINGLE		MARRIED AND YOU AND/OR YOUR EMPLOYER CONTRIBUTE TO RETIREMENT PLAN		
Adjusted Gross Income (AGI) Less Than	*Maximum Deductible IRA Contribution*	*AGI Less Than*	*One Income: Maximum Deductible IRA Contribution*	*Two Incomes: Maximum Deductible IRA Contribution*
$25,000	$2,000	$40,000	$2,250	$4,000
$26,000	$1,800	$41,000	$2,030	$3,600
$27,000	$1,600	$42,000	$1,850	$3,200
$28,000	$1,400	$43,000	$1,650	$2,800
$29,000	$1,200	$44,000	$1,450	$2,400
$30,000	$1,000	$45,000	$1,250	$2,000
$31,000	$ 800	$46,000	$1,050	$1,600
$32,000	$ 600	$47,000	$ 850	$1,200
$33,000	$ 400	$48,000	$ 650	$ 800
$34,000	$ 200	$49,000	$ 450	$ 400
$35,000	$ 200	$50,000	$ 250	$ 400
$36,000	$ 0	$51,000	$ 0	$ 0

*These figures apply whether you or your employer contributes to your retirement plan.

Your strategy in the future is to deposit every dime into an IRA for which you can take a tax deduction before you invest any money anywhere else. The chart opposite, The Magic of Tax-Deferred Growth, should help motivate you. The chart shows, in increments of five years, examples of how money deposited into an IRA every year will compound to age 65 if invested at 12 percent, 15 percent or 20 percent. Locate your current approximate age in column A. Column B shows how much you will have to invest per month in an IRA to end up with the amount shown in column D. Column E then shows how much you could withdraw every month for the rest of your life from your account by averaging only 12 percent per year. For instance, if you are 35 years old now and deposit only $100 per month into your IRA which earns an average of 15 percent per year, you will accumulate $599,948 by the time you reach age 65. You will then be able to withdraw $6,000 per month or $72,000 per year for the rest of your life without touching the principal. That's the best retirement gift anyone can give himself. Once you reach age 50, you will have to go beyond the maximum $4,000 per couple IRA limit to create a significant account by age 65, but you can accomplish your objectives by using a company retirement plan or self-directed annuity, both of which are completely explained in *More Wealth Without Risk*.

THE MAGIC OF TAX-DEFERRED GROWTH

A YOUR AGE	B INVESTMENT AMOUNT	C COMPOUND INTEREST RATE	D ACCOUNT VALUE AT AGE 65	E MONTHLY INCOME INTEREST ONLY AT 12%
25	$40 Mo.	12%	$ 412,388	$4,123
	or	15%	982,057	9,820
	480 Yr.	20%	4,230,061	42,300
30	50 Mo.	12%	290,677	2,906
	or	15%	608,007	6,080
	600 Yr.	20%	2,122,805	21,228
35	100 Mo.	12%	324,351	3,243
	or	15%	599,948	6,000
	1,200 Yr.	20%	1,701,909	17,019
40	200 Mo.	12%	358,400	3,548
	or	15%	587,308	5,873
	2,400 Yr.	20%	1,359,304	13,593
45	300 Mo.	12%	290,514	2,905
	or	15%	424,116	4,241
	3,600 Yr.	20%	806,493	8,064
50	400 Mo.	12%	200,412	2,004
	or	15%	262,640	2,626
	4,800 Yr.	20%	414,920	4,149
55	700 Mo.	12%	165,102	1,651
	or	15%	196,126	1,961
	8,400 Yr.	20%	261,660	2,616
60	1,500 Mo.	12%	128,070	1,280
	or	15%	139,560	1,395
	18,000 Yr.	20%	160,740	1,607

ATTACK #155

Combine all of your individual IRAs into one account for better management, easier recordkeeping and lower fees.

One easy mistake to make with IRA money is to put each year's IRA contribution into a different investment. I have met many well-meaning investors who have six to ten different IRAs. The IRA rules do allow you to choose a different investment for your new contributions each year, but in this case more is not better.

Your objective is to combine all of your IRA money into one or two accounts. The recordkeeping and paperwork get out of control with too many different investments, adding extra work with little chance for extra rewards. Diversifying your IRA investment is certainly a good idea, but adequate diversification can be accomplished by investing in one mutual fund or mutual fund family.

To combine your IRA accounts, use the tax-free IRA rollover rules below. In addition to combining your IRA accounts, there are a number of other reasons, like the following, to move your IRA money to a different investment:

- The yearly trustee's fee is over $30.
- Your investment return is less than 12 percent.
- You want to move your money to an account with which you can get some good financial advice.
- You want to control your IRA money yourself in an investment like a mutual fund family.

DEFENSE #156

Use the tax-free IRA rollover rules to control or combine your IRA money.

You may move your IRA money from one financial institution to another once every 365 days with no taxes or government penalty. You may change investments with your IRA money in the same institution as often as you wish. A rollover occurs when you physically withdraw your IRA money from one institution and deposit it in another IRA at a different institution. A transfer occurs when your money is moved between institutions by the respective trustees. Transfers are safer since you cannot make a timing mistake, but as you may find, are sometimes difficult to accomplish. To roll over your money from one financial institution to another is to ask the financial institution, bank, brokerage firm or credit union for a check for the entire balance in your account. You then have 60 days to the day to redeposit the check in a new IRA. There are no taxes or government penalties.

If your IRA is at a bank or credit union, it is probably invested in an IRA certificate, and the institution may impose its own withdrawal penalty, usually amounting to six months' interest. If your account is earning only 8 percent, the six months' interest penalty is just 4 percent, which is fully tax deductible as an adjustment to income, line 28 on Form 1040. The early withdrawal penalty will normally be shown on the 1099 form the bank or credit union uses to report the interest earned in your account to you and to the IRS. After your tax savings, the real interest penalty is only about 2.8 percent.

To determine if it is mathematically wise to move your money now instead of waiting for your IRA certificate to mature, ask yourself, "How many months in the new investment will it take me to earn 2.8 percent more than I was earning in the old investment?" If the answer is less time than the number of months until your IRA certificate matures, pay the penalty and roll over or transfer your money to the new investment now. If the time it takes to earn the extra interest is longer than the number of months to maturity, wait until your current IRA certificate reaches the maturity date and move your money with no penalty. The same thinking process should be used if you want to move your IRA money out of an insurance company or mutual fund that has a back-end load—a commission charged when you withdraw your money.

Make certain you let your bank, credit union or other institution know of your intent to move your money when your certificate matures. When you opened your account you probably signed an agreement that allows the bank or credit union to renew your IRA certificate automatically without your knowledge or approval, a gimmick that you are told is for your convenience but in truth helps the institution keep its hands on your money.

ATTACK #157

Fund your IRA with OPM (Other People's Money).

Interest paid on money you borrow to invest is tax deductible each year up to the amount that you earn from your investments. Most people, even CPAs, believe that interest paid on a loan to fund your IRA account is not deductible because of the tax shelter interest rule. You cannot take a tax deduction for money you borrow to buy tax-exempt investments like municipal bonds, since the interest on the bonds is already tax-exempt.

However, that rule does not apply to money borrowed for an IRA account, because the interest on the earnings is not tax-exempt, only tax-deferred. You may therefore take a full deduction for the interest on the money you borrow to fund your IRA account. Now you have four incredible tax deductions created by your IRA:

1. You may deduct the interest you pay on a loan to fund the IRA.
2. You may take a tax deduction for the money you contribute to the IRA, even if that money is borrowed.
3. You may deduct or exclude the amount you earn in the IRA from your current taxable income.
4. You may deduct the trustee's fees if billed separately.

What a deal! Let's look at how these deductions might apply to you. Tax deductions shown in the following table are figured at 35 percent, which includes 28 percent federal and 7 percent state tax. Notice that $2,000 IRA money was borrowed for your IRA account at 12 percent interest and the $2,000 IRA money was invested in a mutual fund that also earned 12 percent for the year. The trustee fee is $20. There are four tax deductions you get when you borrow money for an IRA: loan interest paid, contribution, investment earnings and trustee fees. In the example, these deductions total $2,500. The deductions will save you $875 in taxes. If we count the $875 saved in taxes as part of the earnings, along with the actual account earnings of $240, your total return for the year is $1,115. The expenses are $240 for interest paid on the loan plus the $20 trustee fees, leaving net earnings from your IRA of $855, or 43 percent!

Creating Tax Deductions with Borrowed IRA Money

To determine your return on investment, divide $855 by $2,000, which, as you can see, is 43 percent, all created with borrowed money. There is nowhere else you will ever get that kind of no-risk return.

DEDUCTIONS FOR A
BORROWED $2,000 CONTRIBUTION

Loan interest paid 12%	$ 240
Contribution $2,000	$2,000
Investment earnings 12%	$ 240
Trustee fees	$ 20
Total tax deductions	$2,500

Total taxes saved from deductions: 35% × $2,500 = **$875**

NET INVESTMENT INCOME

Investment earnings 12%		$ 240
Tax savings		$ 875
Yearly income		$1,115
Interest paid	−$240	
Trustee fee	−$ 20	
Total expenses		−$ 260
Net earnings from IRA		$ 855
Return on investment		$855 / $2,000 = 43%

Here are some sources for borrowing money to fund your IRA:

- Credit union
- Margin loan on stocks, bonds or mutual fund shares
- Parents/other relatives
- Financially successful children
- Equity loan on your home
- Personal bank loan
- Borrowing against a long-term CD
- MasterCard or Visa loan
- Borrowing against a cash value life insurance policy

Since your IRA contribution can be made each year, make sure you pay back the principal of your IRA loan in one year, especially when using a home equity loan or credit card to fund your IRA. The payments on these loans, if you make only the minimum payments, could stretch out for years. To pay back a $2,000 loan in 12 months, you must pay only $167 a month, plus about $10 to $15 per month interest.

How to Withdraw from an IRA Penalty-Free

ATTACK #158

Use the life expectancy withdrawal method to make penalty-free IRA withdrawals.

Although it is easy to get the money out of your 401(k) or 403(b) without taxes or penalties by borrowing (see *More Wealth Without Risk*, Chapter 18), you cannot borrow from your IRA account. There are strategies, however, that will allow you to take money out of your IRA account without penalties. Getting money out of an IRA early can be an important strategy to those who have rolled over large sums of money from pension plans or retirement accounts to an IRA when they retired early or changed jobs. There are two acceptable methods of withdrawing your money out of your IRA early:

1. Life expectancy withdrawal method.
2. Amortization withdrawal method.

Let's look at each of these methods and how you could use each to your advantage.

To use the life expectancy withdrawal method, you divide your IRA account balance by the number of years in the IRS Ordinary Life Expectancy Table (see page 408). The IRS uses the same number of life expectancy years for men and women, even though in reality women, as a group, outlive men.

To use the table, find your current age and read over to your average life expectancy in years. For instance, if you are currently age 50, the Life Expectancy Table says you have an average of 33.1 years to live. If you have a balance in your IRA account of $100,000, you divide $100,000 by 33.1 to determine your first-year withdrawal of $3,021. The following year your age is 51 and your life expectancy 32.2 years, so you divide the remaining account balance by 32.2 to determine your second-year withdrawal. Withdrawals calculated in this way are penalty-free.

If you are earning 10 percent in your IRA account even though you are making withdrawals beginning at about 3 percent per year, your account is still growing dramatically. Based on a $100,000 initial balance, you are taking out about $250 a month or about $3,000 each year penalty-free and still watching your account balance increase (see the example below). Of course, you will pay taxes on the withdrawal because it is considered income. Create your tax plan to produce enough deductions to offset your withdrawal income. You can use the withdrawal method at any age.

IRA GROWTH WITH LIFE EXPECTANCY METHOD WITHDRAWAL (AGE 50)

$100,000	Account balance
−3,021	Penalty-free withdrawal 1st year (33.1 years)
$96,979	Balance after withdrawal
+9,698	10% investment return
$106,677	New balance
−3,313	Penalty-free withdrawal 2nd year (32.2 years)
$103,364	Balance after withdrawal
+10,336	10% investment return
$113,700	New balance
−3,633	Penalty-free withdrawal 3rd year (31.3 years)
$110,067	Balance after withdrawal

ORDINARY LIFE EXPECTANCY TABLE

AGE	LIFE EXPECTANCY	AGE	LIFE EXPECTANCY
40	42.5	78	10.6
41	41.5	79	10.0
42	40.6	80	9.5
43	39.6	81	8.9
44	38.7	82	8.4
45	37.7	83	7.9
46	36.8	84	7.4
47	35.9	85	6.9
48	34.9	86	6.5
49	34.0	87	6.1
50	33.1	88	5.7
51	32.2	89	5.3
52	31.3	90	5.0
53	30.4	91	4.7
54	29.5	92	4.4
55	28.6	93	4.1
56	27.7	94	3.9
57	26.8	95	3.7
58	25.9	96	3.4
59	25.0	97	3.2
60	24.2	98	3.0
61	23.3	99	2.8
62	22.5	100	2.7
63	21.6	101	2.5
64	20.8	102	2.3
65	20.0	103	2.1
66	19.2	104	1.9
67	18.4	105	1.8
68	17.6	106	1.6
69	16.8	107	1.4
70	16.0	108	1.3
71	15.3	109	1.1
72	14.6	110	1.0
73	13.9	111	.9
74	13.2	112	.8
75	12.5	113	.7
76	11.9	114	.6
77	11.2	115	.5

DEFENSE #159

Slow down required withdrawals from your IRA by using the IRS joint life expectancy tables.

There may be a time before age 59½ when you want to start receiving income from your IRA but want to slow down the withdrawal process to the point where your IRA account won't be depleted as quickly. If so, you can withdraw less money each year with no early withdrawal penalty by using the IRS Ordinary Joint Life Expectancy Table that follows.

To qualify to use this table, you must have a spouse or other named beneficiary on your IRA account. It is assumed in the Joint Life Expectancy Table that one person in a couple will outlive the other, so less can be withdrawn each year than when other withdrawal methods are used.

The joint life expectancy for a 50-year-old couple is 39.2 years, as shown in the joint table, as opposed to 33.1 years for an individual the same age. By dividing the account balance of $100,000 by 39.2 using our earlier example, the first year penalty-free withdrawal would be only $2,551, almost $500 or 15 percent less than when using the life expectancy method in Attack 158.

To use the tables, find the age of one spouse in the left-hand column and the age of the other spouse in the top row. The number at the intersection of their ages is the joint life expectancy in years.

ORDINARY JOINT LIFE EXPECTANCY TABLE

AGES	35	36	37	38	39	40	41	42	43	44
40	51.8	51.2	50.6	50.0	49.5	49.0	48.5	48.1	47.6	47.2
41	51.4	50.8	50.2	49.6	49.1	48.5	48.0	47.5	47.1	46.7
42	51.1	50.4	49.8	49.2	48.6	48.1	47.5	47.0	46.6	46.1
43	50.8	50.1	49.5	48.8	48.2	47.6	47.1	46.6	46.0	45.6
44	50.5	49.8	49.1	48.5	47.8	47.2	46.7	46.1	45.6	45.1
45	50.2	49.5	48.8	48.1	47.5	46.9	46.3	45.7	45.1	44.6
46	50.0	49.2	48.5	47.8	47.2	46.5	45.9	45.3	44.7	44.1
47	49.7	49.0	48.3	47.5	46.8	46.2	45.5	44.9	44.3	43.7
48	49.5	48.8	48.0	47.3	46.6	45.9	45.2	44.5	43.9	43.3
49	49.3	48.5	47.8	47.0	46.3	45.6	44.9	44.2	43.6	42.9
50	49.2	48.4	47.6	46.8	46.0	45.3	44.6	43.9	43.2	42.6
51	49.0	48.2	47.4	46.6	45.8	45.1	44.3	43.6	42.9	42.2
52	48.8	48.0	47.2	46.4	45.6	44.8	44.1	43.3	42.6	41.9
53	48.7	47.9	47.0	46.2	45.4	44.6	43.9	43.1	42.4	41.7
54	48.6	47.7	46.9	46.0	45.2	44.4	43.6	42.9	42.1	41.4
55	48.5	47.6	46.7	45.9	45.1	44.2	43.4	42.7	41.9	41.2
56	48.3	47.5	46.6	45.8	44.9	44.1	43.3	42.5	41.7	40.9
57	48.3	47.4	46.5	45.6	44.8	43.9	43.1	42.3	41.5	40.7
58	48.2	47.3	46.4	45.5	44.7	43.8	43.0	42.1	41.3	40.5
59	48.1	47.2	46.3	45.4	44.5	43.7	42.8	42.0	41.2	40.4
60	48.0	47.1	46.2	45.3	44.4	43.6	42.7	41.9	41.0	40.2
61	47.9	47.0	46.1	45.2	44.3	43.5	42.6	41.7	40.9	40.0
62	47.9	47.0	46.0	45.1	44.2	43.4	42.5	41.6	40.8	39.9
63	47.8	46.9	46.0	45.1	44.2	43.3	42.4	41.5	40.6	39.8
64	47.8	46.8	45.9	45.0	44.1	43.2	42.3	41.4	40.5	39.7
65	47.7	46.8	45.9	44.9	44.0	43.1	42.2	41.3	40.4	39.6
66	47.7	46.7	45.8	44.9	44.0	43.1	42.2	41.3	40.4	39.5
67	47.6	46.7	45.8	44.8	43.9	43.0	42.1	41.2	40.3	39.4
68	47.6	46.7	45.7	44.8	43.9	42.9	42.0	41.1	40.2	39.3
69	47.6	46.6	45.7	44.8	43.8	42.9	42.0	41.1	40.2	39.3
70	47.5	46.6	45.7	44.7	43.8	42.9	41.9	41.0	40.1	39.2
71	47.5	46.6	45.6	44.7	43.8	42.8	41.9	41.0	40.1	39.1
72	47.5	46.6	45.6	44.7	43.7	42.8	41.9	40.9	40.0	39.1
73	47.5	46.5	45.6	44.6	43.7	42.8	41.8	40.9	40.0	39.0
74	47.5	46.5	45.6	44.6	43.7	42.7	41.8	40.9	39.9	39.0
75	47.4	46.5	45.5	44.6	43.6	42.7	41.8	40.8	39.9	39.0

AGES	45	46	47	48	49	50	51	52	53	54
45	44.1	43.6	43.2	42.7	42.3	42.0	41.6	41.3	41.0	40.7
46	43.6	43.1	42.6	42.2	41.8	41.4	41.0	40.6	40.3	40.0
47	43.2	42.6	42.1	41.7	41.2	40.8	40.4	40.0	39.7	39.3
48	42.7	42.2	41.7	41.2	40.7	40.2	39.8	39.4	39.0	38.7
49	42.3	41.8	41.2	40.7	40.2	39.7	39.3	38.8	38.4	38.1
50	42.0	41.4	40.8	40.2	39.7	39.2	38.7	38.3	37.9	37.5
51	41.6	41.0	40.4	39.8	39.3	38.7	38.2	37.8	37.3	36.9
52	41.3	40.6	40.0	39.4	38.8	38.3	37.8	37.3	36.8	36.4
53	41.0	40.3	39.7	39.0	38.4	37.9	37.3	36.8	36.3	35.8
54	40.7	40.0	39.3	38.7	38.1	37.5	36.9	36.4	35.8	35.3
55	40.4	39.7	39.0	38.4	37.7	37.1	36.5	35.9	35.4	34.9
56	40.2	39.5	38.7	38.1	37.4	36.8	36.1	35.6	35.0	34.4
57	40.0	39.2	38.5	37.8	37.1	36.4	35.8	35.2	34.6	34.0
58	39.7	39.0	38.2	37.5	36.8	36.1	35.5	34.8	34.2	33.6
59	39.6	38.8	38.0	37.3	36.6	35.9	35.2	34.5	33.9	33.3
60	39.4	38.6	37.8	37.1	36.3	35.6	34.9	34.2	33.6	32.9
61	39.2	38.4	37.6	36.9	36.1	35.4	34.6	33.9	33.3	32.6
62	39.1	38.3	37.5	36.7	35.9	35.1	34.4	33.7	33.0	32.3
63	38.9	38.1	37.3	36.5	35.7	34.9	34.2	33.5	32.7	32.0
64	38.8	38.0	37.2	36.3	35.5	34.8	34.0	33.2	32.5	31.8
65	38.7	37.9	37.0	36.2	35.4	34.6	33.8	33.0	32.3	31.6
66	38.6	37.8	36.9	36.1	35.2	34.4	33.6	32.9	32.1	31.4
67	38.5	37.7	36.8	36.0	35.1	34.3	33.5	32.7	31.9	31.2
68	38.4	37.6	36.7	35.8	35.0	34.2	33.4	32.5	31.8	31.0
69	38.4	37.5	36.6	35.7	34.9	34.1	33.2	32.4	31.6	30.8
70	38.3	37.4	36.5	35.7	34.8	34.0	33.1	32.3	31.5	30.7
71	38.2	37.3	36.5	35.6	34.7	33.9	33.0	32.2	31.4	30.5
72	38.2	37.3	36.4	35.5	34.6	33.8	32.9	32.1	31.2	30.4
73	38.1	37.2	36.3	35.4	34.6	33.7	32.8	32.0	31.1	30.3
74	38.1	37.2	36.3	35.4	34.5	33.6	32.8	31.9	31.1	30.2
75	38.1	37.1	36.2	35.3	34.5	33.6	32.7	31.8	31.0	30.1

ORDINARY JOINT LIFE EXPECTANCY TABLE (continued)

AGES	55	56	57	58	59	60	61	62	63	64
55	34.4	33.9	33.5	33.1	32.7	32.3	32.0	31.7	31.4	31.1
56	33.9	33.4	33.0	32.5	32.1	31.7	31.4	31.0	30.7	30.4
57	33.5	33.0	32.5	32.0	31.6	31.2	30.8	30.4	30.1	29.8
58	33.1	32.5	32.0	31.5	31.1	30.6	30.2	29.9	29.5	29.2
59	32.7	32.1	31.6	31.1	30.6	30.1	29.7	29.3	28.9	28.6
60	32.3	31.7	31.2	30.6	30.1	29.7	29.2	28.8	28.4	28.0
61	32.0	31.4	30.8	30.2	29.7	29.2	28.7	28.3	27.8	27.4
62	31.7	31.0	30.4	29.9	29.3	28.8	28.3	27.8	27.3	26.9
63	31.4	30.7	30.1	29.5	28.9	28.4	27.8	27.3	26.9	26.4
64	31.1	30.4	29.8	29.2	28.6	28.0	27.4	26.9	26.4	25.9
65	30.9	30.2	29.5	28.9	28.2	27.6	27.1	26.5	26.0	25.5
66	30.6	29.9	29.2	28.6	27.9	27.3	26.7	26.1	25.6	25.1
67	30.4	29.7	29.0	28.3	27.6	27.0	26.4	25.8	25.2	24.7
68	30.2	29.5	28.8	28.1	27.4	26.7	26.1	25.5	24.9	24.3
69	30.1	29.3	28.6	27.8	27.1	26.5	25.8	25.2	24.6	24.0
70	29.9	29.1	28.4	27.6	26.9	26.2	25.6	24.9	24.3	23.7
71	29.7	29.0	28.2	27.5	26.7	26.0	25.3	24.7	24.0	23.4
72	29.6	28.8	28.1	27.3	26.5	25.8	25.1	24.4	23.8	23.1
73	29.5	28.7	27.9	27.1	26.4	25.6	24.9	24.2	23.5	22.9
74	29.4	28.6	27.8	27.0	26.2	25.5	24.7	24.0	23.3	22.7
75	29.3	28.5	27.7	26.9	26.1	25.3	24.6	23.8	23.1	22.4
76	29.2	28.4	27.6	26.8	26.0	25.2	24.4	23.7	23.0	22.3
77	29.1	28.3	27.5	26.7	25.9	25.1	24.3	23.6	22.8	22.1
78	29.1	28.2	27.4	26.6	25.8	25.0	24.2	23.4	22.7	21.9
79	29.0	28.2	27.3	26.5	25.7	24.9	24.1	23.3	22.6	21.8
80	29.0	28.1	27.3	26.4	25.6	24.8	24.0	23.2	22.4	21.7
81	28.9	28.1	27.2	26.4	25.5	24.7	23.9	23.1	22.3	21.6
82	28.9	28.0	27.2	26.3	25.5	24.6	23.8	23.0	22.3	21.5
83	28.8	28.0	27.1	26.3	25.4	24.6	23.8	23.0	22.2	21.4
84	28.8	27.9	27.1	26.2	25.4	24.5	23.7	22.9	22.1	21.3
85	28.8	27.9	27.0	26.2	25.3	24.5	23.7	22.8	22.0	21.3
86	28.7	27.9	27.0	26.1	25.3	24.5	23.6	22.8	22.0	21.2
87	28.7	27.8	27.0	26.1	25.3	24.4	23.6	22.8	21.9	21.1

ATTACK #160

Use the IRA amortization withdrawal method if you want the largest possible payout each year.

The IRA amortization withdrawal method works like a mortgage in reverse. In this case, you figure a reasonable rate of return that you expect your IRA to earn and then determine how much you'll have to withdraw each year in equal payments so that the account balance would be zero by the end of your life expectancy. Using the earlier example, let's say you were a 50-year-old with a life expectancy of 33.1 years. With the amortization method, you compute the money to be paid to you from your IRA each year as if you were a mortgage company that had lent out $100,000. If the interest rate is the same 10 percent we used in the life expectancy example, your yearly payout would be $10,445 a year for 33.1 years, or three times more per year what you would have received from using the life expectancy withdrawal method. This amount per year is the same thing as receiving $870 a month income for every $100,000 that you have invested in your account.

To compute the amount on a financial calculator based on your situation for the above example, n = number of payments = 33.1; I = interest rate = 10%; PV = present value = $100,000. Remember you are using a full year's interest so you would divide by 12, as you would for a monthly payment, or convert to a fraction or a decimal when using your calculator.

Using the amortization method, remember, you choose the interest rate. The higher the rate you choose, the faster you can withdraw your money. The IRS is accustomed to seeing rates of 7 to 9 percent since most people mistakenly keep their IRA money in a bank. If you choose a high return number like, for instance, 15 percent, the IRS may ask you to prove that you are getting, or can get, that high a return. If you are averaging 15 percent per year in your IRA account in a mutual fund, that would be no problem.

ATTACK #161

Borrow cash using a home equity loan and use the IRA penalty-free early withdrawal rules to make the payments.

The only disadvantage to withdrawing your IRA money over a long period of time is that if you are under 59½ years old, you cannot get your hands on the money in one lump sum without paying big taxes and early withdrawal penalties. Using an equity loan on your home in combination with monthly, penalty-free, early withdrawals from your IRA can give you the same benefits as a penalty- and tax-free lump sum withdrawal from your IRA.

Let's say you have $100,000 in taxable equity in your home and about the same amount in your IRA account. You would like to use that amount of money to start up a small business or make other investments. The payments of $1,137 per month for 15 years on a second mortgage at 11 percent interest would be more than you can handle without guaranteed income with which to make the mortgage payments. Your strategy? Borrow the cash using an equity loan on your home and then use the IRA amortization withdrawal method to get the penalty-free money out of your IRA to make most or all of the monthly mortgage payments.

Although you would pay taxes but no penalties on the IRA withdrawals, you are also taking the tax deduction for the interest you pay on the equity loan. One will help offset the other, creating the effect of a tax-free withdrawal from your IRA.

Here are some other interesting IRS rules that apply to IRAs that can be used to your advantage:

- You do not have to tell the IRS how you will use your withdrawal money. The money can be used for any purpose you wish, no limits.
- You can continue to contribute to your IRA even while you are withdrawing.

CHAPTER 20

Create a Rental Property Tax Haven

Under current tax laws, rental properties are still the most powerful and quickest way to cut your income taxes down to size through the deductions allowed for depreciation and the write-off of other rental expenses. You can use real estate to build thousands of dollars of tax deductions for your tax plan. Owning only one or two rental properties will create big tax deductions automatically. Even if you are not interested in managing large numbers of tenants or properties, the extra effort required to produce those thousands of dollars of extra tax reductions on one or two properties is well worth it.

This chapter is not about how to buy rental properties—that's another subject for a later time—but how and why rental properties can create a tremendous tax shelter. For our purposes here, let's assume that you already own rental real estate, but may be unaware of all the ways in which it can generate big tax savings. Or, perhaps you have been considering investing in rental real estate, but need more motivation. If you fall into either one of these categories, you're in for a big, and potentially profitable, surprise.

DEFENSE #162

Treat your rental properties as an investment, not a small business.

One of the questions I am most often asked is, "If I treat my rental properties as a small business, can I get all the small business deductions?" The answer is yes, but by treating rental property as a small business, you could lose the biggest of all your deductions, real estate depreciation.

Those who are actually in the business of real estate are called "dealers" by the IRS and include brokers, agents, builders, developers, contractors and those who buy or build properties to sell quickly, at a profit. Nowhere in the definition does the word "investor" appear. A real estate investor is someone who buys and holds rental properties for current tax benefits and long-term appreciation. There is a major difference in the IRS's eyes. A real estate dealer, the IRS says, technically holds the properties as inventory with the intent to quickly resell, not as long-term investments, and therefore is not allowed to take depreciation deductions. What a loss that would be to an investor! Real estate brokers and agents, although technically dealers, can hold property as investors but must keep good records establishing their intent.

A real estate investor is allowed to compensate for the theoretical wear and tear and age on a property by taking depreciation tax deductions. Real estate investors should claim income and deductible expenses on tax Schedule E, and not Schedule C. Although real estate investors can claim real estate deductions on Schedule C, the IRS will use the form you choose as one indication of whether you are a dealer or an investor. If you use Schedule C instead of E for your real estate investment income and expenses, the IRS may say that you are claiming you are a real estate business and are not entitled to the depreciation deductions. You can have both a small business and real estate investments, but different forms must be used for each. The IRS also applies the following test: If you buy and sell three properties within the same year, you must be a dealer and not an investor and cannot claim depreciation deductions on any of your real estate properties.

Here's the real surprise. As a real estate investor you get exactly the same tax deductions as if you were a small business, but you take your deductions on Schedule E instead of Schedule C. The tax code says that all expenses you incur in the production of income are deductible. The purpose of both a small business and real estate investments is to produce income. Therefore, your investment expenses are just as deductible as business expenses would be. Your strategy: Always fill out Schedule E for your real estate investment income and expenses, never Schedule C.

ATTACK #163

Use the rental real estate passive loss exception to create up to $25,000 of extra deductions.

Under tax reform, Congress revised the concept of passive loss. These rules basically prevent you from using tax deductions that exceed your income from business or investments in which you don't materially participate in order to tax-shelter nonrelated income, like job or retirement income.

For example, a couple, prior to tax reform, had a taxable income of $82,000 a year and invested $10,000 in a business or limited partnership in which they were not actually involved that gave them $20,000 of tax deductions the first year. Subtracting the $20,000 in deductions from the $82,000 income, the couple now paid taxes on only $62,000, saving them as much as $8,000 in taxes. Since the couple only invested $10,000, did no work and saved $8,000 in taxes from their deductions the first year, they made an 80 percent return on their investment just from the tax savings. Tax deductions from tax shelters can far exceed the amount invested, making the investment virtually risk-free. Incredible as it may sound, that process was used by all smart investors prior to the tax reform changes.

Unfortunately, many investors lost big money because they were so eager to get the tax deductions that they seldom did much investigation of the real worth of their investments or the people behind them. If the investments went sour, the investors were often required to recapture or reclaim as income the deductions they had taken. In addition, many supposedly ethical and savvy CPAs and attorneys began putting their stamp of approval on tax shelters that would give off a four-to-one, even a ten-to-one, first-year write-off. Four-to-one meant for every $1,000 you invested you got $4,000 worth of tax deductions. You could apply all of the deductions created through your tax-sheltered investments to your other income, including job, investment or retirement income. It was easy for a smart investor either to get into the zero tax bracket or to lower his taxes from the 50 percent bracket to the 20 percent alternative minimum tax bracket with the right tax shelters.

The tax shelter business was a multibillion-dollar industry, as you might suspect. I'll bet right now you're wishing you had gotten in on some of that good stuff. It was perfectly legal, at least until the IRS challenged and beat many of these outrageous partnerships as having no real economic value or investment potential; they were just a tax scheme. Then investors not only lost their money, they lost their tax deductions and paid penalties and interest to boot. Now I'll bet you're glad you weren't involved.

Under the new tax rule, a taxpayer's losses for rental real estate activities in which he or she materially participates will not be subject to limitations under the passive activity rules. This new rule applies if the taxpayer performs more than half of the personal services he or she performs in trades or businesses during the taxable year and a total of at least 750 hours of service in real estate trades or businesses in which he or she materially participates. A special rule was included for joint returns which provides that these eligibility requirements are met only if either spouse separately satisfies the requirements. Real estate trades or businesses are defined to include any real property, development, redevelopment, construction, reconstruction, acquisition, conversion, rental operation, management, leasing, or brokerage trade or business.

There are several other tests, any one of which will allow you to be considered an active participant, but now you have the idea. If you're an active participant, you can use extra deductions that your business or investment activity generates to offset your other income, like your salary or your spouse's salary. If your activity is considered passive, you can use extra deductions from the passive activity only to offset income from other passive business or investment activities. It's not complicated, it just sounds strange. These rules apply only to businesses or investments that generate more losses than income. If an investor has money in four limited partnerships and is not actively involved, he combines the income and expenses of all the partnerships to determine if there is a net gain or loss. If he has more deductions than income, he must carry the losses forward into future tax years, but cannot use the extra passive deductions to cut the taxes on this year's other income.

Remember, if the investments or businesses are generating more income than expenses, the rules don't even apply. Only investments set up as tax shelters are affected by the passive loss rules. These investments usually generate large amounts of paper deductions, like depreciation deductions for real estate or leased equipment or depletion deductions for oil and gas well drilling and operation.

Here are the rules for real estate investments. In the tax code, section 469, Congress decided to treat all real estate rental activities as passive activities, whether or not the investor was actively involved or to what extent. Then, in the same code section, Congress created what it called the rental real estate limited exception to the passive loss rules. It sounds like that limited warranty you got on the toaster that covers everything except what is probably going to break. But if you are or choose to be a real estate investor, the limited exception can save you up to $10,000 a year in state and federal taxes. The exception includes three rules.

1. All of your excess losses generated by real estate are passive losses, but you may take up to $25,000 of these passive losses each year and use them as tax deductions to offset other income like your job income, retirement income, dividends or interest.
2. You can use all or part of the $25,000 exemption every year. You may even use the $25,000 exemption to put yourself in the zero tax bracket but not below. There are no loss carry-forwards, meaning that you cannot use any unused portion of the $25,000 in some future year.
3. You can use the full $25,000 in deductions against other income as long as your adjusted gross income (AGI) is less than $100,000. The exemption is phased out at 50 cents per income dollar if your AGI is $100,000 to $150,000, and you can't use any of the $25,000 exemption if your AGI is over $150,000. Losses phased out due to these income limits may be carried forward and used to offset future passive income, or if the property is appreciating in value, may be used to offset any capital gains in the year the property is sold.
4. If you are involved in a "real property trade or business" you are not subject to the phase out rules for persons with

an adjusted gross income exceeding $100,000. To qualify for this exception you must, at a minimum:

a. Materially participate in the real estate activity regularly, continuously and substantially in accordance with the provisions of section 469 of the Internal Revenue Service code.
b. More than 50% of your personal services must be performed in real property trades or businesses and must total more than 750 hours per year.
c. Be involved in any or all of the following types of real estate businesses: development, redevelopment, reconstruction, acquisition, conversion, rental, operation, management, leasing and/or brokerage.

For example: If your adjusted gross income is $60,000 and you own enough rental properties to throw off the maximum $25,000 of extra deductions, you could reduce your taxable income that year to $35,000 ($60,000–$25,000), saving you about $7,000 in federal taxes alone. You might save another 7 percent, or about $2,000, in states taxes. Total potential tax savings by using rental property as part of your tax plan is $9,000 per year using the passive loss exception rules. These rules, depending on your income, can cut your tax bill by 25 percent, 50 percent or even 100 percent, putting you in the zero tax bracket.

Some consider the passive loss rules most difficult to understand. In reality, once you have just an idea of what the rules mean, you only have to remember that you can use up to $25,000 of extra deductions from your rental real estate investments to tax-shelter up to $25,000 of your other income, saving you as much as $9,000 in taxes each year and allowing you to apply the money you save to the accomplishment of your other dreams. If that doesn't motivate you, you are probably not fond of money.

ATTACK #164

Combine depreciation deductions with the real estate passive loss exception to create wealth through tax savings.

Now let's turn these tax rules into moneymaking strategies. Whether you presently own rental real estate or are considering buying it, you should structure your investments so that your income from rents equals the sum total of your mortgage payments, taxes, insurance and maintenance costs, minus maybe $400 or $500 per year for vacancies plus some unexpected repairs. Breaking even with income and expenses is called neutral cash flow. You will then be able to generate thousands in real estate depreciation deductions, deductions that don't require you to spend additional cash. Depreciation deductions are often called paper losses or formula deductions because they happen only on paper without negatively affecting your pocketbook.

The concept of depreciation, when applied to real estate, is therefore really an imaginary concept but one that will make you lots of money. When tenants abuse your aging rental properties on the inside and when sun, rain or snow damage them on the outside, the tax code says they will theoretically decrease in value. In truth, real estate has actually increased in value for the past 200 years, yet the tax code allows you to take tax deductions for your property as if it were decreasing or depreciating in value from wear and tear. Depreciation over the past few years has become known in the tax code as cost recovery. That should ease your guilt feelings about claiming tax deductions for depreciating property that is really appreciating.

To determine the amount of depreciation deductions to which you are entitled, you must know or be able to compute three factors.

Cost Recovery Period. The cost recovery period is theoretically the number of years before the property will become old, dilapidated and virtually worthless. With real estate you don't have to guess what the cost recovery period should be. The cost recovery period established under tax reform is 27.5 years for residential rental properties (like homes, condos or apartment buildings) and 39 years for commercial properties (like office buildings or shopping centers). Before tax reform, cost recovery periods were as short as 18 years. The shorter the recovery period the greater your tax deductions each year.

The Depreciation Method. For residential and commercial properties alike, the depreciation method for properties bought after tax reform is called straight line. Straight line is the simplest and most logical of all depreciation methods. To determine the amount of straight-line depreciation you can deduct in one year on a residental rental property, you simply divide the total amount which can be depreciated (your basis) by 27.5. To depreciate 100 percent of the basis of the property equally over the 27.5 years would be the same as deducting 3.636 percent of the total each year (100% ÷ 27.5 years = 3.636%). For every $100,000 worth of depreciable residential real estate you own, each year you are entitled to take $3,636 as a depreciation deduction computed on tax Form 4562 and entered on Schedule E, line 21. For commercial property the life or recovery period is 31.5 years for assets placed into service prior to May 12, 1993. For commercial properties placed into service after May 12, 1993, the recovery period is 39 years. You would take a deduction for 3.174 of the basis each year for 31.5 year property or 2.564 for 39 year property. For every $100,000 of depreciable commercial property you own, your deduction would be $3,174 per year for up to 31.5 years or $2,564 for 39 year property.

The Mid-Month Convention. What about the first year? If you bought and begin renting the property in January, the first month of the year, should you be able to take the same amount of depreciation for the first year as if you bought the property in December, the last month of the year? Congress has said that would be unreasonable so it created a concept called the mid-month convention that applies only to real estate. No matter when you buy a property during the year, the mid-month convention rules require you to treat the purchase as if you bought it at mid-month or on the 15th day of the month in which you actually purchased the property. That means your depreciation the first year will not be 3.636 percent but will be a lesser amount depending on what month you actually closed on the property. In the 28th or last year if you still own the property, you deduct the balance of any depreciation that you couldn't deduct the first year.

To make all depreciation calculations easy, refer to the Depreciation Rate Table for residential and commercial real estate on pages 424 and 428. The numbers across the top of each table, 1 through 12, represent months January through December. You choose the column representing the month you first offered the property for rent. The numbers 1 through 28 shown vertically represent the number of years since you first started depreciating the property. By finding the intersection of the month and year that apply, you will find the percentage factor to be used to determine this year's total depreciation deduction. Only the 1st and 28th year have any significant differences from the normal depreciation rate. Since you probably won't keep the property for 28 years, it is the first year's depreciation amount that will be different. Use these tables to compute your depreciation on

Form 4562 each year and enter the deduction on Schedule E. If you own properties you purchased and started to rent prior to 1987, you can continue to use the old Accelerated Cost Recovery System (ACRS) method of depreciation, which creates greater deductions than the straight-line method in the early years. For all properties purchased after 1986, the new rules apply. These new rules are technically known as the MACRS or the Modified Accelerated Cost Recovery System. Only the government could dream up a mouthful like that. The "modification" is that real estate depreciation is now straight line and no longer accelerated.

What structure should you use, then, to hold title to the real estate? If no one is involved but you or you and your spouse, you will hold title to the property as "tenancy by the entirety." Tenancy by the entirety means that one spouse cannot sell an interest in the property without the permission of the other, and upon the death of one spouse the entire property is then automatically owned by the other. At tax time you fill out a Schedule E, which is attached to your personal 1040 return.

DEPRECIATION RATE TABLE
RESIDENTIAL REAL ESTATE
Straight Line 27.5 Years

IF THE RECOVERY PERIOD IS	AND THE MONTH IN THE 1ST YEAR THE PROPERTY IS PLACED IN SERVICE IS:											
	1	2	3	4	5	6	7	8	9	10	11	12
	The Depreciation Rate Is:											
1	3.485	3.182	2.879	2.576	2.273	1.970	1.667	1.364	1.061	0.758	0.453	0.152
2	3.636	3.636	3.636	3.636	3.636	3.636	3.636	3.636	3.636	3.636	3.636	3.636
3	3.636	3.636	3.636	3.636	3.636	3.636	3.636	3.636	3.636	3.636	3.636	3.636
4	3.636	3.636	3.636	3.636	3.636	3.636	3.636	3.636	3.636	3.636	3.636	3.636
5	3.636	3.636	3.636	3.636	3.636	3.636	3.636	3.636	3.636	3.636	3.636	3.636
6	3.636	3.636	3.636	3.636	3.636	3.636	3.636	3.636	3.636	3.636	3.636	3.636
7	3.636	3.636	3.636	3.636	3.636	3.636	3.636	3.636	3.636	3.636	3.636	3.636
8	3.636	3.636	3.636	3.636	3.636	3.636	3.636	3.636	3.636	3.636	3.636	3.636
9	3.636	3.636	3.636	3.636	3.636	3.636	3.636	3.636	3.636	3.636	3.636	3.636
10	3.637	3.637	3.637	3.637	3.637	3.637	3.636	3.636	3.636	3.636	3.636	3.636
11	3.636	3.636	3.636	3.636	3.636	3.636	3.637	3.637	3.637	3.637	3.637	3.637
12	3.637	3.637	3.637	3.637	3.637	3.637	3.636	3.636	3.636	3.636	3.636	3.636
13	3.636	3.636	3.636	3.636	3.636	3.636	3.637	3.637	3.637	3.637	3.637	3.637
14	3.637	3.637	3.637	3.637	3.637	3.637	3.636	3.636	3.636	3.636	3.636	3.636
15	3.636	3.636	3.636	3.636	3.636	3.636	3.637	3.637	3.637	3.637	3.637	3.637
16	3.637	3.637	3.637	3.637	3.637	3.637	3.636	3.636	3.636	3.636	3.636	3.636
17	3.636	3.636	3.636	3.636	3.636	3.636	3.637	3.637	3.637	3.637	3.637	3.637

18	3.637	3.637	3.637	3.637	3.637	3.637	3.636	3.636	3.636	3.636	3.636	3.636
19	3.636	3.636	3.636	3.636	3.636	3.636	3.637	3.637	3.637	3.637	3.637	3.637
20	3.637	3.637	3.637	3.637	3.637	3.637	3.636	3.636	3.636	3.636	3.636	3.636
21	3.636	3.636	3.636	3.636	3.636	3.636	3.637	3.637	3.637	3.637	3.637	3.637
22	3.637	3.637	3.637	3.637	3.637	3.637	3.636	3.636	3.636	3.636	3.636	3.636
23	3.636	3.636	3.636	3.636	3.636	3.636	3.637	3.637	3.637	3.637	3.637	3.637
24	3.637	3.637	3.637	3.637	3.637	3.637	3.636	3.636	3.636	3.636	3.636	3.636
25	3.636	3.636	3.636	3.636	3.636	3.636	3.637	3.637	3.637	3.637	3.637	3.637
26	3.637	3.637	3.637	3.637	3.637	3.637	3.636	3.636	3.636	3.636	3.636	3.636
27	3.636	3.636	3.636	3.636	3.636	3.636	3.637	3.637	3.637	3.637	3.637	3.637
28	1.970	2.273	2.576	2.879	3.182	3.485	3.636	3.636	3.636	3.636	3.636	3.636

Multiply the depreciation rate from the table times your depreciation basis to determine the amount of your yearly depreciation tax deduction.

NONRESIDENTIAL REAL PROPERTY
MID-MONTH CONVENTION
Straight Line—31.5 Years

For assets placed in service prior to 5-12-93

	MONTHLY PROPERTY PLACED IN SERVICE											
YEAR	1	2	3	4	5	6	7	8	9	10	11	12
1	3.042%	2.778%	2.513%	2.249%	1.984%	1.720%	1.455%	1.190%	0.926%	0.661%	0.397%	0.192%
2–7	3.175	3.175	3.175	3.175	3.175	3.175	3.175	3.175	3.175	3.175	3.175	3.175
8	3.175	3.174	3.175	3.174	3.175	3.174	3.175	3.175	3.175	3.175	3.175	3.175
9	3.174	3.175	3.174	3.175	3.174	3.175	3.174	3.175	3.174	3.175	3.174	3.175
10	3.175	3.174	3.175	3.174	3.175	3.174	3.175	3.174	3.175	3.174	3.175	3.174
11	3.174	3.175	3.174	3.175	3.174	3.175	3.174	3.175	3.174	3.175	3.174	3.175
12	3.175	3.174	3.175	3.174	3.175	3.174	3.175	3.174	3.175	3.174	3.175	3.174
13	3.174	3.175	3.174	3.175	3.174	3.175	3.174	3.175	3.174	3.175	3.174	3.175
14	3.175	3.174	3.175	3.174	3.175	3.174	3.175	3.174	3.175	3.174	3.175	3.174
15	3.174	3.175	3.174	3.175	3.174	3.175	3.174	3.175	3.174	3.175	3.174	3.175
16	3.175	3.174	3.175	3.174	3.175	3.174	3.175	3.174	3.175	3.174	3.175	3.174
17	3.174	3.175	3.174	3.175	3.174	3.175	3.174	3.175	3.174	3.175	3.174	3.175
18	3.175	3.174	3.175	3.174	3.175	3.174	3.175	3.174	3.175	3.174	3.175	3.174
19	3.174	3.175	3.174	3.175	3.174	3.175	3.174	3.175	3.174	3.175	3.174	3.175
20	3.175	3.174	3.175	3.174	3.175	3.174	3.175	3.174	3.175	3.174	3.175	3.174

21	3.174	3.175	3.174	3.175	3.174	3.175	3.174	3.175	3.174	3.175	3.174	3.175
22	3.175	3.174	3.175	3.174	3.175	3.174	3.175	3.174	3.175	3.174	3.175	3.174
23	3.174	3.175	3.174	3.175	3.174	3.175	3.174	3.175	3.174	3.175	3.174	3.175
24	3.175	3.174	3.175	3.174	3.175	3.174	3.175	3.174	3.175	3.174	3.175	3.174
25	3.174	3.175	3.174	3.175	3.174	3.175	3.174	3.175	3.174	3.175	3.174	3.175
26	3.175	3.174	3.175	3.174	3.175	3.174	3.175	3.174	3.175	3.174	3.175	3.174
27	3.174	3.175	3.174	3.175	3.174	3.175	3.174	3.175	3.174	3.175	3.174	3.175
28	3.175	3.174	3.175	3.174	3.175	3.174	3.175	3.174	3.175	3.174	3.175	3.174
29	3.174	3.175	3.174	3.175	3.174	3.175	3.174	3.175	3.174	3.175	3.174	3.175
30	3.175	3.174	3.175	3.174	3.175	3.174	3.175	3.174	3.175	3.174	3.175	3.174
31	3.174	3.175	3.174	3.175	3.174	3.175	3.174	3.175	3.174	3.175	3.174	3.175
32	1.720	1.984	2.249	2.513	2.778	3.042	3.175	3.174	3.175	3.174	3.175	3.174
33							0.132	0.397	0.661	0.926	1.190	1.455

NONRESIDENTIAL REAL PROPERTY
MID-MONTH CONVENTION

Straight Line—39 Years

For assets placed in service on 5-13-93 and after.

	MONTH PROPERTY PLACED IN SERVICE											
Year	1	2	3	4	5	6	7	8	9	10	11	12
1	2.451%	2.247%	2.033%	1.819%	1.605%	1.391%	1.177%	0.968%	0.740%	0.535%	0.821%	0.107%
2–39	2.584	2.564	2.564	2.564	2.584	2.564	2.564	2.584	2.564	2.564	2.584	2.584
40	0.107	0.321	0.535	0.749	0.963	1.177	1.391	1.605	1.819	2.033	2.247	2.461

Partners other than spouses often hold legal title to a property as "tenants in common." Tenants in common means ownership by two or more persons each owning an undivided interest but with no right of survivorship. In other words, no partner can sell the property without the consent of the others but each can will his or her interest to someone other than the surviving partners. If the partners wanted to leave their interest to the other partners, then the deed would be prepared to read "joint tenants." Partners have the choice of holding the property for tax purposes in a partnership by completing tax Form 1065 at the end of the year, distributing a Schedule K-1 to each partner showing the partner's share of the income and expenses. Or partners may choose to hold the property as co-owners. Co-ownership is the simplest of all ownership methods for tax purposes when you and your friends or associates own a property together. Using the co-ownership method, each owner reports his percentage of income and expenses on his own Schedule E and Form 1040. For example, if you have two partners and each of you, according to your agreement, owns one third of the property, total the property income and expenses for the year and divide by three. Each of you claims one third of the income and expenses on Schedule E. You can use the co-ownership method for up to three owners on a property. If your partnership owns more than one property, as co-owners you may use the same approach but treat each property separately on your individual Schedule E. The IRS has taken the position that if the property is used only as a rental, the simple co-ownership reporting method can be used. However, if any other business is conducted on the premises by the partners, then a business partnership does, in fact, exist and you must fill out the more complicated 1065 partnership form.

DEFENSE #165

Allocate 20 percent of the value of a rental property to land and 80 percent to the building before computing the depreciation.

Although you can depreciate the value of a rental property, you cannot depreciate the value of the land on which it sits. Depreciation applies only to buildings, including bricks, concrete, beams, doors, windows, roofs, plumbing, and heating and air conditioning equipment. Depreciation does not apply to land, since land values do not diminish due to wear and tear. Land is considered to have unlimited life unless it contains minerals such as coal or oil and those minerals are being removed. When you bought the property, no distinction was made between the cost of the building and the cost of the land. So how do you figure out which is which?

An acceptable rule of thumb for residential real estate is to allocate 20 percent of the purchase price to the land and 80 percent to the building, unless you have some reason to believe it should be otherwise. If you have a mathematical mind, you'll notice that the smaller the percentage you allocate to the land, the greater will be your depreciation tax deductions on the building. That's why the IRS often looks suspiciously at any allocation where the land is valued at less than 20 percent. Conversely, if you allocate more than 20 percent to the land, your depreciation tax deductions will be less. Many real estate old-timers will tell you that you should visit the county courthouse and get the property tax assessment to see how the tax assessor has allocated the tax base for the property between the land and the building. Interesting but not necessary. The IRS will not automatically accept the tax assessor's opinion, and it may actually hurt instead of help if the tax assessor has allocated greater than 20 percent of the value of the property to the land.

To turn theory into easily understandable numbers, we'll use an example. If you buy a property costing $100,000 and allocate 20 percent to the land, you're telling the IRS that the land value, in your opinion, is $20,000 and, therefore, the value of the building is $80,000. The $80,000 in tax terms becomes your basis for depreciation. It is the $80,000 that will be depreciated over 27.5 years at 3.636 or 3.637 percent per year (except for the first and last years). These are the numbers that will eventually end up on your tax Schedule E.

Your first year's depreciation on a property with a depreciation basis of $80,000 will depend on the month in which you purchased the property. Remember the half-month convention? (See Depreciation Rate Table, Residential Real Estate, pages 424–25.) Each year you rent the property after the first year, your depreciation deduction will be 3.636 percent × $80,000 or $2,909 per year. To determine your total tax deduction for the year for Schedule E, you add to your depreciation deduction all other deductible expenses you incurred and then substract your rents and other income. The difference is your net tax deduction. It's that simple. The important question then becomes how much total property you would need to purchase to get the maximum $25,000 of usable deductions each year. If $100,000 of rental property ($80,000 basis) gives you a depreciation tax deduction of $2,909 per year, you would need to own $859,000 worth of rental properties to get the maximum allowable deduction. The total of $859,000 was determined by dividing the $25,000 maximum deduction by the $2,909 yearly depreciation deduction for $100,000 of property ($25,000 ÷ $2,909 = 8.59). Thus, 8.59 is the number of $100,000 properties that you would need to own to produce the maximum $25,000 yearly depreciation deduction. (See Maximizing Allowable Real Estate Deductions, Part A, page 432).

Another way to compute the formula is to deduct 20 percent of the cost of the land from the total of $859,000 and apply the 3.636 percent factor from the residential real estate depreciation table to the 80 percent balance; 80 percent of $859,000 is approximately $687,000. A $687,000 property deduction basis deducted at 3.636 percent each year gives you the same maximum $25,000 deductions.

Look at Maximizing Allowable Real Estate Deductions, Part B on page 433. This table shows you how much in yearly depreciation deductions you can generate based on the total amount of property you buy between $50,000 and $1,000,000. Notice that from a tax standpoint you get no additional deductions for depreciation once you buy more than $859,000 worth of rental properties. Use this table to plan the growth of your real estate tax haven.

MAXIMIZING ALLOWABLE REAL ESTATE DEDUCTIONS

Part A

Calculating the yearly depreciation for one $100,000 rental property:

$100,000	Cost of property (your purchase price)
× 80%	Percentage of cost allocated to the building
$ 80,000	Depreciation basis (amount you allocated to the building)
× 3.636%	Percentage of depreciation each year (except first and last year)
$ 2,909	Yearly depreciation tax deduction for a $100,000 rental property with an $80,000 depreciation basis

Calculating the number of $100,000 properties you would have to own to get the maximum $25,000 tax deduction from depreciation:

$25,000 ÷ $2,909 = 8.59	Number of $100,000 properties that you would have to own to produce the maximum $25,000 depreciation deduction

Checking your approach:

$859,000	Total value of properties at cost
× 80%	Percentage of cost allocated to buildings
$687,000	Depreciation basis
× 3.636%	Percentage of yearly depreciation
$ 25,000	Total tax deductions from depreciation

MAXIMIZING ALLOWABLE REAL ESTATE DEDUCTIONS

Part B

Your depreciation deduction based on the cost of your rental properties.

COST IF YOUR RENTAL PROPERTY(IES) COST:	*BASIS* AND 80% OF THE COST IS ALLOCATED TO THE BUILDING	*DEDUCTION* YOUR YEARLY DEPRECIATION DEDUCTION IS:*
$ 50,000	$ 40,000	$ 1,500
$ 100,000	$ 80,000	$ 2,900
$ 200,000	$160,000	$ 5,800
$ 300,000	$240,000	$ 8,700
$ 400,000	$320,000	$11,600
$ 500,000	$400,000	$14,500
$ 600,000	$480,000	$17,500
$ 700,000	$560,000	$20,000
$ 800,000	$640,000	$23,300
$ 859,000	**$687,000**	**$25,000**
$ 900,000	$720,000	$25,000
$1,000,000	$800,000	$25,000

***Computed at 3.636% × depreciation basis and rounded to the nearest $100. $25,000 is the maximum deduction you can take each year if your AGI is under $100,000. If you have properties showing a positive cash flow before depreciation, you could use more than $25,000 of depreciation deductions to shelter the additional income.**

DEFENSE #166

Don't incorporate your personal real estate investment plan.

Another question that I am asked frequently is "Shouldn't I incorporate my real estate investments for liability protection?" The answer is a definite no. If you were to put together a regular corporation, known in tax law as a C corporation, you would be double-taxed on any profits—once on the corporate income and again, as an individual, on the dividends distributed to yourself. On the other hand, in the early years a real estate investment is usually showing losses. Since negative dividends cannot be declared, you, as an individual, would stand a good chance of losing the normally allowable deductions for your real estate losses.

The exception to this rule is if you are in a business that owns an office building or other property and there is enough income from the business itself that the losses and expenses of the real estate can be absorbed, you would get the benefit of the deductions. Additionally, a corporation does not qualify for the $25,000 passive loss exception we just discussed, which is the basis upon which you are going to build your personal real estate investment plan.

Forming an S corporation, a corporate entity taxed as an individual, will not help you either. In an S corporation you also lose the $25,000 passive loss exception, and unless you had a tax basis or other income in the corporation high enough to absorb the losses, the tax benefits of your real estate investments would also be lost.

The bottom line is don't incorporate. Always hold title to your real estate investments as an individual, in a partnership or as co-owners.

"Well, what about my liability?" you might be thinking. Do as I do. Carry a landlord's liability policy for each rental property. The cost will average about $200 a year per property for a million dollars of liability coverage, and, of course, it is tax deductible. The agent who writes the fire insurance on your rental property can help you with your liability policy. Now you have accomplished both objectives: You have protected yourself from the financial drain of a major lawsuit but you have also managed to retain all your potential tax deductions.

DEFENSE #167

Carry the same liability insurance limits on each rental property as you do on your automobile, homeowner's or umbrella liability policy.

Any time you are dealing with tenants, you will eventually get into a conflict. My first liability suit occurred in the 1970s when one of my tenants fell through the attic floor of one of my older rental properties and broke his leg when bouncing off the floor below. He had stepped in between the attic 2 × 4s and went right through the insulation and the ceiling board. Having the public presence that I do, any ambulance-chasing, "sue 'em on demand" attorney would gladly handle a suit against me for a percentage even if there was no negligence, and one did. The tenant's story was that he had been up in the attic trying to fix the air conditioner. He had not called the property manager to request that the air conditioner be fixed, so you may wonder what he was doing up there anyway. "Major hassle," you might think. Not at all. I filled out a one-page form for my liability insurance company after I had received notice of the million-dollar lawsuit, and two years later I received a notice from my insurance company that the claim had been settled. I never heard another word before or after the settlement, nor was I ever called as a witness. My liability policy handled the whole process, including the cost.

Handling people is part of the game of life in business, particularly in real estate investing. Liability insurance on your rental properties is an essential part of the process. For most people, a half-million- or million-dollar limit per occurrence is plenty. Use the same formula we used earlier in determining personal liability limits for your home, auto and umbrella liability insurance (see Chapter 8). If you have multiple properties, you can normally combine coverage on the same liability policy and save insurance dollars.

CHAPTER 21

Beat the Capital Gains Tax

The term "capital gains tax" seems to strike terror into the hearts of most investors, business owners and others ready to sell their assets at a profit. The capital gains tax is the tax rate or percentage you pay on profits from the sale of investments that have grown in value over time—investments like stocks, bonds, real estate or a business you own. The capital gains tax is not an additional tax, as many seem to think, but a special set of tax rates and rules that apply only to things you sell at a profit, and is paid *instead of* income tax.

Capital gains taxes are also assessed at the time of sale on all or part of the depreciation deductions you have taken on real estate or business assets, if the sale price is higher than the depreciated value. The difference between the depreciated value and the sale price is called recapture and is subject to capital gains taxes. When you are taking depreciation deductions, you are, in effect, telling the IRS that the property is dropping in value over time. If you then sell the property for $5,000 more than the depreciated value, you are required to pay back the taxes you overdeducted on the $5,000. Therefore, the amount subject to capital gains tax is your real profit plus any extra depreciation you claimed which made the depreciated value less than the sale price.

Until the Tax Reform Act of 1986, the capital gains tax rates were far lower than taxes on income. The maximum tax you could pay on your income was a whopping 50 percent, but the maximum capital gains tax you could pay was only 20 percent, giving a real break to investors and business owners. To qualify for the lower capital gains tax rate, you simply had to own the asset, whether a piece of real estate, a stock or mutual fund shares, for one year or longer before you sold. If you sold within the same 365-day period in which you bought the asset, your profits were taxed at your ordinary or regular income tax rate of up to 50 percent. For a short time, the holding period was even reduced to six months.

In no way, however, could your capital gains tax rate be higher than your ordinary income tax rate. The first 60 percent of your profit was tax exempt by law. The 40 percent balance was then taxed at your ordinary income tax rate. For example, if you sold an investment for a $10,000 profit, the first $6,000 was tax exempt. The other 40 percent, or $4,000, was added to your regular income for the year and taxed at your regular income tax bracket rate. Since the maximum income tax rate was 50 percent, but 60 percent of your profit or capital gain was exempt, the top capital gains tax rate was 20 percent (50% top tax rate × 40% taxable profit = 20%). However, if you were only in the 25 percent income tax bracket, the maximum capital gains tax you could pay was just 10 percent (25% tax bracket × 40% taxable profit = 10%). What a phenomenal break for investors big and small, even though most complained even then at paying any tax on their profits.

Although the capital gains tax rate has never been higher than the regular income tax rate, anytime you pay capital gains taxes on a lump-sum profit the amount sometimes seems outrageous and is currently as much as one third of your profit, or 33 percent. The reason capital gains taxes seem so high is that you pay the tax all at one time on the entire profit from the sale of an asset, a profit that in some cases may have been accumulating for years.

Let's say you've owned five acres of land for the past 10 years, property you originally bought for $10,000 and on which you intended to build. You just sold the property to a developer for $35,000, at a profit of $25,000. You're excited until you learn that, based on your tax bracket, you will pay $8,250 in federal income tax and another $1,750 in state tax, for a total of $10,000. You will only have $15,000 of your profit left! Under current tax law, this is exactly the same amount you would pay on the top $25,000 of your job income, but when the taxes are deducted from your periodic paycheck you don't seem to notice. When you pay in a lump sum, the loss is shocking.

Taxpayers did not appreciate the old capital gains rules until after tax reform. Today's higher capital gains tax rates have brought new meaning to the term, "Ah, the good old days." Under the tax reform rules, the capital gains tax rate you pay is now exactly the same as the income tax rate you pay. Any couple who have over $31,000 of taxable income are paying taxes on their investment gains and profits at 28 percent, or about twice the rate paid under the old rules. On taxable incomes of under $31,000 the capital gains or income tax rate is a flat 15 percent. If your taxable income as a couple is between $75,000 and $155,000, you pay an additional 5 percent hidden surcharge in capital gains taxes, or $500 for each $10,000 of profit. The same is true if you are single with a taxable income of $45,000 to $93,000. An extra 5 percent is, in reality, an 18 percent increase in the total capital gains tax paid. Furthermore, if you live, as most people do, in a state with state income tax and are paying another additional state tax of 7 percent, your total capital gains tax rate is as high as 40 percent, or 40 cents out of every dollar.

One of the most absurd statements from the press and some on Capitol Hill is that lowering the capital gains rate would be a tax break only for the rich. In reality, it is a break that enables the not-so-rich to have a better shot at a piece of the American Dream. Of course, you have to work for it by taking even a small chunk of what you earn and investing it. If a family's adjusted gross income is between $75,000 and $155,000, they are actually paying a higher tax rate on their profits than the super-rich, because of the 5 percent surcharge. It is true that since rich people have more profits (that's how they got to be rich), any tax break is going to mean a greater number of dollars saved. But which is the most meaningful: $3,000 saved through lower capital gains taxes by a struggling family earning $35,000 per year, or $30,000 saved by a high-income investor earning a million a year? The small investors are the big winners; the money they could save in taxes will make the biggest difference in their lifestyle.

For that reason, more and more middle-income earners now realize how duped they were in believing that a lower capital gains tax was a break only for the rich and have begun to complain loudly.

In this chapter we'll explore some very effective strategies you can use to legally reduce the shock and stress of paying capital gains taxes when the time comes. If your goal is building more wealth, you must make a commitment to familiarize yourself thoroughly with the capital gains tax rules and stay current on the constant changes. Your decisions about when and how to sell any investment or asset for the greatest profit are affected by these rules.

If you sell an investment or business for less than you paid, you experience a capital loss, or a loss of your capital, which is deductible. But the amount of capital losses that you can deduct in one year if you've owned the investments for more than one year is a maximum of $3,000 above your total capital gains. We will also discuss strategies for maximizing your deductible losses.

Most assets you own as an individual are capital assets. However, in a business or profession, some assets are capital assets but others, such as accounts receivable, inventory, personal property and real estate used in your business, are not. Thus, the strategies we will discuss in this chapter apply only to the sale of capital assets but not to all business assets.

Most people consider the capital gains and capital loss rules burdensome, cumbersome and worrisome. Here we will simplify all the rules and discuss the strategies in detail. By mastering these strategies, it's not only money, it's *your* money that you will save.

DEFENSE #168

Calculate the gain or loss on the sale of your assets to determine the potential tax effect.

It requires only understanding to stop being intimidated by capital gains taxes. To calculate your exact capital gain or loss from the tax perspective, you must know only four things:

1. The original cost of the asset
2. The adjusted cost basis of the asset
3. The selling expenses
4. The selling price of the asset

The adjusted cost basis is the most important number in determining your tax position. Computation of the adjusted cost basis for a property asset begins with the original cost of the property, also known in tax lingo as the unadjusted cost basis.

To that original cost you add all of the expenses you incurred while buying the property which you have not already deducted, like commissions, legal fees and title insurance. Since all of these items create deductions when you sell a property, check your records carefully. If you made any improvements or additions to the property while you owned it, you add those costs to determine your adjusted cost basis. Obviously with securities investments like stocks, bonds and mutual funds, improvements are not an issue. If you inherited instead of purchased the property, your adjusted cost basis is the market value of the property on the date of death of the decedent, unless the executor of the estate elected to use an alternate valuation date. The estate from which you received the property will have already paid inheritance taxes, if any. If you receive a property that has been held in trust for you, your unadjusted cost basis of the property is the same as while the property was held in the trust.

The selling price of the property includes cash, property and notes received in payment for the property, plus any mortgages given to the buyer. For example, you own a boat and decide to sell. Your boat is worth $10,000, but after negotiations with a potential buyer, you decide to take $4,000 in cash, a note for $2,000 paid to you over the next two years and a less expensive boat in trade, which the buyer says is worth $6,000, all of which would total $12,000. Before completing the transaction, you discover the boat you are getting in trade is worth only $3,000. Your real selling price is only $9,000, which is the total of the cash, the note and the *true* market value of the boat you took in trade. It's that simple. When you sell stock, bond or mutual fund shares, determining the selling price is normally straightforward. If you sell 100 shares of stock at $10 a share, your selling price is $1,000. There are no mortgages, notes or trades involved, although there may be commissions, which are deductible. When you sell an existing piece of real estate, there are normally cash and mortgages involved, but seldom do you take anything in trade.

Now for the selling expenses. Your selling expenses include commissions or fees paid to a broker or anyone else, attorney's fees, plus just about any other money you spent to effect the sale. With real estate, all expenses for last-minute repairs done within 90 days before the sale of the property are also included in selling expenses, as are any fees or interest you pay on behalf of the buyer. Advertising is a selling expense. If you own property outside the area in which you live and selling the property requires that you travel one or more times to that area, your travel expenses are deductible as a selling expense.

The summary that follows demonstrates the steps you use to determine the adjusted cost basis, beginning with your original cost or unadjusted cost basis.

How to Calculate the Adjusted Cost Basis of a Property

Original cost of property (unadjusted cost)

Plus: Commissions
Legal fees
Title insurance
Other purchase expenses not deducted
Additions or improvements to the property

Minus: Depreciation or depletion allowances
Return of capital
Casualty losses or insurance settlement

Equals: Adjusted cost basis of property

Note in calculating your adjusted cost basis that you must subtract any depreciation or depletion tax deductions you have already claimed, plus any return of capital you have received from an investment like a limited partnership. Let's say you originally invested $10,000 in a limited partnership and received from the partnership $2,000 as a return of capital, not as a share of the profit. You reduce your cost basis by that $2,000. If your property, as in the case of real estate, suffered damages during the holding period, casualty losses and any insurance settlement for damages must also be deducted from your original cost. If the property you sold was subject to depreciation or depletion allowances, you must reduce your basis or cost by the actual allowable amount of the depreciation, whether you took the deductions or not. This process is the recapture we talked about earlier.

How to Calculate Your Capital Gain (Loss)

Let's put these rules into an easy-to-understand formula for calculating your capital gain or loss:

Selling price − selling expenses − adjusted cost basis
= capital gain

You bought 100 shares of stock two years ago for $600, or $6 a share, and your broker charged you a $25 commission to make the purchase. Therefore, your adjusted cost basis is $625. You sell the stock for $1,000, or $10 a share (selling price). Your broker charged you $50 in commission to make the sale (selling expense). Now fill in the formula.

Selling price − selling expenses − adjusted cost basis
= capital gain
$1,000 − $50 − $625 = $325

Your capital gain on which you would be taxed is $325. If, when you sell an asset, your adjusted cost basis is higher than your selling price plus selling expenses, you have a capital loss. Say, for example, you bought 100 shares of stock for $1,000, or $10 a share, and you sell your shares for $600 when the stock drops to $6 a share. The commission on the purchase was $50, while the commission on the sale was $25. Here's the way the formula would look now:

Selling price − selling expenses − adjusted cost basis
= capital loss
$600 − $25 − $1,050 = $−475

Keeping your wealth is every bit as important as building it, and your success in part is dependent upon your understanding of the capital gains rules and strategies. Knowing how to calculate gains and losses is the best defense against unnecessary capital gains taxes. Remember, when it comes to the tax system, if you make a mistake in your favor, you'll hear about it; if you make a mistake in the IRS's favor, you may never hear a word.

ATTACK #169

Cut your losses short and run your winners long.

A very wise old man once said to me, "Chuck, the secret to winning in life is cut your losses short and run your winners long." After I thought about it I realized he meant dump the losers and keep the winners. I've used that strategy most of my life and I can assure you he was right.

When you are losing in an investment, get rid of it as quickly as possible; move the balance of your money to a better investment and take the tax deductions for your loss. If you are in the 33 percent tax bracket the government is going to eventually reimburse you for one third of your losses, so deducting capital losses is sort of like filing an insurance claim.

When it comes to winners, whether in investing, real estate or business, hold your winners as long as they keep growing at a reasonable rate. As the tide turns and the growth slows or stops, start making your plans to sell and take your profits. Remember, you cannot lose money by taking a profit.

DEFENSE #170

To offset capital gains taxes, take your profits (gains) early, not late in the year.

If you have an investment that is showing a big paper profit, it is often hard to make the decision to sell because you may have to pay a big chunk of the profits in capital gains taxes. On the other hand, if you don't sell, you cannot enjoy the use of the profit money and the investment could drop in value. If you have an investment that if sold would cause you to lose money, it is all too easy to think, "I'll just hold on and maybe the value will eventually go up to what I paid and I won't feel so foolish as if I sell at a loss now." In the meantime, you are losing money you could have earned by putting the remaining money from a sale into a better investment that would more quickly earn the losses back. Besides, you could then take a deduction for a capital loss. There's the dilemma. What's the solution?

You've heard it said that timing is everything, and with your money that statement is particularly true. Once you have made a decision to sell a capital asset, proper timing can still enable you to save big on taxes.

When you sell a capital asset at a profit, whether stocks, bonds, real estate or a business, you have a choice about when to close on the transaction. Closing is when the seller gives the buyer physical possession of the asset or investment and when title changes from seller to buyer. A transaction occurs for capital gains tax purposes when you close and not when you sign a sales agreement or receive a down payment.

Your strategy is to set up the closing on the sale of a capital asset early in the tax year, like January or February, and avoid closing late in the previous year. The tax effect of this kind of planning is dramatic. Let's say you sell a piece of real estate in September and decide to close December 15 of the same year. If you receive all your money at closing, you will be required to pay taxes on that money four months later on April 15. If, however, you wait just an extra 18 days and close January 2, your taxes will not be due until 16 months later, on April 15 of the following year. That will give you the opportunity to invest your money for more than a year and potentially to earn up to 60 or even 70 percent of the taxes that will be due.

How? The best way to invest your cash proceeds to earn money to offset capital gains taxes is in mutual funds. By averaging a 15 percent return a year, your total return for 16 months would be 20 percent. If the federal taxes you owe on the capital gains are 28 percent, you have earned back about 70 percent of the taxes that will be due. If you closed in December and invested the profit in a mutual fund, four months later in April, you would have gained only 18 percent of the taxes due.

Look at the following example and you will see that a great percentage of the capital gains tax can be offset with smart investing just by timing the closing of a sale correctly. In this example, you sell a property for $100,000 you originally purchased for $70,000, earning a $30,000 profit. If you invested the profit and earned 15 percent per year, or 1.25 percent per month, in a mutual fund family, here is the difference between closing in December and closing a month later in January:

	CLOSING DEC. 15, TAXES DUE APRIL 15, YEAR 1	CLOSING JAN. 2, TAXES DUE APRIL 15, YEAR 2
Number of months until taxes due	4	16
Earnings per month in mutual fund at 15%	1.25%	1.25%
Amount invested	$30,000	$30,000
Total % earned	× 5%	× 20%
Amount earned	$ 1,500	$ 6,000
Taxes due at 28%	$ 8,400	$ 8,400
Subtract earnings	−$ 1,500	−$ 6,000
Balance of tax due	$ 6,900	$ 2,400
% of taxes earned by investment	18%	71%

As a general rule, it is a good financial strategy to put as much time as possible between the sale of a major asset and the date taxes will be due on the profits.

ATTACK #171

Use end-of-year investment losses to claim tax-free investment gains.

Near the end of every tax year, all of America's tax wizards come out with last-minute gimmicks you can use to reduce your taxes. They even appear on local and national television talk shows. The things normally talked about are cute but absolutely worthless, since they apply to almost no one. There are, however, a few little-known end-of-year strategies you can use to make a big difference in the amount of taxes you do or don't pay. For instance, you can create last-minute tax deductible losses from investments at the end of the year to reduce the taxes on your investment profits from the same year.

The tax rules say that before you determine how much tax you must pay on the profits from the sale of investments, you may first subtract any investment losses you incur during the same year. Investment losses or profits are created for tax purposes only at the time of sale, not while you are holding an investment. You may own a piece of land that appreciates 5 percent per year for 25 years, but you pay no taxes on the increase in value until you sell the property. Your strategy is to time sales to reduce the total taxes you pay.

Here's an example: Let's say you have $10,000 in a bond mutual fund which has increased 15 percent in value for the year. In November, you decide to sell your shares, either because you want the money for something else or maybe because the timing is no longer right for bond mutual fund investments. You now have a $1,500 profit on which you will be taxed. However, looking at your investments late in December, you see that your $8,000 investment in a mutual stock fund has lost $1,000 of its value. Maybe the stock mutual fund is a good long-term investment but it just happens to be down at this point.

Here's your opportunity. You sell your shares in the stock mutual fund for $7,000. The $1,000 loss that you incur can then be used to reduce the taxable $1,500 profit on the sale of your bond fund shares by $1,000. Combining these two transactions on Schedule D, which is where you report your capital gains and losses, you have now reduced the amount of profit subject to taxes from $1,500 to $500, which saves you up to $400 in federal and state income taxes. Had you left your money in the stock fund until the following year, you would have paid the extra $400 in taxes no matter what happened to the prices of the shares in the stock fund.

There are, however, restrictions. Congress, realizing that you might get this smart, has created what it calls the 30-Day Churning Rule. Once you sell an investment at a loss, you are not allowed to reinvest the money in the same investment, like the same stock or bond mutual fund, for the next 30 days. If you do, you cannot deduct the loss. What do you do? Use the next strategy.

ATTACK #172

Reinvest your year-end loss capital into a similar investment rather than the same investment.

Rather than waiting for 30 days to reinvest your money in the same investment you sold at a loss, you have another option. Invest the money immediately in a *similar* investment. In the previous strategy, you sold your stock mutual fund shares at a loss to save taxes, even though you believed the fund was a sound investment. There are maybe 10 other *similar* stock mutual funds in the same mutual fund family in which you could reinvest your money. As long as the money is not reinvested in the same investment or mutual fund, you have completely circumvented the churning rules.

For example, you sold shares purchased for $10,000 in Fidelity's Magellan Fund for a $1,000 loss. The same day you reinvest the $9,000 you received from the sale in Fidelity's Capital Appreciation Fund, a mutual fund run with the same investment philosophy. You could actually handle the transaction by telephone. When you change mutual funds, you automatically create a taxable transaction. In this case, a taxable loss of $1,000 is created even though you have exactly the same $9,000 invested in the same kind of mutual fund as the one you sold.

The decision to offset gains with last-minute end-of-year losses is one that should be made every December. As you know, I am a big proponent of mutual funds as an investment, and the mutual fund examples seem the most appropriate here. However, the same strategy can be used whether you are selling land, businesses, individual stocks and bonds, GNMAs or any other type of capital investment on which a loss could be reported.

DEFENSE #173

Time your mutual fund purchases to avoid paying taxes on someone else's gain.

Most mutual funds, particularly stock mutual funds, declare dividends and capital gains distributions in December, usually around the middle of the month. To remain a nontaxable entity, a mutual fund must distribute to investors at least 90 percent of its capital gains for the year. If you were to buy shares in a mutual fund right before the date the dividends or capital gains distributions are declared, a date normally called the ex-dividend date, you would be responsible the following April for taxes on that income, even though you had owned the shares in that mutual fund for a few days of the previous tax year. You would not lose any money overall but you would pay the taxes early on someone else's gain. You wouldn't recover the money until you sold.

When you are selling a loss position in a mutual fund at the end of the year, your strategy is to reinvest your money *after* the ex-dividend date of the new mutual fund in which you are going to invest. You will then have avoided paying taxes on the distributions. Just another method of having your cake and eating it too.

DEFENSE #174

Account for mutual fund distributions on which you've already paid taxes to cut the capital gains tax when you sell your shares.

Millions of mutual fund investors may be paying double taxes on their mutual fund shares when they sell.

Mutual funds are required to distribute at least 90 percent of their interest income, dividend income and capital gains from the sale of individual investments before the end of every calendar year. Distribution means that every shareholder in the mutual fund receives either more shares or cash from the fund. A mutual fund is not taxed on its profits, but its individual investor shareholders are taxed. Dividends received from mutual funds must be reported on tax Schedule B, and the amount is added to the investor's income for the year. No problem if the mutual fund shareholder has been taking out the dividends as monthly cash income, as in the case of bondholders who receive a monthly dividend check for their share of the interest earned by the fund.

But what about a shareholder who receives his or her capital gains and dividend distribution from the mutual fund as extra shares? The investor pays taxes every year on the distribution even though no money was received. The mutual fund notifies the investor of the amount of the distribution on a 1099 form. When a distribution is declared, the price of each share drops by the per share amount of the distribution, but the investor receives more shares instead of cash and is taxed on the value of those shares in the current year.

When the investor sells the shares, the normal method of computing taxes is to subtract the total purchase price of the shares from the total redemption or sales price and include the difference as a profit or loss on Schedule D. But taxes have already been paid on the shares received from each year's distribution, and the investor is about to pay taxes on them again!

The IRS has a record of how much you've received from the sale so you cannot simply deduct the sale price of the new dividend shares from the total you received from the sale. You will likely get an audit notice. The correct way to avoid the double taxation is to add the value of the extra shares on which you have already paid taxes to your purchase price, which you show on Schedule D, at the price shown on your statement at the time of receipt of the new shares. Also add any cash distributions you have taken as income on any of the shares included in the sale. The difference between the total sale and total purchase price of all your shares will then be reduced and thus cut any capital gains taxes due by the correct amount. After looking at dozens of tax returns prepared by tax preparers, I found that not a single one had been adjusted for taxes already paid!

DEFENSE #175

Time the sale of your investments to generate a $3,000 end-of-year deductible net capital loss.

Capital losses are fully deductible if you sell at a loss an investment or asset you have owned less than a year. However, if you have owned the asset longer than one year, it becomes a long-term capital asset, and if you then sell at a loss, you may deduct a maximum of only $3,000 of your losses that are above your actual capital gains. In other words, if your capital gains for the year were $10,000 but your capital losses were $25,000, you could deduct only $3,000 that year. The balance of the loss, $12,000, is carried forward into future years and can be deducted at a maximum of $3,000 per year above that year's net capital gains. Let's turn the rules into a strategy.

If you have one or more investments that are at a temporary loss position at the end of the year, sell to create a tax loss, even if you think they will eventually or even quickly produce a profit. For example, let's say at the end of the year you have $25,000 in a high-yield bond fund that has gone back and forth from the profit to loss column but that you expect will shortly show a big profit. Your investment is currently down 15 percent from what you paid and shows a paper loss of $3,750. Your shares are now worth $21,250 instead of $25,000, and you have no other gains or losses for the year. By switching your investment to another, similar high-yield fund, you will have exactly the same total amount in the account but you can now claim $3,000 of your $3,750 loss as a deduction for that year. The balance of $750 can be subtracted from your capital gains or deducted as a loss the following year.

If you are in the 40 percent combined federal and state tax brackets, by entering the $3,000 loss on Schedule D you will reduce your taxes that year by $1,200. In January, let's say, as you expected, the shares in your new bond fund go up 10 percent, but the taxes on the gain won't be due until you sell or until the year after the mutual fund declares the gain as a distribution. Your year-end strategy is to create, if possible, the maximum $3,000 paper tax loss above your net gains. If at the end of the year all of your investments are in the profit column, just pat yourself on the back and forget this strategy.

ATTACK #176

Deduct a stock as worthless the first year you know the company is in real financial trouble.

Sooner or later you are likely to invest in the stock of a small corporation owned by a friend or relative or even a stranger based on a hot tip. If the company gets into financial trouble, your question should be: "When can I take a deduction for the stock claiming that it is worthless?" You will be surprised to learn that you don't have to wait until the company goes through bankruptcy or even closes its doors. The tax courts have issued an odd ruling that gives you the right to claim an early loss deduction. In one tax case the court ruled, "A taxpayer is often in a very difficult position determining in what year to claim a loss. The safe practice is to claim a loss in the earliest year possible."

Your strategy: If you think a stock you hold is worthless but you can't tell because it is not publicly traded, claim the deduction for the entire cost of the stock on Schedule D of your 1040 form if you think it became worthless in the current tax year, or use Form 1040X (see Chapter 16) if you are claiming that the stock became worthless in a previous year. You may carry forward to the following year any losses that are not deductible the first year. If the company eventually somehow turns around and the stock again has some value, you must then declare any money you receive from the eventual sale of the stock as taxable income.

You have a limit of seven years from the date of your return, instead of the normal three years, to claim refunds based on a deduction for a stock, bond or other security that becomes worthless. You cannot deduct a loss for stock you think is partially worthless or a publicly traded stock that has simply decreased in value until you sell it at a loss. For tax purposes, worthless stock is treated as if it became worthless on the last day of the year.

If you think an investment became worthless in 1989, and it is now 1995, you can still go back and claim the refund, so this strategy may help with investments that became worthless long ago. Let's say you got involved with a local builder in a limited partnership to buy an apartment building as a tax shelter four years ago but it was never bought. You can't seem to get a straight answer as to what is happening, but you think there is little chance of getting your money back. The rules say that you can write off your investment as worthless beginning the year you first believed it to be so, even if it means amending past returns. Many investors miss this opportunity, and so do all but the most savvy tax preparers.

DEFENSE #177

Use the installment sales rules to delay capital gains taxes to future years.

An installment sale is created when you sell an asset or property at a profit, but instead of being paid all cash, you agree to accept one or more payments in later years. The installment sales rules allow you to wait to pay the taxes on a portion of your profit until the year you actually receive the money. To get this great tax deferment, you must fill out Tax Form 6252 to calculate and report your total profit, but using Schedule D you then pay capital gains taxes only on the portion of the profit you receive each year.

Sometimes you will create an installment sale because the buyer doesn't have the full amount to pay you in cash at the time of sale. Other times you may decide to create an installment sale because you don't want to receive the full amount in cash in order to defer some of the taxes to future years. You cannot, however, use the favorable installment sales rules on publicly traded stock, property you sell at a loss or personal property. Installment sales rules and opportunities apply primarily to real estate sold at a profit or gain.

As an example, let's say you sell 10 acres of land you have held for several years for $75,000. You originally paid $40,000 for the land, giving you a profit of $35,000, or 46.6 percent of the sale price. The buyer pays you $30,000 in cash and agrees to pay the balance of $45,000 at $15,000 each year for the next three years. In other words, you receive $30,000, or 40 percent of the sale price, the first year and $45,000, or 60 percent, in future years. Your state and federal tax brackets added together equal 35 percent, and you have no other capital gains or losses that year.

Here's how you report and, thus, defer the taxes on the $45,000 until future years. Without the installment sales rules, you would pay 35 percent of your $35,000 total profit, or $12,250, as a capital gains tax all in the current year. However, by using the installment sales rules, you pay only $4,900 in taxes in the first year and then you pay just $2,450 in taxes each year for the next three years, which totals to the same $12,250.

The basic formula for installment sales is simple. Determine your percentage of profit by dividing your adjusted cost basis by the sale price, in our example, $35,000 ÷ $75,000 = 46.6 percent. Apply that profit percentage to the actual amount received each year to determine the amount of profit you report that year as a taxable income subject to capital gains tax. During the four years the buyer is making payments to you, the income that you would report and the taxes that would be due are shown in the following example.

INSTALLMENT SALES RULE EXAMPLE

YEAR	AMOUNT RECEIVED	% PROFIT	AMOUNT TO REPORT*	TAX PAID AT 35%
Year of sale	$30,000	46.6%	$14,000	$ 4,900
Year 2	15,000	46.6%	7,000	2,450
Year 3	15,000	46.6%	7,000	2,450
Year 4	15,000	46.6%	7,000	2,450
	$75,000		$35,000	$12,250

* Rounded to the nearest $100.

If the total taxes paid amount to the same with or without applying the installment sales rules, why bother—particularly when someone else has the use of your money interest-free? In my opinion, it is almost always a good idea to defer paying your taxes as long as legally possible—unless you already have more deductions than income. Plus, if you do not claim the installment sales election on a transaction in which you were forced to take payments over a period of years in order to make the sale, you could easily end up paying more in taxes the first year than you received in income.

In the Resources at the end of this book you will find more detailed rules you can use when you are actually making an installment sale.

DEFENSE #178

Elect not to use the installment sales rules in a low-taxed year.

Unless you make an election *not* to use the installment sales rules for computing your taxes, you are automatically treated as if you intend to defer the taxes until the money is received.

Let's say your income from your job or business or sales of assets this year will be lower than your income next year, and thus you may be in a lower tax bracket. Wouldn't it make sense, if you could, to take all of the profits from the sale of your assets this year instead of using the installment sales rule to defer profits to years when you will be in a higher tax bracket? If the total amount of taxes you will pay is less by reporting your total profits this year, do so. Do not fill out Form 6252. Instead, report your entire gain on Schedule D. If the property, as in the case of rental real estate, has been subject to depreciation, you must also fill out tax Form 4797 to determine if any of the deductions you took for depreciation must be included in your profit.

Another instance in which you may choose to report your entire profit in the current year is when you have significant losses from other investments. You sell a piece of property that is going to have a significant profit or gain now, even though the buyer is going to pay you over time. You may want to claim the entire gain now to offset the big loss from your other investments, which could only be deducted at a maximum of $3,000 per year above your net gains. So if you can save in taxes by reporting your entire gain from the sale of the profitable asset on Schedule D and using your investment losses from the other investments to offset or tax shelter your gain, do it.

Your objective, of course, is to avoid investment losses, but if one occurs, you can sometimes make smart tax moves by timing your reporting of gains and losses to offset each other. By electing not to report your profits or capital gains using the installment method, you have, in these cases, saved yourself hundreds or even thousands in current capital gains taxes.

DEFENSE #179

Don't use the installment sales rules with sales to relatives.

Those who are trying to get around, instead of using, the tax laws are constantly looking for loopholes or gray areas to do something that was never intended by Congress or the IRS. When the installment sales rules came into play, many people thought, "Why don't I just sell my property to a relative who then resells it? I'll use the installment sales rules to defer the taxes while my relative gets all the cash out front on the resale." Relatives or related parties in this case include a spouse, child, grandchild, parent, brother or sister, family trusts, partnerships or a controlled corporation of which you own 50 percent or more.

Congress and the IRS have plugged this loophole. The installment sales method will not be allowed if you sell to a relative who then resells the property within two years or before you have received all of the payments from the relative. The current rule says, "At the time of the second sale, the original seller must report the income even if not received." You are required to compute the taxes on transactions involving a second sale by a relative on Form 6252.

It is important to note that you may legally sell to relatives on the installment sales plan and defer the taxes if your relative does not dispose of the property for cash under the conditions above. There is also a statute of limitations. When do you transfer property to a related party and notify the IRS on tax Form 6252, the IRS must notify you within two years from the date you filed the form if it intends to assess a deficiency with respect to your transfer to a relative. After the two-year limit, the IRS is powerless to collect any additional taxes on the transfer.

The IRS has also implemented a minimum interest rule. Often there is a temptation, when selling something to a relative, to accept a note or offer a mortgage with a below-market interest rate. Don't even think about it, because the IRS can and often does impute a minimum interest rate of about 9 percent and then charges you taxes, interest and penalties on interest income you never received. As long as you charge your relatives at least 9 percent compounded semiannually, you will have satisfied the imputed interest rule. This rule is covered in Internal Revenue Code sections 1274 and 483, but the language is so complicated and actual percentages so noticeably absent that you would never be able to figure out the actual required rate unless you were a government tax attorney.

DEFENSE #180

Use the interest income from an installment sale to offset the capital gains taxes.

When you sell a piece of real estate, business or other investment using an installment sale, you normally expect to earn and receive interest on the amount that will be paid by the buyer in future years. You can use the interest you receive to pay a part or even most of the capital gains taxes you will owe.

Let's go back to the example we used for an installment sale in Defense #177 but this time add to the contract that you are to receive 12 percent simple interest at the end of each year after the sale on the unpaid balance. Here again are the terms:

Sale price:	$75,000
Down payment:	$30,000
Amount financed:	$45,000
Terms:	$15,000 each year for 3 years
Interest rate:	12 percent on unpaid balance

Now we'll combine the capital gains taxes due with the interest you receive to see how you will fare (see the following page).

	PRINCIPAL BALANCE (A)	INTEREST PAID TO YOU AT 12% (B)	CAPITAL GAINS TAXES PAID BY YOU (C)	DIFFERENCE (D)
Price	$75,000	—	—	—
Down payment	−30,000	$ 0	$ 4,900	−$4,900
End of year 1	45,000	5,400	2,450	+ 2,950
year 2	30,000	3,600	2,450	+ 1,150
year 3	15,000	1,800	2,450	− 650
		+$10,800	−$12,250	−$1,450

Notice that the year you receive the $30,000 down payment, you pay $4,900 out of the $12,250 total tax due. From then on your interest income will cover your capital gains taxes, except in year three. At the end of year one, 12 months after the sale, you receive $5,400 in interest and even after taxes on the interest, you will have plenty left to pay the $2,450 capital gains tax. The same thing is true at the end of year two. Year three the balance owed to you is only $15,000 so your interest income is only $1,800 which is $650 short of covering the balance of the capital gains taxes of $2,450. Overall, however, during the three years of financing you earned a total of $10,800 in interest or almost enough to cover the total of $12,250 of capital gains taxes. In addition you collected a total of $85,800 ($75,000 + $10,800), for a property whose final sale price was $75,000.

CHAPTER 22

Avoiding the AMT—The Alternative Minimum Tax

Everyone talks about it; no one seems to understand it. It's the dreaded AMT, alternative minimum tax. Nothing would be more exciting than to have you already so financially successful that you have to cope with the AMT. If you follow the strategies in this book, you soon will be. But if for some of you this chapter relates more to your future than to your present, it is still important for you to understand the AMT formula and the strategies you can use to protect yourself.

During the seventies and early eighties, those who took the time to analyze income tax rules could easily plan their financial lives, even reaching the zero tax bracket. There are famous examples of those with millions of dollars of income who paid little or no taxes like J. D. Rockefeller, who instead felt obligated to make a contribution to the U.S. Treasury. Taxpayers with incomes of $15,000 to $100,000 could also reach the zero bracket through careful tax planning and investing in real estate and other tax shelters. The problem for those who earned less was they were never taught the first thing about tax planning.

Then someone in Congress decided that for high-income taxpayers, the zero bracket should become an impossibility. Thus, the AMT was born. What Congress giveth, Congress can taketh away. It passes tax laws that can give you thousands of dollars of legitimate tax deductions, but it has also passed the AMT, which can take some of those deductions away. In other words, the AMT can make some of your tax deductions taxable. The AMT does not apply to your income but only to certain deductions called adjustments and tax preference items.

The AMT rules seem to say that a certain amount of tax shelter is the American way, but there is a point at which you are exceeding your fair share. For the most part, the AMT is aimed only at those who invest heavily in tax shelters, but occasionally items such as company stock options or contributions to charity of appreciated property can increase the chance of being nabbed by the AMT, even for those who don't invest in tax shelters.

The AMT is just a different formula for figuring your total taxable income—the amount of income on which you will pay taxes. If your AMT base is higher than your regular taxable income shown on your 1040 form, you pay a 24 percent tax on the difference. If your 1040 taxable income is larger than your AMT base, there is no additional tax.

How do you compute your AMT base income to see if you owe additional tax?

Computing Your Alternative Minimum Tax Base

Your AMT base is figured by adding AMT adjustments and tax preference items as described below to your taxable income shown on your 1040 form, line 37. You then subtract your AMT exemption of $45,000 ($33,750 single) and anything left over is taxed at 24 percent and added to your regular income tax due.

AMT Adjustments and Tax Preference Items

Out of all the possible tax preference items and adjustments that are subject to the AMT, chances are you will encounter only these few in your financial life. The line numbers refer to Form 6251, Alternative Minimum Tax, a copy of which is at the end of the chapter.

EXERCISED COMPANY STOCK OPTIONS

Line 4p

Executives of corporations often receive options to buy company stock at a discount as part of their compensation package. An option is a right to buy a share of stock at a predetermined price by a specific date ranging from one to ten years. When the option is exercised and the stock purchased, the difference between what was paid and the market value of the stock becomes an adjustment in determining the AMT base. Often this adjustment is missed because the words "Stock option" do not appear on Form 6251, line 4p, which instead says, "Adjusted gain or loss."

DEDUCTION FROM A TAX SHELTER FARM

Line 4r

Lots of Americans have purchased or inherited farmland which they don't actively farm but lease to someone else. Certain tax deductions are allowable as described in IRS Publication F, but an operating loss, which is normal on a leased or tenant-run farm, must be included in determining a taxpayer's alternative minimum tax. No farm? Don't worry.

LOSSES FROM A PASSIVE INVESTMENT (PASSIVE ACTIVITY LOSSES)

Line 4s

Passive investments are securities or business interests that you own but in which you don't take an active part in management. Under the new income tax rules you are allowed to deduct passive losses in any one year only up to the amount of income you receive from your passive investments. Passive losses are often created by investments in real estate or oil and gas limited partnerships. Stock or bond investments don't count, since investors are not allowed to claim losses until the investments are sold. Net losses from passive activities must be included in calculating the AMT base.

PRIVATE ACTIVITY BONDS

Line 5b

Private activity bonds are tax-exempt investments sold by brokers that are used to finance public projects like sewage disposal plants, public housing and mass transit facilities. Private bonds are treated differently from regular tax-exempt municipal bonds. The tax-exempt interest received on private activity bonds must be included on Form 6251, line 5b, as a tax preference item, but only if the bonds were issued after August 7, 1986.

DEPLETION

Line 5c

Depletion is depreciation on a property that contains natural resources, including coal, oil, timber, gas or other resources. As the resources are removed, tax law assumes the property becomes worth progressively less, and the reduction in value is called depletion. You are allowed to take the deduction for depletion on tax Schedule E. Investing in partnerships or properties containing natural resources can be one of the best remaining tax shelters, because the depletion deduction formula actually allows you to take more deductions than the total value of the property. Depletion deductions, believe it or not, can be taken indefinitely, even after the adjusted basis in the property reaches zero. However, there is a catch or limit. The amount of depletion deduction you claim that exceeds the value of the property must be added to your tax preference items to determine your alternative minimum tax base.

INTANGIBLE DRILLING COSTS

Line 5h

During the search for oil and gas fields and the subsequent drilling of wells, there are lots of expenses that have nothing to do with the value of the land. These costs, known in tax law as intangible drilling costs, include:

Labor
Repairs
Tools
Depreciation on drilling equipment
Fuel

Practically any cost that is connected with the drilling, testing or completion of an operating oil or gas well can be an intangible drilling cost. To encourage oil and gas exploration in the United States, owners and investors in companies involved in this industry are able to deduct all of these costs in the year the money is spent, even though the well is not yet producing. Although investments in oil and gas exploration are among the riskiest, the up-front tax deductions are a big attraction. The deductions are valid even for dry holes—wells that produce no oil or gas. Even though you get the deduction for intangible drilling costs on tax Schedule E, part or all of these deductions become a tax preference item when computing your alternative minimum tax base. There is no tax preference effect for a dry hole; 100 percent of the expenses are immediately deductible.

Alternative Minimum Tax Adjustments

In addition to adding tax preference items to determine your AMT taxable income, you must also include in your AMT tax base several adjustments that you took as deductions on your 1040 form. These adjustments include your standard deduction, if you did not itemize, or most Schedule A deductions if you did itemize. These adjustments are listed on Form 6251, lines 4a through 4h (see example at end of chapter).

The Alternative Minimum Tax Exemption

Congress has concluded that a certain amount of tax shelter is healthy, at least for middle-income taxpayers, and exempts that amount from any potential AMT. The amount of potential exemption depends on your filing status and your income as shown here:

ALTERNATIVE MINIMUM TAX EXEMPTION

TAX FILING STATUS	AMT EXEMPTION AMOUNT	PHASE-OUT BASE
Married—filing jointly	$45,000	$150,000
Married—filing separately	$22,500	$ 75,000
Single or head of household	$33,750	$112,500
Estates and trusts	$22,500	—

The exemption is phased out at $.25 per $1 of AMT income above the phase-out base shown in the table above. Married couples filing joint returns whose income is above $310,000 ($232,500 single) get no AMT exemption because their entire exemption has been phased out.

The Tax Benefit Rule

Before you pay an alternative minimum tax instead of your regular income tax rate, you must have received a financial tax benefit from the adjustments and tax preference items. If your regular taxable income shown on your 1040 form is negative, you are in the zero tax bracket and receive no tax benefit from the additional deductions that cause your taxable income to be less than zero. These deductions are not subject to the AMT. Only the deductions, tax shelters or adjustments necessary to reduce your 1040 taxable income to zero are subject to the tax.

Here is an example of a situation in which you would owe additional taxes because of the AMT rules. You and your spouse earned $115,000 last year, but because of your deductions, only $55,000 was taxable, and you file jointly. From your 1040 form you see that your regular tax owed is $10,460. However, you calculate that your AMT adjustments plus tax preference items equal $46,000. How much, if any, additional tax do you owe?

Taxable income: Form 1040, line 37	$ 55,000
AMT adjustments and tax preference items	+$ 46,000
AMT tax base	$101,000
Minus the AMT exemption (couple)	−$ 45,000
AMT taxable amount	$ 56,000
AMT tax rate	× 26%
	$ 14,560
Minus regular tax from From 1040, line 47	−$ 10,460
Additional tax owed because of AMT	$ 4,100

The Alternative Minimum Tax is entered on your 1040 form, line 48.

There are a number of strategies you can use to avoid the AMT, or at least soften its impact. But just like regular income tax strategies, you can't wish you had used them when you are filling out your annual tax returns. By then it's too late. You should be aware of AMT consequences throughout any given year. Use AMT strategies wherever they are applicable, and make them an integral part of your overall financial plan.

ATTACK #181

Calculate your potential AMT tax before the end of the tax year and defer triggering AMT adjustment items.

If you suspect that you will be subject to the AMT in the current year, you can choose to wait until the following year to take actions that may cause you to pay additional tax. Making donations of appreciated property or exercising company stock options at a discount are two examples of decisions that affect the AMT. Time these decisions to shift the deductions into the year when you are least likely to be subject to the AMT. To determine the best year, you or your tax preparer should pencil in a tentative Form 1040 and a Form 6251—Alternative Minimum Tax. Complete two Form 6251s, one with and one without the proposed contribution or exercised stock option. If the AMT is not triggered, make your move and take the deductions in the current year. If most of your deductions or profits will be subject to the AMT, wait until after January 1 and defer the taxes another 16 months. Once the new year arrives it is too late to plan.

DEFENSE #182

If you're subject to the AMT, get rid of some deduction-generating investments.

Choose your investments so that you do not trigger the AMT. Investments in private activity bonds or limited partnerships that throw off income or deductions that must be included in calculating your AMT may be excellent choices until you have exceeded your AMT exemption. When that happens, you may want to get rid of some of these investments. By reinvesting in higher-return investments not subject to the AMT, such as mutual funds or partnerships that throw off high income instead of deductions, you may end up better off financially even after you pay the taxes. Money in private activity tax-exempt bonds, for instance, can be shifted to high-yield tax-exempt municipal bonds, which are not subject to the AMT. If you do have tax preference items or adjustments subject to the AMT created by investments like tax-shelter limited partnerships or private activity tax-exempt bonds, the investment may not make economic sense without the full benefit of the deductions.

DEFENSE #183

To avoid the AMT, sell your stock the year you exercise your stock options.

If you sell stock acquired through a stock options employment incentive package in the same year you exercise the options, you are not required to include the gain as an adjustment in determining if you owe an additional AMT. However, to sell stock in a down market just to avoid extra taxes would not be in your best interest. Consider both factors when making your decision.

Form **6251** Department of the Treasury Internal Revenue Service (O)

Alternative Minimum Tax—Individuals

▶ See separate instructions.

▶ Attach to Form 1040 or Form 1040NR.

OMB No. 1545-0227 **1993** Attachment Sequence No. **32**

Name(s) shown on Form 1040 | Your social security number

Part I Adjustments and Preferences

		Line	Amount
1	If you itemized deductions on Schedule A (Form 1040), go to line 2. If you did not itemize deductions, enter your standard deduction from Form 1040, line 34, and skip to line 6	1	
2	Medical and dental expenses. See instructions	2	
3	Taxes. Enter the amount from Schedule A, line 8	3	
4	Certain interest on a home mortgage not used to buy, build, or improve your home	4	
5	Miscellaneous itemized deductions. Enter the amount from Schedule A, line 24	5	
6	Refund of taxes. Enter any tax refund from Form 1040, line 10 or 22	6	( )
7	Investment interest. Enter difference between regular tax and AMT deduction	7	
8	Post-1986 depreciation. Enter difference between regular tax and AMT depreciation	8	
9	Adjusted gain or loss. Enter difference between AMT and regular tax gain or loss	9	
10	Incentive stock options. Enter excess of AMT income over regular tax income	10	
11	Passive activities. Enter difference between AMT and regular tax income or loss	11	
12	Beneficiaries of estates and trusts. Enter the amount from Schedule K-1 (Form 1041), line 8	12	
13	Tax-exempt interest from private activity bonds issued after 8/7/86	13	
14	Other. Enter the amount, if any, for each item and enter the total on line 14.		

a Charitable contributions		g Long-term contracts	
b Circulation expenditures		h Loss limitations	
c Depletion		i Mining costs	
d Depreciation (pre-1987)		j Pollution control facilities	
e Installment sales		k Research and experimental	
f Intangible drilling costs		l Tax shelter farm activities	
		m Related adjustments	

		Line	Amount
		14	
15	**Total Adjustments and Preferences.** Combine lines 1 through 14 ▶	15	

Part II Alternative Minimum Taxable Income

		Line	Amount
16	Enter the amount from **Form 1040, line 35.** If less than zero, enter as a (loss) ▶	16	
17	Net operating loss deduction, if any, from Form 1040, line 22. Enter as a positive amount	17	
18	If Form 1040, line 32, is over $108,450 (over $54,225 if married filing separately), enter your itemized deductions limitation, if any, from line 9 of the worksheet for Schedule A, line 26	18	( )
19	Combine lines 15 through 18 ▶	19	
20	Alternative tax net operating loss deduction. See instructions	20	
21	**Alternative Minimum Taxable Income.** Subtract line 20 from line 19. (If married filing separately and line 21 is more than $165,000, see instructions.) ▶	21	

Part III Exemption Amount and Alternative Minimum Tax

22 **Exemption Amount.** (If this form is for a child under age 14, see instructions.)

If your filing status is:	**And line 21 is not over:**	**Enter on line 22:**
Single or head of household	$112,500	$33,750
Married filing jointly or qualifying widow(er)	150,000	45,000
Married filing separately	75,000	22,500

If line 21 is **over** the amount shown above for your filing status, see instructions. — 22

		Line	Amount
23	Subtract line 22 from line 21. If zero or less, enter -0- here and on lines 26 and 28 ▶	23	
24	If line 23 is $175,000 or less ($87,500 or less if married filing separately), multiply line 23 by 26% (.26). Otherwise, see instructions	24	
25	Alternative minimum tax foreign tax credit. See instructions	25	
26	Tentative minimum tax. Subtract line 25 from line 24 ▶	26	
27	Enter your tax from Form 1040, line 38 (plus any amount from Form 4970 included on Form 1040, line 39), minus any foreign tax credit from Form 1040, line 43	27	
28	**Alternative Minimum Tax.** (If this form is for a child under age 14, see instructions.) Subtract line 27 from line 26. If zero or less, enter -0-. Enter here and on Form 1040, line 48 ▶	28	

For Paperwork Reduction Act Notice, see separate instructions. Cat. No. 13600G Form **6251** (1993)

☆ U.S. GPO:1993-345-414

EPILOGUE

A New Beginning

Financial success is simply a matter of applied knowledge, not intellectual regurgitation—knowing a lot but doing little.

The strategies in *Financial Self-Defense* combined with the strategies in *More Wealth Without Risk* are not just good ideas or theories, they represent a plan of action a way of life, a total approach to money and your financial future. Applying one, two or 10 strategies will make or save you lots of money this year as well as in the years to come. But the real power in this knowledge is using it to develop automatic wealth-building skills.

The only difference between a pro and an amateur in sports or wealth building is that the amateur, even though he or she may know all the right moves, has to think and make a conscious decision to apply them. The pro has practiced the right moves for so long that the conscious thinking process is not required—the correct, winning responses are automatic. In wealth building, becoming a pro means practicing the right moves or strategies until they become habits. Anyone can become a pro at the wealth-building process simply by applying the correct strategies at every decision-making point—again and again.

Practiced strategies become wealth-building skills.

There are three ways to involve yourself in the wealth-building strategies in this book: as a spectator, an amateur or a pro. Spectators will read the table of contents, then skim the rest of the book. They forget that in wealth building, just as in sports, spectators are not permitted to score points. Only the players are. No matter how many times the spectator shows up at a game, skills do not increase because he never really plays the game. The spectator may have dreams of glory, but these dreams will never be fulfilled.

The amateur at least plays the game, but having read the book, he will apply only a few of the strategies. The amateur will spout financial strategies at work and at cocktail parties like an expert but will see only a few hundred to a few thousand extra dollars each year from the limited use of the strategies.

The pro, on the other hand, will make a total commitment to maximizing the power of the strategies of this book. He has read the book carefully, followed its instruction and applied all of its strategies as part of his financial game plan. He has sharpened the financial skills he already has and developed the new ones that he will need as he moves toward financial success. The pro has the attitude "I will not be denied."

There is a lifetime's worth of knowledge in your hands. Better than seeing the future, the application of these strategies will allow you to design your future—that is, if you approach your future like a pro.

If along the way you attention wavers or you are pulled in too many directions, return to this chapter and read the experiences of those who have been using my strategies for many years. These strategies are meant to do far more than just change the size of your bank account. Use them like a pro and they will positively change your entire life.

If you want to get personal help every step of the way, join the Charles J. Givens Organization, as 650,000 individuals and families have done. Call:

1-800-333-3556

Most of all, remember, everything you dream of for yourself and your family is not only possible but probable when you have the plan, the knowledge and the willingness to take action.

To your success,

What the Readers Say About the Charles J. Givens Strategies

"With the increase in taxes recently proposed by the Clinton administration, we have used the Charles J. Givens strategies to find new ways to protect our earnings."

Robert J. Anderson
New Hampshire

"It's truly amazing to speak with bankers, real estate agents, insurance agents, and other professional people and realize they aren't aware of these proven strategies. I have to suppress a grin when they begin asking questions and taking notes."

Wanda Arndt
Minnesota

"In a few short months we've gone from a no-win situation to full control of our financial future. Our phone, which once carried the dreaded calls of bill collectors, now rings off the hook with opportunity."

Pat and Sandy Arthur
Maine

"Thanks to the Charles J. Givens strategies we are a success. We were like the lion in the Wizard of Oz—you gave us encouragement, support, and guidance as needed throughout our endeavors."

Loman and Alta Atkin
California

"We are thrilled with the knowledge and confidence we've gained using the Givens strategies. You can imagine how we felt when we met with a financial adviser and he had to admit we really didn't need his services."

Cindy Barshinger
Illinois

"I really could not afford not to have the membership. I know for sure—without the membership, my family's paycheck-to-paycheck existence (despite my 80-hour-a-week income) would have been a lifelong experience for me."

J. Batucan
Maryland

"Strategies of goal setting are awesome. Visualization of our dreams soon become reality."

Bill and Jana Boese
Oklahoma

"PAID IN FULL are the magic words that now echo through my mind."

Loretta Bond
California

"The psychological changes are priceless to us, and the monetary rewards are growing day by day!"

Rick and Lea Boyd
Wisconsin

"It's truly wonderful to be able to wake up each morning knowing we're winning financially."

Keith and Jeannine Brickey
Missouri

"After working five years for brokerage firms and banks as financial planners, we have something to admit: we have learned more in the past 45 days from the Givens strategies than we have learned in our entire careers as financial planners!"

Rob and Heidi Bryant
California

"As I began to use your strategies in running a couple of small businesses, it became crystal clear to me that if people would just listen to you, and then act accordingly, there would be a lot more happy, successful people."

Robert W. Bunke
Minnesota

"At a time in our history when it is so easy to turn to the Federal Government for all the solutions, it is truly a breath of fresh air to read and use the Givens approach to personal success."

Robert W. Bunke
Minnesota

"I honestly believe that the Givens strategies are one of the major vehicles we have to fight the ongoing deterioration of the free enterprise system here in the United States."

Robert W. Bunke
Minnesota

"Everyone, and I mean everyone I have talked to or worked with in the Givens Organization was always positive, knowledgeable, enthusiastic, professional and courteous. It is rare that you find an entire organization of this caliber."

Phyllis Carter
Georgia

"Today, after applying and trusting the Givens strategies, I live a proven life of financial competence and peace of mind."

Tom Cecil
Louisiana

"I believe most people like me felt that trying to understand all the terminology was beyond their comprehension. But if you attack one step at a time you will not only be amazed on how fast you catch on but on how simple a lot of it really is."

Frank Ceravolo, Jr.
Florida

"We've realized that we could be like everyone else and rely on others for a monthly paycheck, or we can assume some risk and hard work and with the help of Charles Givens be on the road to *our own* financial success."

Doug Christensen
Iowa

"Grand total of savings and additional income generated is $137,930. If interest saved is included the total would be $417,930. Incredible. Before you came into my life, I had no savings, no retirement plan, and no investments."

Darnell Clarke
Georgia

"It doesn't matter how big or small you are financially, these strategies work for anyone who is willing to apply them."

Laurie Clark-Gruber
Michigan

"Since using these strategies, we have more self-esteem, feel more self-confident, feel more in control of our lives, and we are now less likely to ever bother buying another lottery ticket even if the lottery does come to North Carolina."

Jerry and Carmelita Daniel
North Carolina

"The results are kind of staggering when you look at the small things involved to produce the changes and attitudes we now have in regard to life and finances."

James and Wanda Davis
Arkansas

"In a way, you could say the Givens strategies helped make it financially possible for our daughter to get a second chance at life."

Kristi and Larre Draper
Texas

"To think that I am getting the equivalent of yet another advanced degree through the Givens strategies is absolutely unbelievable. My master's degree cost me close to $50,000."

Karin Elizabeth Clark Edmiston
Ohio

"I could tell you all of the details describing the wonderful changes that we have made . . . but that would take pages and pages."

Gerald Graham
Oklahoma

"With every accomplishment, the excitement is rejuvenated and it just motivates us all the more to obtain those goals/dreams that seemed so unreachable before."

Mr. and Mrs. Gregory Kapelewski
Ohio

"My husband and I were able to develop skills and accomplish goals that before were seemingly unattainable. We developed confidence in coping with our finances."

Fern Levine and Russell Klein
Pennsylvania

"The Givens strategies have given us the support, tools and most important the confidence we needed to take hold of our own destiny instead of leaving our destiny in the hands of others."

Bob and Lenora Pasch
Michigan

"My family and I have found that it takes the same amount of time to do income management as it did to do debt management. The only difference is that income management is more fun."

Dr. Gerald Stotts
Ohio

Resources

A. Declaration of Life Insurance Trust

This Declaration of Insurance Trust is made this _____ day of __________, 19__, by and between __________________, of ____________________, hereinafter called the Trustor, and ____________________, of ____________________, hereinafter called the Trustee.

I.

The Trustor, as owner of certain life insurance policy or policies listed below, and desiring to establish a Life Insurance Trust, with power in the Trustee upon the death of the Trustor to purchase assets from Trustor's estate, assigns to the Trustee all his rights, title, and interest in the policy or policies of insurance, to be held by Trustee in trust, and to receive the proceeds of the policy or policies of insurance when they become due and are paid, for the purposes and on the conditions set forth herein. The Trustor reserves the right to add to this trust from time to time additional life insurance policies which, when delivered to the Trustee, shall be held by him subject to the terms herein.

(DESCRIPTION OF LIFE INSURANCE POLICIES)

II.

The Trustee is vested with all rights, title, and interest in the life insurance policy or policies, and is authorized and empowered to exercise and enjoy, for the purposes of the trust and as absolute owner of the policy of insurance, all the options, benefits, rights and privileges under the policy or policies. The Trustor relinquishes all rights and powers in the life insurance policy or policies which are not assignable and will, at the request of the Trustee, execute all other instruments reasonably required to effectuate this relinquishment. The Trustee shall receive and hold said life insurance policies, together with any additions thereto, in trust for the use and benefit of:

(List Names of Beneficiaries)

III.

Upon the death of the Trustor, the Trustee may, within his discretion, purchase assets from Trustor's estate at a fair value. The propriety of the purchase, the amount of such assets purchased, and the ascertainment of fair value shall be solely within the discretion of the Trustee, and the Trustee shall incur no liability as a result of the purchase or purchases whether or not the assets constitute investments which may be legally made by Trustee.

IV.

If the Trustee uses all or any portion of the proceeds of the policy of insurance to purchase assets from the estate of the Trustor, as authorized above, then the net income produced from the assets, or the proceeds of any sale, exchange, or reinvestment of the assets, shall be paid to the spouse of the Trustor during the spouse's lifetime.

V.

If any beneficiary of this trust who is at the time receiving income would otherwise, in the opinion of the Trustee, be subject to hardship or suffering, the Trustee shall have the authority to pay over and distribute, at any time and from time to time, to the beneficiary the amounts of the principal of this trust, from which the beneficiary shall then be entitled to receive income as the Trustee, in his sole discretion, shall deem necessary to provide for the maintenance, comfort, support and medical care of the beneficiary.

VI.

This Life Insurance Trust shall be irrevocable and unamendable. I am aware of the consequences of establishing an irrevocable trust and hereby affirm that the trust created by this agreement shall be irrevocable by me or any other person, it being my intention to make to the beneficiary/beneficiaries named herein an absolute gift of the life insurance policies described in paragraph I above.

VII.

This agreement and the trust created hereby shall be administered, managed, governed and regulated in all respects according to applicable statutes of the State of __________.

VIII.

The Trustee, in addition to all other powers granted by this agreement and by law, shall have the following additional powers with respect to the trust, to be exercised from time to time at the Trustee's discretion:

MANAGEMENT OF THE TRUST

To invest and reinvest, lease, rent, mortgage, insure, repair, improve or sell any of the real and personal property of the trust as he may deem advisable.

MORTGAGES, PLEDGES AND DEEDS OF TRUST

To enforce any and all mortgages, pledges and deeds of trust held by the trust and to purchase at any sale thereunder any such real estate or personal property subject to any mortgage, pledge or deed of trust.

LITIGATION

To initiate or defend, at his discretion, any litigation affecting the trust.

ATTORNEYS, ADVISORS AND AGENTS

To employ and pay from the trust reasonable compensation to such attorneys, accountants, brokers and investment, tax and other advisors as he shall deem advisable.

ADJUSTMENT OF CLAIMS

To submit to arbitration, to compromise or to release or otherwise adjust with or without compensation, any and all claims affecting the trust estate.

IX.

No bond for the faithful performance of duties shall be required of any Trustee appointed under this agreement.

X.

The trustee shall receive reasonable compensation for the services performed by him, but such compensation shall not exceed the amount customarily received by corporate fiduciaries in the area for like services.

XI.

No Trustee of the trust created by this agreement shall at any time be held liable for any action or default of himself, or of his agent, or of any other person in connection with the administration and management of this trust unless caused by his own gross negligence or by commission of a willful act of breach of trust.

XII.

The Trustee, by joining in the execution of this agreement, hereby signifies his acceptance of this trust.

XIII.

The Trustee shall have sole authority to determine what shall be defined as income and what shall be defined as principal of the trust established by this agreement, and to determine which costs, taxes and other expenses shall be paid out of income and which shall be paid out of principal.

XIV.

In the event that any portion of this agreement of the trust created hereby shall be held illegal, invalid or otherwise inoperative, it is my intention that all of the other provisions hereof shall continue to be fully effective and operative insofar as is possible and reasonable.

IN WITNESS WHEREOF, the parties hereto have executed this agreement the day and year first above written.

____________________ ____________________
Trustor

____

____________________ ____________________
Trustee

____

STATE OF ________________ COUNTY OF ________________

On this ____ day of __________, 19 __, before me personally came and appeared ____________________, known, and known to me, to be the individuals described in and who executed the foregoing instrument, and who duly acknowledged to me that he executed same for the purpose therein contained.

IN WITNESS WHEREOF, I hereunto set my hand and official seal.

____

My commission expires: ________________

B. Additional Installment Sales Rules

The concept of an installment sale is not complicated, but there are some rules to follow to be certain you calculate correctly the selling price, the profit percentage and the reportable amount of any payment you receive.

1. The sales price of your capital asset includes:
   - Cash you receive
   - Fair market value of any property you receive
   - Notes given to you by the buyer at face value
   - Existing mortgages whether or not assumed by the buyer

   If the buyer pays off an existing mortgage, pays the sales commission or agrees to pay off liens on the property, these items must be added into the sales price.
2. In order to determine the amount of taxes you owe using the installment method, you must also be able to compute

the total amount of each payment received. If the amount of payment is in cash, there's no problem. However, payment can also include the fair market value of any property given to you in lieu of cash and interest and principal payments you receive on the buyer's notes and mortgage held by you.

3. Payments received do not include notes, which are not yet paid. If someone owes you a $15,000 installment payment in cash and instead gives you a note because he is unable to pay, the amount of the note is not included in computing your taxes that year unless the note is payable upon demand and you don't demand the money. This rule prevents you from asking for a note in lieu of cash to defer the taxes into yet another year.
4. Your total gross profit on a property you sell is the total sales price you computed less the adjusted cost basis. Selling expenses such as brokers' commissions and legal fees are deducted from the gross profit before you compute your net profit percentage.
5. If you change or renegotiate the selling price during the years that installment payments are being made, you are required to refigure the profit percentage. By completing lines 1 through 15 on tax Form 6252, you will recompute your profit percentage.
6. If the buyer assumes a mortgage when purchasing your property or buys the property subject to a mortgage, the formula for the calculation of the gain or profit that you must report each year changes. You now have a contract price that is different from the sale price according to tax law. The formula for reporting your taxable gain is your profit divided by the contract price times the payment you receive. The principle is: The larger the mortgage assumed (or taken subject to) by the buyer, the less your contract price and the greater the amount you will have to report for tax purposes. See tax Publication 537, Installment Sales.

Acknowledgments

This book was written on all seven continents including Antarctica. Adena, my wife, was always there with encouragement and patience. We spend two and one-half months a year exploring the world, and there is no more peaceful time to write.

For this new edition, countless hours of research, updating, and typesetting were spent by Elaine Wilson, Steve Romeo, John Super, Marsha Shilts, Amy Detwiler, Mary Ann Swiderski, Susan Jackson, Tim Copello, Dana Delaney, and Deena Lyle. Thanks also to Randy Reynolds, Jim Robinson, Steve Butler, Dave Phillips, Roger Easton, Karan Newbold, Buddy Hewell, and Mike Belton for their assistance in reviewing the material in this updated edition. Special thanks to my literary agent Lois de la Haba for her recognition of the importance of the book and her zealous efforts in bringing it to print.

Index

About the Author

Charles J. Givens has built a business and investment empire that includes banks, brokerage firms, television production, radio stations, a quarter billion dollars of commercial real estate and the biggest financial planning and education organization in the world.

Described by one national publication as "fearless, determined, eloquent, and flamboyant," he has made it his personal mission to "stamp out financial ignorance in America," attacking the systems and policies in business and government that he feels impede the progress of individuals and families toward their dreams.

He has been featured on major television shows with Oprah Winfrey, Phil Donahue, Regis Philbin and Kathie Lee Gifford, Geraldo Rivera and Larry King, as well as *The Today Show* and every major radio show, and in leading magazines and newspapers nationwide.

Charles J. Givens knows about money because he learned at an early age about poverty. As a child he saw his parents' alcoholism destroy their business and family. He watched as a moving van pulled up to their home in Decatur, Illinois, and confiscated everything the family owned to be sold at auction to pay unpaid bills and taxes.

Charles J. Givens was 18 years old, earning 85 cents an hour bagging groceries, when having gone through years of depression, shyness and feeling beaten, he made up his mind to take control of his life once and for all. He began by writing a dreams list—a list of everything he would do with his life if he had unlimited time, talent and money.

Along the way he had more than his share of personal and financial setbacks. Three times in his twenties he lost everything—his home, his furniture, his automobiles, his investments—but he never lost his dreams.

So far he has seen most of those original dreams come true, including becoming one of America's wealthiest men; exploring the most remote areas of the earth—Africa, Sumatra, Borneo and Antarctica; owning a jet, a castle in Europe, a professional sports team; and, most important, developing a beautiful relationship with his family.

His wife, Adena, and sons, Rob and Charles III, are involved in everything he does and are deeply committed to the Charles J. Givens Organization. The author is based in Altamonte Springs, Florida.